OPPORTUNITIES IN THE

NUTRITION
AND
FOOD SCIENCES

**Research Challenges and the
Next Generation of Investigators**

Committee on Opportunities in the Nutrition and Food Sciences

Food and Nutrition Board

INSTITUTE OF MEDICINE

Paul R. Thomas and Robert Earl, *Editors*

NATIONAL ACADEMY PRESS
Washington, D.C. 1994

National Academy Press • 2101 Constitution Avenue, N.W. • Washington, D.C. 20418

NOTICE: The project that is the subject of this report was approved by the Governing Board of the National Research Council, whose members are drawn from the councils of the National Academy of Sciences, the National Academy of Engineering, and the Institute of Medicine. The members of the committee responsible for the report were chosen for their special competences and with regard for appropriate balance.

This report has been reviewed by a group other than the authors according to procedures approved by a Report Review Committee consisting of members of the National Academy of Sciences, the National Academy of Engineering, and the Institute of Medicine.

The Institute of Medicine was chartered in 1970 by the National Academy of Sciences to enlist distinguished members of the appropriate professions in the examination of policy matters pertaining to the health of the public. In this, the Institute acts under both the Academy's 1863 congressional charter responsibility to be an adviser to the federal government and its own initiative in identifying issues of medical care, research, and education. Dr. Kenneth I. Shine is president of the Institute of Medicine.

This study was supported by Reference Log No. 89-01306-000 from the Pew Charitable Trusts; Contract No. N01-DK-1-2270 from the National Institutes of Health, U.S. Department of Health and Human Services; the Kellogg Foundation; Contract No. 59-32U4-0-35 from the U.S. Department of Agriculture; and General Mills, Inc.

The serpent has been a symbol of long life, healing, and knowledge among almost all cultures and religions since the beginning of recorded history. The image adopted as a logotype by the Institute of Medicine is based on a relief carving from ancient Greece, now held by the Staatlichemuseen in Berlin.

Dedication

This report is dedicated to DeWitt S. Goodman, M.D. (1930-1991), who served as the original chairman of this committee. Dr. Goodman was a renowned nutrition researcher and educator as well as a developer and great supporter of this study. His untimely death is a tragic loss to the biomedical community. We believe that this report reflects his desire to enhance research and training in the nutrition and food sciences.

COMMITTEE ON OPPORTUNITIES IN THE
NUTRITION AND FOOD SCIENCES

RICHARD J. HAVEL (*Chair*),°† Cardiovascular Research Institute,
School of Medicine, University of California, San Francisco,
California

JOHN W. ERDMAN, JR. (*Vice Chair*), Division of Nutritional Sciences,
University of Illinois, Urbana, Illinois

CUTBERTO GARZA (*Vice Chair*), Division of Nutritional Sciences,
Cornell University, Ithaca, New York

ALAN G. GOODRIDGE (*Vice Chair*), Department of Biochemistry,
University of Iowa, Iowa City, Iowa

JANET C. KING (*Vice Chair*), Department of Nutritional Sciences,
University of California, Berkeley, California

FERGUS M. CLYDESDALE, Department of Food Science, University
of Massachusetts, Amherst, Massachusetts

ROBERT J. COUSINS, Center for Nutritional Sciences, University of
Florida, Gainesville, Florida

ADAM DREWNOWSKI, Human Nutrition Program, School of Public
Health, University of Michigan, Ann Arbor, Michigan

SUSAN K. HARLANDER, Dairy Foods Research, Technology, and
Engineering, Land O'Lakes, Inc., Minneapolis, Minnesota

LAURENCE N. KOLONEL, Cancer Research Center of Hawaii,
University of Hawaii, Honolulu, Hawaii

GILBERT A. LEVEILLE, Research and Technical Services, Nabisco
Foods Group, East Hanover, New Jersey

MARTHA CONSTANTINE-PATON, Department of Biology, Yale
University, New Haven, Connecticut

F. XAVIER PI-SUNYER, Division of Endocrinology, Diabetes, and
Nutrition, St. Luke's/Roosevelt Hospital Center, Columbia
University College of Physicians and Surgeons, New York, New York

SARA A. QUANDT, Department of Anthropology, University of
Kentucky, Lexington, Kentucky

SYED S.H. RIZVI, Department of Food Science, Cornell University,
Ithaca, New York

IRWIN H. ROSENBERG, USDA Human Nutrition Research Center on
Aging, Tufts University, Boston, Massachusetts

A. CATHARINE ROSS, Division of Nutrition, Department of
Biochemistry, Medical College of Pennsylvania, Philadelphia,
Pennsylvania

° Member, National Academy of Sciences
† Member, Institute of Medicine

SACHIKO T. ST. JEOR, Nutrition Education and Research Program, University of Nevada School of Medicine, Reno, Nevada

ALBERT J. STUNKARD,† Department of Psychiatry, University of Pennsylvania, Philadelphia, Pennsylvania

DAVID VALLE, Departments of Pediatrics, Molecular Biology and Genetics, Johns Hopkins University School of Medicine, Baltimore, Maryland

WALTER C. WILLETT, School of Public Health, Harvard University, Boston, Massachusetts

M.R.C. GREENWOOD (*Food and Nutrition Board Liaison*),† Office of Graduate Studies, University of California, Davis, California

Staff

PAUL R. THOMAS, Project Director
ROBERT EARL, Program Officer
CONNIE ROSEMONT, Research Associate (through June 1992)
SHEILA A. MOATS, Research Associate (from August 1993)
JANIE B. MARSHALL, Project Assistant (through April 1993)
SUSAN M. KNASIAK, Project Assistant (from November 1993)

STEVE L. TAYLOR (*Ex Officio*), Department of Food Science and Technology, University of Nebraska, Lincoln, Nebraska

ARTHUR H. RUBENSTEIN (*IOM Council Liaison*),† Department of Medicine, University of Chicago, Chicago, Illinois

Staff

CATHERINE E. WOTEKI, Director

MARCIA S. LEWIS, Administrative Assistant

SUSAN M. WYATT, Financial Associate

Foreword

Food is fundamental to life and health. Observations over millennia and scientific research have demonstrated that what and how much we eat can affect profoundly how we grow, develop, and age and our ability to enjoy life to its fullest. Dietary patterns are linked to risks of developing a variety of chronic diseases that are disabling and terminate life prematurely.

Fundamental scientific inquiry is essential to advances in the nutrition and food sciences or to any of the biomedical, social, and physical sciences. Especially noteworthy is the promise of the biological and genetic revolutions in biomedicine and agriculture. With disease prevention becoming more important in this time of health care reform, continued research and advances in the nutrition and food sciences provide great opportunities to improve the lives of millions of Americans. The United States' preeminent role as a feeder of the world is a stunning example of how advances in science and technology have led to improved food production and processing practices. As a result, citizens in this country and in much of the world are assured an adequate amount of nutritious and safe foods at reasonable prices.

Public health researchers and practitioners face many challenges in facilitating the adoption of healthy eating patterns by the majority of the public. These include developing improved measures to assess the nutritional status and health of individuals and groups, as well as developing individualized dietary recommendations that are based on individual susceptibilities to disease. The range of problems is broad—from dietary excesses contributing to chronic disease, to inadequate food contributing to hunger—and their solutions will require changes in both individual behaviors and public policies. This report identifies research that will link the nutrition and food sciences even more closely with agriculture, economics, and the social and behavioral sciences in order to develop research-based programs and policies to improve public health.

Given the vital importance of the nutrition and food sciences to the wealth of nations and the health of their citizens, it is unfortunate that nutritionists and food scientists have reasons to be concerned about the future and long-term vitality of their disciplines. As described in this report, research in the nutrition and food sciences appears to be inadequately funded in relation to its potential contribution to society. These fields face an identity crisis given their interdisciplinary nature and the diversity of institutional settings in which research and training occur. How to recruit and train students to address the interdisciplinary research opportunities of the future is a critical challenge. Such opportunities highlight the need for collaborative efforts among nutritionists, food scientists, and their colleagues in disciplines ranging from basic biology and chemistry to the social and engineering sciences.

The members of the Committee on Opportunities in the Nutrition and Food Sciences have produced a timely and important report. Special thanks are due to Richard Havel, a member of the National Academy of Sciences and Institute of Medicine, who agreed to chair this committee following the untimely death of DeWitt Goodman, another Institute of Medicine member. The report reflects the dedication of the committee members, who gave large amounts of their time and energy over several years. It should be an important reference work that will spark needed discussion about shaping the future directions of the nutrition and food sciences into the twenty-first century.

Bruce M. Alberts
President
National Academy of Sciences

Kenneth I. Shine
President
Institute of Medicine

Preface

The Institute of Medicine's (IOM) Food and Nutrition Board (FNB) has long wished to examine needs and opportunities in the nutrition and food sciences, as others have done under the auspices of the National Academy of Sciences for the fields of chemistry, biology, hydrology, astronomy and astrophysics, and several others. We were able to initiate this study with the generous support of the Pew Charitable Trusts, the National Institutes of Health, the U.S. Department of Agriculture, and National Research Council funds from the Kellogg Foundation. The objectives of this 2.5-year study were:

- to identify the most promising opportunities in research in the nutrition and food sciences and the means of enhancing research, and
- to examine the organizational structure and quality of education and training in nutrition and the food sciences and to propose recommendations for improving them.

The Committee on Opportunities in the Nutrition and Food Sciences, whose members wrote this report, consists of 21 scientists who are recognized leaders in research and who were recommended by one or more scientific or professional associations. These individuals work in a wide variety of settings, including land-grant colleges, public and private universities, medical schools, and industry. They are familiar with education and training issues and, as a group, with the work of practitioners in nonacademic settings, including various institutions, hospitals, and public health agencies, as well as field settings and the food industry.

Because no committee of manageable size could adequately cover the range of topics within the purview of the nutrition and food sciences, we requested the help of many outside experts. First, we contacted more than 100 professional scientists and practitioners, asking them for information, ideas, or contributions on specific topics. In addition, we organized public sessions at the 1992 annual meetings of the Federation of American Societies for Experimental Biology and the Institute of Food Technologists. Furthermore, we encouraged contributions by publishing a study summary and a list of six questions in numerous professional journals and newsletters, including *American Institute of Nutrition Notes, Food Technology, The Journal of the American Dietetic Association, Journal of Nutrition Education,* and the newsletter of the American College of Nutrition. The questions were:

1. What do you consider to be the top three research findings in your own area?

2. What do you see as the three most important new frontiers and opportunities for research in the nutrition and food sciences that should be addressed?

3. What new technologies are required or need to be developed to meet these challenges?

4. What do you regard as the essential elements of training needed to meet the future research opportunities that you listed above?

5. What changes in current institutional and organizational structures would enhance research and training and thereby lead to progress in the nutrition and food sciences?

6. If you could hire a new faculty member or employee, what expertise would you seek?

We evaluated all contributions and incorporated many of them in this report. With our sincere thanks for their help, we list these contributors by name and affiliation in Appendix B.

The full committee met five times during the course of this study. We established four working groups to develop drafts of Chapters 3 through 6, which identify needs and exciting opportunities for research related to nutrition in the basic biological sciences, food science and technology, clinical sciences, and public health. Working groups held innumerable special meetings and conference calls to prepare their papers and coordinate the contributions of outside experts. Our draft report was formally reviewed under the auspices of the National Academy of Sciences' Report Review Committee by a panel of experts whose identities remain unknown to the committee. We have incorporated many of their thoughtful and constructive suggestions.

This report describes a wide range of interesting and exciting needs and opportunities for research in the nutrition and food sciences. However, by necessity in such diverse and applied disciplines, we were selective rather than encyclopedic in our coverage. We examined recommendations for research made in a variety of reports by the FNB, government, and other sources. We established three criteria to help us decide which areas of research to highlight. First, the research must be likely to enhance individual and public health substantially, by preventing and treating nutrition-related diseases and improving the quality, safety, and availability of our food supply. Second, the research must provide important opportunities and challenges for investigators. Third, the research was seen as important by one or more of the outside experts who contributed to this report. Our selections were made difficult by friendly differences of opinion and the fact that the nutrition and food sciences are expanding as new techniques and ideas are developed in the basic sciences on which these disciplines depend.

With few exceptions, the research accomplishments and opportunities we have identified are of domestic interest. The constraints that led to this limitation precluded a discussion of the exciting challenges faced by the nutrition and food sciences in improving global health. The nature of immigrant populations worldwide and common health problems faced by them and by many rural and urban communities in this country present special challenges that we were unable to review. We hope that the opportunities highlighted in this report succeed in capturing the imagination of new professionals and encourage them to tackle problems of domestic and international significance.

In addition to identifying research opportunities and needs to enhance the education and training of the next generation of investigators, this report also speaks to the need for facilitating the application of available knowledge in the nutrition and food sciences to clinical and public health programs and policies. However, this latter topic—one of vital importance to the future of the nutrition and food sciences—deserves a separate study of its own. Most nutritionists and food scientists are practitioners who translate and apply the research results of investigators into programs and initiatives to improve dietary patterns in this country, treat diet-related diseases, or improve the nutritional value and safety of our food supply.

We have prepared this report for a large audience, from nonscientist policymakers to well-trained nutrition researchers. We hope to reach decision makers in Congress, academic institutions, foundations, and governing boards of accrediting programs, who are in positions to support the growth and well-being of the nutrition and food sciences. We also direct our report to students who are contemplating careers in science, as we hope to convey the excitement and challenge of careers in these disciplines. Our goal is to provide all readers with some understanding of and appreciation for the diversity of problems and opportunities that challenge nutrition and food scientists. Realization of these opportunities will provide us in some cases with a better understanding of the basic biological mechanisms that may improve health in the future and in others with immediate improvements in our lives through medicine, agriculture, and our choices in the supermarket.

ORGANIZATION OF THIS REPORT

This volume begins with a summary of the report that sets forth our conclusions and recommendations for research, education, and training priorities to ensure adequate support for the nutrition and food sciences. In Chapter 1, we present what we believe to be some of the most promising directions for research, organized into five themes and illustrated with two examples. Chapter 2 describes several important accomplishments that are based upon modern concepts of biology and available technologies. Our examples show how the nutrition and food sciences have enormously improved human health around the world and suggest how further research promises even greater health benefits.

Chapters 3 through 6 make up the bulk of this report. They describe numerous current and future opportunities for exciting, challenging research to advance the nutrition and food sciences and to improve human health and the healthfulness of the food supply. Research opportunities in the basic biological sciences and the food sciences are presented, followed by opportunities in clinical nutrition research and public health nutrition. While these are necessarily the most technical chapters in the report, their main points are presented in nontechnical fashion in the summary and conclusions.

The future health of the nutrition and food sciences depends almost entirely on a continued supply of outstanding researchers in these areas, as well as adequate financial support. In Chapter 7, we address the education and training of nutrition and food scientists. While our primary focus is on the training of competent researchers at the graduate and postdoctoral levels, we do not neglect undergraduate education. Chapter 8 reviews the various sources of financial support for the nutrition and food sciences and trends in that support over time. Our list of references is intentionally short; we have listed review articles and particularly important research studies to steer the interested reader to more detailed information on the topics we address. The report concludes with three appendixes: a list of acronyms, acknowledgment of contributors to this report, and brief biographies of the committee members and staff.

This report, while ostensibly a product of this committee, incorporates the contributions of hundreds of individuals, many of whom are recognized leaders in the nutrition and food sciences. We have benefited greatly from their ideas and suggestions and hope that, as a result, this report represents somewhat of a consensus of expert opinion on how to shape the directions of the nutrition and food sciences into the twenty-first century.

Richard J. Havel, *Chair*
Committee on Opportunities in the
Nutrition and Food Sciences

Acknowledgments

This committee acknowledges the important contributions of Paul Thomas, Project Director of this report, as well as Catherine Woteki, FNB Director, and Robert Earl, Program Officer. Their attention, skill, and dedication to all aspects of the production of this report and their service to the committee have been invaluable.

We also appreciate the assistance provided by Research Associates Connie Rosemont and Sheila Moats and Project Assistant Janie Marshall. Mike Edington of IOM's Reports and Information Office helped to prepare the final manuscript for publication, and Blair Burns Potter served ably as copy editor. The staff of the National Academy Press, particularly Sally Stanfield in publishing this report and Barbara Kline in marketing it, were professional and helpful, as always. Special thanks are also due to Kenneth Shine, IOM President, Enriqueta Bond, IOM Executive Officer, and the members of the FNB for their support, advice, and encouragement.

Richard J. Havel, *Chair*
Committee on Opportunities in the
Nutrition and Food Sciences

Contents

Summary and Conclusions

> When you get right down to it, food is practically
> the whole story every time.
>
> —Kurt Vonnegut (Galápagos)

This report describes how the nutrition and food sciences have advanced enormously in this century and contributed to the development of an abundant, health-promoting food supply and better health for people around the world.* We make the case that the nutrition and food sciences will continue to advance, providing even greater health benefits to the nation, as long as research is supported adequately and highly qualified students are attracted to these disciplines and trained to become outstanding investigators and practitioners in settings that range from laboratories to communities.

Nutrition is involved to some extent in almost all of the processes of human life. It clearly plays a role in the majority of the chronic degenerative diseases that cripple and kill most people in the United States. We believe strongly that investing more resources in basic and applied research in the nutrition and food sciences by the federal government, food

---

*Throughout this report we use the phrase "nutrition and food sciences" as a convenient way to refer to both nutrition (or nutritional) science and food science in the same sentence. The reader should not misconstrue our use of this phrase as a recommendation that the two disciplines be homogenized or blended into a single area of study. While more collaborative efforts among nutrition scientists and food scientists are needed to meet some of the research opportunities described in this report, these disciplines are separate but related, and each confronts important challenges.

industry, foundations, and nonprofit organizations will pay big dividends in improved health and well-being of the nation. In addition, many opportunities exist to improve the public's knowledge of nutrition and to increase their practice of good nutrition. Improving the food supply will make it easier for many more people to meet current dietary guidelines and enable this country to increase its export of processed food products.

A PRESIDENTIAL INITIATIVE FOR THE NUTRITION AND FOOD SCIENCES

This is a propitious time for developing a mechanism to bring greater attention to the nutrition and food sciences. Such a mechanism must provide for a public debate on the support society will provide these disciplines in terms of research, education, and training of professionals; education of the public; and the development and evaluation of public policy. In fact, the Food and Nutrition Board in 1991 recommended that the executive branch consider establishing a single, high-level entity to coordinate and direct government activities to improve this country's diet and health.

Expanding on this concept, **we recommend the establishment of a Presidential Initiative for the nutrition and food sciences within the Executive Office of the President, under the auspices of the Federal Coordinating Council for Science, Engineering and Technology (FCCSET) of the Office of Science and Technology Policy (OSTP)**. OSTP assists the President in providing leadership in various areas of science and technology, in part by evaluating the scale, quality, level of coordination, and effectiveness of federal efforts. OSTP plays an important role in coordinating science policy and enhancing cooperation between the public and private sectors.

FCCSET-supported initiatives often bring high-level attention to issues not easily encompassed or well attended to within individual government agencies and programs. Furthermore, these initiatives often lead to greater government commitment and financial support, better coordination of activities, and spinoff activities within the private sector. Federal research on global warming, for example, is coordinated by FCCSET under the direction of the President's Science Adviser. Among the many benefits of this initiative is much more funding for research on climate change. A Presidential Initiative in the nutrition and food sciences would bring needed attention, coordination, and support to federal and private efforts in research, education, training, and the development of science-based public policy in these areas. Furthermore, such an initiative would establish a comprehensive system to set goals, monitor activities, and document progress.

Further support for an FCCSET-supported initiative in the nutrition and food sciences comes from the council itself. Recently, a FCCSET committee studying federal food safety research activities recommended that FCCSET establish a standing committee to coordinate food safety research among agencies and ensure that this research receives adequate attention and budgetary support. Of particular note, that committee concluded that many future research needs in food safety are linked closely to other facets of nutrition and food science described in this report, including the relationship of nutrition to health.

In our judgment, an ideal opportunity to launch a Presidential Initiative in the nutrition and food sciences is in conjunction with a second White House Conference on Food, Nutrition, and Health. The first such conference was held 24 years ago by then-President Richard Nixon. That three-day meeting focused the country's attention on the quality of the food supply, the prevalence of hunger and malnutrition, improving the nutrition of vulnerable groups, nutrition education efforts, and the surveillance of the nutritional health of the nation. Most important, it led to actions that continue today, including expanded food assistance programs and nutrition education efforts, nutrition labeling of foods, and better efforts to monitor nutritional status. We urge the administration to hold a second White House Conference on Food, Nutrition, and Health—perhaps in 1994, the twenty-fifth anniversary of the first conference—to assess progress over this time period, examine the future of the nutrition and food sciences and their role in maintaining health and preventing and treating disease, identify means of providing additional resources to these disciplines, and improve the use of available resources.

Together, the Presidential Initiative and White House conference would bring needed attention, support, and focus to enhancing research, education, and training in the nutrition and food sciences. We direct readers to Chapters 3 through 8 of this report to review all our several hundred important recommendations in these areas. Only some of them can be summarized in this chapter.

Research

In Chapter 1, we note that the most promising directions for research in the nutrition and food sciences are encompassed by five themes that together address human health and well-being and the prevention and treatment of disease. Here we use these themes to illustrate some important opportunities for research.

Nutrients and Biologically Active Food Constituents in Development,
Cell Differentiation, Growth, Maturation, and Aging

Macronutrients (carbohydrates, fat, and protein), micronutrients (vitamins and minerals), and other biologically active constituents in food (e.g., carotenoids and fiber) play important roles in maximizing physiological functions and supporting health. Current research is showing how nutritional quality at critical points throughout the life cycle—from pregnancy, lactation, and childhood to old age—profoundly affects development and risk of disease. Optimizing growth, development, resistance to disease, and longevity requires more information on the interactions among nutrients and other biologically active constituents in food, since these relationships affect the absorption, bioavailability, and functions of these important dietary components in the body.

One important function of nutrients is to regulate gene expression. Developments in molecular biology and genetics promise to increase dramatically our understanding of this function of nutrients throughout the life cycle. Using various approaches to manipulate the mammalian genome will also make it possible to identify and study rate-limiting enzymes in metabolic pathways that direct the flow of nutrients throughout the body under conditions of both health and disease. Furthermore, these approaches will lead to a better understanding of the functions of vitamins and minerals within cells. As the human genome is mapped, it will be possible to identify, then clone additional genes whose products play important roles in the physiology, metabolism, and functions of nutrients.

For example, the development and differentiation of many tissues, including those of the nervous system during embryonic development, are regulated in part by retinoids derived from vitamin A. These tissues contain in the nucleii of their cells receptors for the retinoid compounds. Vitamin A directly affects cell differentiation. At the other end of the life cycle, some aspects of the aging process are being linked to cumulative damage to body fats, proteins, and DNA as a result of oxidation. Antioxidant nutrients such as vitamins C and E, selenium, and the sulfur-containing amino acids—as well as other important constituents of food such as beta-carotene, zinc, and copper that help to prevent and repair the damage from oxidation—may help slow the aging process or at least the extent of cellular damage that accompanies it.

Genes, Food, and Chronic Diseases

Dietary patterns and inheritance are linked in fundamental ways to one's state of health and the risk of a wide variety of diseases, including cardiovascular disease, cancer, diabetes, hypertension, and obesity. We have learned a great deal and continue to learn about how to reduce the genetically determined risk of these diseases in many individuals by improving dietary patterns and lifestyles. Better knowledge of the genetic basis of these diseases will make it possible to tailor individual nutritional approaches to prevention and treatment of them. The new and emerging field of gene therapy (the introduction of a functional gene to replace or supplement the activity of a resident defective gene) has vast potential for preventing and treating nutrition-related genetic diseases, such as atherosclerotic heart disease brought on by high concentrations of cholesterol in the blood. Mapping the human genome will help us to identify some of the genes involved in multifactorial disorders (those with more than one cause) such as diabetes, obesity, and hypertension.

Determinants of Food Intake

Genetic, metabolic, sensory, and sociocultural factors (such as age, sex, and income) and the characteristics of our food supply affect food preferences and choice of food. At present, we have a limited understanding of how these factors, individually and in combination, affect individual actions. Research is elucidating the role of neurotransmitters such as serotonin and the opioid peptides, whose concentrations in the brain are determined in part by diet, on food selection and preferences, and on the amounts of food consumed. Research is also needed to understand how sensory preferences for foods are affected by body weight and various sociocultural and behavioral factors.

Research on diet and health and our ability to identify individuals and groups at risk of diet-related illnesses depend on our ability to measure intake. Current methods of assessing dietary patterns and nutrient intakes are extremely limited and need to be improved. In addition, much more remains to be learned about the behaviors and motivations of people who have improved their diets compared to those who have not. Basic and applied studies are needed to understand the obstacles to, and opportunities for, dietary change.

Improving Food and Nutrition Policies

Research to improve our knowledge of current dietary patterns and the individual and social forces that influence eating habits is vital if we are to develop effective public policies that will improve eating habits in this country. Efforts to monitor and assess the nutritional health of all segments of our population should be continued and the methodologies improved. In addition, our knowledge of food composition needs to be enhanced, and databases to accommodate this information need to be expanded and improved. More information is required about subgroups of the population who are at the highest nutritional risk in this country, including the poor and homeless, adolescent girls, the elderly, and various ethnic minority groups. At the same time, we need to understand better how dietary patterns may protect some groups from certain diet-related diseases. Our abilities to assess the nutritional status of individuals and populations and their risks of disease will improve dramatically with the development of novel biomarkers (e.g., concentrations of the zinc-inducible protein metallothionein in red blood cells to assess zinc nutriture or concentrations of vitamin A labeled with a stable isotope to measure total body stores of this nutrient). In addition, methodologies to be expanded and improved include anthropometry, which is widely used to assess growth and body composition, and biochemical and functional assessments of nutritional status.

Targeted interventions are still needed to improve dietary patterns in this country, reduce inequities in access to food, and provide food assistance to individuals in need. However, for these interventions to be more successful than they currently are, they must be designed with a sophisticated understanding of diet-related and social behaviors. Furthermore, interventions need to be evaluated to determine whether they are accomplishing their goals, to learn which components are the least and the most successful, and to aid in the design of more effective interventions in the future.

Enhancing the Food Supply

Given consumers' preferences for more convenient and healthful foods, improved knowledge of human nutritional needs and technological developments are enabling the U.S. food industry to develop a wider variety of products. These include fortified foods, low-fat and low-calorie foods, functional foods (in which concentrations of one or more food constituents have been manipulated to enhance their contributions to a healthful diet), and, most recently, foods produced by the emerging techniques of biotechnology (such as cereal grains with greater nutritional value and better-tasting vegetables with longer shelf life). Taking a raw commodity, such as wheat or soybeans, and making it more nutritious, safer, more convenient, more acceptable, easier to prepare, or specific to the needs of special populations adds value to the commodity. Techniques of adding value to foods in the future include improved methods of manufacturing, preserving, and packaging. Our abilities to prepare high-quality value-added foods will increase as we learn more about the physical and engineering properties of food, develop better technologies to separate food ingredients, and make more use of computers and biosensors in food-processing systems to increase product quality and safety and process efficiency while minimizing wastes.

Innovative and practical approaches must be developed to minimize food contamination and educate the public about proper food preparation and storage techniques. Food safety issues pertaining to naturally occurring toxicants in foods, as well as food allergies, sensitivities, and idiosyncrasies, also should be better studied. By understanding the chemical structure, reactivity, and physical properties of food at the molecular level, food scientists and technologists will be better positioned to use more readily available, less expensive, and nutritionally or functionally superior ingredients to improve our food supply. Areas of study to be emphasized include the roles of water in food, the architecture of the macronutrients in food, free-radical reactions (which are involved in food spoilage), and the effects of food processing on the cellular membranes of plant and animal foods.

Education and Training

Success as a scientific investigator in the nutrition and food sciences requires graduate education, usually at the doctoral and frequently at the postdoctoral level. Current institutional infrastructures should be examined as these disciplines advance to meet the research challenges identified in this report. Faculty will need to engage in interdisciplinary efforts with each other and with basic biological and social scientists. This could lead, for example, to graduate programs being offered by groups of faculty with a common interest in nutrition or food science rather than by a specific department or division. Students in these disciplines will need to develop an understanding of a related discipline such as molecular biology or political science, depending on their career paths, to become successful investigators and practitioners.

Undergraduate Education

The best undergraduate programs in the nutrition and food sciences help students understand the interrelationships of nutrition, food, and health and to develop critical-thinking and problem-solving skills. A core curriculum for nutrition undergraduates should include general and organic chemistry and biochemistry; biology and integrative biology (e.g., physiology); nutrition science; microbiology; food chemistry; mathematics through elementary calculus; physics; statistics; and behavioral sciences. Students interested in food science need the same basic science training in biology, chemistry, and physics, plus food engineering, food processing, and coursework in regulatory policy. Many fine research universities and colleges without specialized undergraduate programs in nutrition or food science face special challenges in identifying students in these settings who may have interests in the critical problems facing these disciplines, excite their curiosity, and identify opportunities for them to begin to study these issues within their institutions.

Summer courses in the nutrition and food sciences would provide great opportunities to acquaint undergraduates with a range of research problems in these disciplines and the approaches and technologies used to solve them. Several models of these programs exist; each provides students with lectures and opportunities to conduct research. Summer training programs should be organized and offered by nutrition science and food science departments and by the U.S. Department of Agriculture (USDA) through their Human Nutrition Research Centers and Regional Research Centers across the United States. Funding for competitively awarded fellowships and travel grants to attend these programs could come from professional societies in the nutrition and food sciences, industry, USDA, and the National Institutes of Health (NIH).

Tension may exist between institutions that offer baccalaureate degrees in the nutrition and food sciences and the American Dietetic Association and Institute of Food Technologists, which accredit or approve many of the programs. Both disciplines benefit from this credentialing or approval process, but meeting the requirements outlined by these professional associations makes demands on departmental curricular resources and can limit student development. We recommend that departments take the initiative and develop, in cooperation with the appropriate professional societies, a credentialing and approval process that is fully congruent with future opportunities in the nutrition and food sciences, clearly allied to the rapid advancements in knowledge and technology, and increasingly competitive in attracting bright undergraduates who wish to pursue advanced degrees.

Graduate Education

Graduate students who intend to become investigators in nutrition or food science receive education and training that is configured around their undergraduate background and career goals. Required courses in nutrition often include graduate-level basic cellular and molecular biology, biochemistry, physiology, perhaps genetics and epidemiology, and one or more courses in the social sciences. In food science, core courses include graduate-level food chemistry, food microbiology, food engineering, and basic science or engineering. Many different academic structures exist to educate and train students in the nutrition and food sciences; each has its strengths and weaknesses. Departments of nutrition, food science, and combined departments are perhaps the most visible. The graduate programs in nutrition in several medical schools are varied, reflecting both the lack of nutrition departments and a school-by-school approach to developing the medical-nutrition curriculum. We concur with past reports of the great need to improve nutrition education in medical schools. In addition, several graduate nutrition departments are located within schools of public health. To ensure that these schools have a strong nutrition component, we recommend that nutrition be one of the public health disciplines required for accreditation.

Graduate Education Support

Increasing the number of training grants and fellowships will help attract more investigators to the nutrition and food sciences. (It is worth noting that the number of doctorates awarded in the nutrition and food sciences is only about 3.7 percent of the number awarded in the life sciences.) We recommend a new national combined pre- and postdoctoral awards program to provide more flexible and comprehensive training support for nutrition and food scientists. Graduate students would compete for awards that would guarantee the winners stipends for the last three years of graduate work and the first three years of postdoctoral work. Student who obtained a Ph.D. degree in nutrition or food science would enter a postdoctoral laboratory in a complementary discipline that is not located in a nutrition or food science department. Students who obtained a Ph.D. in a supporting discipline (such as molecular biology, physical anthropology, or engineering) would select a postdoctoral laboratory within a department or program in nutrition or food science. We envisage such a program being funded by NIH and USDA, perhaps with the help of the National Science Foundation (NSF) and private foundations. To create and maintain a viable program, at least 10 awards should be provided each year.

Support

Meeting the research challenges and opportunities summarized above requires that the research enterprise itself be supported adequately. We are acutely aware that the current funding climate limits the financial support for meritorious research and training in the nutrition and food sciences and in the biomedical sciences generally. Among the reasons are the huge federal debt, restructuring and consolidation within the private sector, and the plethora of important social needs that require financial support from private, nonprofit organizations and foundations. We suggest that the major supporters of the nutrition and food sciences conduct self-assessments of their research and training programs in these disciplines to ensure that available funds are spent wisely and efficiently.

It is not possible to estimate accurately the total resources applied to research in the nutrition and food sciences, in part because the centralized government system for compiling and reporting does not include private sector investments in research and does not impose uniform requirements on agencies reporting data. Documenting the government's research effort would be substantially improved if federal agencies were to become consistent in their definition of nutrition- and food-related research, consistent in the inclusion or exclusion of overhead costs in the estimates of research costs, and use the same system throughout government to account for their contributions. Ideally, such a system could be used by the private sector and nonprofit institutions as well.

Federal Government

The federal government estimates its annual expenditures on research and research training in the nutrition and food sciences to be more than $400 million each year. However, expenditures in constant dollars reached a peak in fiscal year (FY) 1988, declined for two years, then increased somewhat in FY 1991, indicating overall that investments in nutrition and food science research are not keeping place with inflation.

National Institutes of Health   NIH leads all federal agencies in financial support of nutrition research and training, contributing about three-quarters of total federal expenditures in these areas. It supports both basic and clinical research on nutrition throughout the life cycle and nutritional factors in the development, prevention, and treatment of disease. NIH does this through various mechanisms, primarily investigator-initiated research grants but also through eight Clinical Nutrition Research Units (CNRUs) and four Obesity Nutrition Research Centers (ONRCs). We recommend that the level of support from NIH for nutrition research reflect the important role of diet in health promotion and the prevention and treatment of disease. This is currently not the case. Two important mechanisms for NIH to accomplish this goal are through its Bionutrition Initiative and by ensuring that the nutrition sciences have strong representation throughout the institutes. NIH should also ensure that nutrition scientists are adequately represented on all of its study sections that evaluate proposals for nutrition research. In general, too few nutrition experts sit on study sections that evaluate proposals with significant or strong nutrition components. The committee also recommends that the training functions of CNRUs and ONRCs be expanded and strengthened to enhance the trainees' expertise in nutrition through formal didactic and laboratory-based training. In addition, consideration should be given to increasing the financial support to the CNRUs and ONRCs and initiating a process to determine the desirable number of centers, as they have successfully encouraged multidisciplinary research and training in clinical nutrition within biomedical research institutions. Funds to implement these recommendations should not come at the expense of support for investigator-initiated research.

U.S. Department of Agriculture For more than a century, USDA has supported research in the nutrition and food sciences. Today, it contributes approximately one-seventh of total federal expenditures for research in these areas, focusing on the nutritive value of foods, human nutrition needs, food consumption patterns, food quality and safety, and strategies for improving diets and the food supply. We recommend that USDA develop a strategic plan that places research in the nutrition and food sciences more in the center of its agricultural research initiatives. Congress should provide full funding for USDA's National Research Initiative, which would lead to a tenfold increase in spending on its program in human nutrition, food safety, and health. Increased support for research on developing and applying new and emerging food and engineering technologies is also needed to enable food scientists to develop more value-added food products for export. USDA should also explore the possibility of changing the way it allocates monies to states for agricultural research, emphasizing competitively-awarded, peer-reviewed grants in the nutrition and food sciences, in contrast to automatic entitlements. In addition, some of the funding for USDA's food assistance programs should go to competitively awarded research proposals to evaluate the success of these programs and ways of improving them.

National Science Foundation NSF does not have a research program in the nutrition or food sciences, so its direct support of research in these areas is small. We recommend that NSF play a greater role in supporting the nutrition and food sciences in two ways. First, more nutrition and food scientists should be members of NSF advisory panels that review research grant applications. NSF would then be likely to support more basic food science and food engineering research as well as basic behavioral research related to food intake patterns and other sociocultural determinants of food behavior. Second, NSF should support more students in food science and engineering through its Graduate Research Traineeship Program and establish at least one Center of Excellence in food engineering.

Industry

The food industry supports a considerable but nonquantifiable amount of research in the nutrition and food sciences, although recent corporate restructurings and economic recession have led companies to shift resources from basic research and development to the support of business operations. We recommend that the private sector establish better links with academic departments of food science and nutrition. These alliances would provide universities sources of new funds, enable them to keep their best and brightest faculty, and speed the transfer of research results from their laboratories to the marketplace. Industry, in turn, would have a larger pool of qualified food and nutrition scientists from which to select. We urge the meat and dairy industries—as well as other commodity groups concerned with plant foods that participate in USDA-administered programs of research and promotion—to be generous in allocating funds to competitively awarded research on their products and encourage investigator-initiated research. The entire food industry should increase its spending on research related to value-added food processing, which is needed to increase this country's international competitiveness and trade balance.

Private, Nonprofit Organizations

Foundations such as the Pew Charitable Trusts and voluntary health agencies like the American Heart Association have made limited but important contributions to research in the nutrition and food sciences, particularly in strengthening university research programs. We encourage these sources to continue their support and hope that more foundations of the food industry and those with a public-health orientation begin to support these disciplines. Specifically, we recommend new initiatives along the lines of one begun by the Pew Charitable Trusts to award fellowships and help several institutions develop and give direction to their nutrition and food science programs. Support from a wide variety of private, nonprofit organizations will become even more important if federal support of research and training remains level or is capped.

CREATING THE FUTURE

These are among the best of times for the nutrition and food sciences, yet their future is far from certain. Few investments promise comparable returns in terms of improved quality of life for individuals and productivity of society as do those in the nutrition and food sciences. For these disciplines to take advantage of the many opportunities identified in this report, more financial support is needed for research and the training of students, and greater efforts must be made to attract a new generation of high-quality, achievement-oriented, career-seeking scientists. To achieve these goals in today's political and economic climates, nutrition and food scientists will need to become more politically active through their professional societies and as individuals to advocate more government and private support of their disciplines. In addition, as potential role models, they must become more visible and available to students in elementary and high school to promote the appeal of careers in the nutrition and food sciences.

In addition to pursuing research challenges identified in this report, it is important that investigators and practitioners in the nutrition and food sciences provide ongoing evaluations of the consequences and policy implications of meeting these challenges. The research required to do so is important and must be supported adequately. Research agendas recommended in this report and by others can raise moral and ethical questions that should be identified and addressed. One such question is raised by the two fundamentally different approaches to improving dietary patterns in this country: modifying people's food habits through lifestyle changes versus modifying the food supply to make the foods people eat more health-promoting. Many views exist as to which approach is more efficacious, practical, acceptable, safe, and affordable and how resources should be allocated between the two to achieve the goal. Some of these views can and should be investigated experimentally; others must simply be based on judgments made by those who can influence policies. Our task has been to describe research opportunities that exist to further each approach (see especially Chapters 4 and 6).

The heightened federal effort to study and combat global warming came in large measure as a result of coordinated efforts by individual scientists and their professional societies, who insisted on, and proved the need for, greater government participation. Today's nutrition and food science communities hold the future of these disciplines in their collective hands. How the nutrition and food sciences are perceived in the next century and the level of support they receive for research, education, and training depend a great deal on our activities today.

1

Introduction

The nutrition and food sciences are among the most interdisciplinary of all sciences. They bring together the chemical, physical, biological, medical, agricultural, social, behavioral, and engineering sciences to examine how food affects health—from the basic molecular and cellular levels to the organ, organism, and even population levels. Another major area of study in these fields is how food systems can be designed to enhance the physical and economic well-being of individuals and groups, as well as the adequacy and safety of their food supply. Progress in the nutrition and food sciences has accelerated dramatically during this century. We have moved from defining the chemical nature and biological role of macronutrients (carbohydrates, fats, and proteins) to discovering vitamins, minerals, and other biologically active food constituents and now to establishing a scientific basis for the role of food and dietary patterns in long-term health. Various technological achievements have enabled scientists to conduct research more effectively and to develop a more abundant and health-promoting food supply.

As we approach the twenty-first century, the nutrition and food sciences will be profoundly affected by the rapid advances being made in molecular biology. Understanding the molecular and genetic aspects of health and disease and how food components modulate biological processes and the expression of our genetic makeup will continue to be a significant, possibly the predominant, component of the health-related research of the new century. Research findings are likely to play a critical role in developing strategies to prevent and manage genetically and environmentally governed diseases. Therefore, nutrition and food scientists, academic educators and administrators, and public- and private-sector policymakers need to consider the trends developing in these disciplines, their research needs and opportunities, the adequacy of education and training programs for researchers and practitioners, and the speed with which knowledge in the nutrition and food sciences is being transferred from science into policies and practice.

WHO WE ARE AND WHAT WE STUDY

Research in nutrition in the early part of this century was focused almost entirely on discovering essential nutrients and characterizing their physiological and biochemical roles in the body. Researchers used a unique method of determining essential nutrients and their requirements—the animal growth model—that was unique to nutrition.

More than 40 years ago, the first issue of the *American Journal of Clinical Nutrition* defined nutrition as "the cornerstone of preventative medicine, the handmaiden of curative medicine and the responsibility of every physician." Almost two decades later, in the same journal, Alfred Harper suggested that nutrition be called an "integrating science," or perhaps an "applied science," since it is concerned with solving practical problems. Harper added, "There is no such thing as *a* nutritionist; there are nutritionists. . . . We are chemists, biochemists, physiologists, pathologists, microbiologists, physicians, dentists, economists, dietitians, sociologists, animal scientists and husbandmen, food technologists, toxicologists, and many others." Admittedly, he added, "[t]his makes it much more difficult to decide where we are and where we are going because we are in different places going in different directions."

Today, no single methodology unites the nutrition and food sciences. Some contend that food science is concerned with food from its production to the point where it is consumed, at which time food becomes the interest of nutrition investigators. A more inclusive description of the nutrition and food sciences is that they are a collection of interests centered around food and human well-being and, therefore, part of a continuum.

In Figure 1.1, we present one of many possible diagrams to illustrate the scope of the nutrition and food sciences. These disciplines are roughly divided into four overlapping areas of concentration—within cells or *in vitro* environments; specific organs, entire human, or animal; populations; and food supply—each of which depends on a variety of supporting areas of study.

We have decided not to establish or debate definitions of the nutrition and food sciences. We will use the terms "nutrition science" and

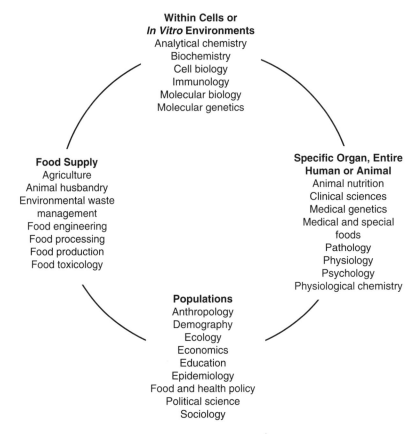

FIGURE 1.1   One illustration of the scope and coverage of the nutrition and food sciences. Each box represents one focus of the nutrition and food sciences with examples of areas of study. The areas of study listed are examples; many of them could be placed in more than one box.

"food science" and refer to both as disciplines or fields of study. We concur with Harper that they are integrating, applied disciplines that apply knowledge about food and nutrients and their effects on health derived from the basic chemical, physical, biological, medical, social, behavioral, and engineering sciences to improve human well-being.

To prepare a readable report of reasonable size, we have had to be selective rather than encyclopedic in our coverage of the nutrition and food sciences. Many topics within the purview of these diverse disciplines, such as those relating to agriculture or the environment, receive little or no attention. In addition, we have focused on the United States in examining research opportunities, issues of training and support, and applications of research to public policy.

THEMES

Chapters 3 through 6 identify what we consider to be among the most promising directions for research in the nutrition and food sciences to improve human health and ensure the vitality and importance of these disciplines into the next century. Most of our research recommendations can be encompassed by five themes. These themes, described below, integrate the remaining chapters in this report and provide a basis for developing the major components of a national research program that we propose in Chapter 9.

Uniting these themes is the underlying premise that our long-term health is determined by both genetics and environment. The environment as used here includes diet and other life-style factors (including both health-promoting and risk-taking behaviors) in addition to physical and chemical exposures (such as ionizing radiation and toxic substances in the workplace). For the majority of Americans who do not smoke, do not drink excessively, and are not exposed to environmental hazards in their work, the food they eat is the largest controllable factor determining their long-term health.

Theme 1: Nutrients and Biologically Active Food Constituents in Development, Cell Differentiation, Growth, Maturation, and Aging

Understanding how nutrients and other biologically active compounds in food influence human development from conception to death has been and remains a fundamental line of inquiry for the nutrition and food sciences. Research in these areas has led to the development of the Recommended Dietary Allowances (RDAs), which have been established for groups of healthy individuals of both sexes and different ages as levels of intake of essential nutrients judged to be adequate to meet known nutritional needs. RDAs have been revised periodically to include new research results.

Research is showing, for example, how retinoic acid, a derivative of vitamin A, affects the expression of specific genes that regulate cell division and differentiation (whether a cell, for example, becomes a liver cell or epithelial cell on the inside of the mouth). In addition, carotenoids (found in fruits and vegetables; several have provitamin A activity) seem to enhance communication among cells, which may reduce the risks of cancer, characterized by uncontrolled cell division. Scientists are discovering how malnutrition during critical periods in early development—before birth or during the first three years thereafter—can compromise normal growth and development throughout childhood and into adolescence. They are learning how peak bone mass can be achieved with the help of dietary patterns that include adequate calcium and other nutrients, thereby lowering the risks of osteoporosis in later life. Not only are nutrients necessary for development, but they may also be used to extend human life. Research suggests that the aging process and risk of diseases such as heart disease and some cancers are amenable to influence by antioxidants. Nutrients with antioxidant properties such as vitamins C and E and selenium, as well as carotenoids and possibly other nutrients and food components help protect the proteins, lipids, and DNA in cells—on which most of our basic life processes depend—from damage by oxygen. Scientists are just beginning to learn how nutrition can affect the ability of the immune system to protect us against infectious diseases and influence our risk of developing chronic degenerative diseases. Tests to determine how well the immune system responds to various challenges may become very sensitive tools to measure a person's nutritional status.

Theme 2: Genes, Food, and Chronic Diseases

Over the past half century, scientists have investigated the role of dietary patterns, specific foods, and nutrients in maintaining health and reducing the risk of developing chronic diseases such as heart disease and cancer. Laboratory, clinical, and epidemiological research has enabled them to identify dietary constituents that influence specific diseases and their underlying biological mechanisms. As a result, nutrition scientists have developed dietary guidelines that not only help ensure nutritional adequacy, but offer some protection against the diseases that kill most people in the United States. As we learn more about how genetic factors influence specific diseases and their underlying mechanisms, dietary guidelines will likely be modified to incorporate our knowledge of the interactions of genes and diet. At some point in the future, it may be possible to individualize dietary guidance through knowledge of a person's genetic endowment and lifestyle. At the present time, dietary guidelines are directed to most of the U.S. population to help protect the largest number of people from diet-related chronic diseases.

Perhaps the most significant new development in nutrition science is the growing understanding of the role of diet and hormones in regulating the expression of our genetic endowment. Dietary patterns interact with genetic predispositions to alter the risk of disease. Using the techniques of gene transfer with animals and with cells in culture, it will be possible to learn the mechanisms by which specific food constituents interact with DNA to cause or affect disease processes. These basic studies can then be related to applied clinical questions. For example, studies of twins and adopted children strongly suggest that obesity has a genetic component, as do studies of the Pima Indians, whose rates of obesity and diabetes are among the highest in the world. But studies of primitive peoples who undergo rapid modernization provide strong evidence that changed dietary patterns and lifestyles also affect powerfully the risk of disease, since the spectrum of diseases in these peoples changes much more rapidly than can be accounted for by genetic accommodations.

Theme 3: Determinants of Food Intake

A person's food selections and dietary patterns are profoundly influenced by a variety of metabolic, sensory, cognitive, cultural, and economic factors. Although genetic and physiological factors shape individual food preferences and aversions, the translation of these into behavior—diet selection—is mediated by a variety of sociocultural factors. The study of nutrition and behavior has traditionally dealt with the impact of foods or nutrients on brain function and their subsequent influences on behavior. Less attention has been paid to the ways in which behavior influences nutritional status. In fact, until recently, research on food preferences and choices and the selection of a habitual diet was often regarded as peripheral to the nutrition and food sciences.

We need to conduct much more multidisciplinary research into the relationships between food intake, nutritional status, and behavior. The results of this research should enable us to develop strategies to help more people to follow dietary guidelines. At the basic biological level, we need to understand how neurotransmitters function and how they influence appetite and food choice. While genetic and physiological factors may shape individual food preferences and aversions, socioeconomic and cognitive factors definitely do. Learning how all of these factors interact to determine what and how people eat is a challenging, long-term opportunity for research in the nutrition and food sciences.

Theme 4: Improving Food and Nutrition Policies

Food and nutrition policies and programs rely on research for their formulation, implementation, and evaluation. The essential components of a comprehensive policy on food and nutrition includes (1) the availability of adequate food for everyone, (2) a high-quality, safe, and wholesome food supply, (3) consumer education about dietary patterns that promote health and prevent disease, (4) opportunities for individuals to put their increased awareness and improved dietary knowledge to practice, (5) access to nutrition services within the medical care system, and (6) effective food assistance programs for those in need.

To improve policy formulation, we need to determine what combination of social and economic indicators best predicts an individual's need for help in obtaining food. We also need to develop a uniform understanding of what constitutes desirable dietary behavior. For policy implementation, it is important to learn how to deliver nutrition information to people in such a way that they will act upon it and on identifying the most appropriate strategies for changing the eating behavior of subpopulations. Implementation also depends on learning what incentives will prompt producers and processors to modify the food supply to meet health concerns while simultaneously maintaining its quality, safety, acceptability, and profitability. We also need research on better ways to evaluate the effectiveness of programs by government and others to provide food to those in need or to improve eating habits.

Theme 5: Enhancing the Food Supply

Food science and the food industry are responding to emerging research findings, consumers' changing dietary preferences, and government policies by providing a wide variety of foods reduced in calories and modified in fat, cholesterol, and salt content. Enhancing the food supply involves producing health-promoting, high-quality, economical, and wholesome foods with reduced adverse effects on the environment and better use of raw materials.

Challenges facing the food industry are to continue to conduct research to develop better products; minimize microbiological and chemical contamination of food products; minimize the environmental impacts of food production and processing by developing sustainable agricultural practices and environmentally sound packaging; increase the availability of health-promoting foods, such as vegetables, fruits, and whole-grain products; and use newer technologies to maintain the low food costs that U.S. consumers have come to expect. Biotechnology that utilizes recombinant DNA or genetic engineering techniques to improve plants, animals, and microorganisms selectively should provide more desirable, predictable, controllable, and health-promoting products than conventional crossbreeding technologies. Another area of intense research interest involves modifying foods to help people meet dietary guidelines. Some of these products incorporate newly developed fat and sugar substitutes. Modified foods of the future will contain enhanced or reduced amounts of biologically active components, thereby helping to maximize health and reduce an individual's risk of disease.

Crosscutting Examples of Our Themes

Most of the research recommendations we make in this report illustrate one or more of the themes described above. In the last section of this chapter, we provide two examples—understanding the functions of vitamin D and combating atherosclerotic heart disease—to show the interdisciplinary nature of most nutrition and food science research. They are simply two of many examples that could have been chosen. The vitamin D example pertains to an essential substance that is sometimes not obtained in adequate amounts. The heart disease example, in contrast, pertains in part to dietary excesses. Both examples illustrate how research in the basic sciences has led to clinical research, which in turn has driven improvements in the food supply and contributed to the development of food and nutrition policy.

Understanding the Functions of Vitamin D

For centuries, rickets, a disease in which the bones do not have enough calcium and therefore become deformed, was common among urban children in temperate zones of the world and in young animals raised indoors. Early this century, a substance in animal fat was identified that prevented or cured rickets when given orally. In 1920, this substance was named vitamin D. Soon afterward, it was discovered that sunlight could convert a derivative of cholesterol in the skin to vitamin D. Most people can meet their vitamin D requirements without food as long as their skin is regularly exposed to a sufficient amount of sunlight or artificial ultraviolet light.

Vitamin D has many functions in the body. The first identified and best known function is that it enables the small intestine to absorb calcium and thereby plays a role in the proper formation and maintenance of bones. Vitamin D occurs in abundance in only a few foods, such as eggs, butter, and liver. In 1925, it was demonstrated that certain molecules similar to cholesterol in various foods, including cow's milk, developed vitamin D activity when exposed to ultraviolet radiation. Vitamin D-fortified cow's milk, which became available as a result of this basic research, is credited as the major factor in the disappearance of infantile rickets in this country in the second quarter of this century. Using the tools of physical chemistry and engineering, food scientists developed techniques to add fat-soluble vitamins to water-based foods. To this day, vitamin D-fortified milk and milk products, margarine, ready-to-eat cereals, and several other foods are dependable sources of this nutrient and help prevent rickets around the world.

Currently, there is renewed research interest in vitamin D because of its relationship to calcium and osteoporosis, a disease in which the bones lose calcium and become weak and subject to fractures. In addition, vitamin D regulates the activities of some genes whose exact purposes in most cases are unknown.

The active form of vitamin D in the human body induces the production of calbindin, a protein that shuttles the calcium released from food in digestion from the small intestine to the bloodstream. Vitamin D also appears to activate a molecule on the intestinal cell membrane that pumps calcium from the intestine into the bloodstream so that it reaches bone, muscle, and nerve cells where it is needed. Acting with parathyroid hormone, vitamin D also mobilizes calcium from the bones, when necessary, so that there is enough of the mineral in the blood for the muscles and nerves to function properly.

There are many potential applications for vitamin D and its various forms in clinical care. Patients with chronic kidney failure, for example, have a severely limited ability to convert vitamin D to its active form and therefore often develop a variety of bone diseases. Research is needed to determine how they may benefit from treatment with active forms of vitamin D or synthetic analogues of this nutrient. Children with genetic defects, such as vitamin D-dependency rickets type II, will benefit from work to correct a defect in their cells that prevents vitamin D from being utilized. There is continuing study of the effects of calcium, vitamin D, and estrogen to treat or prevent osteoporosis.

Clearly, research to define in detail the exact functions of vitamin D is in its infancy. There is still much to be learned about how vitamin D and the compounds into which the body transforms it regulate calcium absorption from food and the movement of calcium and phosphorus within the various tissues of the body, as well as their roles in preventing and treating osteoporosis and a variety of other diseases. How vitamin D and derivatives activate genes associated with growth and development is another question that will provide research opportunities with this nutrient.

Combating Atherosclerotic Heart Disease

Atherosclerosis is a disease process in which arteries that bring nutrient- and oxygen-rich blood to the cells of the body become narrowed with intrusive plaques formed by cholesterol and fibromuscular tissue. The coronary arteries of the heart are particularly susceptible to atherosclerosis, which can begin in childhood and progress silently for decades. When a coronary artery becomes narrowed by atherosclerotic plaque and then becomes obstructed, a heart attack occurs. In the United States each year, more than 1.25 million people (two-thirds of them men) suffer a heart attack; more than 500,000 of them die as a result. The major risk factors for heart disease are high concentrations of cholesterol in the blood, high blood pressure, cigarette smoking, obesity, non-insulin-dependent diabetes mellitus, and physical inactivity.

Although coronary heart disease (CHD) is the leading cause of death in this country, the age-adjusted death rate from it has dropped substantially since 1964. The nutrition and food sciences have helped to reduce the impact of this killer substantially by determining how foods and nutrients influence the development of atherosclerosis and by developing clinical and population-based strategies to reduce blood cholesterol.

Cholesterol and other fat-soluble substances, or lipids, necessary to health are carried in the blood by proteins called lipoproteins. Low-density lipoproteins (LDLs), which carry most of the cholesterol in the blood, are most strongly linked to CHD. As described in Chapter 3, molecular biologists and physiologists have discovered the basic pathways in which the LDLs are formed and function and how the body's production of cholesterol is regulated. Diets high in saturated fat and cholesterol reduce the number of receptors for LDLs in the liver; this, in turn, leads to elevated concentrations of LDLs in the blood. We have learned how cholesterol production is regulated at the molecular level and how people differ genetically in their susceptibility to CHD. The work of Michael Brown and Joseph Goldstein in this area was highlighted when they received the Nobel Prize for Physiology or Medicine in 1985.

There are many opportunities to study further the relationship between diet and CHD. For example, antioxidant nutrients such as carotenoids and vitamins E and C may help protect against damage to the artery wall caused by oxidized lipids (unstable fatty molecules that carry extra oxygen). Much work remains to investigate this association and the mechanisms of action. In addition, research is needed to determine how the body regulates the amount and distribution of its fat tissue, factors that have been linked to CHD. An increasing number of genetic abnormalities that may help predict the risk of atherosclerosis is being identified, suggesting that we may soon be able to identify an individual's risk of CHD by tests that determine whether or not their cells contain certain "biomarker" genes. Ultimately, people could receive dietary recommendations based on their personal risk of disease.

Even though a number of fats in food are linked to CHD, there is no doubt that most people in the United States like fatty foods. Half the calories consumed in industrialized nations come from only two ingredients—refined sugar and fat. Fats are responsible for the texture, flavor, and aroma of many foods, enhancing their palatability. The preference for fat in foods may be controlled in part by neurotransmitters, chemicals that enable the cells of the brain to communicate with each other. This is a fertile area for study. It may be possible in the future to design chemicals that will affect neurotransmitters, thereby influencing the amounts and kinds of food people choose to eat.

Dietary guidelines have been developed and widely disseminated to make people aware of the links between diet and disease and how to modify their eating habits to reduce the risk of developing these diseases. Many federal and state programs and private sector initiatives have undertaken to teach and apply these guidelines in homes, food assistance programs, cafeterias, supermarkets, schools, and a wide variety of other venues. The National Cholesterol Education Program (NCEP), for example, has helped increase the awareness of both the public and health professionals of the need to reduce cholesterol in the blood. A new, federally mandated food-labeling program that will make it easier for consumers to adopt lower-fat diets will go into effect in 1994. To date, however, most Americans are not meeting dietary guidelines. Much more research is required to identify the determinants of long-term dietary change and to find the best ways to apply this knowledge to increase healthful eating (and healthful life-styles generally) in this country. With improved methods of monitoring dietary intake coupled to genetic biomarkers of food intake and disease risk, surveys could identify subgroups of the population at greatest risk for various diseases. Intervention programs could then be designed to help modify those risks.

Food technologists are actively involved in modifying the food supply to enhance health. The food industry is continuing research to produce high-quality, safe, good-tasting, and desirable foods that are low in fat, sugar, and salt. Some of the new foods use fat substitutes produced from ingredients like microparticulated proteins, a variety of modified starches and gums, and newly created nonabsorbable fats. By applying advances in biotechnology and animal nutrition, researchers can make the meat of animals raised for food leaner. Gene transfer technology can be used to increase the unsaturated fat and lower the saturated fat content of oilseeds (such as cotton, sunflower, and safflower). In the future, it will be possible to create "functional" or "designer" foods containing biologically active compounds that may reduce an individual's risk of CHD and other diseases. Making the food supply more healthful will require research to clarify further the biochemistry and genetics of fat, protein, and carbohydrate metabolism in plants, animals, and microorganisms as well as continued improvements in food production technologies. The aim is to provide people with even more appealing food choices and increase the availability of health-promoting food so they can consume a healthful diet, no matter what their life-styles.

CONCLUDING REMARKS

Our two crosscutting examples illustrate a pattern in the nutrition and food sciences that often leads to important improvements in public health. First, a clinical condition or problem is clearly identified (e.g., rickets in children and atherosclerotic heart disease). Through research, we gain some, though usually not a complete, understanding of the biological mechanisms involved in its genesis, prevention, and treatment. Concurrent advances in food science and technology enable the food supply to be modified appropriately (e.g., adding vitamin D to foods and modifying the fat content of food products). Finally, government policies are brought to bear on the problem (e.g., mandating vitamin D fortification of milk and establishment of the NCEP). Chapters 3 through 6 identify many opportunities for research and the development of new and improved technologies in the nutrition and food sciences. By taking advantage of these opportunities and meeting the challenges they offer, further improvements to public health in the next century are certain.

In the next chapter, we provide a brief history of the nutrition and food sciences and more examples of how these disciplines have contributed so importantly to improving our health and well-being.

2

Accomplishments in the Nutrition and Food Sciences

Throughout history, people have observed connections between food and health. In 400 B.C., Hippocrates wrote of the relationship between diet and health. One hundred years later, beriberi was described in Chinese texts, as were other nutrient-deficiency diseases in early writings. Hippocrates and Galen often used the word *diet*, but the term *nutrition* did not come into popular use until the latter half of the nineteenth century. The concept of nutrition—that human beings require a steady intake of specific components of food in defined amounts—is thus clearly a modern one. Food science and technology are concerned with the vehicle—food—in which essential and desirable food components are delivered to the body in adequate amounts and in safe, acceptable forms.

The earliest efforts in nutrition science are often attributed to Antoine Lavoisier. This French chemist demonstrated in 1789 that oxygen breathed in from the air is used by the body to produce carbon dioxide and water in what we know today as the central metabolic process in which food is "burned" to provide the energy needed for all bodily functions. Lavoisier showed that the amount of oxygen used was related to the amount of food consumed and the amount of physical activity. Later, other scientists observed that citrus fruits prevented scurvy, iodine prevented goiter, and unmilled rice prevented beriberi. Canning was invented and added to the processor's means of preserving food, along with the traditional fermentation, drying, and salting. Louis Pasteur developed the process of pasteurization, which saved countless lives and provided milk in a safe and palatable form. It was only early in this century, however, that scientists defined human nutritional requirements, identifying the amino acids, vitamins, fatty acids, and minerals in foods essential to health. Diseases such as scurvy, beriberi, rickets, and pellagra were found to be caused by vitamin deficiencies.

After World War II, people in the United States were generally eating better, thanks to improved transportation systems (which made a wider variety of foods available), home refrigeration, frozen foods, and nutrient-fortified foods such as bread and milk. The war stimulated improvements in dehydration, heat processing, and other technologies to minimize spoilage of food while maintaining quality and taste. Nutrient-deficiency diseases became much less prevalent in the United States and other industrialized countries.

For several decades, nutrition scientists have been examining the relationships of modern dietary patterns to deadly chronic diseases such as heart and blood vessel diseases, cancer, and diabetes. Responding to the dietary guidelines developed by the nutrition community, food scientists have developed a wide range of technologies to lower the fat, salt, and sugar in food. In addition, they have developed and implemented a variety of quality control procedures to make processed foods generally safe and of high quality.

As the nutrition and food sciences have evolved and expanded in this century, they have assumed a growing role in public policy. By 1979, the federal government was involved in more than 350 programs to ensure an adequate and safe food supply for consumers. These programs covered areas such as support to farmers, food safety and regulation, food fortification, food assistance, nutrition services and training, monitoring of food intake and nutritional status, food and nutrition research, and food and nutrition education.

In the past several decades, the federal government has become the largest funder of research in the nutrition and food sciences, now contributing more than $400 million dollars annually. Much of that research is conducted in academic laboratories at colleges and universities. The land-grant colleges and universities (with their focus on agriculture, rural communities, and the needs of consumers) have been largely responsible for the growth of the nutrition and food sciences in the United States. Much of the research in these disciplines has been conducted in departments of animal science, food science, and nutrition in schools of agriculture and home economics. Increasingly, research on diet's role in chronic disease is conducted by scientists in medical schools and schools of public health. Fundamental nutrition research is now conducted as well in more general university and professional school departments. Today, government at all levels, the private sector (particularly the food industry), biomedical researchers, health-care practitioners, foundations, and others are working individually and together to support research in the nutrition and food sciences, to bring the fruits of that research to the public, and to use it to develop programs and policies that will improve the health of the public.

As we rapidly approach a new century, new challenges in the nutrition and food sciences are emerging. Research opportunities that await us include defining and determining "optimal" nutrition (ensuring maximal health and resistance to disease throughout the lifespan), determining the role of nutrition in the expression of our genetic material, learning the role of important substances in food (such as fiber and carotenoids) that are not traditional essential nutrients, and developing more effective strategies for promoting healthful dietary change. To meet these new challenges, the science of human nutrition is becoming more interdisciplinary, drawing on food science, biochemistry, molecular biology, genetics, physiology, toxicology, epidemiology, and the social and behavioral sciences (such as sociology, psychology, anthropology, and political science) to understand the role of human nutrition in health and disease.

EXAMPLES OF ACCOMPLISHMENTS AND CHALLENGES

In the remainder of this chapter, we present examples of how research in the nutrition and food sciences has led to discoveries and applications that have substantially improved the health and well-being of people throughout the world. Chapters 3 through 6 describe future research opportunities and challenges that stem from these accomplishments.

There are many examples that might be chosen to illustrate the accomplishments of the nutrition and food sciences. The following eight are representative examples and are organized around three topics: the interactions of genes with nutrients, improving the food supply, and nutrient delivery and nutritional assessment. Further research in each of these areas is likely to result in improved health, greater resistance to disease, and better treatments for disease.

Gene-Nutrient Interactions

Iron

Iron, a constituent of hemoglobin in red blood cells, is essential for carrying oxygen from the lungs to all the body tissues. Several crucial enzymes involved in general metabolism require iron as well. Iron deficiency remains one of the most common nutritional deficiencies around the world. Groups most subject to deficiency are pregnant women, infants, children, and menstruating women. Iron deficiency impairs physical

NOBEL PRIZES FOR RESEARCH APPLICABLE TO THE NUTRITION AND FOOD SCIENCES

The Nobel Prize, established by Alfred Nobel at the turn of the century to honor "those who . . . shall have conferred the greatest benefit on mankind," is perhaps the most prestigious award one can receive for one's work in certain fields. We list here Nobel laureates in physiology or medicine and in chemistry whose work falls within the nutrition and food sciences.

Year	Name	Accomplishment
1902	Emil Herman Fischer (Germany)	Research on the synthesis of sugars and purines
1904	Ivan P. Pavlov (Russia)	Work on the physiology of digestion
1923	Sir Frederick G. Banting (Canada) and John J.R. MacLeod (Canada)	Discovered the hormone insulin
1928	Adolf O.R. Windaus (Germany)	Research on sterols and their connection to vitamins
1929	Christiaan Eijkman (Netherlands) and Sir Frederick G. Hopkins (Britain)	Discovered the antineuritic vitamin (thiamin) and several growth-stimulating vitamins
1929	Sir Arthur Harden (Britain) and H. von Euler-Chelpin (Sweden)	Investigated the fermentation of sugars by yeast juice, leading to later studies of the basic metabolic processes of life
1934	George R. Minot, William P. Murphy, and George H. Whipple (United States)	Discoveries concerning liver therapy against anemia (Years later, it was shown that vitamin B_{12}, found in liver, could prevent or treat pernicious anemia.)
1937	Sir Walter Norman Haworth (Britain)	Research on carbohydrates and vitamin C
1937	Paul Karrer (Switzerland)	Research on carotenoids and vitamins A and B
1937	Albert Szent-György (Hungary)	Research on basic metabolic processes, with an emphasis on vitamin C
1938	Richard Kuhn (Germany)	Research on carotenoids and vitamins
1943	Henrik Dam (Denmark) and Edward A. Doisy (United States)	Discovery of vitamin K and research on its chemical nature

1945	Artturi Virtanen (Finland)	Development of several inventions in agriculture and nutritional chemistry, especially a method to preserve fodder
1947	Carl F. Cori and Gerty T. Cori (United States)	Research on glycogen and its conversions by enzymes
1953	Sir Hans Adolf Krebs (Britain) and Fritz A. Lipmann (United States)	Discovery of the citric acid cycle in the metabolism of carbohydrates
1955	Vincent Du Vigneaud (United States)	Studies on the biochemistry of sulphur compounds and contributions to knowledge about the vitamin biotin
1957	Sir Alexander Robertus Todd (Britain)	Research on nucleotides and their coenzymes (Early in his career, he synthesized thiamin and worked on vitamins E and B_{12}.)
1964	Konrad Bloch (United States) and Feodor Lynen (Germany)	Research on the metabolism of cholesterol and fatty acids
1964	Dorothy Crowfoot Hodgkin (Britain)	Determined the structure of vitamin B_{12}
1965	Robert Burns Woodward (United States)	Developed techniques for synthesis of organic molecules, including cholesterol, chlorophyll, and vitamin B_{12}
1967	George Wald (United States)	Research on vision and the identification of a vitamin A metabolite as the critical molecule of the visual pigment rhodopsin
1970	Luis F. Leloir (Argentina)	Discovered sugar nucleotides and their role in the biosynthesis of carbohydrates
1982	Sune K. Bergström (Sweden), Bengt I. Samuelsson (Sweden), and John R. Vane (Britain)	Research on the biochemistry and physiology of prostaglandins
1985	Michael S. Brown and Joseph L. Goldstein (United States)	Research into the regulation of cholesterol metabolism and the development of cholesterol-related diseases

and work performance as well as immune function. Sustained deficiency eventually leads to anemia.

Pregnant women are perhaps the most at-risk population in this country for iron deficiency. Iron deficiency and anemia during pregnancy—which are more common in African-American women and those of low socioeconomic status, with multiple gestations, and with limited education—may be harmful to the fetus, but the data are not conclusive. Iron deficiency is of special concern for infants and young children because it may affect permanently their physical and mental development. Infants with even mild iron deficiency anemia have impaired ability to attain skills that involve mental and muscular activity, such as crawling, talking, and solving cognitive problems. It is not clear whether these psychomotor delays are ever completely reversed after the deficiency is corrected. In children, iron deficiency can cause apathy, short attention span, irritability, and reduced ability to learn. Iron deficiency also increases the risk of lead toxicity, which can impair cognitive function permanently. Iron deficiency is linked with increased concentrations of lead in the blood of preschool children.

In contrast, dietary iron toxicity is rare in this country. Several hundred children each year experience acute iron poisoning from iron supplements, mistaking them for candy. People who carry a gene from both parents (who are homozygous) for hemochromatosis may experience chronic iron toxicity from consuming iron in food. Hemochromatosis is a hereditary disorder of iron metabolism that results in the slow accumulation of iron in the tissues. The primary defect appears to lie in the intestine. Intestinal iron absorption is abnormally high, resulting in excess iron being absorbed from food and supplements. If not identified and treated, hemochromatosis can lead to cirrhosis, cardiovascular disease, diabetes, arthritis, impaired immune function, cellular damage (since excess iron is an oxidant that attacks the fat molecules in cell membranes), and possibly liver cancer. While these clinical features represent the end point of a chronic condition of iron overload, children as young as two years of age with this disease may have high concentrations of iron in their blood. Hemochromatosis is believed to be the most common inherited metabolic disorder, with 1 in every 400 to 500 individuals possibly having both genes and being likely to develop the disease. The responsible gene has not been identified. Nutrition scientists are eager to understand this abnormality of iron absorption and to explore the molecular mechanisms of iron absorption in normal individuals (see Chapter 3).

There is no definitive biochemical marker in the body to diagnose hemochromatosis. The usual method of screening for this disorder in a general population is to draw blood to identify individuals with markedly elevated concentrations of ferritin (the form of iron stored in tissues) or elevated transferrin saturation (a test of the protein that carries iron in the blood). Where possible, these individuals should have the presumptive diagnosis confirmed with a follow-up liver biopsy. The treatment for this disorder is to bleed patients periodically, which removes some red blood cells and forces the body to use some of its stored iron as it replenishes its supply of these cells.

Given the relatively high prevalence of hemochromatosis in the U.S. population, it is clear that there are many more people who carry a hemochromatosis gene from one of their two biological parents (that is, who are heterozygous for this gene). These carriers—a group that may represent as many as 10 percent of people in the United States—are at increased risk of some of the diseases caused by hemochromatosis. However, blood tests to determine iron status are not sensitive enough to distinguish between heterozygotes for hemochromatosis and normal individuals. Research is needed to develop noninvasive screening tools to identify the large population of these heterozygotes. Research leading to the identification of the hemochromatosis gene and the metabolic products of its expression could open new vistas both for identifying affected individuals and for improving the treatment.

The prevalence of iron deficiency in the United States and the risks of iron overload to a significant minority raise important public policy questions and pose significant challenges for intervention. The iron fortification policies of this country have been very effective in combating iron deficiency, but we must be vigilant to ensure that iron-fortified foods reach those populations at high risk of deficiency without putting those with hemochromatosis, or those prone to the disorder, at risk. An alternative approach involves identifying the 10 percent of the population that may be at increased risk of iron overload and learning whether they need to decrease their iron intake.

Energy Balance and the Risks of Diabetes and Obesity

Diabetes exists in various forms, but they all have in common abnormal metabolism of carbohydrates, which leads to hyperglycemia (excess sugar, or glucose, in the blood). Non-insulin-dependent diabetes mellitus (NIDDM), the most common form of this disease, occurs when the body loses its ability to respond to insulin, the hormone produced by the pancreas to lower blood sugar concentrations. NIDDM is linked to obesity for reasons that are unclear. Researchers assume that at least some obesity-associated diabetes results from the interaction of the genetic backgrounds of populations and specific genetic traits in individuals, along with a variety of lifestyle factors, including what and how much one eats. These interactions are undoubtedly behind the high prevalence of obesity and diabetes among certain populations, such as the Pima Indians in the Southwest.

NIDDM has a strong genetic basis. Several gene mutations linked to NIDDM have been identified recently, including 40 different mutations of the insulin receptor on cells. (This receptor binds insulin, one of several compounds the body uses to control blood glucose concentrations, and thereby lets glucose into the cells.) Although obesity is also influenced by genes, no specific human gene mutation has yet been identified.

To study the contribution of genetic background and lifestyle to obesity, researchers have developed inbred strains of animals that are either very susceptible or very resistant to this disorder. As a result, there is an immense amount of information on the metabolic derangements and altered patterns of behavior that accompany the various forms of genetic obesity in animals. To date, however, we do not know the series of events that leads from the presence of a known gene or a specific experimental manipulation (e.g., feeding diets high in fat or sugar) to the development of full-blown obesity.

Scientists are using cellular and molecular genetic techniques to identify and isolate genes that promote obesity in laboratory rodents. One animal model shows sex-related differences in obesity-associated diabetes. The model is relevant to humans because when men and women are matched for body fatness, men are clearly at greater risk for diabetes. Studies suggest that diabetes is linked to the distribution of body fat (where in the body it tends to collect) as well as to how much there is.

The type of obesity associated with diabetes and its complications is called central, or android, obesity. In this type, the enlarged fat cells are found primarily in the abdomen. Where in the abdomen the fat is found—just under the skin (subcutaneous) or deeper (visceral)—also affects the risk of disease. The more benign form of obesity is known as gynoid obesity, in which excess fat is deposited mainly in the hips and thighs. Obese men tend toward android obesity; obese women are of both types. How the distribution of excess body fat influences metabolism and the risks of disease is unclear, but stimuli (such as the concentrations of sex hormones) have different effects on fat cells depending on where in the body they are. Much more research is needed to define the link between distribution of body fat, insulin resistance, the influence of sex hormones, and the risk of diabetes and other chronic diseases.

As will be discussed in Chapters 3 and 5, many opportunities exist to study the underlying causes of these two disorders, particularly the mechanisms through which genetic and dietary factors interact. Progress will be made toward this goal through further research on inbred strains of animals and by using transgenic animals (animals into which DNA from a different species of animal or plant has been inserted; see section on biotechnology later in this chapter).

Folate and Neural Tube Defects

During this century, we have learned much about the biochemistry and physiology of vitamins in relation to human nutritional requirements, but we continue to learn more. For example, foods or vitamin supplements containing the B vitamin folic acid, taken prior to and during the first trimester of pregnancy, can prevent some neural tube defects (NTDs)— birth defects in which the spinal column does not close during embryonic development.

We hypothesize that NTDs result from interactions between the genes of the developing embryo and its intrauterine environment. The genetic component, which probably involves several genes, is complex and not well understood. Epidemiological studies (in which population groups are compared) and other evidence indicate a strong environmental component as well. The nature of these environmental factors, especially the supposed role of micronutrients (vitamins and minerals), is not well understood. Animal models support the hypothesis that vitamin deficiencies contribute to some human NTDs.

Growing evidence from observational and intervention studies in humans suggests that supplements of folic acid [0.1 to 4.0 milligrams (mg) per day] taken around the time of conception (one to three months before conception and during the first six weeks of pregnancy) can reduce the risk of NTDs. On the basis of these studies, the federal government has recommended that fertile women consume 0.4 mg of folic acid each day, slightly more than twice their current recommended dietary allowance (RDA). While it is not difficult to obtain this amount from food with a well-selected diet, most women fail to do so.

More research is needed to determine the amount of folic acid that prevents NTDs most effectively, to learn the molecular mechanisms by which folic acid reduces the incidence of NTDs, and to determine the risks to the population at large of significantly increasing folic acid intake. It is known that folic acid converted to forms that participate in reactions that lead to DNA synthesis. Therefore, it may prevent delays in DNA synthesis, delays in fetal development through abnormal expression of genes, and thus the failure of the neural tube to form completely.

Recommendations have been made to fortify foods with folic acid so that all women capable of becoming pregnant can more easily consume 0.4 mg per day in their diets. However, this strategy presents some difficult public policy issues, because it would lead to most of the public consuming significantly more folic acid than they do now, and this could pose risks to some. For folate, as for most nutrients, we know little about the long-term effects of ingesting considerably more than the RDA, particularly in forms that are very well absorbed by the body. We have no information about how ingesting 1 or more mg of folic acid daily over months and years may affect individuals with conditions that may predispose them to unanticipated harmful effects. For example, approximately one-quarter of the elderly population may be at risk for vitamin B_{12} deficiency because their ability to absorb B_{12} from foods or supplements is impaired. Since folic acid masks the characteristic anemia of vitamin B_{12} deficiency, widespread fortification of foods with this nutrient could permit vitamin B_{12} deficiency to go undiagnosed.

We encourage readers interested in this topic to peruse Chapter 5, which presents many opportunities for investigating the role of nutrition and its relation to various pregnancy-related outcomes and conditions and the long-term consequences of nutritional insults and inadequate nutrition on early development. Chapter 6 provides a discussion of the research opportunities in assessing growth, development, and nutritional status, as well as understanding the motivations for and barriers to changing food habits.

Oxidative Damage to DNA, Proteins, and Fats

Research using methods that range from the test tube to an entire population suggests that forms of oxygen produced in our bodies in the course of daily living can cause significant damage, affecting the aging process and increasing our risks of a variety of chronic diseases. These "active oxygen" species include singlet oxygen and oxygen radicals containing an unpaired electron, which makes them likely to interact with important molecules in the body and produce undesirable by-products. For example, oxidized genetic material (DNA) can initiate or promote the development of cancers of the lung, colon, breast, and uterus and cause chromosomal abnormalities. Oxidative damage to proteins is linked to the formation of cataracts. Oxidized fatty acids and the products formed from them are linked to damage to the arteries leading to the buildup of fatty plaques. Oxidative damage caused by active oxygen species also may compromise the immune system.

Given the constant, inevitable production of active oxygen species, it is no surprise that the body has evolved mechanisms to prevent their damaging consequences, some of which are influenced by what we eat. The enzymes superoxide dismutase (which contain essential trace minerals such as copper, manganese, and zinc) and glutathione peroxidase (which contains the essential trace mineral selenium) provide two such mechanisms to inactivate these forms of oxygen. Many carotenoids (including those that are precursors of vitamin A) can quench singlet oxygen, and vitamin E can prevent the propagation of oxygen radical-initiated reactions. Vitamin C regenerates vitamin E that has become oxidized in the course of fighting oxidation, thereby contributing to the efficacy of this fat-soluble vitamin. Several studies of population groups link low intakes and low blood concentrations of these antioxidant nutrients with several diseases, including heart disease, several cancers, and cataracts of the eye. Evidence of health benefits from supplements of these nutrients is suggestive but not yet convincing.

Each of the diseases mentioned above has important genetic components. The predisposition to coronary heart disease that occurs in middle age can be explained in significant measure by genetic disorders that involve the transport of cholesterol and other fats in the blood. However, the known risk factors underlying heart disease (such as high blood cholesterol, high blood pressure, and cigarette smoking) fail to account for much of the individual susceptibility to this major cause of death in the United States. Although there is considerable evidence that oxidation of blood lipoproteins within the arterial wall, particularly the low-density lipoproteins (LDLs) that carry most of the cholesterol in the blood, underlies the early development of atherosclerotic plaques, the factors that regulate formation of oxidized LDL are still largely unknown. That such factors could be critical is supported by observations that the susceptibility of individuals with familial hypercholesterolemia, a common genetic disease, to the development of coronary heart disease varies widely among families and cannot be explained simply by the concentrations of LDL in the blood. What may underlie these differing susceptibilities are important interactions between nutrients and genes that are influenced by diet or how the body metabolizes critical nutrients. Similarly, the genetic determinants of metabolism and the way the body handles various nutrients may underlie some of the genetic susceptibility to other chronic diseases that can develop as a result of oxidative damage.

The fact that one's genetic endowment can influence the aging process is suggested by observations in the fruit fly. Strains specially bred to be long-lived tend to have a more active form of the enzyme superoxide dismutase. In one strain into which genetic material was inserted, leading the flies to produce greater than normal amounts of this enzyme, the average life span (though not the maximum life span) was increased.

These examples provide some indication of the types of research in antioxidant biology that have considerable potential to improve human health. For further details, see Chapter 3.

Improving the Food Supply

Sensory Biology and the Development of New Foods

The typical person in the United States derives more than one-third of his or her daily calories from fat and one-fourth from sugars, both natural and added. Fat and sugar together account for more than one-half the total daily energy intake. Diets low in carbohydrate and fiber but rich in simple sugars and fat are linked to a high prevalence of obesity and increased risk of chronic disease, including coronary heart disease, diabetes, and some forms of cancers. Excessive fat intake has been called the number-one problem in the U.S. diet, and current dietary guidelines recommend reducing fat consumption to 30 percent or less of total calorie intake.

Reducing fat consumption is no easy task. We generally like the taste of high-fat foods and are reluctant to give them up. High-fat diets are flavorful, varied, and rich. Fats are largely responsible for the texture, mouthfeel, and flavor of many foods and play an important role in determining the palatability of the diet. Poor adherence to low-fat regimens is a documented problem in the dietary management of people with high cholesterol counts, while cravings for sweet, high-fat foods are a major obstacle to weight reduction. Even highly motivated cardiac patients often find it difficult to follow diets composed of grains, vegetables, fruit, and low-fat dairy products.

One approach to implementing dietary guidelines is to apply existing strategies and models of behavior change to the dietary behavior of communities and populations. The National Cholesterol Education Program is a classic example of this approach to lower total fat, saturated fat, and cholesterol consumption in this country. Another approach to implementing dietary guidelines is to alter the available food supply, because dietary compliance may increase if low-fat foods offer the same eating pleasure as foods high in fat. Recent advances in food technology, particularly the development of fat-replacement products, offer one way of reducing fat consumption while satisfying natural sensory preferences for a varied, palatable diet. Similarly, the use of intense sweeteners offers a way of reducing excess sugar consumption.

Sensory preferences for sweetness and fat are deeply ingrained and appear to be universal. The pleasure response to sweetness is innate and has been observed in human infants at birth. The pleasure response to fats is most likely learned early on; sensory preferences for high-fat foods have been observed in children, adolescents, and adults. The pleasure response to palatable foods may involve central brain mechanisms. The neurotransmitter serotonin and endogenous opioid peptides may mediate preferences for carbohydrates, sugar, and fat. Taste preference profiles for sugar-fat mixtures also change with age and may be modified further by repeated cycles of weight loss and gain.

At the same time, large-scale epidemiological and agricultural studies suggest that the amount of fat in the typical diet is strongly influenced by socioeconomic factors. Indeed, the amount of fat in the typical Western diet may be influenced not so much by physiological variables as by the amount of fat available in the food supply. Consequently, strategies for reducing fat consumption must be planned carefully.

The food industry has made impressive progress in increasing the range of palatable yet low-fat products available to consumers. One promising area is the production of leaner beef, leaner pork, and eggs with less cholesterol. The food industry is using new technologies to develop new generations of low-calorie or zero-calorie fat replacement products and new versions of intense sweeteners.

Biotechnology

Since first domesticating plants and animals, people have exploited the genetic diversity of living systems to improve the food supply. Over the centuries, we have developed well-accepted techniques for selectively breeding plants and animals for desirable characteristics. Producing fermented foods such as cheese, bread, and wine in a wide variety of forms depends on an ability to manipulate and alter microorganisms. Biotechnology provides a new set of tools for improving the variety, productivity, and efficiency of food production and the nutritional quality of foods. Genetic engineering provides a mechanism for producing specific genetic improvements in plants, animals, and microorganisms in less time and with greater precision, predictability, and control than possible with traditional methods of breeding and selection.

Plants Genetic engineering can be used to improve dramatically the nutritional quality of plants by making minor modifications in their genetic makeup. For example, cereal grains, which are the main source of protein for the vast majority of the world, are deficient in essential amino acids. Improving their amino acid composition would make them a higher-quality, more complete source of protein. It is now possible to improve the nutritional value of oilseeds, which supply almost half the fat in our diets. Gene transfer technology has been used to alter composition and reduce the degree of saturation of fatty acids in major oilseed crops such as sunflower and safflower.

The many studies linking diet to cancer have led to research to identify the responsible components in food. Over 600 plant-derived chemicals (phytochemicals) have cancer-preventing potential, including antioxidants such as beta-carotene and vitamins C and E. In the future, genetic engineering will make it possible to manipulate the amount of these chemicals in food. In addition, plant tissue culture techniques may be used to produce phytochemicals that could be added to processed foods.

An emerging technology that promises to have a dramatic effect on the genetic engineering of plants involves inserting a single gene normally present in a plant in the opposite orientation. This antisense technology has already been used to block the expression of single genes involved in the ripening process in tomatoes (thereby reducing losses caused by premature spoilage) and in caffeine production in coffee beans. It could also be used to block the production in food of antinutrients such as phytates and oxalates, which bind to minerals and make them unavailable for absorption. By improving the taste, texture, and shelf life of fresh fruits and vegetables, this technology should entice more consumers to eat more of these nutritious foods.

Animals   Genetic engineering will be increasingly important in animal agriculture. The most obvious applications involve directly manipulating an animal's body composition, growth rate, and disease resistance. There is also a growing interest in using transgenic animals (which have incorporated genetic material from an unrelated animal, plant, or microorganism) to produce novel proteins in milk, blood, and urine that can be extracted and purified.

Many complex biological processes affecting fertility, ratios of lean meat to fat, growth rate, and milk yield are regulated by hormones. The genes directing the production of many of these hormones have been cloned, providing opportunities to manipulate the physiology of farm animals. For example, somatotropin (growth hormone) genes from several animal species have been identified, characterized, and integrated into the gene pool of related and unrelated animal species. Supplements of bovine somatotropin (BST) improve the feed efficiency of cows and increase their milk production without altering the milk's composition. Porcine somatotropin (PST) enables the pig to form muscle rather than fat, dramatically reducing the fat content of pork.

Genetic changes that improve disease resistance and feed digestion in food-producing animals will have an indirect but very positive effect on the nutritional quality of their meat and milk. Several economically important diseases might be combated by transgenic strategies, thereby decreasing dependence on antibiotics and broad-spectrum chemical treatments and reducing drug residues in the food supply. Genetic approaches have been proposed to increase the digestive capacity of ruminant animals. One option is to add transgenic bacteria that produce digestive enzymes into the rumen of these animals. For example, enzymes called phytases increase the availability of phosphorus, which is essential for forming bone, in plant foods. Incorporating phytase-producing bacteria in the rumen of cows, for example, would reduce both the amount of expensive phosphorus needed in their diet and the amount excreted in their feces. The latter would reduce phosphorus contamination of groundwater from farm wastes.

Food-processing biotechnology   Bacteria, yeasts, and molds have been used for centuries to produce fermented foods such as cheese, yogurt, sausage, pickles, sauerkraut, wine, beer, soy sauce, and bread. Biotechnology can be used to alter the metabolic processes of these microorganisms in ways that will improve production efficiency and extend shelf life, improve nutritional content, or ensure the safety of the product. Microorganisms with a long history of safe use can be manipulated to produce food flavors and flavor enhancers, sweeteners, thickeners, and nutritive additives such as vitamins, amino acids, and fiber.

Biotechnology will enable us to develop systems that rapidly detect pathogenic and spoilage organisms, microbial and fungal toxins, and chemical and biological contaminants in foods. In addition, it will provide innovative ways of treating food-processing waste with microorganisms and enzymes to help prevent environmental contamination and convert some of this waste to higher-value food and nonfood products.

To make the most of biotechnology, we must learn much more about metabolism in plants, animals, and microorganisms. Many opportunities exist, for example, to study the biochemistry and genetics of carbohydrate, protein, and fat metabolism. There is little doubt that this powerful technology will improve dramatically the nutritional quality of the food supply in the coming years. (For further details, see Chapter 4.)

Preventing Childhood Morbidity and Mortality

Oral Rehydration Therapy

The development of oral rehydration therapy (ORT) represents a milestone in the history of public health nutrition. Use of an oral solution containing sugar and electrolytes to help replenish fluids lost during acute diarrhea can be traced back thousands of years to traditional folk remedies and non-western medical traditions. The scientific rationale for such a therapy emerged with the recognition in the 1800s that the mortality associated with cholera was due primarily to diarrhea and the resulting loss of body fluids and electrolytes.

Basic research in the 1950s established the mechanisms by which sodium and organic solutes are transported in intestinal cells. By the l960s, clinical studies of the effectiveness of ORT were being carried out in several Asian countries. These were followed by studies that confirmed the efficacy of oral rehydration and extended it as a therapy to patients suffering from acute diarrhea of any origin.

Diarrhea is the most frequent cause of death of young children in the world. To combat this scourge, the World Health Organization (WHO) in 1971 formulated a simple and standard oral rehydration solution; it began worldwide distribution of packets of this solution and instructions to prepare the solution at home. Efforts to promote ORT have targeted the household, as ORT is a simple, inexpensive primary health care intervention that can be used effectively by family members. The initial mass health education programs to encourage widespread use of ORT had only limited success. Public health workers have learned that they must recognize and work within the health beliefs and childcare practices of various cultures if they are to succeed in increasing the acceptance and use of ORT.

Vitamin A

The first scientific paper describing the discovery of vitamin A appeared in 1913. Investigators soon learned that rats made deficient in this nutrient stopped growing, became more susceptible to infections, and died. Those that managed to survive the longest ultimately developed xerophthalmia, a term for eye problems caused by vitamin A deficiency. Human xerophthalmia is very dramatic; the most severe manifestation is keratomalacia, in which the cornea literally melts, often in just a few hours, causing blindness. Children who develop keratomalacia die at a high rate, because they are not only severely deficient in vitamin A, but also badly malnourished in general, usually suffering from respiratory diseases and diarrhea.

For many decades, scientists and health workers focused on the ocular changes resulting from vitamin A deficiency. As a result, they did not recognize or become sufficiently alarmed by the other potential consequences of this deficiency, particularly in impoverished developing nations. This situation began to change in the early 1980s after investigators followed a group of 4,000 pre-school-age children in Indonesia who appeared well-nourished and healthy, but who had night blindness and other mild manifestations of xerophthalmia. Over time, the children with mild xerophthalmia died at a greater rate than children whose eyes were clinically normal at the beginning of the study. This association had a strong dose-response relationship; that is, the more vitamin A-deficient the child, the more likely he or she was to die, suggesting that the observation went beyond mere coincidence. However, it was always possible that other, unrecognized factors associated with vitamin A deficiency accounted for the increase in the death rate (mortality). The next logical step was to conduct controlled clinical trials to eliminate potential confounding factors and to determine whether reversing vitamin A deficiency could reduce mortality.

By 1993, these clinical trials had been conducted in several countries in Southeast Asia, Africa, and Central America. The overwhelming conclusion based on the combined results is that improving vitamin A status can reduce mortality, mainly from diarrhea and respiratory diseases, in childhood by 25 to nearly 40 percent. In fact, some studies suggested that the reduction in mortality might be as high as 72 percent if every child targeted for vitamin A treatment had actually received all the treatments.

These phenomena are one side of an emerging equation. The other side concerns measles-related mortality. Measles in Africa is a devastating disease; it has a high mortality and is the major cause of blindness among African children. Studies of children hospitalized for severe measles in Africa have shown that providing vitamin A can save lives and reduce the severity of sickness brought on by the disease. WHO and the United Nations International Children's Emergency Fund (UNICEF) recommend that vitamin A be routinely used to treat children with measles in all countries where vitamin A deficiency is known to be a problem or where the fatality rate from measles exceeds 1 percent.

Initiatives must be developed to ensure that all children get enough vitamin A to prevent even subclinical deficiencies (those that are not readily apparent). Among the initiatives proposed or already adopted are encouraging breastfeeding, promoting cultivation of foods rich in beta-carotene (which the body converts to vitamin A), changing dietary habits, fortifying commonly used ingredients, and providing supplements of vitamin A to children to build up their stores of this nutrient in the liver.

We have learned that vitamin A supports the growth and development of body tissues soon after conception and on through life. This nutrient is also required for the health and integrity of the skin and other organs, such as the lung and intestine, that help prevent microorganisms from entering the body. Growing evidence points to the importance of vitamin A and its metabolites (compounds the vitamin is converted into) and to precursors of vitamin A (carotenoids such as beta-carotene) in maintaining health and reducing the risk of certain cancers and possibly heart disease. Yet we have much to learn about optimal intakes of vitamin A and the carotenoids as well as the mechanisms by which they promote growth and health. Exciting advances in molecular and developmental biology described in Chapter 3 have led to the discovery that a metabolite of vitamin A, retinoic acid, directs the expression of a large number of genes. Future research will undoubtedly help us to understand how vitamin A acts in organs throughout the body to maintain their health, control infection, and protect against various chronic diseases.

New Concepts of Nutrient Requirements

Nutrient requirements are currently defined as the amounts of nutrients needed to maintain normal body functions. The most widely used methods to determine requirements have been nutritional balance, or depletion-repletion, studies. In such studies, the requirement for a nutrient was assumed to be met if intake equaled output (i.e., balance) or if body functions dependent on that nutrient remained "normal." Recently, we have learned that nutritional balance can be achieved without maintaining normal or optimal function. This was evident, for example, in studies of zinc nutrition in lactating Amazonian women. Although their usual intake of zinc was only 8.4 mg per day (about two-thirds of the amount recommended), they achieved a positive zinc balance by absorbing a high proportion of the intake. When these women were given zinc supplements, their milk supplied adequate zinc and larger amounts of vitamin A, and their nursing infants had less risk of developing diarrhea. Apparently, the usual zinc "balance" of these women was not without cost to them and their infants in terms of other biological functions. We therefore cannot assume that all zinc functions are fully met just because balance is achieved.

During the past decade, we have made significant advances in using heavy isotopes as tracers to study the metabolism of nutrients. Methods have been developed to administer these isotopes to humans, as have analytical methods for measuring them in biological samples. These techniques have enabled us to measure body stores, turnover, kinetics (movement), and recycling of nutrients in people with very different eating habits and physiological states (e.g., adolescence and pregnancy). It is now possible, with the help of computers and appropriate software, to use this information to develop mathematical models that depict the movement of nutrients through the digestive system, into the bloodstream, and to specific sites within tissues. These kinetic models have been built for several nutrients, including zinc, selenium, copper, calcium, and vitamins A and D.

A kinetic model can be used, for example, to determine whether particular dietary patterns place individuals at risk of depleting their body stores of zinc by reducing zinc absorption from the intestine or increasing its excretion in urine and sweat. An adequate zinc intake might be defined as the amount required to maintain zinc stores at some specified level at an appropriate rate of absorption from the intestine. A diet poor in zinc could then be defined as one that leads to a drop in body stores or that maintains body stores by forcing the body to substantially increase zinc absorption or markedly decrease excretion. Dietary zinc requirements could then be formulated for a variety of different types of diets consumed around the world, such as cereal-based (moderate-zinc) diets, red-meat-based (high-zinc) diets, or poultry-based (low-zinc) diets. In this way we can begin to individualize dietary zinc requirements and recommend intakes for populations based on their usual dietary patterns.

As we begin to think about possible changes in dietary allowances, we must revisit the criteria for establishing requirements for all nutrients in healthy people in a manner similar to that described above for zinc. Also, these same models and novel approaches can be used to study nutrient requirements of people with various diseases. For example, the wasting syndrome associated with acquired immunodeficiency syndrome (AIDS) places those patients at particular nutritional risk. They could be studied using isotopic tracers to determine how this disease alters nutrient balance. However, apart from the relevance of such research to specific diseases, learning how disease disrupts nutrient balance can provide new insights into nutrient metabolism in health.

We have learned a great deal about our vulnerability to specific nutrient deficiencies and the detection and consequences of these deficiencies based on a quarter century of experience in delivering nutrients to individuals with various diseases who cannot eat normally. These patients require nourishment delivered entirely through a vein (total parenteral nutrition) or with synthetic formulas either by mouth or via a tube in the stomach or intestine (enteral nutrition). Some receiving this specialized form of nutrition support have developed nutrient deficiencies—particularly of trace minerals such as zinc, copper, selenium, molybdenum, and chromium—that are often clinically dramatic. The good news, however, is that identifying these deficiencies has enabled investigators to determine the essentiality and practical importance of these trace minerals in human nutrition and to design more effective formulations. For example, studies of patients fed entirely intravenously have provided the only evidence that humans are vulnerable to a dietary deficiency of molybdenum and some of the strongest evidence that chromium deficiency may impair our ability to metabolize carbohydrates properly.

It is in providing specialized nutrition support that we have also detected deficiencies of vitamins, minerals, essential fatty acids, and certain amino acids. The amino acid glutamine is one such example. Glutamine is not regarded to be a dietary essential because it can be synthesized in adequate quantities by our muscles. It then enters the blood circulation and is taken up, in part, by other tissues where it is needed, especially the immune system, kidneys, and the cells lining the intestine. The intestine, which uses glutamine as a source of energy, derives what it needs in part from the diet, as this amino acid is present in protein-containing foods. A patient fed entirely by vein will depend entirely on the supply from his or her muscle, as the present generation of intravenous amino acid preparations does not contain glutamine. Patients receiving this form of nutritional support who experience trauma or infection may not make enough glutamine in their muscles to meet their needs.

Enteral and parenteral nutrition will become increasingly important in the nutritional management of patients with a variety of disabling diseases and medical problems. Continuing research in this area in both animals and humans should yield further insights into the occurrence and consequences of deficient and excessive intakes of various nutrients.

In the future, it may be possible to use functional tests of nutrient-dependent functions to establish nutrient requirements, either alone or in conjunction with other endpoints (such as body stores or turnover rates). For example, since we need adequate zinc in our diets to detect and discriminate various tastes, requirements for zinc might be defined as the amount that maintains taste acuity and enables the body to store a specific amount of the mineral. In addition, we may wish to broaden the criteria for establishing dietary allowances to encompass the goal of maximizing healthy lifespans through the prevention of chronic diseases and by slowing the aging process. Earlier in this chapter, for example, we noted that antioxidant nutrients such as vitamins C and E consumed in adequate amounts from food or taken as supplements might help to protect against heart disease, several cancers, and cataracts. Clinical trials are needed to determine the levels of intake of nutrients and other biologically active constituents in food (such as dietary fiber and carotenoids) that enhance health and reduce the risk of disease. (For further details, see Chapter 6.)

CONCLUDING REMARKS

In the next four chapters, we describe in detail a variety of current and future opportunities for exciting and challenging research to advance the nutrition and food sciences and to meet critical human needs. Many of these opportunities stem from the accomplishments described above. Chapter 3 presents opportunities in the basic biological sciences applicable to nutrition, followed by food science and technology in Chapter 4. In Chapter 5, we present opportunities in clinical nutrition research, followed by Chapter 6 on public health nutrition. Some opportunities in these latter two areas are clearly dependent on technological advances, but many also depend upon research in basic biology and food science.

3

Understanding Genetic, Molecular, Cellular, and Physiological Processes

The biological well-being of humans is a composite of genetics, nutrition, and other environmental influences that may explain the renaissance of research in nutrition science. In this chapter, we present selected opportunities in the nutrition sciences at the molecular and cellular levels. The development of the techniques of molecular genetics and of analytical equipment and powerful computer-based techniques to analyze the resulting data has driven much of the progress and created many of the research opportunities in the basic sciences related to nutrition. Much of this technology is described in this chapter, but it is also relevant to many sections in Chapters 4 and 5.

Research in nutrition, as in any field, evolves as a mosaic of information gathered from technological advances and conceptual breakthroughs. Two disciplines have made particularly important contributions: nuclear physics and molecular biology. During the first half of this century, developments in nuclear physics led scientists to produce radioactive and stable isotopes. In the mid-1930s, stable isotopes were used to show that body lipids labeled with deuterium are in a dynamic state, with constant interaction among the body pools and substantial influence by absorbed dietary lipids. Experiments with ^{15}N-labeled amino acids provided early insights into the dynamics of protein synthesis. The knowledge of nutrient metabolism gained during the last half century would not have been possible without use of radioisotopes.

Molecular biology made its impact on nutrition through advances in understanding the regulation of gene expression. In the early 1960s, studies of the regulation of lactose metabolism in the bacterium, *Escherichia coli* began our understanding of nutrient metabolism at the molecular level. Lactose was found to stimulate the synthesis of enzymes involved in the conversion of lactose to galactose and glucose and in transporting galactose into the cell. As we discuss later, nutrients regulate the metabolic fate of mammalian cells and control the metabolism of other nutrients.

Nutrition as a field of scientific inquiry poses important questions that can be investigated from many perspectives. Major contributions of basic biological research to the understanding of nutrient metabolism and function at the cellular level include: (1) nutrient transport in the brain and intestine, (2) uptake and utilization of nutrients by cells, (3) control of gene expression by nutrients, and (4) hormonal regulation of nutrient metabolism. Results of research in these areas of biology provide the framework for understanding nutrient assessment, dietary recommendations, and the interactions of nutrients in disease and health. In this chapter, we briefly review several examples of contemporary discoveries in nutrition where basic science was skillfully applied to illuminate a physiological process. We also describe several rapidly advancing technologies creating new opportunities for basic research in nutrition science. These examples illustrate several of the many opportunities that lie ahead.

ACCOMPLISHMENTS AND RELATED POSSIBILITIES

Brown and Goldstein and Lipid Metabolism

Cholesterol, a small lipid molecule, is essential to membrane integrity and is the precursor of bile acids, steroid hormones, and vitamin D. Yet elevated cholesterol in blood plasma (hypercholesterolemia) is one of three major risk factors, along with smoking and hypertension, of atherosclerotic heart disease, the major cause of death in the United States. Atherosclerosis is characterized by an accumulation of esterified cholesterol within the smooth muscle cells and macrophages of the artery wall, eventually leading to cell death and hardening of the arteries. The resulting obstruction of the vessel can reduce or cut off blood flow, causing heart attack or stroke.

Cholesterol is both synthesized in the body and contained in foods commonly found in most Western diets. A fundamental problem in cell biology is understanding how cells control their cholesterol content. Epidemiological studies identified elevated concentrations of low-density lipoprotein (LDL), carrier of the major portion of cholesterol in human plasma, as the main factor causing atherosclerosis. Diets high in saturated fat and cholesterol elevate LDL levels in most individuals. A genetic disease called familial hypercholesterolemia (FH) causes severe hyper-cholesterolemia in a few people that can be improved, but not normal-ized, through dietary treatment alone.

By the early 1970s, it was known that FH exists in two clinical forms: a severe, homozygous form, in which LDL cholesterol is elevated 6 to 10 times normal and heart attacks may begin in childhood; and a less severe, heterozygous form, in which plasma LDL cholesterol is elevated 2 times normal at birth and heart attacks begin in the fourth to fifth decade of life. Heterozygous FH occurs in approximately 1 person in 500; the ho-mozygous form affects about 1 in 1 million persons.

In 1972, Michael Brown and Joseph Goldstein hypothesized that FH might be caused by a failure of cells to repress cholesterol synthesis. The concept of feedback inhibition was well established, but genetic defects in end-product regulation had not previously been associated with human or animal disease. But how could cholesterol regulation, then thought to be the provenance of the liver and intestine, be studied in patients? Using an assay for the rate-limiting enzyme in cholesterol synthesis, Brown and Goldstein found that cholesterol synthesis increased in normal fibroblasts when lipoproteins were removed from the culture medium. Conversely, synthesis was rapidly suppressed when LDL was added back. Moreover, cells from patients with homozygous FH had a high rate of cholesterol synthesis even when LDL was added. These studies identify LDL as a regulator of cellular cholesterol synthesis and FH as a disease of impaired end-product regulation of cholesterol biosynthesis.

Studies originally undertaken to explore how LDL cholesterol is de-livered to cells provided new insight into fundamental pathways of protein movement across cell membranes. Studies of Brown and Goldstein and others showed that the regulated uptake of LDL could be separated into distinct steps: (1) binding to the LDL receptor on the plasma membrane, (2) movement of LDL receptors into regions of the plasma membrane (coated pits) that invaginate to form endocytic vesicles that contain LDL, (3) dissociation of LDL from the LDL receptor in lysosomes at acid pH, (4) lysosomal degradation of the LDL protein and hydrolysis of LDL's esterified cholesterol, and (5) recycling of LDL receptors to the plasma membrane. The elucidation of the LDL receptor pathway was possible in large part because LDL uptake in FH fibroblasts contained mutations in the proteins that mediate most of these distinct steps. Eventually, the combination of genetic, biochemical, and molecular analyses revealed at least five separate classes of mutations, each of which causes the FH phenotype (Figure 3.1). The concepts of LDL receptor saturation, inter-nalization, and down-regulation of LDL receptor synthesis also helped to explain why diets high in fat stimulate production of LDL from its precur-sors and elevate circulating LDL levels.

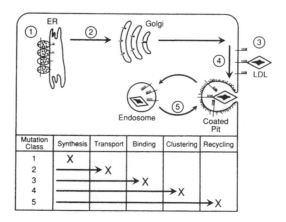

Mutation Class	Synthesis	Transport	Binding	Clustering	Recycling
1	X				
2		X			
3			X		
4				X	
5					X

FIGURE 3.1 Five classes of mutations at the LDL receptor locus. These mutations disrupt the receptor's synthesis in the endoplasmic reticulum (ER), transport to the Golgi, binding of apolipoprotein ligands, clustering in coated pits, and recycling in endosomes. Each class is heterogenous at the DNA level. From Hobbs et al. (1990). Reproduced, with permission, from the Annual Review of Genetics, Vol. 24, copyright 1990 by Annual Reviews Inc.

As this example illustrates, elucidating the LDL pathway has had an impact far beyond that of understanding cholesterol homeostasis. Receptor-mediated endocytosis also applies to receptors for nutrients and hormones. The significance of these observations has been recognized frequently and ultimately led to the awarding of the Nobel Prize in Physiology or Medicine to Brown and Goldstein in 1985. The role of cholesterol and blood lipids in atherosclerosis is discussed further in Chapter 5.

Retinoic Acid

Shortly after "fat-soluble A" was described as a required dietary factor in the early 1900s, investigators recognized that vitamin A must play essential roles in reproduction and in maintaining normally differentiated epithelial cells in many organs throughout the body. Epithelia of the ocular conjunctiva and respiratory and genitourinary tracts showed especially marked histopathological changes during vitamin A deficiency. By 1931, the chemical structure of vitamin A was identified as retinol, and in the 1950s, the retinol metabolite, 11-cis-retinaldehyde, was identified as the critical light-absorbing molecule of the visual pigment rhodopsin.

Further chemical studies led to the synthesis of retinoic acid, the carboxylic acid derivative of retinol, and the demonstration that retinoic acid could substitute for retinol in growth assays and in maintaining normal cellular differentiation. In the late 1970s, it was discovered that retinoic acid regulates growth and causes embryonic stem cells to differentiate—that is, to undergo a permanent change in the pattern of gene expression. At the same time, it was found that vitamin A inhibited the promotion phase of carcinogenesis. Together, these studies implied that retinoic acid functioned in the nucleus to regulate the transcription of specific genes.

A major recent landmark in vitamin A research was the discovery of retinoic acid receptor (RAR) proteins in the nuclei of cells. These receptors function as transcription factors that regulate retinoid-responsive genes. Critical features of the nuclear receptors that mediate the actions of steroid hormones and thyroid hormones were already understood. Knowledge of these receptors served as a base for a search for additional homologous proteins with unknown ligands. Investigators cloned a cDNA encoding a novel protein structurally related to the steroid/thyroid hormone receptors. In cultured cells expressing the new receptor, addition of retinoic acid activated specific genes (see box). Subsequent experiments identified more RARs. These RARs are now recognized as members of the steroid/thyroid hormone gene superfamily. This research has established retinoic acid as an important "hormonal" form of vitamin A that acts through a mechanism analogous to that of the steroid hormones.

This basic discovery has had important consequences for nutrition, development, and cancer research. For example, previous studies of embryonic development had identified retinoic acid as a morphogen that could control the form of body parts during embryonic development. Chemical methods showed that retinoic acid is present in the embryo early in development. Researchers now hypothesize that retinoic acid provides a signal for normal cell migration.

Vitamin D—Receptors and Metabolism

Continuing interest in vitamin D derives from its importance in enabling the body to make use of available calcium. Early in this century, vitamin D was shown to cure or prevent rickets, a bone disease common at the time and a major public health problem (see Chapter 1). Our current interest in this nutrient centers on the influence that natural and synthetic analogues of vitamin D have on human diseases such as osteoporosis, endocrine disorders, skin disease, and cancer. Sufficient calcium deposition in bone, as stimulated by vitamin D (particularly early in life), minimizes the risks and consequences of osteoporosis, a painful, debilitating disorder that afflicts millions of older women.

CLONING THE FIRST NUCLEAR RETINOIC ACID RECEPTOR (RAR)

The discovery of the first nuclear RAR, RAR-alpha, occurred nearly simultaneously in laboratories in France and the United States. The estrogen and glucocorticoid receptors have modular "cassette" structures comprised of six main domains (see illustration below). The DNA-binding domain (domain C) mediates binding of the receptor to the promotor region of specific genes. The ligand-binding domain (domain E) mediates activation of the receptor complex by ligand. Investigators postulated that new genes with strong sequence similarity to the steroid/thyroid receptor genes might code for as-yet-unidentified nuclear receptors. They used cDNA probes specific for the highly conserved regions of known nuclear receptors to screen human cDNA libraries. This search identified a "candidate receptor," one similar in size and domain structure to the known nuclear receptors.

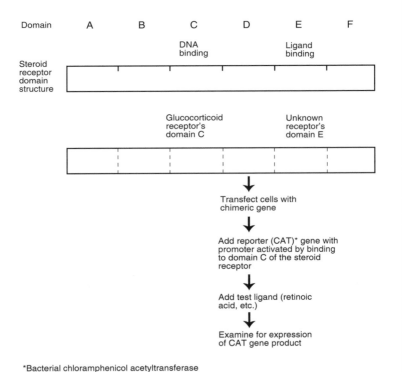

*Bacterial chloramphenicol acetyltransferase

How could the ligand for this new receptor be identified when its target genes were unknown? An ingenious strategy, the swap experiment, provided the key. Molecular cloning techniques were used to construct a new gene. Region C of the candidate receptor was replaced with region C of the glucocorticoid receptor. When the new hybrid (or chimeric) receptor was expressed, it interacted with its novel ligand through its unique domain E and bound to known glucocorticoid response elements through domain C. When cells were cotransfected with plasmid DNA that directed synthesis of the chimeric receptor and with DNA that contained a glucocorticoid-sensitive promotor linked to a reporter gene, candidate ligands could be tested for their ability to activate the reporter gene. Several natural and synthetic molecules were added as putative ligands for the chimeric receptor. Only retinoic acid was a strong activator. Based on the sequence similarity between the nuclear RAR and steroid/thyroid receptors and on the ability of RAR to activate gene transcription, the RARs are new members of the steroid/thyroid superfamily of ligand-dependent nuclear receptors.

Metabolism from Vitamin to Steroid Hormone

In the late 1960s, researchers demonstrated that vitamin D is hydroxylated to a biologically active form in the liver and kidneys. This research demonstrates the application of multiple approaches, a characteristic of nutrition research. Chromatographic methods were developed and used to show that vitamin D_3 (cholecalciferol) undergoes hydroxylation to biologically active polar metabolites, mainly 1,25 dihydroxyvitamin D_3 (calcitriol). Specialized chemical syntheses and analytical mass spectrometry were used to identify these structures. The side-chain conformations of these vitamin D derivatives were identified using high-resolution proton nuclear magnetic resonance. The structure and relationships of vitamin D and its key metabolites are shown in Figure 3.2.

Over 30 metabolites of vitamin D have been described. Calcitriol, the active form of vitamin D, is generated in the kidneys from the 25-hydroxylated metabolite produced in the liver. The enzyme responsible for hydroxylation in liver, calciferol-25-hydroxylase, is regulated by a feedback mechanism that protects against vitamin D toxicity (which would cause abnormal calcification) and helps to conserve vitamin D when dietary intake is low or formation of vitamin D in the skin is decreased.

Physiological Actions via Genomic and Nongenomic Pathways

Calcitriol regulates metabolism of calcium and phosphorus and the expression of many genes of known and unknown function. This contem-

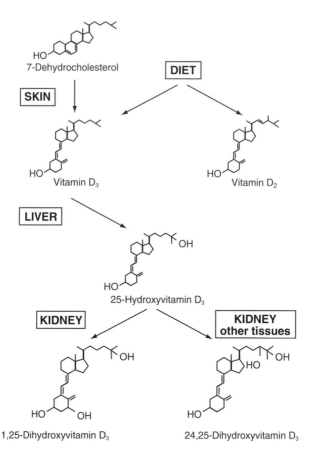

7-Dehydrocholesterol

DIET

SKIN

Vitamin D₃

Vitamin D₂

LIVER

25-Hydroxyvitamin D₃

KIDNEY

KIDNEY
other tissues

1,25-Dihydroxyvitamin D₃

24,25-Dihydroxyvitamin D₃

FIGURE 3.2 Vitamin D metabolism in the skin, liver, and kidney. From Henry, H.L., et al. 1992. The cellular and molecular regulation of $1,25(OH)_2D_3$ production. J. Steroid Biochem. Molec. Biol. 41:401-407. Copyright 1992, reprinted with kind permission from Pergamon Press Ltd.

porary biomedical research is at the interfaces of physiology, biochemistry, nutrition, and molecular biology. Our understanding of the calcium-related functions of vitamin D was enhanced with the discovery of the calcium-binding protein calbindin. Vitamin D stimulates the production of this protein by increasing transcription of the calbindin gene. Calbindin, by a mechanism not yet defined, transports calcium across intestinal cells and delivers it to a calcium pump on the basolateral membrane that is regulated by calcitriol. The pump transports calcium across the membrane into the blood and then to bone and soft tissues. Calcium metabolism is controlled by parathyroid hormone (PTH) and calcitriol (Figure

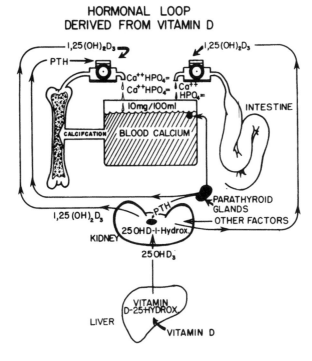

HORMONAL LOOP
DERIVED FROM VITAMIN D

FIGURE 3.3 Diagrammatic representation of the regulation of plasma calcium (ECF) concentration by the vitamin D endocrine system and the parathyroid glands. Low plasma calcium is detected by parathyroid glands. Parathyroid hormone stimulates production of $1,25(OH)_2D_3$. The two hormones act either independently or in concert to mobilize calcium from bone, kidney tubules, and small intestine, bringing about an elevation of plasma calcium concentration that in turn suppresses parathyroid hormone secretion. H.F. DeLuca, from *Nutrition: An Integrated Approach,* third edition (p. 149), by Ruth L. Pike and Myrtle L. Brown, John Wiley & Sons, copyright 1984. Reprinted with permission.

3.3). A subnormal concentration of calcium in the blood stimulates secretion of PTH, which in turn increases the synthesis of calcitriol in the kidneys. Increased expression of the calbindin gene stimulates intestinal transport of dietary calcium, which increases calcium concentrations in the blood. In addition, calcitriol, in conjunction with PTH, increases mobilization of calcium and phosphorus from bone to the blood. Through these mechanisms, calcium in the blood is maintained at concentrations sufficient to calcify bones and perform important intracellular functions such as signal transduction.

In addition to regulating calcium metabolism, vitamin D increases or decreases expression of 50 other genes. The vitamin D receptor is a member of the gene family for steroid/thyroid receptors and functions accordingly. The hormone-receptor complex binds to DNA and regulates transcription of specific genes. Learning more about the cellular distribution of this receptor may shed light on other important roles of vitamin D.

Despite the advances described above, knowledge of calcium's role in intracellular processes and for maintaining the skeletal system remains incomplete. We do not know (1) how dietary calcium homeostasis, regulated by vitamin D metabolites, contributes to bone calcium turnover, (2) the significance of the trans-acting vitamin D receptor system in differentiating tissues, or (3) how this receptor system interacts with cytokines and growth factors during development or nutritional deprivation or in diseases such as osteoporosis. These questions represent important opportunities in nutrition research.

Neurotransmitters—Regulation and Action

Molecular and immunocytochemical techniques and newly developed drugs have increased our understanding of the development and regulation of neurotransmission. We have achieved a new understanding of the relationships between neurotransmitter function, behavior and cognition, and the molecular and biophysical basis of the dominant excitatory and inhibitory receptor systems in the brain. During brain development, these systems are regulated at the level of the gene, and their functions may be influenced by dietary factors such as low protein intake. At least one class of excitatory receptors is involved in neurotoxic damage, some of which may occur early in development and be detectable only with careful cognitive testing over an extended period of time.

Influences on Eating Behaviors

Monoamine neuropeptides and hormones appear to affect food intake and aspects of feeding behavior in animals as well as humans. Concentrations of amines and neuropeptides in the brains of animals are highly responsive to circulating nutrients and hormones and to environmental variables that may contribute to eating disorders in humans. Injecting specific transmitters into the hypothalamus causes satiated animals to overeat or hungry animals to stop eating. Understanding the brain pathways involved in eating motivation and satiety is vitally important to improving health. For example, altering the concentrations of serotonin (5HT) and norepinephrine (NE) in the medial hypothalamus may modulate the temporal pattern of carbohydrate and protein intake by activating or inhibiting satiety mechanisms. Activation of serotonin receptors may directly antagonize the action of alpha-2-adrenergic receptors that normally function to increase carbohydrate intake. *In vivo* microdialysis enables scientists to measure the actual concentrations of small molecules such as serotonin, dopamine, and cyclic-AMP in small, defined regions of the brain and has advanced this field considerably. Despite these new findings, much more needs to be learned about the interrelationships among the areas in the brain where particular neurotransmitters act as well as how these actions are coupled to dietary and environmental variables that influence food intake.

Excitatory and Inhibitory Receptor Systems in the Brain

The amino acids glutamate and aspartate and the amino acids glycine and gamma amino butyric acid (GABA) are the transmitters in the dominant excitatory and inhibitory pathways, respectively, of the vertebrate brain. Molecular cloning techniques have been used to learn the primary structures of many of the subunits that make up the complex receptors for these transmitters. Subunit composition varies dramatically from region to region in the brain, providing the receptors with different kinetics, binding affinities for the transmitters, and susceptibilities to cytoplasmic or extracellular modulators. Receptor composition also changes during development; thus the receptors on neurons in the young brain may produce markedly different responses than the same receptors on the same neurons in the adult brain.

There are two types of receptors in eukaryotic cell membranes. Ion-passing receptor complexes are ion channels, and at least three types are regulated by the excitatory amino acid glutamate. In contrast, metabotropic cell surface receptors transmit their signals to intracellular modifying enzymes which, in turn, activate signaling pathways that lead to specific end effects. One receptor subtype for glutamate, the N-methyl-D-aspartic acid (NMDA) receptor, deserves particular mention because it has been implicated in a wide range of normal and pathological processes in the central nervous system. The NMDA receptor has a high affinity for the synthetic glutamate analog, N-methyl-D-aspartate. The complexity of the ligand-binding and voltage-gating properties of this receptor make it unique among the known ion-passing receptors. Certain brain traumas cause glutamate to be released into the extracellular fluid and cause neuron death; the NMDA receptor has been implicated in this brain cell death. In addition, overactive NMDA receptors have been implicated in various forms of epilepsy. The other major class of ion-passing "glutamate" receptors—the alpha-amino-3-hydroxy-5-methyl-4-isoxazole propionic acid/kainic acid (AMPA/KA) receptors—have much lower binding affinities for NMDA, thus allowing the properties of the NMDA receptor channel to be studied selectively.

The NMDA receptor also may be involved in the actions of some toxins in food. Several toxins found in food cause the death of brain cells. Overactivation of NMDA receptors may mediate some of these effects. In the Pacific Islands, an endemic neurological disease producing symptoms of amyotrophic lateral sclerosis (ALS), parkinsonism, and dementia has been linked to ingestion of seeds from the cycad plant; these seeds contain large quantities of beta-N-methylamino-L-alanine. *In vitro*, this toxin has excitotoxic properties that are blocked by NMDA receptor antagonists. ALS has been linked to loss of neurons expressing high numbers of NMDA receptors. Although no history of unusually high short- or long-term exposures to excitatory amino acids has been found in victims of ALS, parkinsonism, or dementia, the NMDA receptor complex may play a role in the etiology of these conditions. A familial form of ALS is caused by mutations in the gene encoding Zn^{++}/Cu^{++} superoxide dismutase. This suggests that free radicals may modulate the NMDA receptor, disrupt cytoplasmic Ca^{++} homeostasis, and lead to degeneration of motor neurons.

Dietary factors may play a role in the onset of NMDA-linked neurodegenerative diseases. Wernicke-Korsakoff syndrome, for example, is associated with thiamin deficiency and frequently results from alcoholism in humans. The impairment of memory and cognitive function characteristic of this syndrome is associated with damage to specific sites in the central nervous system. In thiamin-deficient rats, homologous sites in the brain are damaged. The effect of thiamin deficiency can be attenuated with a NMDA receptor antagonist.

Among the elderly, altered amino acid receptor function may be caused by altered subunit expression, accumulated dietary deficiencies, altered transport functions for amino acids, or altered dietary intake of amino acids. One or more of these may be important in senile dementias. Understanding the function of amino acid receptors in the aging brain is an important area for future research. The availability of molecular probes for the individual subunits of these receptors should facilitate this research.

Iron Metabolism and Regulation

Iron deficiency remains the most common nutritional deficiency in the world, despite the fact that it is preventable with iron supplementation. Much is known about the metabolism of iron, but we still need more research on physiological control mechanisms, regulation of the involved genes, and relative benefits of different forms of iron provided in the diet or as dietary supplements. These issues provide important opportunities for future research.

Iron is an essential dietary constituent; from primitive to advanced forms of life, it is required for aerobic metabolism. Nevertheless, iron is also deleterious because it can catalyze formation of reactive oxygen radicals. This property has been exploited in iron-containing drugs to treat specific malignancies. Furthermore, high iron intake may influence the growth of certain microorganisms associated with disease. Consequently, the uptake and metabolism of cellular iron must be carefully regulated.

Iron absorption, metabolism, and storage in mammalian systems involve a poorly understood interplay among transferrin, the transferrin receptor, ferritin, iron complexes, and transport and storage forms of this ligand. Over 50 years ago, nutritionists showed that absorption of iron is proportional to body needs. The major circulating forms of iron are in erythrocytes as hemoglobin and in plasma as transferrin. Within cells, iron is distributed to the proteins that make up the respiratory chain, enzymes of the cytochrome P-450 system, lipoxygenases, reductases, and ferritin. Transferrin has a high affinity for iron and is the main component of iron transport. Ferritin has a high capacity for iron and is the major component of iron storage.

Transferrin and the Transferrin Receptor

Transferrin is a glycoprotein with two iron-binding domains. Expression of the human transferrin gene is stimulated by glucocorticoid hormone and cytokines. Regulation of the transferrin receptor is the key to understanding iron transport in plasma. In the transferrin cycle, transferrin binds to the transferrin receptor and undergoes endocytosis. In tissues that require a large amount of iron (e.g., erythroid cells and hepatocytes) and during cell proliferation, expression of the transferrin receptor is high. Furthermore, expression is increased when cellular iron concentrations are low, allowing iron-poor cells to acquire more transferrin-bound iron.

The transferrin receptor mRNAs have specific sequences in the untranslated region called iron-responsive elements (IRE). A protein called the iron-responsive-element-binding protein (IRE-BP) binds to these IREs. The IRE-BP is also the cytosolic enzyme aconitase that may help regulate low molecular weight iron pools via citrate. Affinity of the IRE-BP for the IREs of transferrin receptor mRNA is increased when cellular iron is low (Figure 3.4). When the IRE-BP binds to the IREs, the mRNA for transferrin receptor becomes more stable, thereby increasing the mRNA concentration and the rate of receptor synthesis. Increasing the number of receptors increases the uptake of iron bound to transferrin. When iron supplies are sufficient for cellular needs, IRE-BP binding to transferrin receptor mRNA is decreased, so the mRNA degrades more rapidly (i.e., translation decreases). Consequently, synthesis of the receptor is decreased.

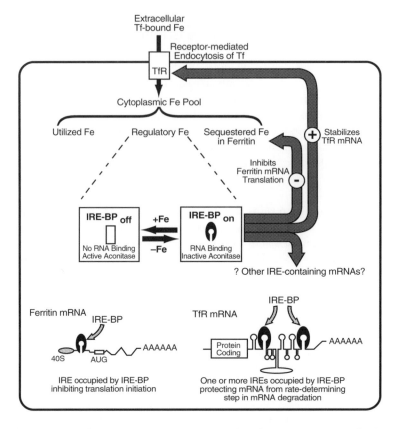

FIGURE 3.4 Cellular iron homeostasis is regulated posttranscriptionally through iron-dependent changes in the IRE-BP. Iron enters dividing cells of higher eukaryotes via the transferrin receptor. Once inside the cell, the iron may be considered to be in 1 or 3 pools, although overlap and interchange between these pools may occur. Iron is utilized in a variety of metabolic processes, or iron may be sequestered in ferritin. Intracellular iron also serves to regulate the IRE-BP such that when iron is abundant (e.g., in hemin-treated cells) the IRE-BP is in its [4Fe-4S] state, which has high aconitase enzymatic activity but low affinity for IREs (IRE-BP$_{off}$). When iron is scarce (e.g., in desferrioxamine-treated cells), the IRE-BP is in its high affinity state for RNA binding (IRE-BP$_{on}$) with negligible aconitase activity. The IRE-BP$_{on}$ state results in decreased translation of ferritin mRNA and increased stability of the transferrin receptor mRNA by binding to the IREs contained in these transcripts. The IRE-BP system may also regulate other IRE-containing mRNAs (e.g., mRNAs encoding eALAS and mitocondrial aconitase). From Klausner et al. (1993) with permission. Copyright 1993 by Cell Press.

This is an example of a nutrient that controls the concentration of a protein by regulating the degradation rate of its mRNA.

Regulation of Iron Storage as Ferritin

The second way in which cells regulate iron metabolism is to control the amount of free iron within the cell. This is accomplished by regulating synthesis of ferritin, an iron-binding protein. Nearly two decades ago, dietary iron was found to stimulate the efficiency with which ferritin mRNA is translated. Within the last few years, investigators have shown that the factor that inhibits translation of ferritin mRNA is the same IRE-BP that binds to transferrin mRNA. In the case of ferritin mRNA, binding of the IRE-BP to the IRE of ferritin mRNA inhibits synthesis of ferritin by inhibiting the efficiency of translation, as opposed to altering the degradation rate of the mRNA. When cellular iron concentrations are high, IRE-BP dissociates from the mRNA and translation of ferritin mRNA increases.

Understanding the regulation of expression of transferrin and ferritin has increased our understanding of iron nutrition and metabolism. However, both physiological and molecular questions about iron metabolism remain to be answered. For example, how do IRE-BP and IREs influence iron absorption in the intestine? Do they control the availability of iron involved in the production of H_2O_2, a process that leads to formation of deleterious hydroxyl radicals? These and other aspects of the transferrin-ferritin system and other components of iron pathways offer exciting future research opportunities.

TECHNOLOGIES CREATING NEW OPPORTUNITIES FOR BASIC RESEARCH IN NUTRITION SCIENCE

Genetics

Manipulation of the Mammalian Genome

In prokaryotes, genetics has been a powerful tool for establishing definitive cause-and-effect relationships between molecular mechanisms that regulate enzyme activity and flux through metabolic pathways. Molecular nutrition as a field brings the tools of genetics and genetic engineering to the analysis of metabolism in animals. Using the techniques of gene transfer with both cells in culture and whole animals, it is now possible to introduce functional promoter-regulatory DNA attached to reporter genes to (1) analyze mechanisms involved in the regulation of gene expression, (2) express a gene's protein product in a specific subcellular compartment or organ, (3) express measured concentrations of gene products by using regulatable heterologous promoter-regulator DNAs joined to structural genes, and (4) delete specific proteins and replace them with altered genes. These are a few examples of the experiments that modern molecular genetics has made possible in animals and that are applicable to important questions in nutrition approached at the molecular level.

The most significant impact of these powerful tools on nutrition research has been in the analysis of the regulation of gene expression by hormones and diet. Other areas, such as regulation of the functional efficiency of proteins, have received less attention. In this section, we will describe methods for introducing normal and mutant DNA into cells and animals. In a later section, we show how these methods might be applied to nutritionally significant research problems. Nutrient absorption and utilization and disease-related nutritional problems involve either altered gene expression or altered functional efficiency of key proteins. The new genetic approaches are critical to understanding in these new fields.

Introduction of DNA into cells in culture   There are several ways to introduce DNA into cells in culture. Agents that precipitate DNA or bind it to liposomes are effective, as is electroporation, a procedure that makes transient holes in the cell membrane. Once inside the cells, foreign DNA probably uses the same cellular machinery that guides infective viral DNA to the nucleus. Initially, the DNA is present as an episomal element, separate from genomic DNA. If the test DNA contains a structural gene with appropriate eukaryotic regulatory elements, it can be expressed transiently (i.e., for a few days). Thereafter, most of the DNA is lost by cell division and degradation. DNA taken up by cells in culture is inserted into the genome, usually at random sites, at a frequency of about 1 in 1,000. The low frequency of this event necessitates a selection process to identify and purify cells with integrated DNA. Usually this involves adding a poison that is detoxified by a second gene on the test plasmid or by co-uptake of the plasmid containing the test DNA from a second plasmid containing the detoxification gene. Transiently and permanently expressed transgenes are used for different purposes.

Introduction of genes using viral vectors   Infective viruses contain nucleic acid encoding the viral genome coated with viral proteins. Depending on the type of virus, the nucleic acid may be either DNA or RNA. Viruses gain entrance to cells by mimicking the ligand for a natural cell-surface receptor. Once inside a cell, the genome of RNA viruses is reverse transcribed to produce a DNA copy. Viral DNA makes its way to the nucleus, where the viral genes can be transcribed. For some viruses, the DNA version of the viral genome can become integrated into the host cell's DNA. For some commonly used retroviral vectors, integration of viral

DNA appears to require ongoing replication of cellular DNA. This limits the usefulness of retroviral vectors to dividing cells. In gene therapy for cancer, this may be an advantage, because in many tissues only the tumor cells are undergoing rapid division.

Viral DNAs often contain coding sequences for proteins that are not essential for replication or infection. Once a viral DNA has been cloned, the unnecessary DNA can be replaced with sequences that will generate a product of interest. Once integrated, the viral sequences become part of the cell's genome and are passed to daughter cells at each division. Infection of cells with viral vectors is more efficient than transfection of naked DNA and results in better control of the number of DNA copies introduced into the cell.

Replication-competent viral vectors, such as those described above, are infective and have the disadvantage that infected cells are continuously synthesizing and shedding virus particles. Viral vectors that undergo only a single round of infection are also available and will be particularly useful for gene therapy of domestic animals and humans.

Introduction of genes into animals Cells in culture are good models for testing hypotheses that involve levels of organization simpler than those of intact organs; they clearly are not adequate models for intact animals. Tests of the more complex interactions that take place in whole animals have been made possible by the development of procedures for making transgenic animals. There are two methods for introducing genes into the germline of animals. In one method, DNA is injected directly into the male pronucleus of the fertilized egg. The second method involves insertion of the DNA into pluripotent embryonic stem cells in culture, followed by injection of the transgenic cells into developing embryos. The latter procedure is less efficient, but it can be used to inactivate specific host-cell genes by homologous recombination (gene knockout) and will be explained in a later section.

Direct injection of fertilized eggs has been used in mammals, fish, and amphibians. Fertilized eggs of these organisms are large enough to permit injection of DNA directly into a pronucleus. Integration of the injected DNA into the host's genome occurs during subsequent cell division. Numerous lines of transgenic animals have been developed using this technology, and these animals are used for a variety of experimental and commercial purposes. Overexpression of growth factors or hormones can lead to changes in body size and composition. Overexpression of specific apolipoproteins has profound effects on lipid metabolism, suggesting possible therapeutic strategies for human hereditary hyperlipidemias. Other examples of disease-related advances will be discussed in a later section.

Why transgenes are useful   Transgenes have two key uses.

Defining the function of upstream regulatory regions   In most genes,
DNA upstream (in the 5' direction with respect to the coding strand) from
the transcription start site contains a promoter. This element binds RNA
polymerase and initiation factors, determines the nucleotide at which transcription will start, and bestows a basal rate of transcription on the gene.
Additional upstream regions contain nucleotide sequences that act in *cis*
(i.e., are present in the same molecule) to regulate transcription. These
vary as a function of cell type, nutritional state, hormonal status, and
pharmacological conditions. *Cis*-acting regulatory elements are, in turn,
regulated by *trans*-acting proteins (diffusible regulatory molecules) that
bind to the DNA sequences or to proteins bound to those sequences.

The concentrations of most proteins are regulated by controlling the
initiation of transcription of the corresponding genes. An important step
in molecular analysis of the signaling pathways by which hormones or
nutritional states regulate protein concentration, therefore, is identification and characterization of *cis*-acting DNA elements and *trans*-acting
proteins that regulate transcription. Knowledge of the structure and function of regulatory elements is also essential for constructing vectors that
will drive expression of structural genes in specific cell types under specific physiological or pharmacological conditions both in cells in culture
and in intact animals.

The *cis*-acting elements can be defined functionally by introducing
them into an appropriate cell type linked to a reporter gene. The reporter
gene usually encodes an easily assayed enzyme or protein that is not normally expressed in vertebrate cells. The bacterial gene for chloramphenicol
acetyltransferase and the insect gene for luciferase are examples. By systematically testing mutated versions of the regulatory DNA, we can define
the nucleotide sequence required for a given response. A steroid response
element confers sensitivity to cholesterol on the gene for 3-hydroxy-3-
methylglutaryl coenzyme A (HMG-CoA) reductase and has been defined
in this manner.

Testing the function of specific proteins   Different forms of structural genes can be tested by introducing them into cells in culture using
transient or permanent transfection techniques or by constructing transgenic
animals. The expression of such genes can be regulated by an inducible
promoter or can be maintained at a high, essentially unregulated level
with viral promoters. The function of gene products can be studied by
introducing the gene into a cell type that normally does not express that
product. For example, a *trans*-acting factor postulated to activate tran-

scription in a particular tissue might be introduced into a different cell type along with an appropriate regulatory sequence linked to a reporter gene. Expression of the reporter gene would be evidence that the factor was required for transcription. By introducing mutant versions of the gene for the *trans*-acting factor, structural requirements for the function of the *trans*-acting factor could also be tested. A similar protocol could be devised to analyze structure, function, and regulation of any gene product for which a suitable assay system could be devised. This technology was used to identify retinoic acid receptors (see page 51). Identifying the mechanisms by which nutrient intake regulates the function of *trans*-acting factors will be critical to understanding how nutrients regulate gene expression.

Deletion of specific gene products Just as important as the ability to express or overexpress a particular protein is the ability to suppress expression. Three general methods have been developed: dominant negative mutations, antisense RNA or DNA, and homologous recombination. The ability to delete the protein products of specific genes provides the nutrition research community with opportunities to examine the roles of these proteins in nutrient function.

Dominant negative mutations This strategy requires that the product of the targeted gene be a multimeric protein. A mutant version encoding a stable but inactive subunit is overexpressed by one of the means described above. If the ratio of mutant to wild-type subunits is high enough, virtually every multimer will contain one or more mutant subunits and the resulting multimers will be inactive.

Antisense RNA or DNA To suppress gene expression using antisense RNA, researchers insert into the cell a transgene that expresses an RNA complementary to the target messenger RNA. At sufficiently high ratios of antisense RNA to mRNA, the mRNA will be partially double-stranded and translation will be inhibited. Generally, this technique is successful only for target mRNAs expressed at low levels.

Antisense oligodeoxynucleotides work on a similar principle but are added to the outside of cells. Once inside the cell, the oligomers hybridize to the target RNA and inhibit translation or stimulate degradation of the mRNA. Stability and efficiency of uptake are potential problems, but new methods are being developed to resolve these difficulties without altering the specificity or affinity of the antisense DNA for its complementary RNA. Antisense oligodeoxynucleotides are important experimental agents at the present time, and they are widely expected to become important therapeutic agents in the future.

Homologous recombination   This procedure permits researchers to target specific mutations to specific genes. DNA introduced into cells readily recombines with the host cell's genomic DNA. In most cases, the recombination does not have sequence specificity; the foreign DNA is inserted randomly. In rare instances, however, recombination is sequence-specific and the introduced DNA is inserted at exactly the same location as its endogenous homolog. Strategies have been developed to purify the cells with homologous recombination events from those containing the more frequent random, nonhomologous events.

Additional developments were necessary before scientists could use homologous recombination to produce intact animals (mice) with targeted mutations. Primary cell lines were established from the pluripotent stem cells of the mouse embryo. These cell lines maintain an undifferentiated pluripotent state even after substantial manipulation. Embryo-derived stem (ES) cells containing a disrupted target gene are isolated by one of several procedures and injected into the blastocoele of a mouse embryo. The manipulated embryo is implanted in the uterus of a pseudopregnant foster mother, and development proceeds to term. If successful, the resulting mouse will be a chimera composed of cells derived from the mutated ES cell line and the recipient embryo. Typically, the ES cells are derived from a mouse with one coat color and the recipient embryo from a mouse of another coat color so that the chimeric offspring will have patches of both colors and be easily detectable. If the chimerism extends to the germ cells, interbreeding will yield animals homozygous for the desired mutation.

Gene knockout provides the opportunity to study the consequences of designed mutations of selected genes in an intact animal. This enables investigators to use genetic methods to dissect such complex integrative processes as development, nutrition, and disease pathophysiology. Mice with targeted disruptions, or knockouts, of several genes have been produced. Genes presumed to have important roles in development and genes known to be defective in certain hereditary human diseases have been the favorite targets so far. Structure-function studies in the natural environment of a gene product will be of great value in nutrition-related studies. Once a knockout has been achieved, mutant versions of the gene product can be introduced by standard transgenic methods. Tissue specificity can be ensured by using the appropriate promoter-enhancer region to drive transcription of the mutant transgene. Gene knockout work is still in an early stage, and we anticipate increased activity in the years to come with improvements in homologous recombination and ES cell technologies and the application of these approaches to additional animal models.

Approaches to Analysis of Multifactorial Traits

Genetic disorders are typically classified into three groups. The first includes the monogenic disorders, caused by defects in a single gene and inherited in classical Mendelian fashion as autosomal dominant, autosomal recessive, and X-linked traits. Over 5,000 monogenic traits have been recognized. Nearly all are rare, with frequencies in the general population of less than 1 per 10,000. Phenylketonuria, cystic fibrosis, and Tay-Sachs disease are well-known examples.

The second group of genetic disorders involves abnormalities of chromosomal structure or number or both, in which many genes are present in abnormal amounts. Although as many as 10 percent of all conceptions yield a fetus with a chromosomal aberration, the vast majority of chromosomally abnormal conceptuses are aborted spontaneously. Trisomy 21, or Down's syndrome, is an example that frequently survives this *in utero* selection.

Multifactorial disorders account for the third and most challenging group of genetic diseases. For the most part, these are common diseases of adult life that tend to run in families but follow no simple inheritance pattern. Examples are obesity, hypertension, diabetes, and hyperlipidemia. Multifactorial diseases result from the interplay of multiple genes and environmental factors, many of which are nutritional. There are multiple susceptibility genes for each disorder, and the genetic determinants among individuals may differ. This combination of great complexity and high frequency makes the multifactorial disorders a daunting challenge for medical and nutritional investigators.

Recent advances have enhanced our ability to identify the genes that contribute to multifactorial phenotypes. First, the human gene map has grown more dense and informative. The recognition and characterization of a large number of highly polymorphic microsatellite markers at sites spread evenly about the map is particularly important. These markers can be analyzed rapidly and are highly informative, so genetic linkage studies can examine nearly every region of the genome with high resolution.

The second major advance has been the development of statistical methods to study complex non-Mendelian traits. Earlier methods required large, well-characterized multigenerational families, a particularly difficult problem for disorders that appear in middle-aged people in a highly mobile society. The development of multipoint linkage analysis, using an affected-sib-pair method, makes it possible to analyze small nuclear families with two or more affected siblines and unaffected parents. The method is based on the notion that affected relatives share alleles for a susceptibility gene at a higher frequency than that predicted by their genetic relationship. The method requires a large number of nuclear pedigrees,

but provides a robust and workable method for detecting disease susceptibility genes.

Advances in the study of animal models, particularly mice, have also
been of great value for the identification of susceptibility genes in humans. Elucidating the extensive similarity between human and murine
genomes makes it possible to predict with reasonable confidence where a
gene homolog will map in the one species, given its location in the other.
Thus, identification of a susceptibility gene in mice quickly points to a
chromosomal location in humans. Using this method, researchers are making
progress in identifying genes involved in obesity, hypertension, and non-
insulin-dependent diabetes mellitus.

Clarifying the genetic factors that contribute to the development of
multifactorial disorders will provide us with a better understanding of the
environmental factors. The latter may be more amenable to change, and
we can anticipate a time when individuals will be informed of their own
particular genetic susceptibilities and advised as to how to adjust their
diets and other behaviors to compensate for these susceptibilities.

Identification, Isolation, and Tracking of Specific Cell Types

Identifying specific cell types during development, pathology, or in
culture systems where their normal morphology or relations with other
cells may be disturbed is a particularly pressing problem for investigators.
Frequently, cells must be removed from their normal environment for
experiments, or they must be grown in culture to obtain adequate amounts
of tissue for analysis or experimentation. Several techniques are used to
identify phenotype in such situations. Most of these depend on a particular molecular species being diagnostic for a particular cell type.

Monoclonal Antibodies

Monoclonal antibodies are homogeneous immunoglobulins secreted
by an immortal line of hybridoma cells formed by fusing a normal B-
lymphocyte and one of several well-defined myeloma (tumor) cell lines.
Several attributes of monoclonal antibody technology make it useful for
identifying specific cell types. For example, in order to generate a monoclonal antibody, as opposed to a polyclonal antiserum, it is not necessary
to purify the antigen. Purified antigen or crude homogenates containing
the antigen of interest can be injected into mice or rats. Cells from the
animal's spleen or lymph nodes or both are fused with a myeloma line that
supplies enzymes critical to the use of an alternative pathway for synthesis
of thymine. Successful somatic cell hybrids are selected by growth on a
medium that selects cells capable of using the alternative pathway. Cell

extracts are assayed by enzyme-linked immunosorbent assays (ELISA) or immunohistochemistry to determine which of the surviving colonies produce specific antibodies. Monoclonal antibodies thus provide a method for identifying cell types that express rare or difficult-to-purify antigens. Monoclonal antibodies are also used to screen libraries of recombinant bacteria containing eukaryotic cDNAs or genomic DNAs. They can identify recombinant bacterial clones that express specific proteins.

In addition to identifying specific cell types, monoclonal antibodies can detect specific antigens in serum and tissue extracts and facilitate assessments of nutrient status. As we learn more about plasma antigens as tools for assessment of nutrient status, banks of monoclonal antibodies will become extremely valuable tools to the nutrition scientist.

Visualization

Histochemistry, immunohistochemistry, and radioimmunoassay   If a cell type produces a particular enzyme or hormone, its phenotype can be identified by histochemistry, antibodies against the specific molecule, or radioimmunoassay. For example, histochemistry for alkaline phosphatase and radioimmunoassay for gonadotrophic hormone have been used to identify the phenotypes of placental cell lines. Antibodies against different keratins have been used to identify various epithelial cell lines.

In situ hybridization   *In situ* hybridization uses antisense RNA as a probe to localize cells expressing mRNA for a particular gene of interest. In this technique, radioactively or chemically labeled nucleotide sequences (probes) hybridize specifically to their complementary nucleotide strands. These probes can be used to examine a complex tissue or organ to determine which cells are expressing a particular gene. *In situ* hybridization is used, for example, to show where in the brain transcripts for various neurotransmitter subunits are expressed and how they change with time.

The new limits of microscopy   Over the past two decades, the explosion in computer and laser technology has produced a revolution in microscopy that affects all fields of biological science. The new technology makes possible resolution and analyses with light microscopes that are well beyond the capabilities of standard optical microscopes. Most of these techniques use the light microscope to obtain an image, then digitize the image using a video microscope, and finally process the digitized image to improve spatial resolution and increase signal detection.

The initial stages of signal gathering (a microscope and good objectives) are similar for all varieties of image analysis. Coherence of the light representing the image, filtering of diffracted and scattered light, spatial resolution, spectral sensitivity, and temporal response of the system are variables that differ dramatically in the new forms of digitized microscopy. Silicon-intensifier video cameras are used for signals with low light intensity, such as those obtained in many kinds of fluorescence microscopy. High-resolution and charge-coupled device cameras are used for high spatial resolution. Depending on the computer hardware and software available, the signal can be amplified relative to "noise" at a chosen level, and various aspects of the image, its movement, fluorescence, or density can be analyzed. The processed image can be saved either on an optical monitoring disk recorder or on a videotape recorder.

This technology makes possible dynamic imaging of cell migration. Scientists can follow and experimentally manipulate organelle movement in the cytoplasm of cells and can watch the polymerization of actin and microtubules. Silicone-intensifier cameras permit biologists to analyze living cells at exceptionally low light levels, thus avoiding the heat and light damage usually encountered with standard microscopy. These same cameras, in association with fluorophores specifically designed to fluoresce in the presence of certain ions, also permit detailed visual analyses of fluxes through membrane channels or from intracellular stores. Much of the activity with ion imaging has concentrated on subcellular analysis of cell motility and transmission of neural signals. However, there is an enormous potential for new information at the interface of nutrition science and cell biology. In particular, these techniques will apply to specific transport systems and to receptor-mediated endocytosis in polarized epithelial cells.

The laser-scanning confocal microscope reduces the collection of scattered light by sandwiching the specimen between two lenses that focus an entrance and an exit pinhole on the same (confocal) point in the specimen. Resolution is further enhanced by the coherence of laser illumination. These microscopes produce thin optical sections of fluorescence images that eliminate out-of-focus fluorescence. In larger fields, we can examine fine detail in thick sections and living tissue. Moreover, series of optical sections can be stored in the memory of the image processor so that, in a matter of seconds, alternative views, or stereopairs, of an image can be presented on a monitor screen. Confocal microscopy can also produce digital movies of subcellular events such as mitosis and changes in cellular Ca^{++}.

These new techniques, taken together, reveal the organization of cells and tissues with resolution and specificity that were unimaginable even a decade ago. It is now possible to see the transmembrane proteins of the brush border cells of the intestine with submicron resolution and to follow the intracellular migrations of vesicles and vacuoles as cells take up materials from the outside. These and other applications will provide exciting new opportunities to analyze the interactions of nutrients, nutrient transport, and cell function.

Tagging and following cells in living tissue   Tracking the movements of or morphological changes in specific cell types in complex tissue is a difficult problem. Ideally, the markers should be suitable for use with living tissue, give high resolution, and allow continuous monitoring. One approach, if cell surface antibodies are available, is to label these antibodies with a fluorescent tracer. In thin embryonic tissues or in organs or tissue slices in culture, these labeled cells can then be followed with a confocal microscope without phototoxic damage. A more direct approach to following cells is being used to trace the development and migration of cells in the nervous system. Nontoxic, fluorescently tagged dextran is injected into individual cells in organs or slices in culture. It also may be possible to label cells using retroviral vectors to deliver specific reporter genes to specific cell types.

Fluorescence-Activated Cell Sorting

Fluorescence-activated cell sorting (FACS) is a technique that separates a population of heterogeneous cells into separate groups on the basis of their relative fluorescence. If particular cells or cell type-specific molecules can be labeled fluorescently with any of the techniques mentioned above, and if sufficient quantities of cells are available, an investigator can obtain a reasonably pure population of the labeled cells. The FACS technique, underutilized at present, could be tremendously powerful in conjunction with techniques for immortalizing cells, because it would permit the small number of specifically tagged cells recovered from FACS of a complex tissue to be expanded for biochemical, genetic, molecular, or cell biological analyses.

Cell and Tissue Culture Systems

Nutrition requires an eclectic approach to studies at the cellular and molecular levels. Cell lines and culture systems make possible experimental control of multiple variables and the gathering of large amounts of homogeneous tissue. Useful culture systems are those that closely mimic the state of the cells of interest in the whole animal. Nevertheless, findings must be verified by comparing them with observations in the intact organism. Three kinds of culture systems are used. Mass maintenance cultures are used for differentiated cells that do not grow in culture. They are usually limited to a few days in culture and may be obtained by collagenase perfusion of intact organs. Primary cells grow in culture and survive numerous passages; ultimately, however, they senesce and die. Permanent cell lines contain immortal cells; these cells do not senesce and can be maintained in culture indefinitely.

Immortalization of Cells

Five methods are used to obtain continuously propagating cell lines: (1) growth in culture of cells isolated from tumors, (2) isolation of immortal cell lines from primary cell cultures, (3) transformation of cells in culture with carcinogens, (4) somatic cell hybridization of normal, terminally differentiated cells with a defined tumor cell line, followed by selection and subcloning in a selective medium, and (5) immortalization of a terminally differentiated cell type by introduction of an oncogene, followed by subcloning and selection of a line on the basis of some phenotypic characteristic. The technologies described in the previous section can be used to develop cell lines with methods 4 and 5 because they provide a means of selecting, from complex tissue, the type of terminally differentiated cell to be hybridized or transformed. They also provide means of selecting continuously propagating lines on the basis of the molecules they express. In addition, the availability of cloned oncogenes and oncogenic viruses makes it possible to use method 5 to develop cell lines from terminally differentiated cells.

Many cell lines have been derived from tissues of potential interest to the nutrition scientist. One established cell line, Caco-2, deserves special mention in the context of nutritional studies. This human intestinal cell line was established from a human adenocarcinoma and has many of the properties of differentiated intestinal absorptive cells, or enterocytes. Many other tumor- or intestine-derived cell lines fail to maintain a differentiated state. Caco-2 cells, however, spontaneously assemble a brush border when cultured on a filter and grown to confluence. They express normal intestinal brush border proteins such as hydrolases, alkaline phosphatase, and amino- and dipeptidases. They have secretory proteins, growth factor responses, intestinal polypeptide receptors, and transport systems that appear similar to normal human fetal enterocytes. Additional well-differentiated cell lines are essential to progress in several areas of nutrition and food safety research. The American Type Culture Collection maintains a large collection of cell lines.

Complex Culture Systems

Normal endodermal cells may differentiate into intestinal epithelial cells if the endodermal cells are cultured with fibroblasts or undifferentiated mesenchymal cells. Unfortunately, actual contact between the two cell types is required, making it difficult to obtain pure cell types for biochemical studies. Undoubtedly, changes in the extracellular matrix caused by one cell type influence differentiation of the cocultured cell type.

Another complex culture system has been used to study differentiating neural epithelia. In this system, 200- to 400-micron slices of tissue are cultured on a plasma clot, usually at an air-water interface. Neurons and glia from various regions of the fetal or neonatal central nervous system and retina appear to undergo relatively normal differentiation in such cultures, providing the investigator access to the cells for visual monitoring or perturbation. Differentiation and transport properties of various epithelial tissues may be amenable to analysis in such systems.

Animal Models

The ultimate goal of biological research is to understand how individual genes and their products function in the intact organism, interacting with other genes and gene products in the complex networks required to program and achieve normal development and physiological homeostasis. Similarly, medical researchers want to understand how defects in one or a few genes disrupt normal development and physiological homeostasis to produce genetic disease and how to devise effective therapies. The integrative approaches required to reach these goals will depend heavily on animal models of genetic diseases.

Great progress has been made in the methods for producing animal models and in the ways in which these models can be used to provide insight into normal and abnormal human biology. Much of this progress has involved the laboratory mouse, *Mus musculus*. Over the last century, mouse geneticists identified and characterized scores of models resulting from naturally occurring mutations or from selective breeding strategies aimed at producing animals with phenotypes such as obesity or hypertension. Ambitious strategies to mutagenize mice with agents such as N-ethyl-N-nitrosourea and scrutinize their offspring for mutant phenotypes have paid off with identification of several important new models (Table 3.1). More recently, the rapid development of technologies to manipulate mouse gametes and early embryos has opened the way to rational, preplanned development of specific models and greatly reduced dependence on the serendipity of other methods. Introduction of disease-producing genes into mouse zygotes has enabled researchers to develop animal models of atherosclerosis, anemia, and other common ailments. Alternatively, as described earlier in this chapter, specific target genes can be disrupted or modified by homologous recombination (gene knockout) in embryonic stem cells. Models of cystic fibrosis, Gaucher's disease, and several other disorders have been produced in this fashion. Although most of this work

TABLE 3.1 Examples of Animal Models Useful for Nutrition Research

Disease/Phenotype	Model	Source	Useful for Study of
Phenylketonuria (PKU)	hph-5 mouse	Chemical mutagenesis	Pathophysiology of central nervous system (CNS) damage
			Treatment
Hyperammonemia due to deficiency of ornithine transcarbamylase	spf mouse	Naturally occurring	Pathophysiology of CNS damage
			Treatment
Hyperlipidemia/ atherosclerosis	Human lipoprotein (a) transgenic mouse	Transgenic	Pathogenesis of atherosclerosis
			Treatment
	Apoprotein E knockout mouse	Knockout	Treatment
	Watanabe rabbit	Naturally occurring	Treatment
			Gene therapy for LDL deficiency
Hypertension	Dahl rat	Selective breeding	Identification of genetic factors in hypertension
	NaCl-resistant		
	NaCl-sensitive		
	Lyon rat	Selective breeding	
Obesity	ob mouse	Naturally occurring	Identification of genetic factors in obesity
	db mouse	Naturally occurring	
	Zucker rat	Naturally occurring	
Diabetes	nod mouse	Naturally occurring	Identification of genetic factors in diabetes

has been done with mice, important models have been developed in other species.

Animal models are extraordinarily valuable and are used in many ways. First, as outlined earlier (see page 66), genes responsible for a variety of monogenic and multifactorial disorders can be identified. Animal models also are valuable in sorting out the genetic and environmental contributions to complex multifactorial traits. For example, investigators are beginning to use genetic linkage methods to identify the genes responsible for hypertension and obesity in rat and mouse models. The contribution of these same genes to the corresponding human condition can then be examined. The final proof that genes identified in this fashion contribute to a particular multifactorial trait can be obtained from transgenic and gene knockout experiments in mice. Several genes thought to be involved in atherosclerosis have been tested in this fashion; overexpression of the human LDL receptor gene protected mice against massive cholesterol feeding, while knockout of the apolipoprotein E gene confirmed its role in cholesterol homeostasis and atherogenesis.

A third use of animal models is to elucidate the pathophysiology of disease. For many human genetic disorders we know the clinical features and have identified the responsible gene and many causative mutations. Nevertheless, there is still much uncertainty regarding pathophysiological mechanisms. Genetic heterogeneity, variation in clinical severity, and difficulty in obtaining samples of the affected tissues at all stages of the illness contribute to this lack of understanding. For example, the clinical features, biochemical abnormalities, and molecular defects in phenylketonuria (PKU) are well known, but the mechanism(s) by which elevated blood phenylalanine produces mental retardation, the principal phenotypic feature of PKU, remains unknown. The recently described Pah[hph-5] mouse appears to be an excellent model for PKU. Homozygous animals have less than 3 percent of normal hepatic phenylalanine hydroxylase activity, and phenylalanine in the drinking water causes hyperphenylalaninemia and urinary excretion of phenylketones. Studies of neurotransmitter metabolism and myelinization in these animals may provide insight into the pathophysiology of the mental retardation in human PKU.

A final important use of animal models is to develop and test disease treatments. This includes a variety of conventional therapies, including nutritional manipulations, pharmacological interventions, organ transplantation, and other forms of surgery. The results and experiences with trials in animal models guide the design of studies in humans with the same disorders. The recent explosion of interest in strategies for gene therapy is closely tied to availability of animal models, as discussed elsewhere in this chapter.

Imaging Technologies for Metabolic Studies

Traditional approaches to elucidating the relationships between nutritional variables and intracellular metabolism have involved repeated sampling of accessible body fluids such as blood and urine or direct assays of tissue samples. These methods have limited value for studying metabolism in humans because most tissues cannot be easily and repeatedly sampled. Understanding the rapidly changing, region-specific metabolism of the central nervous system is a prime example of this challenge.

Two new technologies offer investigators the opportunity to examine metabolism of the human brain and other tissues in real time. Positron emission tomography (PET) uses positron-emitting radionuclides (^{11}C, ^{15}O, ^{13}N, and others) that are incorporated into metabolically important molecules such as water or glucose. After administration of tracer amounts, these compounds are detected by paired, integrated crystal detectors positioned outside the body. With the assistance of a computer, these signals are reconstructed into a three-dimensional image of the organ. Quantitative estimates of the metabolism of labeled compounds can be determined from metabolic rate constants, which, in turn, can be calculated from consecutive scans. PET is sensitive and painless, but it does expose the subject to radiation and requires an on-site cyclotron to produce the short-lived positron-emitting isotopes.

Nuclear magnetic resonance (NMR) is the second technique. Certain atomic nuclei become energized when placed in a magnetic field. When the field is relaxed, a detectable signal is created as the nuclei dissipate their energy by oscillating briefly at a characteristic radiofrequency. The resulting data can yield three-dimensional images (diagnostic NMR imaging) or quantifiable spectra. The latter can be used for regional assessment of metabolism (NMR spectroscopy). For clinical NMR spectroscopy, ^{31}P and ^{1}H metabolites are observed in defined regions (e.g., the brain). NMR is less sensitive than PET, but it is harmless and can be repeated many times.

PET and NMR continue to be refined to enhance sensitivity, expand applications, and, in the case of PET, reduce exposure to radiation. Even at their current stages of development, however, both technologies provide real-time analysis of regional metabolism in complex tissues and organs.

Approaches to Determining the Structure of Macromolecules

Understanding the molecular basis of the function of enzymes, receptors, structural proteins, and other important macromolecules requires that we understand their three-dimensional structures. The most powerful method for determining the three-dimensional structures of molecules, with or without bound effectors, is X-ray diffraction. This approach requires a homogeneous protein and formation of a protein crystal, and it allows us to characterize the structure at near-atomic resolution.

In this technique, an X-ray beam is diffracted by the electron cloud surrounding the atomic nuclei in the crystal with an intensity proportional to the number of electrons around the nucleus. From the distribution of electrons within the molecule, we infer positions of the nuclei. The diffraction patterns are recorded on photographic film or electronic area detectors. The amplitude and phase angle measurements of the diffracted radiation are mathematically reconstructed by Fourier synthesis, which in turn generates a three-dimensional electron-density map of the diffracted object. When thousands of reflections are collected and analyzed, resolution at 1.4 angstroms can be achieved. Using advanced computer graphic techniques, the known amino acid sequence of the protein is fitted to the electron-density pattern. The primary structure adds a large number of constraints in the form of allowable bond angles and known volumes occupied by side chains. Refinement of the three-dimensional structure is obtained by aligning the amino acid sequence to the electron-density map to obtain the best fit.

Proteins do not function *in vivo* in a crystalline environment. The physical structure of proteins in solution has been more difficult to approach, but it is now being attacked by techniques such as nuclear magnetic resonance (NMR) imaging. Like X-ray crystallography, high-resolution structural analysis of proteins in solution requires knowledge of the protein's amino acid sequence. At present, NMR spectroscopy is limited to small proteins, but it is an advancing field and should be capable of greater and greater resolution with more and more complex proteins. NMR measurements suggest that the crystal structures are good approximations of protein structures in solution.

Prior to the advent of recombinant DNA technology, amino acid sequences were determined directly, a laborious procedure that required many months for even small proteins. Primarily for this reason, only a few three-dimensional structures had been discovered. Now, the amino acid sequence of a protein can be deduced from the nucleotide sequence of its cloned complementary DNA. The recombinant DNA revolution also provided a way to produce large quantities of proteins, even those that are present at very low concentrations in tissues or are difficult to purify from natural sources. The cloned complementary DNAs are linked to promoter-regulatory DNAs of either bacterial, insect, yeast, or vertebrate origin and inserted into the appropriate host. Under appropriate conditions, the host will overproduce the encoded protein, facilitating purification and resulting in high yields of the purified protein. These developments greatly accelerated the pace of structural determinations. Two other developments also stimulated the increase in structural analyses—automated data collection and advances in computerized analysis of the collected data.

FUTURE OPPORTUNITIES

We have chosen some examples of future opportunities for research in basic nutritional science. Earlier in this chapter, we described recent accomplishments in the basic biological sciences relevant to nutrition and some of the new technologies that are, in part, responsible for these recent breakthroughs. It is this new understanding of biochemistry, molecular biology, and cell physiology and the development of powerful new technologies that make it possible to describe these opportunities. Many of these opportunities involve increasing our understanding of molecular, cellular, and physiologic processes that are influenced by nutritional state. In some cases, the opportunities involve the development and perfection of techniques that will lead to greater understanding of the basic processes as well as to effective therapeutic strategies to treat human disease. Many important health and disease problems linked to nutrition are discussed in detail in Chapter 5. In this chapter, however, we have not linked each opportunity identified below to a specific human disease or health problem.

Manipulation of the Mammalian Genome to Understand Gene Function and Normal Metabolism

The ultimate goal in analyzing metabolic regulation is to determine the molecular basis of physiological events. This requires a physiological milieu for conducting the analysis and methods for establishing cause-and-effect relationships between organ-specific metabolic processes, extra- and intracellular effectors, molecular changes in key enzymes, and altered flow of metabolites through metabolic pathways. New molecular genetic approaches can be used to accomplish those goals. Some examples particularly relevant to nutrition are described below.

Rate-limiting Enzymes in Metabolic Pathways

Conversion of a nutrient to a metabolically useful product often requires the concerted action of many enzymes. Each enzyme usually catalyzes a single chemical transformation, but the pathway leads ultimately to a product greatly different from the starting nutrient. Tightly controlled regulation of the flux of carbon and nitrogen through metabolic pathways makes it possible for the constant energy demands of a living organism to be met by its irregular eating patterns, which vary greatly with respect to both quality and quantity. Understanding the molecular means by which the catalytic activity of pace-setting enzymes is regulated is crucial to understanding the regulation of flux through an overall pathway and to designing ways to correct pathophysiological changes that cause disease.

Correlations between the concentrations of intermediates in metabolic pathways and the flux of carbon through those pathways have provided indirect evidence that some key enzymes are rate-limiting in their metabolic pathways. The ability to inactivate a single gene by homologous recombination should permit unequivocal identification of such enzymes and extensive characterization of the molecular mechanisms involved. The process would start with insertion of a mutation into the gene for a putative rate-limiting enzyme. The resulting transgenic animal should have a null phenotype with respect to that enzyme activity. The issue of rate limitation could be tested in one or both of two ways. First, the structural gene for a normal enzyme could be linked to a promoter-regulatory region regulated by a mechanism not usually used by the gene. This transgene would be inserted into the genome of the null mouse by the egg-injection method. Graded levels of expression of the protein would be obtained by treating the mouse with an agent specific to the promoter-regulatory region linked to the structural gene. The other possibility would be to link the promoter-regulatory region of a constitutively expressed gene to a set of structural genes that specified mutant enzymes of different catalytic efficiencies. This would create strains of mice that express different levels of enzyme activity. In either model, changes in pathway function that paralleled changes in catalytic activity of the putative rate-limiting enzyme, when those activities were in the same range as those in normal mice, would provide compelling evidence that the enzyme was a rate-limiting step in the pathway *in vivo*.

Physiological Relevance of Regulatory Phenomena Characterized with Purified Proteins

The catalytic activity of many purified enzymes is regulated by metabolites that bind to the enzyme noncovalently. Often, physiologically induced changes in the concentrations of the relevant metabolite *in vivo* correlate with changes in flux through a metabolic pathway, consistent with the allosteric regulation deduced from action of the metabolite on the purified enzyme *in vitro*. Such correlations, however, do not constitute proof that flow through a pathway is regulated by controlling the catalytic activity of the enzyme involved. The new analyses would begin with characterization of the physical and kinetic properties of purified proteins by site-specific mutagenesis. This process could also lead to identification of those amino acids in the overall sequence that are essential for specific, high-affinity binding of the metabolite to the enzyme. Homologous recombination would then be used to knock out the natural gene in intact mice. A mutant form of the enzyme that cannot bind the effector could be reinserted into the null mice by egg injection. If the effector is physiologically important, the normal regulatory phenomenon should be absent in null mice expressing a site-specific mutant that cannot bind the effector. The physiological relevance of phosphorylation-dephosphorylation—another common mode of regulation of rate-limiting enzymes in intermediary metabolism, in transcription regulation, and in other cellular processes—could be analyzed using a similar strategy. Identification of the physiologically relevant regulatory mechanisms would be only the first step in such an analysis. Characterization of the structural requirements for function of both the regulated protein and the regulatory protein or ligand would then follow.

Intracellular Signaling Pathways

The influence of diet on intracellular metabolism is often mediated by changes in the concentrations of hormones in the blood. When a hormone binds to a specific receptor on the exterior surface of a cell's plasma membrane, it sets in motion a series of events that ultimately leads to a biological response. That response could be a change in catalytic efficiency of a specific enzyme, in rate of transcription of a specific gene, or in the rates of numerous other processes. A series of molecular events along a signaling pathway connects the extracellular event to the eventual biological response. Proteins involved in intracellular signaling can be identified in a manner analogous to that described above for identifying pacesetting enzymes in metabolic pathways. The physiological significance of putative molecular mechanisms can be tested as described above for regulation of the catalytic efficiency or phosphorylation of pace-setting enzymes. Such information is essential for designing drugs or nutritional therapies to restore normal signals in pathways disrupted by disease or genetic mutations.

Importance of Tissue-specific Expression in Metabolism

Many enzymes and transcription factors, and in some cases their isoforms, are expressed tissue-specifically. Different isoforms of the same enzyme or transcription factor may be selectively responsive to the metabolites characteristic of a given tissue. Eliminating the gene for a specific isoform of an enzyme by homologous recombination would provide mice with a null background for testing the validity of this hypothesis. Mixing and matching the structural genes for the different isoforms linked to tissue-specific promoter-regulatory regions and expression of them in a null background will provide the test itself. Similarly, expression of enzymes and transcription factors in inappropriate tissues can test hypotheses about their roles in interorgan metabolism.

Gene Therapy

Treatment of genetic diseases by conventional strategies has proven difficult. Many of the successes have involved nutritional approaches to inborn errors of metabolism. Nevertheless, the majority of genetic diseases have resisted our therapeutic efforts. The opportunities provided by the advances in molecular biology have focused attention on a more direct approach to treating genetic disease, namely, gene therapy—the introduction of a functional gene to replace or supplement the activity of a defective gene.

Two gene therapy strategies that differ in the nature of the recipient cells have been contemplated—germline and somatic. In the germline approach, foreign DNA is introduced into the zygote or early embryo with the expectation that it will contribute to the germline of the recipient and be passed on to the next generation. In somatic gene therapy, genetic material is introduced only into somatic cells and will not be transmitted to the next generation. Somatic gene therapy could be implemented in the perinatal period or any time thereafter.

A third approach to gene therapy involves activation of an endogenous gene(s) to augment or circumvent a defective gene. One experiment already in progress involves inhibition of the normal developmental silencing of the fetal globin gene to treat genetic defects of the adult beta-globin gene, particularly sickle cell anemia. Agents such as hydroxyurea and sodium butyrate increase production of fetal globin to levels in the range required to ameliorate the symptoms of sickle cell anemia. Many interesting questions remain to be answered. What is the mechanism for these effects and what are their specificities? In what other gene families are there fetal forms that could be activated to replace a defective adult form? What are the side effects of these perturbations in gene regulation?

Considerable experience with germline gene therapy has been acquired with transgenic mice. Germline gene therapy has been used to treat several monogenic diseases of mice, including deficiency of growth hormone, myelin basic protein, and beta-globin. In general, the disease phenotype is markedly ameliorated. These experiments have provided enormous amounts of information on the regulation of gene expression and the pathogenesis of genetic disease, but application to humans is still problematic. Only 15 to 20 percent of injected eggs produce transgenic animals, and of these, only 20 to 30 percent express the introduced gene.

Furthermore, random insertion of foreign DNA poses the risk of damage to resident genes. In most instances, the certainty of having an unaffected child, as established by prenatal diagnosis, is preferable to the risks and uncertainty of the transgenic approach. For these reasons, germline gene therapy is unlikely to be applied to human genetic disease. Nevertheless, future research on transgenic experimental animals will continue to yield new understanding of the nutritional regulation of gene expression and its role in pathogenesis.

By contrast, somatic gene therapy experiments for human genetic disease are under way. The first transfer of cells with intentionally altered genes took place in 1989. The first attempt to correct a genetic disease began in 1990. In this latter experiment, the T cells of two young girls with adenosine deaminase (ADA) deficiency were isolated and transduced in culture (ex vivo) with a retroviral vector containing a human ADA gene. The transformed T cells were then infused into the patients. Preliminary results indicate that gene therapy caused an improvement in the girls' immune function, although the long-term consequences of this approach have yet to be reported. Additional experiments in somatic gene therapy of familial hypercholesterolemia, alpha-1-antitrypsin deficiency, and cystic fibrosis have begun or will begin soon. Many of them will have important relevance to nutrition.

In order to develop rational somatic gene therapy strategies, it is important to understand the biology and pathophysiology of the target disease. These research questions provide important opportunities. Is the disease local (within the cell manifesting deficient activity of the gene product) or systemic (with cell injury resulting from metabolic disturbances caused by functional deficits in a remote cell type)? Neuronal death caused by local deficiency of hexoseaminidase A activity in Tay-Sachs disease is an example of the former. An example of the latter is phenylketonuria, where neuronal damage is secondary to high extracellular phenylalanine levels caused by the deficiency of hepatic phenylalanine hydroxylase (PH) and dietary intake of phenylalanine. In the former, gene therapy requires expressing the introduced gene in the neurons themselves. In the latter, expression of PH in any population of cells with access to the extracellular fluid should reduce phenylalanine levels and prevent neural damage. Considerations of this type influence the choice of recipient cell for the introduced DNA. Initially, attention focused on bone marrow stem cells, but these have proved difficult to isolate and transduce in adequate amounts. More recently, investigators have worked with hepatocytes, endothelial cells, skin cells, and myoblasts, depending on the requirements imposed by the particular disorder.

Another important methodological variable concerns access to the target cell. In the ex vivo strategy, cells are removed from the body, transduced in culture, and then reintroduced into the patient. The ADA replacement experiment described above is an example of this approach. Alternatively, the target cells are transduced *in situ*, without being removed from the body. This direct delivery strategy leaves the target tissue intact, but the new genes may not reach an adequate number of cells.

What we know about gene therapy is dwarfed by what remains to be learned. We need more research on vector design, delivery systems, manipulation of the recipient cells, biology of the affected cells and tissues, and pathophysiology of the disease processes. Given the complexity of the systems involved, many genetic diseases may continue to resist our therapeutic efforts. Nevertheless, somatic gene therapy will likely prove to be effective for some disorders and may truly cure others. It is likely to be used to treat common diseases such as cancer and acquired immune deficiency syndrome (AIDS). Generally, somatic gene therapy approaches will introduce genes whose protein products are toxic to the diseased cells or make these cells more sensitive to pharmacologic agents.

The Human Genome Project and Nutrition

The Human Genome Project was launched in 1988. Its short-term goals are to produce several types of maps of the human genome and to enhance technologies required for the task. The long-term goal is formidable: to determine the nucleotide sequence of the human genome by the year 2005. The human genome is estimated to contain 50,000 to 100,000 genes encoded in 3 billion base pairs. Completion of the sequencing will require 3,000 to 10,000 person-years of effort. A considerable informatics capability will be necessary to collect and maintain the sequences in usable forms. With industrial-scale use of current technologies, a focused group of 300 people may be able to obtain the entire sequence in 10 years.

The short-term goals are also impressive. The first of these will be a genetic map of the human genome at a relatively high resolution. In addition, two types of physical maps will be constructed. One will show the location of certain landmark sequences or sequence-tagged sites at intervals of about 100,000 base pairs. The other will be an assembly of overlapping sets of cloned DNAs covering large portions of the genome. These physical maps will allow manipulation of the genome and identification of genes of interest. Early versions of the map have assisted with identification and cloning of genes for adrenoleukodystrophy, amyotrophic lateral sclerosis, Menkes' syndrome, choroideremia, Norrie's disease, and Huntington's disease.

The third short-term goal is to obtain limited sequence information in humans and certain model organisms. The experience gained with the model organisms will be utilized to improve sequencing and informatics technology and provide information for evolutionary comparisons of gene sequences and genome organization. Additional short-term goals include developing informational, training, and technological resources necessary to support the effort, as well as study of the ethical, legal, and social implications of the information to be acquired.

What opportunities might this rapid expansion of our knowledge of the human genome provide to the nutritional sciences? First, new genes will be identified, cloned, and mapped at an ever-increasing pace. Many of them will be of importance to nutrition research, including genes encoding proteins involved in epithelial transport of small molecules, enzymes in intermediary metabolism, transcriptional regulators, cytokines, and cell cycle regulators. Some will be genes directly involved in nutritional diseases. Others will be genes whose products play important physiological roles not yet associated with particular diseases. Many genes may be unanticipated by our current view of the genome. For example, even in such a thoroughly studied organism as yeast, *Saccharomyces cerevisiae*, approximately 60 percent of the genes identified by sequencing chromosome 3 encode unknown proteins. With molecular reagents in hand, nutrition investigators can ask how the encoded proteins function and interact to produce normal growth and physiological homeostasis.

Regulation of Gene Expression

Transcriptional Mechanisms

The phenotype of a cell is the sum of the developmentally regulated expression of a tissue-specific set of genes and the influence of environmental factors such as nutrients, hormones, and growth factors on expression of those genes. Understanding the molecular mechanisms by which development and environment regulate the expression of specific genes is thus crucial to understanding how nutrition influences metabolism and other processes. For many genes, the quantitatively most important type of regulation is exerted when transcription is initiated. Earlier in this chapter we described the importance of *cis*-acting DNA sequence elements flanking the 5' region of genes vis-à-vis regulation of transcription initiation. Specific sequence elements, usually fewer than 20 base pairs in length, determine which genes will be expressed in which tissues after treatment with which hormones (or growth factor, drug, or, in some cases, micronutrient). How do intracellular signaling pathways interact with these *cis*-acting elements to regulate gene expression?

Trans-acting proteins bind to *cis*-acting sequence elements and connect intracellular signaling pathways to regulation of transcription. Two types of binding assays help to define the exact nucleotide sequence of *cis* elements and protein involved. In one assay, binding of the protein to a radiolabeled DNA fragment alters the mobility of the DNA during gel electrophoresis. In the second assay, binding of the protein to the DNA protects a region of the DNA from degradation by DNAse or chemical agents. Adding unlabeled DNA fragments of the same sequence will create competition for the relevant protein and prevent the alteration in mobility or the protection from degradation. By systematically altering the base sequence of the unlabeled competitor fragments, one can define the length and nucleotide sequence of the DNA that constitutes the binding site for a *trans*-acting factor. If the protein binding in the *in vitro* assay is physiologically relevant, introduction of the same mutations in DNA tested in the functional assay should lead to proportional changes in the ability of that DNA to activate transcription of a linked reporter gene. Numerous *trans*-acting factors involved in tissue-, hormone-, and micronutrient-specific expression of genes have been identified and purified using these binding assays. The nutritional significance of many of the already purified proteins is not known. Furthermore, many nutritionally significant DNA-binding proteins remain to be identified and characterized.

The experimental work described in the previous section usually uses defined cell lines in culture and transient transfection systems. Unfortunately, the chromatin structure of transiently expressed genes is not the same as that of natural genes. It is thus important to test *cis*-acting elements in their natural environment by creating permanent cell lines or transgenic mice carrying the test genes. Such experiments are much more time-consuming than transient expression experiments, but they are essential to understanding the physiologically relevant events.

Identification of the *cis*-acting sequence elements and the *trans*-acting proteins to which they bind does not solve the problem of how intracellular signaling mechanisms control transcription initiation. Two problems are relevant. First, the molecular mechanisms whereby binding of a *trans*-acting factor regulates transcription initiation are obscure. Additional proteins that "connect" the DNA-binding protein with the general transcription apparatus appear to be involved. Second, little is known about how intracellular signaling pathways regulate activity of the *trans*-acting factors. In some cases, the amount of the DNA-binding protein is regulated, and in others the "catalytic" activity is regulated by covalent modification or allosteric mechanisms. Either the DNA-binding protein itself or the "connecting" protein(s) could interact with the signaling pathway. In some cases, binding of the protein to DNA is altered by activation of the signaling pathway, whereas in others the ability of the bound protein to activate transcription appears to be the regulated event. There is much to be learned about regulation of transcription in general and dietary regulation of gene expression in particular.

Posttranscriptional Mechanisms

Initiation of transcription is only the first of several steps that lead to the production of a mature, biologically active protein. Regulation at any of the subsequent steps has the potential to regulate production of the mature protein. In the nucleus, transcription initiation is followed by elongation and then termination of transcription; all three are potential steps at which gene expression may be regulated. Little is known about regulation of elongation or termination in higher animals. Similarly, little is known about regulation of the processing of primary transcripts that precedes transport from the nucleus to the cytoplasm. Transport of the mature transcript to the cytoplasm may also be a regulated step, but little is known about this process.

In the cytoplasm, protein synthesis can be regulated by two general mechanisms. First, the rate of degradation of the mature mRNA will influence the steady-state concentration of mRNA and thus the rate of synthesis of the corresponding protein. Some examples of this type of regulation involve hormones. Examples of regulation of this reaction by specific nutrients have also been reported (such as that for iron, discussed on page 58); however, the molecular mechanisms involved remain a mystery. Second, selective changes in the rate of translation of a specific mRNA will influence production of the protein product. As noted in an earlier section, regulation of ferritin concentrations by dietary iron is controlled by a protein that binds to a specific sequence in the 5' end of the ferritin mRNA and regulates its rate of translation. Substantial regulation also occurs after the protein product has been synthesized. Among the posttranslational processing events that cause altered activities of proteins are proteolytic cleavage, phosphorylation, glycosylation, methylation, acylation, isoprenylation, and carboxylation. In each case, the ability of recombinant DNA techniques to facilitate identification of the modified amino acid residues, to create site-specific mutations, and to express normal and mutant forms of the involved proteins in a variety of cell types provides a powerful approach to understanding the molecular basis of regulatory phenomena. There are numerous examples of nutrient-related posttranslational regulation.

Gene-Environmental Interactions in
Complex Disease Phenotypes

Complex disease phenotypes may involve both genetic and environmental components. Dietary intake of a particular nutrient is an environmental component that we can potentially control. Identifying genes that are involved in these diseases and characterizing their functions should enable us to develop dietary interventions that improve function. Obesity is an important example of this type of disease. It is characterized by excessive deposits of fat in adipose tissue and is caused by ingesting more calories than needed. It is imperative that we understand more about the genetic, physiological, and biochemical bases of weight control. Research on the development and function of adipose tissue is crucial to understanding the etiology of this common and potentially devastating problem. Obesity has a significant genetic basis, although in some cases interactions with the environment may be necessary before the genetic propensity manifests itself. The complexity of the metabolic and neurological changes that accompany the onset and maintenance of obesity has made it difficult to determine which of the observed changes are causing the problem. Interestingly, there are a number of mouse and rat models of obesity that are unequivocally the result of changes in single genes. In keeping with the multigenic character of obesity, different genes appear to be involved in the different animal models. Obesity in these animal models is inherited in a simple Mendelian fashion. Despite the obvious importance of this debilitating disease, these genes have not been identified.

Identification of these genes must be a priority for nutritional research. Positional cloning, or reverse genetics, has already identified some genes that cause diseases in humans, even though the molecular bases of these gene defects were unknown. Using approaches outlined earlier in this chapter, it should be possible to identify the genes that cause obesity in various animal models. This will have two important consequences. First, we will be able to examine the structure of those same genes in humans to see if any forms of human obesity have the same causes. Second, we can analyze the effects of early diet, stress, and other environmental factors on the expression of those genes in normal animals to determine the roles of those genes in nongenetically determined obesity. Other approaches to identifying obesity genes in humans have been outlined earlier in this chapter.

Structural Biology

Techniques such as two-dimensional NMR and X-ray crystallography, described earlier in this chapter, have created unprecedented opportunities to determine, at the atomic level, the three-dimensional structures of enzymes, enzyme-substrate complexes, and other proteins (with and without ligands such as hormones, vitamins, drugs, and metal ions). These techniques will enable us to also determine RNA and DNA structures and those of protein-DNA and protein-RNA complexes.

These opportunities are related to nutrition. Determination of the atomic structure of a receptor protein with and without its ligand will enable investigators to identify the optimal chemical structure of a ligand for interaction with its protein partner. This type of interaction initiates virtually all regulatory activity in the body. Knowing the optimum structure of the ligand will be useful in synthesizing effective agonists and antagonists for use in conventional drug therapy and therapy with modified nutrients. Some of these therapeutics will be modified micronutrients such as vitamins or antioxidants. Others may be modified versions of macronutrients, because it is clear that macronutrients or their metabolites regulate the activity of some enzymes by binding directly to them and altering their enzymatic activities. Alternatively, macronutrients or their metabolites may bind to and regulate the activity of proteins that control production of the enzyme; for example, by binding to proteins that regulate transcription of the gene for that enzyme. Understanding the structure and function of proteins that interact with regulatory ligands will facilitate the synthesis and effective use of therapeutic agents. The same principle can be applied to the synthesis of substrate analogs to be used as inhibitors of specific enzymes involved in intermediary metabolism.

Understanding the three-dimensional structure of proteins will also lead to the design of more effective enzyme catalysts. These improved catalysts will be useful to the food industry (see Chapter 4). To get improved catalytic properties, we can apply the same principles described above. In this case, however, the goal will be to modify a protein's structure to give it optimal binding or catalytic properties with respect to a specific ligand or substrate. Alternatively, the structure can be modified to make it more stable or to function in a non-aqueous environment. Enzymes with improved catalytic properties may also be useful in gene therapy. If only a small amount of an enzyme can be introduced by gene therapy, a very efficient one would be very useful.

A large number of enzymes and proteins are involved in nutritional processes, nutritional regulation of metabolic function, and food processing. Determining their structures, characterizing their functions, and designing therapies for improving their functions in specific situations provide important opportunities in basic science with clear relevance to nutrition and food science.

Stem Cell Biology

Stem cells are critical for the development and maintenance of the organism. Their properties include the ability to self-renew, divide asymmetrically, and generate one or more irreversibly differentiated progeny cell types (Figure 3.5). In the adult organism, continuously proliferating tissues such as skin, bone marrow, and intestinal epithelium depend on their respective stem cell populations to replace obligatory cell losses. The

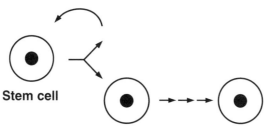

FIGURE 3.5 Stem cell asymmetric division, producing one daughter that is committed to terminal differentiation and another that remains as a stem cell.

Terminally differentiated cell

magnitude of the replacement is considerable; approximately 10^{11} epithelial cells are shed by the human small intestine each day and must be replaced by new cells originating from the division of stem cells located deep within the intestinal crypts. Because of their high synthetic rates, these same tissues are particularly sensitive to nutritional inadequacies.

Despite the importance of stem cells, our understanding of how their differentiation is regulated and how they function is limited. Until very recently, it was not possible to recognize and purify stem cells in sufficient numbers to perform meaningful experiments. In addition, we lacked *in vitro* systems appropriate for the culture and analysis of stem cells. Finally, our understanding of the factors regulating cell division, even in the less complicated case of non-stem cells, was limited. Recent basic science developments in all these areas, particularly with stem cells from the bone marrow, offer great opportunity and promise for improved understanding of the biology of stem cells.

The quintessential characteristic of stem cells is their ability to undergo asymmetric cell division: that is, one daughter retains its stem cellness while the other undergoes terminal differentiation. How this is accomplished is a fascinating, unanswered question and research opportunity. How nutritional state regulates this process is even more obscure and an equally important area for future research. These problems are made all the more difficult by our limited knowledge of the factors that control the normal mitotic cell cycle. The asymmetric cell division of stem cells probably represents a special case of the normal mitotic cell cycle modified by internal or external signals that ensure the different fates of the two daughters. Recent work in a variety of organisms, including yeast, flies, amphibians, and mammals, has led to a general model of cell cycle control. It should now be possible to determine the factors responsible for the special characteristics of stem cells.

A second area of great progress in basic research relative to stem cell biology has been the identification of several cytokines and growth factors. The interleukins, granulocyte macrophage colony-stimulating factor, erythropoietin, insulin-like growth factors, basic fibroblast growth factor, and many others have been described and made available for experimental use in culture systems. Supplementation of culture medium with various combinations of these growth factors allows culture of stem cells with preservation of their characteristics. Available evidence suggests that these potent molecules are a necessary part of the microenvironment of stem cells. In fact, one hypothesis for the mechanism of asynchronous cell division suggests that each stem cell has an optimal microenvironment, or niche, and that when the cell divides, only one daughter can remain in the niche—the other is physically forced out. Away from the optimal microenvironment, the displaced cell commits to differentiation. How nutritional state regulates concentrations of the growth factors and composition of the microenvironment is a largely unexplored research opportunity.

Great progress has been made in the identification and isolation of stem cells, particularly of bone marrow. The search began with the recognition that lethally irradiated mice suffered bone marrow failure and that this could be reversed by injection of unirradiated bone marrow cells. This assay for the ability of cells to reconstitute the hematopoietic system made it possible to sort through the complex mixture of cells found in the marrow to identify stem cells. Work in several laboratories led to the development of monoclonal antibodies that identify cell surface differentiation antigens characteristic of various stages in the lineage of hematopoietic cells. Availability of these reagents, coupled with advances in purification of cells by fluorescence-activated cell sorting (FACS) and other antibody-based cell-separation techniques, allowed mouse hematopoietic stem cells to be purified to virtual homogeneity. As few as 30 of these cells are sufficient to reconstitute all blood cell types in a lethally irradiated mouse. Similar cells have now been identified in human marrow. An even more primitive cell gives rise both to hematopoietic stem cells and the marrow stromal cells that produce cytokines essential for the hematopoietic microenvironment. Hematopoiesis is one of several processes essential to maintenance of the immune system. The importance of maintaining good immune function is discussed in Chapter 5.

These advances in basic research set the stage for studies that will analyze the role of nutrition in regulating the function of stem cells. Nutrition scientists will be able to study stem cells of the intestinal mucosa to learn how these cells function in health and disease. We can anticipate learning how stem cells accomplish asynchronous cell division, what signals are responsible for a commitment to terminal differentiation, and what factors determine how often stem cells divide. The answers to each of these questions will be important landmarks in nutrition research.

Nutrient Transport Systems of the Blood-Brain Barrier

The blood-brain barrier (BBB) refers to the selective permeability of the vasculature in brain capillaries in the central nervous system. The blood-cerebrospinal fluid (CSF) barrier represents the permeability of the capillaries of the dense vascular beds of the third and fourth brain ventricles, known as the choroid plexus. These vessels separate the blood from the CSF. Thus, the interstitial fluids that bathe nerve cells and the CSF of the ventricles and subarachnoid space are different from each other and significantly different from the fluid that bathes other cells of the body. The term "barrier" is something of a misnomer derived from early studies in which lipid-insoluble dyes were perfused intravenously and shown to be excluded from brain tissue. In fact, the permeability characteristics of the BBB and the blood-CSF barrier are complex, as is the relationship between the two.

Endothelial cells act as molecular sieves, passing hydrophilic molecules of up to 40,000 molecular weight. In contrast to other capillary beds of the body, the endothelium of the brain capillaries is essentially impermeable, in either direction, to proteins and ions in the blood. Morphologically, these reticuloendothelial cells show tight junctions completely blocking the intracellular spaces, and they are not interrupted by gap junctions. If free flow between cell junctions is ruled out as a common route of passage for molecules in the normal adult brain, what are the alternative routes? For small molecules, these include a variety of pumps and active transport systems.

There is general agreement among workers in the field that the brain endothelium itself is the major component of the BBB. However, there is another structural difference between brain capillaries and the capillary beds of other body organs that could play an important role in BBB permeability, either by acting as another filter or by modulating endothelial cell permeability. Specifically, brain capillaries are completely enclosed by the endfeet of astrocytes, separating them from direct contact with neurons. There appear to be no gaps in the junctions between these endfeet. Thus, the sequence of potentially specialized surfaces separating the blood plasma from brain cells is as follows: the luminal wall of the brain endothelium, the basal wall of the epithelium, an unusually thick basement membrane, and the two surfaces of the endfeet of astrocytes. In short, most of the molecules that enter the brain have to travel through specialized transport systems or, if they are lipid-soluble, to navigate successfully two types of cells. On the other hand, plasma-borne molecules of a wide range of sizes can enter the brain when there are disruptions of the physical endothelial barrier. Such disruptions can be brought about by disruptions in osmolarity or by physical damage.

Basic Research in Nutrition and the Blood-Brain Barrier

Recent work in the private sector has concentrated on developing molecules that will cross the BBB. In addition, there has been considerable basic research on extracellular matrix proteins in basement membranes and the way these molecules interact with neuronal and glial cell surface receptors. Molecular microbiology has created a wealth of new knowledge on specialized glial pumping systems, "transmitter" receptors in glia, and complex peptide and growth-factor-mediated interactions between neurons and glia. In contrast, there is a paucity of basic research on interactions between various types of endothelial cells. Whether particular molecules entering the bloodstream after ingestion and intestinal absorption are harmful to neurons or brain function and whether nutrients are adequate to support healthy brain function are complicated issues. Answers will have to be determined not only on the basis of epithelial permeability, as measured under some controlled conditions, but also on how long the molecules in question remain in brain fluid and on the final concentrations they reach in the brain. The latter depends on how effectively they are cleared into CSF and on the efficacy of active uptake systems for them in particular brain regions, in the neurons themselves, and in the endothelia and glia that surround brain capillaries. Moreover, like other aspects of nutrition, these factors will undoubtedly vary in individuals of differing age and genotype.

The specialized properties of brain endothelial cells apparently derive from their contact with brain cells. Long-term cultures would provide the easiest approach to studying the selective permeability or transport systems of brain endothelia. However, such cultures apparently do not retain the selective permeability characteristics of brain endothelia in the intact animal. Thus, in the area of nutrition in the brain, many of the required basic research models are simply not available. This is a particular concern with respect to the effects of food additives and nutrition on the developing brain. There is considerable controversy over differences between fetal and adult BBBs and over when the fetal BBB is established for molecules of various sizes. The CSF-brain barrier of the young fetus is less permeable to large proteins than is that of older fetuses or adults. Many receptors and ionic pumps present in the adult brain differ in their subunit composition and probably, therefore, in their function in the fetal brain. Consequently, the young differentiating neurons in the fetal brain may be relatively unprotected from potentially dangerous molecules in the blood. Basic aspects of the nutrition of the brain thus provide the molecular bases for the diet-related cognition studies described in later chapters.

The topic of what passes into the developing brain has become contentious in some areas, such as that of glutamate and other excitatory amino acids used as additives in many foods, largely because of the increasing number of research reports suggesting an important role for glutamate receptors in neural development and increasing evidence that amino acids can function as excitotoxic agents. For fetal development, the issue becomes the degree of permeability of the blood-placenta barrier. One study in primates during late gestation indicated very little transfer of even high concentrations of infused glutamate through the placenta. In addition, several studies suggest that ingestion of large amounts of glutamate has relatively little effect on glutamate concentration in circulating blood or in the milk of nursing mothers. However, some scientists studying brain development or excitotoxicity feel that the existing studies are inadequate. We lack sensitive longitudinal behavioral assessments of the development of cognitive and motor skills in children exposed to large amounts of glutamate in their diet and good basic research studies on when and how the developing BBB is established and maintained. Thus, the issue of the high concentrations of potentially toxic additives in food regularly ingested by children and women of childbearing age should not be dismissed. Behavioral biologists have begun to develop and employ in humans and nonhuman primates the kinds of analyses that might identify effects of long-term exposures to low levels of excitotoxins in the diet.

Prevention and Repair of Oxidative Damage

Structural changes in lipids, proteins, or nucleic acids caused by chemical or photochemical oxidation have been linked to aging, cancer, and other degenerative diseases. Because a host of oxidative processes are essential for life, it is critical to distinguish pathophysiological changes from physiological ones and to determine how the pathological ones can be prevented or reversed. Dietary factors, especially the antioxidant vitamins C and E, beta-carotene, the sulfur-containing amino acids, and proteins with redox functions, may prevent or control oxidative damage. Various metals have either pro-oxidant or antioxidant properties, and some may have both, depending on their chemistry, concentration, and environment. Thus, both pro- and antioxidant activities exist together in cells, and a major challenge is to elucidate the mechanisms of each and the factors that balance their actions in physiological situations.

The results of clinical investigations support the preventive or therapeutic value of antioxidant vitamins in certain diseases. For instance, vitamin E may prevent retinal damage (retrolental fibroplasia) in infants undergoing oxygen therapy, and high levels of beta-carotene may be efficacious in the genetic photosensitivity disorder erythropoietic protoporphyria. In addition, beta-carotene or other dietary antioxidants in fruits and vegetables may be beneficial in reducing the risk of some cancers, including lung cancer, a tumor that is often associated with oxidative damage from smoking. The dietary components that mediate the protective effects of fruits and vegetables need to be identified; advances in chromatography and spectroscopy are likely to facilitate this research. Another area in need of research is the interaction of antioxidants with intestinal bacteria. Such studies should increase our understanding of the role of antioxidants in reducing the production of metabolites with the potential for pro-carcinogenic activity in the colon.

The effects of antioxidants on tumor cell biology, including the ability of cells to elaborate growth factors, proteases, and cell-surface antigens associated with metastasis, also may be explored by new methods of molecular biology, electron spin resonance spectroscopy, and immunocytochemistry. Little is known about the effects of antioxidants on the activation of cellular oncogenes, another promising area for future research. Likewise, the relationship of oxidants to DNA damage and the ability of antioxidants to promote repair deserve further study.

Some recent intervention trials were designed to examine the association of antioxidant vitamin intake and cancer. Unexpectedly, the antioxidant vitamins also benefited sufferers of other diseases, such as heart disease. In cells in culture, oxidative damage to lipids and sterols has been linked to changes in lipoprotein metabolism reminiscent of those that occur in atherosclerosis. Oxidation of lipoprotein fatty acids can stimulate cells of the artery to release mediators that attract monocytes from the blood. Oxidation of apoproteins can trigger lipoprotein uptake by the scavenger receptor pathway instead of the LDL receptor pathway. There is some evidence that vitamin E and possibly carotenoids in plasma LDL can prevent such oxidation.

Antioxidants also may play important roles in tissue repair following injury. Studies of the effects of dietary antioxidants on tissue repair, including new vessel formation (angiogenesis), may be aided by advances in microscopy (e.g., confocal), use of molecular probes (e.g., for cytokines and growth factors), and identification of cell surface changes related to cell adhesion or migration (e.g., cell adhesion molecules).

The "oxidative burst" of polymorphonuclear leukocytes and macrophages is a normal process critical to antimicrobial activity. Little is known of the effects of dietary antioxidants on the normal function of these cells. The relationship between nutrients with antioxidant activity and cytokine production also requires investigation in a variety of systems. Recent evidence supports synergistic interactions between retinol, formed in cells from beta-carotene, and various cytokines on cell functions, including oxidative metabolism and proliferation. The cellular levels at which these effects are exerted (e.g., transcription, translation, and secretion) remain to be learned.

There are also new opportunities to study the functions and requirements for sulfur-containing amino acids, seleno-proteins, and metalloproteins as antioxidants. With molecular techniques it should be possible to express specific proteins in bacteria that depend on sulfur or selenium for growth. Incorporation of isotopic sulfur or selenium into newly expressed proteins will facilitate molecular and structural studies. Our future ability to follow metabolism in intact cells using NMR and other methods may lead to new understanding of the influence of oxidation state on growth and cell function. Genetic manipulations and transfection of cells to maintain more oxidized or reduced states may lead to new insight into the role of oxidation status on cell proliferation, function, and survival.

Clearly, the functions of dietary oxidants and antioxidants pose a great variety of intriguing basic science questions. Research in this area, capitalizing on new techniques for manipulating cells and monitoring their metabolism, has great potential for improving our understanding of how disease can be prevented or its onset delayed. Some additional discussion of oxidative damage and its control by diet can be found in Chapters 2 and 5.

Retinoic-Acid-Regulated Nuclear Receptors

The recent discovery of the retinoic-acid-regulated nuclear receptors RAR and RXR and their expression during early embryonic development has opened new opportunities for learning how retinoids regulate differentiation and development in many tissues. Retinoid receptors have been identified in neural tissues not previously recognized as targets of retinoid action. A family of genes known to regulate the pattern of development of body parts in lower organisms (e.g., the *HOX* genes in Drosophila) also play an important role in mammalian development. The discovery that certain genes, first identified by virtue of their rapid response to retinoic acid, are in fact homologous to genes in the *HOX* family opens the way to a new understanding of when and how retinoids function in development and how they act as morphogens. Similarly, the discovery of RAR and RXR proteins in embryonic neural tissue has opened the way for detailed studies on retinoid-directed development throughout the nervous system.

Information concerning the RAR can also be applied to a better understanding of the mutations related to certain cancers. A hallmark of acute promyelocytic leukemia (APL) is an abnormal chromosomal pattern in which part of human chromosome 17 is translocated to chromosome 15. After the gene for RAR-alpha was identified, it was localized to chromosome 17. Investigators found that the translocation resulted in fusion of a portion of RAR-alpha with another, uncharacterized gene (now termed

PML) in a number of APL patients. This new information implies that disruption of RAR-alpha has profound consequences on the differentiation of blood cells. The future holds great promise for understanding the relationship between abnormalities of retinoid metabolism and certain cancers such as APL. Understanding the roles of RAR and *PML* in the formation of blood cells is now a high priority in cancer research. Both molecular and metabolic studies may lead to important insights into specific cellular requirements for retinoic acid or other newly identified retinoids during differentiation.

Knowing that the actions of the nuclear RAR and RXR are controlled in a concentration-dependent manner by retinoic acid or other retinoids, investigators have refocused attention on understanding the enzyme pathways through which bioactive retinoids are formed from their nutrient precursors. These enzymic transformations take place in the cell's cytoplasm, where certain retinoid-binding proteins are also known to exist. New studies have pointed to the importance of these proteins in controlling the metabolism of vitamin A. They control ligand concentration and direct retinol, retinaldehyde, or retinoic acid to specific enzymes that catalyze important esterification, hydrolytic, and oxidation reactions. Future research must address how cells take up retinol or retinoic acid from plasma, how cells regulate the conversion of retinol to retinoic acid, and what types of catabolic reactions prevent the buildup of bioactive retinoids.

The relationship of vitamin A nutrition, including the consumption of carotenoids and preformed vitamin A, to cellular retinoid metabolism is not well understood. There are many opportunities for nutritional biochemists and cell or cancer biologists to work together to understand how vitamin A and the carotenoids exert their effects on cell differentiation. The demonstration of a link between an abnormal RAR-alpha and APL suggests that other abnormalities of retinoid metabolism might also be linked to cancer susceptibility. Such basic science discoveries may lead to tests to identify individuals with a genetic predisposition to cancer. As noted earlier, providing vitamin A to children at risk of vitamin A deficiency decreases their rate of death. There are clearly opportunities for basic studies on the relationship of vitamin A deficiency to immune defenses and cellular growth; such studies would contribute to improved strategies for nutritional supplementation for children in vulnerable populations and to our knowledge of the underlying effects of retinoids on the immune system.

CONCLUDING REMARKS

We have learned much, but there is still much more to be learned! In this chapter, we have tried to convey a sense of some recent accomplishments and future opportunities in basic biology related to nutrition science. One reason for doing so is to demonstrate how new technologies are resulting in more powerful approaches to the resolution of long-standing research problems in nutrition science. These technologies have made possible increased understanding of basic biological phenomena at the cellular, molecular, and physiological levels. Our increased understanding, in turn, provides the intellectual foundation for pursuing future opportunities.

Continued technological advances give us the ability to meet our intellectual challenges. Two areas of technology have been particularly important in creating the new opportunities. The first of these is the transgenic technology that has grown out of the revolution wrought by the development of recombinant DNA procedures. The second is the evolution of instrumentation that, with the ever-growing power of computers, permits us to measure the amount and identity of almost any small molecule with precision and exquisite sensitivity and to analyze the structure of large molecules at the atomic level of resolution. We have tried to convey how these two great technologies will contribute, separately and jointly, to the solution of a number of research problems in basic nutritional science. A growing number of these techniques are being applied to important research concerns in clinical nutrition, food science, and public health. Subsequent chapters provide numerous examples of this sort.

4

Enhancing the Food Supply

It should be a goal of our country to provide a sufficient variety of foods throughout the year to meet the energy and nutrient needs of its citizens, promote health, and export value-added food products that improve our international competitiveness and trade balance and create jobs. Our food supply should be safe and properly preserved to maintain high quality, yet should be low enough in cost for all to have access to a nutritionally adequate diet, irrespective of income.

Because of the numerous technological advances in food preservation, some of which are noted in this chapter, and the productive system of agriculture in the United States, we enjoy a relatively abundant, safe, and nutritious food supply. Furthermore, the amount we spend on food at home—about 12 percent of disposable personal income—is the lowest in the world among countries for which comparable data are available.

Micronutrient-deficiency diseases and foodborne illnesses that plagued our nation earlier this century have largely disappeared as a result of the improved supply, preservation, and enrichment and fortification of foods. In addition, technologies developed by food scientists since the 1940s are helping to reduce nutrient deficiencies throughout the world, although the challenges are still great.

Current dietary needs in the United States go beyond providing sufficient food and nutrients. They involve modifying and enhancing the food supply to help combat coronary heart disease, cancer, and other chronic diseases. The safety of the food supply continues to be of concern as we learn more about microbial contamination and the toxic effects of some components of food.

Food technologists are producing modified foods to help people meet dietary recommendations (for example, to consume foods with fewer calories or less total fat, saturated fat, and cholesterol). Many of these products incorporate newly developed fat and sugar substitutes. More "functional foods," as these products are called, will be developed through collaborative efforts among plant geneticists, biotechnologists, and food technologists to enrich or reduce the amounts of biologically active components in these foods. Functional foods are the wave of the future: for example, a cancer-preventing compound may be increased in a food through addition or by biotechnology.

Exciting opportunities and challenges lie ahead as we enhance the food supply for optimal health. Nutritional recommendations per se will not be effective unless people can meet them by eating generally available food products. Technological responses to consumers' concerns and nutritional recommendations have already changed the food-product landscape. Low-calorie, low-fat, low-salt, higher-fiber, and fortified foods, as well as decaffeinated coffee, cholesterol-free egg products, and fat and sugar substitutes are all familiar examples.

As the driving forces for a healthier, safer, more convenient, competitively superior, seasonally invariant, and environmentally friendly food supply have accelerated in recent years, new technical needs have begun to emerge, with actions and contributions in one area affecting the others. The next generation of novel materials, new and hybrid technologies, and unique applications will emerge from the progressively specialized frontiers of scientific research. Their synergistic linkages with the scale and range of existing food-manufacturing practices will offer new opportunities and fresh challenges worthy of special efforts. The impetus for safe foods also requires new technologies and associated biological, physical, and engineering concepts. Success will indeed vitalize the science and engineering basis for enhancing the quality, safety, and sustainability of the U.S. food system and for long-term amelioration of increasingly serious global competition. In the following examples, applications of biological, physical, and engineering principles form the basis of theoretical and experimental understanding of foods and food systems.

ENGINEERING FOODS FOR DIETARY COMPLIANCE

Dietary recommendations may be perceived by much of the public as promoting a shift to less food and perhaps to less aesthetically pleasing foods, often resulting in noncompliance. Technology can play a key role in this scenario by creating new formulated foods and modifying whole foods

THE FOOD-PROCESSING INDUSTRY

Based on the value of its shipments, the food-processing industry is the largest manufacturing industry in the United States, employing 1.6 million people. The U.S. food system—stretching from farms to grocery stores—plays a distinctly vital role in the national economy. As a total system, it employs 14 million people directly and another 4 million in related industries. It contributes nearly 20 percent of the gross national product (GNP).

The overall contribution of the food-processing industry to this country is far greater than the mere dollar value of its shipments, the number of its employees, or its position in worldwide competition would indicate. The recent evolution of a scientifically based, integrated, efficient system of food engineering, processing, and packaging allows Americans the unique luxury of acting as if food were a constant around which other activities can be planned. This has considerably enhanced the quality of life that we enjoy today. Its total contribution is considerably greater than its cost to U.S. consumers—on average, about 12 percent of disposable income in 1991 (15 percent including beverages). This is much lower than food costs in any other country in the world.

The importance of food engineering, processing, and packaging in this area cannot be overestimated. Adding value not only captures the benefit of economic output, but also provides employment and generates government revenues. In today's global economy, value-added processing of consumer-oriented foods has assumed new dimensions. In 1990, international trade in consumer-oriented foods grew at a 4 percent annual rate, while growth in bulk and intermediate commodities was up by only 1 percent. In the same year, 53.8 percent of U.S. agricultural exports were exported in bulk form, 22.7 percent in intermediate form, and 23.5 percent in consumer-oriented form. However, the United States accounts for only 8 percent of the $140 billion world market for consumer-oriented foods. It is reasonable to assume that as disposable income increases across the globe, there will be new demands for consumer-oriented food products. A 15 percent U.S. share of the high-value product market would generate a 1 to 2 percent increase in GNP ($52 to $104 billion in 1991) and create about 1.5 million new jobs.

A critical question is how to tailor a vigorous and dynamic research program to meet the demands and dimensions of the international food trade and take advantage of growing markets. It has been recognized for some time that competition from abroad is favored by lower labor costs and that competing on the basis of cost alone is less successful than competing on the basis of new products and product quality. Improvements in cost and quality can be achieved effectively through developing new technologies and by applying recent engineering and manufacturing advances.

The food system comprises the biggest complex of businesses in the United States, involving the production, processing, manufacturing, wholesaling, retailing, and importing or exporting of food. Infrastructures to produce and supply people with their food and drink are enormous and tightly linked. They are dependent on, and use, natural resources as fundamental as air, water, soil, energy sources (e.g., solar, coal, and oil) and elements necessary for materials (e.g., glass, steel, and aluminum). There are an estimated 3 million farmers and an additional 11 million employees in the food industry. Approximately 53 percent of those employed in the food industry work in eating and drinking places, 27 percent in food stores, and 20 percent in food manufacturing and wholesaling. The 380,000 firms that process, wholesale, and retail the nation's food supply have become more international in character, deeper in debt (primarily due to mergers and leveraged buyouts), and more concentrated, productive, and profitable.

or ingredients to be used in whole foods and enhancing both their health benefits and acceptability.

Fortification and Enrichment

As knowledge of nutrient needs evolved earlier this century, it became apparent that nutrient deficiency diseases were a critical problem in the United States and the rest of the world, and various approaches to solving them were considered. In the end, these public health problems were solved in large part by enriching and fortifying foods. Enrichment of cereal-grain products with iron, thiamin, riboflavin, and niacin has been a remarkably effective and efficient means of enhancing the nutrient quality of the food supply and is a classic example of an effective, well-designed public health approach to providing needed nutrients. Cereal grains were selected for enrichment because they are eaten frequently by virtually all populations groups. Subsequently, breakfast cereals were fortified. The result has been a significant increase in the amount of these enrichment nutrients available for consumption (Figure 4.1). Other nutrient-deficiency problems were addressed by fortifying various foods with specific nutrients (e.g., iodized salt and vitamin D-fortified milk). Recently, the Food and Drug Administration (FDA) began examining the feasibility of fortifying flours and other foods with folic acid to reduce the occurrence of neural tube defects in infants.

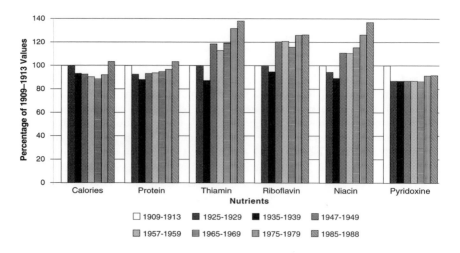

FIGURE 4.1 Nutrients available for consumption, 1909-1988. From U.S. Bureau of the Census, Statistical Abstract of the United States: 1992 (112th edition), Washington, D.C.

Research Opportunities

Provide nutrients that are bioavailable yet stable in food   Iron, zinc, calcium, and folic acid fortification of adult and infant foods would benefit from increased knowledge of the bioavailability of micronutrients.

Iron deficiency is the most common nutritional deficiency in the United States, affecting young children, women of childbearing age, pregnant women, and poor people. The typical U.S. diet is estimated to provide only 6 to 7 milligrams (mg) of iron per 1,000 kilocalories (kcal) of food, and women of childbearing age have difficulty achieving their recommended dietary allowance (RDA) of 15 mg per day because they generally eat fewer calories. Premenopausal women risk developing a negative iron balance because of menstrual blood loss. Iron deficiency may also be exacerbated by the relatively low amount of iron available from grains, legumes, fruits, and vegetables. Such problems exist in many parts of the developing world where there is little meat consumed and in this country among those choosing diets low in red meat. Iron deficiency may increase because all the major dietary guidelines recommend increasing the consumption of grains, fruits, and vegetables.

Readily bioavailable forms of iron are often the most chemically and biologically reactive, thereby creating color and flavor problems in fortified food. Stabilized forms of iron and other fortificants would allow for more effective fortification.

Identify and understand the mechanisms by which meat and ascorbic acid enhance iron absorption Both ascorbic acid (vitamin C) and meat enhance the bioavailability of non-heme iron in foods. However, ascorbic acid, an unstable nutrient, is often not a good candidate for processed food or food that might be stored in warm, humid climates. Therefore, we need to discover how meat enhances iron absorption. Several investigators have offered data to support the notion that meat's action is attributable, in part, to amino acids or a peptide. If meat's potent enhancing factor is a peptide (at least in part) and that peptide can be isolated, it would prove a tremendous boon to the 500 million cases or so of nutritional anemias worldwide. Such a peptide could be added to food; even more important, the major grain crops might be genetically engineered to produce it. Such a development would not only provide relief to the developing world but would allow a greater shift to plant foods in the United States without creating concerns about iron deficiency.

Define and resolve potential dietary inadequacies of other nutrients such as folic acid, vitamin B$_6$, copper, zinc, and calcium These problems could be addressed by adding nutrient mixtures to traditionally fortified foods such as flour. Issues of bioavailability and reactivity of these nutrients with foods have only been partially addressed by food scientists. Consideration should be given to fortifying traditionally unfortified foods such as beverages and snacks.

Low-Fat and Low-Calorie Foods

Compliance with dietary recommendations to reduce fat and calorie intake will not be easily achieved by the general population. Gains in this area require changing behavior as well as modifying and reformulating traditional foods.

Because of the energy density of macronutrients (protein, fat, and carbohydrate), one goal is to lower consumption of all of them, but particularly fat. Now the problems begin—how do we achieve this laudable modification and still have enough foods with desirable sensory characteristics? This offers some great technological challenges, including, in some cases, the development of low-calorie substitutes for sugars, starches, and fat. However, substitutes cannot directly replace macronutrients unless they have equivalent properties for their intended use. Indeed, eliminating certain macronutrients from food, whether replaced or not, can create serious sensory problems related to flavor and texture. The safety and health aspects of these macronutrient manipulations must also be considered while providing the consumer with acceptable sensory characteristics.

Some reduction in the fat content of foods of animal origin has been achieved through applied genetics and altered livestock feeding practices. However, technologies exist to further reduce fat in foods. The most common approach to date is to replace a portion of the fat with an aqueous dispersion of a hydrocolloid such as starch, dextrins, or gums. The objective is to structure carbohydrates or proteins, or both, in such a way that they feel in the mouth like the high-fat food.

Interestingly, certain cellulose ethers can be used in a different context to reduce fat. These polymers have unique thermal gelation properties that, when put in fried-food batters, act as a barrier to oil absorption. Another fat-reduction technology involves the use of microparticulated proteins processed into spheroidal particles so small that they feel to the tongue like a fatty, creamy liquid. In this case, 4 kcal can replace 27 kcal of fat in an ice-cream-like product, since the fat substitute is a hydrated protein at 1.33 kcal per gram (g), which replaces 1 g (9 kcal) of fat. The practical applications are almost exclusively in nonheated foods such as frozen desserts, yogurt, and margarine because these proteins are dispersed and denatured if heated and lose their fat-like mouthfeel.

Macronutrient replacement has had a significant impact on dietary patterns. Two-thirds of adults in the United States consume "light" products an average of nearly four times each week. Approximately 10 percent of the new food products introduced in 1990 claimed to be low-fat or nonfat products. Among the new dairy products, 41 percent were low- or nonfat. And 31 percent of new products in the category of processed and fresh meat, poultry, seafood, and eggs were low- or nonfat products. Lower-fat products are not confined to supermarket shelves. Restaurants, fast-food establishments, and school cafeterias are also increasingly offering low-fat fare, although none of these has taken full advantage of this technology, particularly school cafeterias (see box).

EATING LESS FAT

The Institute for Science in Society has developed a report card on fat-reduction activities, using the goals set by the *Healthy People 2000* report of the U.S. Department of Health and Human Services (DHHS):

Development of Low-Fat Products—A

The food industry has surpassed the year 2000 goal calling for more than 5,000 products to be developed, with the Food and Drug

Administration reporting more than 5,600 new and improved lower-fat products on the market since the publication of *The Surgeon General's Report on Nutrition and Health* in 1988. As new ingredients are introduced, such as those designed to replace fat, the numbers can be expected to rise.

Restaurants—B+

Industry-wide surveys of table service and fast-food restaurants show steady progress in adding lower-fat items to menus. According to the National Restaurant Association, 78 percent of restaurants offer at least one lower-fat menu option, such as salads or skinless chicken breasts. Even fast-food restaurants are beginning to provide healthful options. Some restaurants, including a number of hotel chains, are completely revamping their menus. Good progress toward the year 2000 goal is evident among at least 90 percent of restaurants offering low-fat choices.

Nutrition Labeling—B+

Spurred by the Nutrition Labeling and Education Act of 1990, the marketplace will see a complete overhaul of labeling within the next two years. The year 2000 goal is nutrition labeling on all processed foods and at least 40 percent of fresh foods. Under the comprehensive regulations proposed by the DHHS and U.S. Department of Agriculture (USDA), nutrition labeling will be on all processed foods by 1993, as mandated by Congress. Labels will include vital information on fat content. They should be clearer, with less opportunity for misleading health claims and vague descriptors. Important labeling format issues are still to be resolved.

The National School Lunch Program—C

USDA has steadfastly refused to mandate that school lunches meet the recommendations on fat in its joint publication with DHHS, *Dietary Guidelines for Americans, 3rd edition*, and it has no plans to do so. The year 2000 goal calls for at least 90 percent of schools to meet the guidelines. USDA has promised comprehensive data on the amount of fat in school lunches nationwide when its survey is completed at the end of 1992. But sporadic evidence consistently points out that 35 to 45 percent of calories in school lunches are derived from fat. While supporting the dietary guidelines in school nutrition education programs, USDA's failure to require the fat limits in school meals suggests that schoolchildren must eat much less fat during the rest of the day to keep within the fat recommendations of the dietary guidelines.

SOURCE: Institute for Science in Society (ISIS), 1992. Eating Less Fat: A Progress Report on Improving America's Diet. ISIS, Washington, D.C.

Clearly, technology has improved the nutritional value and convenience of these foods. There is as yet no unequivocal evidence that low-fat or low-calorie foods are lowering fat or energy intake in the total diet, since all the compensation mechanisms have not yet been fully studied. However, foods with lower fat content are available in a convenient, attractive, and, for the most part, acceptable form for consumers.

Research Opportunities

Develop new low- or no-fat and low-calorie substitutes   Critical to the success of low-fat and low-calorie food products is presentation of the sensory attributes (taste, aroma, and mouthfeel) of such foods. Altered lipids and structural fats with modified fatty acid profiles are providing challenging opportunities for research. Consumers are not yet satisfied with the mouthfeel and taste of some low-fat products.

Compensation mechanisms in humans should be clearly established   If low-fat technology is to succeed in providing clear health benefits to consumers, we must understand if and how humans compensate for lowered macronutrient intake.

Develop an understanding of how macronutrient replacement might affect the overall diet   Micronutrient intake might be affected in individuals who significantly alter their diet to consume better-tasting, lower-fat, or low-calorie products. As the total fat content of their diets decreases, the ratio of saturated to unsaturated fat might actually increase.

Develop barriers to reduce fat uptake in fried foods   Since fried foods form a high percentage of appealing fast foods, the development of compounds to inhibit fat absorption by the food will provide interesting opportunities.

Sensory Needs of the Elderly

One of the most crucial problems facing the elderly is their voluntary reduction of food and beverage intake, with a consequent reduction in fluids, calories, essential nutrients, and fiber. The anorexia of aging is multifactorial, having both physiological and pathological causes. Obviously, food technology cannot address all the causes of this reduced food intake, but it certainly can make some major contributions.

One of the reasons for decreased caloric intake may be impaired dentition. One study of older subjects with teeth or dentures showed that, compared to subjects with teeth, the denture wearers had a drop of almost 20 percent in the nutritional quality of their diets (including calories and most of the 19 nutrients studied). Such a drop could accelerate nutritional deficiencies or poor health. Decreases in caloric intake have also been seen in people with full dentition. Nonetheless, it must be assumed that, at the least, difficulties in chewing certain foods might affect variety in the diet and certainly would affect enjoyment of foods and quality of life.

Taste and smell perceptions are reduced markedly in the elderly, with losses occurring at both threshold and suprathreshold concentrations for taste and especially smell. Flavor, odor, color, and perception also play an important role in food acceptance in the elderly. Designing foods to override these challenges would provide a valuable service to this increasing population.

Research Opportunities

Enhance our understanding of the sensory physiological processes The operation of individual receptors and the physiology and biomechanics of the sensation process are age-dependent. Therefore it will be necessary to correlate objective measures of sensation such as flavor, taste, texture, and color, with physiological mechanisms in various age groups in order to better understand how to optimize food acceptability at every age. Further, it has been observed that sensory stimulation is linked to physiological changes in immune response in humans and gene expression in animals. Therefore, providing good tasting, high-quality food will not only increase the quality of life but may also increase the length of life.

Develop products for the elderly and other people with special needs It is possible, for example, to increase fragility and maintain crunchiness of foods or to make chewy foods that require less chewing in order to minimize fatigue. Texture, although most directly involved with dentition, is not the only sensory attribute important to the enjoyment of food and food intake.

Design foods and beverages with enhanced flavor to increase fluid and food intake Foods for the elderly population should have enhanced flavor and aroma to compensate for the reduced perception of these sensory characteristics. Experiments suggest that the thresholds for many odors are often as much as 12 times higher in the elderly than in young persons. As a result, it is not surprising that the elderly have been found to prefer flavor enhancement in a wide variety of foods. Technology can provide almost any flavor, but it can also provide high-intensity flavors. Enzymatic and other biotechnological techniques are available to produce these flavors, and their use in this nontraditional approach might prove beneficial to an elderly population. Such high-intensity flavors could be manufactured independently or, through genetic engineering, be produced within the food by the plant or animal itself.

Extract objectionable compounds in food   Technology could also be used to remove food constituents that are objectionable from a sensory or physiological viewpoint. For instance, compounds in the Brassica genus of plants (e.g., cabbage and broccoli) that cause stomach upset might be removed by supercritical fluid extraction (a process now used to decaffeinate coffee) with little effect on the food itself. Oligosaccharides like stachyose and raffinose, found in soybeans and other legumes and responsible for the flatulence experienced by people who consume them, could be removed by selective extraction or genetic manipulation of the plants.

Develop visual cues to replace losses in flavor and taste   Studies have shown that color influences the perception of sweetness in flavored and unflavored foods. Color interferes with judgments of flavor intensity and identification and in so doing dramatically influences the pleasantness and acceptability of foods.

Functional Foods for Health

Traditionally, food scientists and nutritionists have focused their research and development efforts upon providing a food supply that is both safe and acceptable from sensory, economic, and nutritional standpoints. The guiding light for nutritional content of foods and diets has been the RDAs. The RDAs were first established in 1943 to provide "standards to serve as a goal for good nutrition." Over the years, good nutrition has typically meant avoiding nutrient-deficiency diseases and maintaining ideal weight. Thus, the traditional view has been that the food supply should provide sufficient energy, macronutrients, and micronutrients to meet the needs of consumers. With the recent surge of research into the role of nutrients in promoting optimal health and the recognition that nonnutrient components of foods may increase or alleviate the incidence of various diseases has come increased interest in designing foods and diets for optimal health, not just to prevent classic nutrient-deficiency diseases.

Modern genetic engineering techniques make it possible to enhance, suppress, or even transfer genes from one species to another to attain health benefits. Food-processing techniques may achieve the same goal by selectively removing or concentrating components of interest or by developing more acceptable products with a high concentration of health-promoting constituents in whole foods.

Various terms are used to describe this new class of foods. "Designer foods" has been used extensively. They have been defined as processed foods supplemented with food ingredients naturally rich in cancer-preventing substances. Extracts of garlic, cabbage, licorice, soybeans, and other foods and spices are sources of such ingredients. "Medical foods" encompasses enteral formulas used to feed hospitalized patients and foods for people with rare diseases. Medical foods have been a legal classification under the jurisdiction of the FDA for decades. The medical foods industry has been a large one in this country for some time, with numerous companies and hundreds of products. We will use the term "functional foods" to encompass potentially healthful products. A functional food may include any modified food or food ingredient that may provide a health benefit beyond the traditional nutrients it contains.

Research Opportunities

Use technology to enhance whole foods   In order to increase consumption of important physiologically beneficial components of fruit, vegetables, and grains, it will be necessary to create foods that have substantially enhanced amounts of these ingredients as whole foods. This will create many technical and functional challenges.

Develop disease markers to test the efficacy of foods and food constituents   Markers will be needed to monitor the effectiveness of these foods in improving health. Intermediate markers to indicate risk of development of cancer, heart disease, and other chronic diseases are needed. In addition, methods are needed to assess the impact of the intake of these functional foods on health end points.

Resolve the debate on the regulatory and ethical aspects of genetically modified and functional foods   The FDA has several regulatory mechanisms governing the approval of new food ingredients and additives that are distinct from the approval requirements for new drugs. A new functional food may fall between a food and a drug. For example, a new food with greater than usual amounts of a phytochemical that may lower the risk of a chronic disease may be, for legal purposes, neither a food nor a drug. The manufacturer of this functional food lacks a clear set of guidelines to follow to ensure the efficacy and safety of the product. Moreover, the Nutrition Labeling and Education Act of 1990 places great restrictions on manufacturers' health claims on product labels.

Regulatory mechanisms must be developed to govern the approval, naming, labeling, and advertising of functional foods. In the case of a genetically modified food or ingredient, a scientific consensus on the ethical issues surrounding its consumption should be established prior to introducing it into the market. For example, if it becomes possible in the future to use ingredients in functional foods that alter mood or increase physical performance, these foods will require strict safety testing and assessment of any potential psychological impact.

IMPROVING FOOD SAFETY

Ensuring a safe food supply is a goal of all food producers and food providers. Protection from microbiological spoilage and pathogen contamination is the major concern. However, there are naturally occurring toxicants in foods that can cause illness and even death. In addition, certain food components cause allergies in sensitive people. The risk of adverse effects from these food components must also be minimized.

Microbiological Food Hazards

A profusion of food-related illnesses, largely associated with raw milk and dairy products, in the early 1900s led to the introduction of processing techniques and safeguards that have made processed foods in the United States today among the safest in the world. Paradoxically, foodborne illnesses are prevalent, ranging from an estimated 6.5 to 81 million cases each year. Most of these illnesses, however, result from improper handling of food in the home or in food-service establishments. The leading culprit is improper holding temperature or cooling of foods by food handlers. Other major contributing factors include the use of contaminated raw food or ingredients, food preparation by an infected person, and inadequate cooking of foods.

Many recent innovations in food processing increase the quality, stability, and shelf life of foods. Several of them present safety concerns. Examples include modified atmosphere packaging, *sous vide* processing (in which foods are packaged under vacuum and cooked at low temperatures, usually less than 71°C), and aseptic packaging. All three of these technologies delay or prevent microbial spoilage by suppressing or killing the spoilage microorganisms normally present in foods. The principal safety concern is that these practices may provide conditions that allow *Clostridium botulinum* spores to grow and produce toxin if appropriate safeguards are not implemented.

Several newly recognized foodborne pathogens emerged in the 1980s. Among them were *Campylobacter jejuni*, enterohemorrhagic *Escherichia coli* 0157:H7, *Listeria monocytogenes*, and *Vibrio vulnificus*. Considering that the causative agent of more than 50 percent of foodborne outbreaks reported annually is never identified, it is likely that more hitherto unidentified pathogens will become recognized agents of disease. The agent responsible for the chronic diarrhea syndrome associated with drinking unpasteurized milk is an example of a yet-to-be-identified pathogen.

An issue of emerging importance is the increasing number of immunocompromised and elderly people. It is estimated that more than 20 percent of the U.S. population will be over age 65 by 2020. In addition, with major advances in medical treatment, the survival time and number of patients with life-threatening illnesses that result in an impaired immune system continue to increase dramatically. People infected with human immunodeficiency virus, for example, are at increased risk of acquiring foodborne illness—not only through commonly recognized pathogens, but also through pathogens that may be frequently ingested but do not normally cause illness in healthy persons.

Reducing foodborne illness will require research in all aspects of the food system, from production to consumption. For example, studies are needed to identify the foods most responsible for transmitting foodborne illness, identify and characterize previously unrecognized foodborne pathogens, reduce the prevalence of pathogens in animals used in food production, develop real-time procedures to detect foodborne pathogens, and develop innovative approaches to educate food handlers.

Research Opportunities

Identify the foods involved most frequently in foodborne illness At present, the best sources of information for identifying trends in foodborne illness and its prevalence are reports of outbreaks. This information is not derived from statistically designed studies that identify foods most frequently involved in foodborne illnesses. Well-designed prospective epidemiological studies are needed for this purpose. The results of such research will enable public health officials to address major problem areas more effectively by targeting those foods responsible for the most illnesses.

Identify and characterize new foodborne pathogens The causes of many outbreaks of food-associated illnesses are unknown, sometimes because the agent responsible is not a recognized pathogen. Uncovering the identity of new pathogens that may be agents of foodborne disease requires extensive detective work. New technologies are needed to produce appealing pathogen-free processed foods for immunocompromised populations. In addition, studies are needed to verify the microbiological safety of reformulated foods, such as functional foods.

Develop innovative ways to produce pathogen-free foods from animals Animals often carry microbial pathogens within their intestinal tract and on hide, skin, feathers, and feet. With the frequent occurrence of internal and external contamination of animals by harmful microorganisms, present-day slaughter and primary processing procedures cannot reliably produce pathogen-free raw foods. We need to develop innovative, practical approaches to reduce the conveyance of pathogens that are harmful to humans by animals used in food production. In addition, foolproof safeguards are needed for new processing techniques such as modified atmosphere packaging and *sous vide* cooking. Much of the food industry uses hazard analysis and critical control points (HACCP) procedures to identify and control for potential health hazards or quality loss during the processing of foods. HACCP programs should be designed and put in place for handling all raw foods of animal origin.

Develop procedures for detecting pathogens in foods that take only minutes or hours to complete Classical testing procedures for microbial pathogens in foods usually take days to complete. This time period is too long to allow for an effective monitoring system or recall for many foods. Innovative approaches to developing real-time assays would allow for the rapid detection of potential microbiological risks in foods.

Develop innovative ways to educate food handlers The incidence of salmonellosis, which is principally transmitted by foods, has increased dramatically during the past two decades. Several approaches have been taken to educate food handlers and consumers about proper food-handling practices, yet the occurrence of foodborne illness continues unabated. Reducing the incidence of foodborne disease is a challenge for the future, with a principal problem being the improper handling of foods by consumers and those involved in commercial food preparation. Innovative approaches of educating consumers and commercial food preparers about proper food-preparation techniques are needed. In addition, consumers should be made aware of the risks of foodborne illness from eating raw or undercooked foods of animal origin.

Naturally Occurring Toxicants in Foods

Many naturally occurring substances in foods have significant toxic potential. If toxicity can be manifested under any likely circumstances of exposure, then the substance can be classified as a naturally occurring toxicant. The dose of exposure is extraordinarily important. Some of these substances are hazardous at certain doses and beneficial at lower doses. Several categories of naturally occurring toxicants exist:

•   Natural and normal constituent substances that affect normal consumers ingesting normal amounts of the offending "food." Examples include poisonous plants and mushrooms.

•   Natural, though abnormal, contaminant substances that affect consumers ingesting normal amounts of the offending food. Examples include
mycotoxins from contaminating molds (e.g., aflatoxin in peanuts) and algal
toxins in seafood (e.g., paralytic shellfish poisoning and ciguatera poisoning).

•   Natural and normal constituent substances that affect consumers
ingesting normal amounts of the offending food if it is prepared in an
abnormal fashion. An example would be the lectins in kidney beans, which
are inactivated by typical heat processing and cooking.

•   Natural and normal constituent substances that affect normal consumers who ingest abnormally high amounts of the offending food. An
example would be the cyanogenic glycosides in lima beans.

•   Natural and normal constituent substances that affect some people
with food allergies and sensitivities (e.g., to shellfish and to gluten in
wheat).

Research Opportunities

*Identify and evaluate the toxicity of naturally occurring toxicants in
foods*   While all naturally occurring substances are toxic at some level, we
are unable to identify all naturally occurring substances that can exert
toxic effects at comparatively low doses of exposure. Assessment of the
doses of these substances and the circumstances of exposure that pose
hazards to consumers is woefully inadequate. Evaluation of the effects of
these substances on human health, especially as they relate to cancer, has
received very little scrutiny. Systematic study of naturally occurring toxicants is needed, especially in light of attempts to develop functional foods
with improved health benefits and the increased development of genetically engineered foods (which requires an assessment of the toxicity of the
new varieties).

*Develop methods for easily detecting and quantifying most naturally oc-
curring toxicants in foods*   Methods are needed to assess the extent of
consumer exposure to naturally occurring toxicants. Without this information, we cannot establish the magnitude of the exposure and the hazard
that might be posed by these substances. Such methods would permit us
to identify the food sources that contain the highest concentrations of
potentially hazardous toxicants. Methods are also needed to screen for
toxicants that might be transferred to new plant varieties through genetic
engineering.

Improve methods for assessing the degree of hazard posed to humans by naturally occurring toxicants   Current toxicological testing methodologies that use experimental animals and isolated cell and organ systems create controversies about the accuracy of extrapolating results from animals to humans and from the high doses administered in the laboratory to the typically low-dose exposure of humans. Toxicological assessments should focus more on the biochemical and physiological mechanisms of action for individual toxicants as a function of dose. Comparative human data should be sought from existing and typical doses and circumstances of exposure. Extrapolations should be made from experimental animals that have metabolic profiles similar to humans'. Other toxicological end points, such as neurobehavioral, developmental, and immunological indexes, need to be included in toxicological assessments. Some substances (e.g., vitamin A and selenium) are essential at low doses but hazardous in excess. Recognition of these "U-shaped" toxicity relationships will be critical to the successful development of functional foods.

Develop genetic engineering technologies to remove undesirable traits from foods   Genetic engineering offers the opportunity to remove or decrease naturally occurring toxicants in food selectively and specifically. An improved understanding of the formation of toxicants in foods will be needed to accomplish such feats. The effect of such genetic alterations on the overall safety of the resultant food must also be studied carefully.

Assess the effects of processing on food components and their toxicity   There is a need to develop processing technologies that reduce the toxicity of potentially hazardous naturally occurring toxicants (e.g., heating to inactivate lectins in kidney beans). However, traditional and novel processing can also lead to the formation of potentially hazardous chemicals. The identity, concentration, and toxicity of the chemicals induced by processing need to be determined. Methods are needed to screen for potential toxicants that might be formed during processing and food preparation and for techniques that might diminish the number and potency of such toxicants.

Food Allergies and Sensitivities

Food allergies and sensitivities are those foodborne diseases that affect only certain individuals in the population. A variety of mechanisms may be involved. True food allergies involve abnormal immunological responses to the offending food. The best-known examples are the immediate hypersensitivities, true food allergies involving allergen-specific immunoglobulin E (IgE) response to naturally occurring food proteins.

IgE-mediated food allergies affect less than 1 percent of the adult population but as much as 5 percent of children. Symptoms can range from a mild and transitory rash to life-threatening anaphylactic shock or asthma.

Celiac disease is probably a true food allergy, involving an abnormal response of the gut-associated lymphoid tissue to proteins from wheat, rye, barley, and oats. However, despite the fact that celiac disease affects 1 in every 3,000 Americans, we do not know the mechanism of the disease or the proteins responsible.

Other forms of food sensitivities do not involve the immune system. A good example is lactose intolerance, which affects millions of consumers and results from a deficiency of the enzyme lactase in the intestinal tract and the resulting intolerance to dairy products containing lactose.

A host of food idiosyncrasies also exist. In these cases, the role of specific foods or food ingredients in the adverse reaction is often unproven, and the mechanism of the illness is unclear. Some food idiosyncrasies, such as sulfite-induced asthma, have been well established, although their mechanisms of action remain unknown.

Research Opportunities

Investigate the prevalence of, and mechanisms behind, food allergies and sensitivities   While the mechanism of immediate hypersensitivities is understood, many unknowns remain, such as the prevalence of IgE-mediated food allergies, the nature of most food allergens, and the effects of food processing on these allergens. Other forms of true food allergies probably exist, but the mechanisms remain uncertain. The role of delayed hypersensitivities or immune complex reactions in food allergies should be studied and methods of diagnosing them developed. While lactose intolerance has been studied extensively, improved diagnostic procedures and treatment modalities are needed. The role, if any, of food and food ingredients in many other food sensitivities and idiosyncrasies remains to be established. Examples include alleged adverse reactions to monosodium glutamate, aspartame, FD&C Yellow #5, other food dyes, butylated hydroxytoluene (BHT), and butylated hydroxyanisole (BHA).

Develop methodologies for assessing the allergenicity of novel proteins created by genetic engineering or other procedures   Any novel protein introduced into a food through genetic engineering or other procedures (direct addition or through conventional breeding) has the potential to become an allergen, although the risk is probably remote in most cases. Decision-tree approaches need to be developed to assess the allergenic potential of novel proteins in foods, including an evaluation of the source material and the transferred protein, the level of expression of the novel protein in the new variety, and the digestibility of, and effect of processing on, the novel protein.

Improve the diagnosis and management of IgE-mediated food allergies and celiac disease   Improved diagnostic procedures are needed to evaluate adverse reactions to foods. They require better-defined and more readily available materials for oral-challenge studies, wider adoption of appropriate challenge protocols, and better-characterized and -standardized food extracts for skin testing and radioallergosorbent tests in IgE-mediated food allergy. Simpler *in vitro* diagnostic procedures are needed for celiac disease. While there exist pharmacological approaches to treat the symptoms of true food allergies, the allergies cannot be cured. The key to prevention is avoidance of the offending food. Research is needed to provide the food industry with methods for the detection of allergenic contaminants of food that can become part of its quality assurance programs.

VALUE-ADDED FOOD MANUFACTURING

Traditionally, the United States is viewed as the prime example of a technologically superior society that is able to harvest, mine, or purchase raw commodities and, through technology, add value to them for the benefit of our citizens and for export. This situation is undergoing a dramatic change, particularly in relation to agricultural products. We are fast becoming a supplier of inexpensive raw materials to the world and an importer of value-added products. Unfortunately, this means fewer jobs, a poorer standard of living for citizens, lower profits, and a poor balance of payments for our country.

These changes call for the United States to seize the opportunities offered by developments in the food-processing industry and international food trade. If nutrition is a key to maintaining good health, then food is the vehicle whereby nutrition is delivered in adequate and appropriate amounts and in a safe and acceptable form. This means that consideration of value-added technologies only in terms of economics is too narrow. Value can be added in many forms. A food can be made more nutritious, safer, more convenient, more acceptable, easier to prepare, or more suited to the specific needs of special populations, such as the elderly. All of these examples add noneconomic value and increase the desirability of the raw commodity.

Methods of Preservation

Drying and fermentation are probably the oldest methods of preserving food. They have been vastly refined over the millennia to increase quality, safety, nutritional value, and output. Refrigeration and freezing are also traditional methods of preservation that have become commonplace. Preservation techniques rely on creating an environment that is hostile to harmful microorganisms, either destroying them or rendering them less active or dormant. Newer preservation techniques include microwave processing, irradiation, extrusion, and various forms of packaging that control the environment or atmosphere in which the food resides.

Research Opportunities

Learn how to use aseptic packaging with low-acid foods   Preservation of low-acid products through aseptic processing (with conventional or ohmic heaters), especially those containing particulates, is on the horizon. Using aseptic processing for high-acid products, such as tomatoes, has been so successful that a package failure or the introduction of a pathogen after processing carries little risk. Mathematical models must be developed to predict accurately and control the thermal treatments given to complex combinations of low-acid foods.

Enhance our understanding of how foods interact with packaging (or vice versa) during manufacturing and storage   The effects of radionuclide irradiation or microwaves on packaging materials, packaging that protects foods better from freeze-thaw cycles, improved sealants, better reclosures for flexible packages, improved water-based inks, and improved functional barriers all await further research to improve food safety and quality. Compatibility between foods and the materials they come in contact with needs investigation under actual conditions of use to improve their safety and performance.

Expand the study of microwaves and use of microwave sterilization in food manufacturing and processing   The design of industrial-scale microwave sterilization systems and greater scientific understanding of microwave-induced changes in food products is needed so that microwave technology can be used to help solve these problems. Implementation of integrated statistical process control systems in food manufacturing (such as HACCP) will enhance the safety and quality of end products and should be integrated with on-line sensors and probes. The application of microwave heating to food processing presents many new questions related to the process controls to ensure safety of both low-acid and high-acid foods.

Physical and Engineering Properties

The quality of a food is a combination of several attributes with a definite range of values. These include nutritional profile, microbiological characteristics, cost, convenience, stability, and sensory properties. The ability of the U.S. food system to provide consumers with high-quality, safe food for proper nutrition depends on improvements in current processes and equipment and development of new ones. The food manufacturing industry has traditionally lagged behind other manufacturing sectors in the introduction of new and advanced technologies. The reason for this gap is that food materials are heterogenous, their properties change with processing conditions, and on-line sensors for monitoring food quality and safety are not available. The following research priorities have been identified to alleviate some of these problems.

Research Opportunities

Establish a basic understanding of the biological, chemical, and physical properties of food ingredients, products, processes, and packages To design efficient processes, it is essential to understand the macro- and microproperties of food and food ingredients and to minimize undesirable changes caused by processing. The present lack of sufficient data on physical properties (such as rheological, thermal, mass, and surface properties) of basic food components under real-use conditions is a problem and a great opportunity for well-trained food scientists.

Expand our understanding of water dynamics and of glass and other temperature-based transitions in food materials Water dynamics is the study of the physical properties of water as, for example, a solvent, transferrer of heat, and controller of solute diffusion. Studies of water dynamics in food materials and changes in their diffusional and mechanical properties are essential for understanding a number of phenomena in food processing and preservation. We also need to evaluate critically the relative importance of glass transitions and other temperature-based transitions in amorphous and semicrystalline foods and their effects on the stability of dehydrated and frozen foods. In addition, investigations are needed into the effects that pore structure and composition of foods can have on moisture mobility during various operations such as drying, baking, puffing, and extrusion. An understanding of these properties is important in designing continuous processes and their theoretical simulations.

Develop new models of process and equipment design Quantitative data on the changes caused by processing are needed to incorporate nutritional and quality attributes in models of processing. We should create appropriate data banks and develop predictive models of chemical, physical, and transport properties of foods on the basis of these data. Comprehensive understanding of the properties and structures of food materials can assist in predicting nutrient retention during different phases of manufacturing or in tracing toxic materials in the food-processing stream, thereby enhancing both quality and safety of food. It will also provide food processors with a catalog of properties that can be transformed into both food values and controllable variables, which should lead in turn to increased productivity and the manufacture of better foods.

Separation

Separation processes are central to most of the unit operations employed in food processing. Distillation, extraction, leaching, stripping, and various combinations of these processes are widely used to separate edible foods, flavoring and coloring compounds, and other desirable or undesirable components from their natural locations in food. The common factor in these techniques is the use of solvents, such as alcohols, hexane, methylene chloride, and other organic compounds. The past two decades have witnessed ever-tightening regulations restricting the use of organic chemicals in food processing, while over the last decade, the energy costs of conventional separation processes have risen sharply. In many cases, bioseparation steps pose the greatest impediment to scaleup and commercialization of a new process. Given current trends in food manufacturing and recent developments in genetic engineering research, bioseparations are likely to become increasingly critical in terms of cost and safety in coming years. Pressure-driven separation techniques such as microfiltration, ultrafiltration, and reverse osmosis, along with chromatographic methods and supercritical fluid extraction, are increasingly being used to obtain desirable end products.

Research Opportunities

Expand our understanding of both phase equilibrium and mass transfer characteristics of supercritical solvent-biomaterial mixtures   Supercritical fluid extraction is an important example of an underresearched, emerging technique that offers very interesting possibilities for bioseparations. It uses nontoxic, environmentally clean solvents, such as carbon dioxide, that have high dissolving power at moderate temperatures. Because the dissolving power of supercritical solvents can be varied by manipulating temperature and pressure, refluxing processes may be designed to operate as extractive distillation. This process has been successfully applied to biomaterial separations that would be extremely difficult, if not impossible, to perform on a large scale using conventional separation techniques. Original methods using chlorinated solvents to decaffeinate coffee imparted minute traces of these compounds to the coffee. The first large-scale production plant using supercritical carbon dioxide to remove caffeine from green coffee beans was constructed in the United States and has been operating since 1979.

Scaleup and commercialization of other supercritical fluid extraction processes are currently impaired, for several reasons. Little data on phase equilibrium and mass transfer characteristics of supercritical solvent-biomaterial mixtures have been reported in the literature. Moreover, models of phase equilibrium and mass transfer that are known to apply to simple molecules at moderate temperatures and pressures have been applied only rarely to biomaterial mixtures. Indeed, it is not known which, if any, of the models currently applied to simple systems can be successfully applied to multicomponent mixtures of biomaterials at supercritical temperatures and pressures. This is a barrier to developing promising applications such as removal of cholesterol from eggs and dairy products, fractionation of animal fats to enhance ratios of unsaturated to saturated fatty acids, and enzymatic reactions in supercritical fluids.

Develop new membrane technologies   Membrane separation technology is being used on a limited scale for energy-efficient concentration and separation of value-added products or pollutants, or both, from a process stream. Other separation techniques may involve adding natural polysaccharides with unique binding characteristics to bind certain food components. More research is needed to explore the potential of these separation concepts and to use them in food and nonfood applications.

Biosensors and Process Control

Computer-integrated manufacturing and biosensors hold great potential for increasing product quality and process efficiency while minimizing waste. Areas of interest range from the design and control of individual unit operations to the synthesis, design, operation, control, and optimization of integrated food-processing systems.

A substantial amount of the cost-effectiveness of manufacturing foods lies in how we handle, sort, and prepare raw materials. Not only are these processes labor-intensive, they also create waste; and poor-quality raw materials produce poor-quality end products. We need to introduce smart conveyor technology, machine vision, and custom design in order to handle substantial production rates in an optimal manner.

Research Opportunities

Develop biosensors with simulation capabilities   Biosensors are needed that can simulate steady-state and non-steady-state unit operations;

semicontinuous and continuous processes; process control strategies; optimization of unit operations, processes, and plants, including consideration of utilities and waste; scheduling and production planning (e.g., operations research and just-in-time production); and equipment design. We must develop sanitary sensors that determine the dynamic state of food processes on-line and in real time. In addition to controlling processes, such sensors should provide objective measures of food safety and such attributes of quality as color, flavor, composition, and texture. One new approach is to sense quality changes through rheological properties (see page 122). To do this, we must develop suitable sensing devices and determine the rheological properties of various materials, their correlation with the sensory properties, and their changes during the processes.

Nondestructive testing for quality management during processing and packaging can be accomplished by developing lower-cost—but sensitive and versatile—sensors. Use of near-infrared absorption for specific quality measurements and on-line applications is under way in many research laboratories. In the visible and ultraviolet ranges, spectral properties, image analysis, and pattern recognition techniques offer possibilities that have already resulted in some practical applications.

Improve and use technologies such as nuclear magnetic resonance, magnetic resonance imaging, ultrasonics, laser, and infrared for biosensor development Such on-line safety sensors can detect pesticides in flesh foods and fruits and vegetables, lethal quantities of microbes in thermally processed foods, foreign objects in ground meats, and so on. By adapting integrated time-temperature sensors, we can better monitor shelf life of foods. Full utilization of automatic process control, a road already traveled by other industries, will enable us to take greater advantage of modern developments such as fuzzy logic and neural networks.

Apply computer-based management and control systems to food-processing operations The advent of advanced computers has afforded new opportunities for automation of food engineering, processing, and packaging operations. While decision- and implementation-controlled operations such as scheduling, off-line quality control, logistics, inventory control, and database management have become feasible and practical with computers, knowledge-controlled operations such as closed-loop process control and automation are constrained by our lack of knowledge of food properties, adequate on-line sensing systems, and appropriate models of the process.

Apply fuzzy logic to food-processing control systems "Fuzzy logic" is a heuristically based advanced control technique with potential applications in difficult-to-model systems that have multivariable and nonlinear processes. It is equally effective in dynamic systems where information is incomplete or imprecise. Development and implementation of a self-learning fuzzy control algorithm could offer advantages not available through other means and should be investigated.

Rheology

Rheology, the study of the deformation and flow of matter, provides insight into the behavior of materials when they are stressed and strained. Understanding and using rheology is essential to improving new product development, processing operations, product quality and shelf life, and correlating food texture to sensory data. Rheological studies have been conducted extensively to relate food structure to physical and chemical aspects of food. Because of their complexity, measurements of rheological properties of food have been largely subjective and generally instrument-dependent.

Research Opportunities

Expand our understanding of the rheological behavior of food   More knowledge is needed about the rheological behavior of foods as it relates to their structural and physical-chemical aspects. Interaction between heat transfer and rheology (e.g., heat transfer properties of gelatinized systems) needs to be considered. The role of rheological and physical properties in extrusion, baking, and puffing should be studied, and efforts to provide mechanistic bases for the rheological behavior of foods should be expanded. This includes the development of suitable sensing devices, systematic study of the rheological properties of various food materials and their correlation with sensory properties, and changes in food materials during processing.

Improve and extend extrusion technology to other high-value-added products   Rheology will be more fully applied to food-processing systems when more is known about the effects of extrusion on the macro- and microconstituents of foods, ingredient interaction, and nutrient and flavor retention during processing, and how the extruder modifies textural properties of ingredients or final products.

Packaging

Without packaging, goods would rot at the farm, dock, and warehouse, becoming infested with insects and other vermin, while food poisoning, disease transmission, and product losses would increase substantially. Understanding this puts the importance of packaging in perspective. All too often there is so much concern about the disposal of packaging materials that we forget that its major role is the preservation of the safety, quality, and nutritional value of food.

To food scientists, packaging is a rigorous scientific discipline that includes all the physical, chemical, and biological interactions of the package, the product, the filling and sealing system, and the environment. In the past 50 years we have seen an evolution in the food package that has increased dramatically the health and quality of life of consumers and has reduced food waste. We have reduced the volume and weight of material used, extended the shelf life of products to permit national distribution, increased strength to meet the rigors of handling abuse, and improved product access and convenience (e.g., dispensing, childproofing, closing, and storability). Currently, food waste accounts for only 3.3 percent of the municipal solid waste in the United States, while in countries with limited access to food packaging, it can reach 10 times that volume.

Metals, glass, paper, paperboard, corrugated plastics, and mixed materials such as the retort pouch and containers for aseptic processing are the major substrates used in packaging in the United States today (Figure

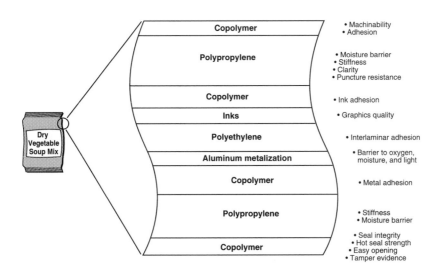

FIGURE 4.2 Cross section of a package of dry vegetable soup mix, adapted from the Council on Packaging in the Environment. This cross section illustrates the complexity of modern packaging. The package is approximately 0.002 inches thick and consists of nine different layers, each with a specific function. While such complexity can inhibit recycling efforts, it also can reduce the overall weight of the package and keep food fresher, thus providing waste-prevention benefits.

4.2). Environmental concerns will provide a legion of opportunities in food packaging, including the development of new sensors, edible films, new films made from nonpetrochemical sources, and materials amenable to recycling and biodegradation.

Research Opportunities

Develop new packaging methods and materials that improve food safety and expand consumer acceptance and convenience   As important as environmental issues are, the food-safety function of packaging is paramount. Controlled- and modified-atmosphere packaging will have the greatest impact in the near future because of the shift from shelf-stable and convenience products to freshly prepared and catered products. Some estimates predict that more than half of all food consumed will be in this category by the year 2000. The implications for the food-processing and packaging industry are obvious.

Depending on the product involved, reduced oxygen or elevated carbon dioxide can modify respiration and influence microbiological growth. As a result, shelf life in a well-controlled distribution system can be extended from a small number of days to many days or several weeks. Unquestionably, packages have been and will be developed which can achieve some of these goals. However, because of the distribution distances and safety problems inherent in such products, other technologies will have to combine with packaging to make them an economic success.

Sensor technology will be important in packaging. At present, there are sensors that warn of exposure to nonrefrigeration temperatures, as well as color-changing closure systems for moisture-sensitive products. In the future we will see more sophisticated sensors that provide an easy-to-read check on the condition of the contents of a package, such as the awareness indicators now being used on some microwavable food packages. This kind of simplicity is a step in the right direction, but we must go further. We must provide easy-to-read, understandable labeling in an easy-to-open package with a built-in measuring device that delivers easy-to-prepare single servings. When this is accomplished, technology will have indeed contributed to the needs of all consumers, particularly the elderly. Additional specifications for future food packages are outlined in the box.

BIOTECHNOLOGY

Biotechnology has been defined as a collection of technologies that employ living systems, or compounds derived from these systems, for the production of industrial goods and services. Biotechnology is not new to

THE MODERN FOOD PACKAGE

For a modern food package to meet safety requirements, it must:

• Meet all regulatory requirements with regard to materials of construction;
• Provide acceptable package integrity through final consumer usage, provide a barrier to microorganisms and other potential contaminants, and provide protection against infestation by insects, rodents, and other vermin; and
• Meet the rigors of processing, distribution, storage, and other performance requirements.

To meet specific product-protection requirements, the package must provide:

• A barrier to the inward or outward transfer of flavors and odors;
• An oxygen barrier adequate to preserve color, flavor, and nutrients;
• An appropriate barrier to the inward or outward transfer of moisture;
• A carbon dioxide barrier to retain internal pressure (e.g., carbonated beverages);
• A barrier adequate to preserve gases such as nitrogen or carbon dioxide used for preservation in applications such as controlled- or modified-atmosphere packaging;
• An adequate light barrier for vitamin or color protection, or both; and
• A thermal barrier—that is, insulation for the purpose of maintaining temperature.

Other considerations in developing a modern food package involve:

• Physical protection of food and package;
• Labeling to provide critical information (i.e., product brand identification; net weight; ingredients; content; manufacturer's name, address, and codes; date by which product should be sold or used; preparation instructions; and nutrition labeling);
• Means of discouraging and indicating tampering;
• Visibility of contents (in some cases); and
• Opening, reclosing, microwavability, dispensing, shatter resistance, safety in handling, and size of serving features.

SOURCE: Institute of Food Technologists, 1990.

the agricultural and food sectors—people have been exploiting living systems for the production, processing, and preservation of food for centuries. Significant improvements in the food supply have been realized through traditional agronomic and laboratory methods.

The "new" biotechnology employs recombinant DNA technology or genetic engineering (see Chapter 3) to selectively improve plants, animals, and microorganisms. Genetic engineering has the potential to be more predictable, controllable, and precise than classical breeding and selection. In addition, genetic improvements can proceed at a much faster pace, and the ability to cross species barriers greatly expands the available gene pool.

Genetic Engineering of Crops

The efficiency and profitability of producing raw agricultural commodities could be dramatically improved by increasing crop yields and decreasing agricultural inputs such as fertilizer, herbicides, and pesticides. Although current methodology has been limited for the most part to dicotyledonous plants such as tobacco, which have little value from a food-production standpoint, significant progress has been made in developing the tools of genetic engineering and in verifying its potential for improving agronomic properties of crop plants. Examples of agronomic properties amenable to genetic manipulation include disease and virus resistance, insect resistance, herbicide tolerance, and stress tolerance (i.e., saline soil conditions, temperature). In many cases, single genes code for these traits. Introduction of these genes into a variety of plant species and regulation of their expression therein are relatively simple tasks. Successful examples of the introduction of genes into plants by genetic engineering include those coding for toxin from *Bacillus thuringiensis* (insect resistance), viral coat proteins (virus resistance), silk moth antibacterial proteins, lysozymes, cecropins, and attacins (to counteract bacterial diseases). To date, over 35 varieties of plants have been genetically engineered, including many important crops used in processed foods.

Cereal grains serve as the main source of protein for the vast majority of the world, yet most cereals are deficient in one or more of the essential amino acids, isoleucine, lysine, methionine, threonine, or tryptophan. An understanding of the regulation and rate-limiting steps in the metabolic pathways involved in amino acid biosynthesis opens the door to application of genetic engineering for improving the nutritional quality of cereal grains. Genetic engineering is being used to increase the concentration of sulfur-containing amino acids (methionine and cysteine) in soybeans, phaseolin (the major storage protein) in legumes, and the amino acids lysine and tryptophan in maize. Increasing the content of essential amino acids in cereal grains eliminates the need for supplementation in animal diets and ensures a more complete protein source for human consumption.

Almost 50 percent of dietary fat is derived from oilseeds. Gene transfer technology has been developed for rapeseed (canola), flax, cotton, sunflower, and safflower seeds, and the tools of biotechnology could be used to improve the fatty acid composition of plant oils. Changes in the amount of unsaturation in the fatty acids of canola oil have been achieved by cloning a desaturase enzyme that plays a central role in determining the ratio of saturated to unsaturated fatty acids in vegetable oils. Transfer of the gene encoding an enzyme, lauroyl-ACP thioesterase, from the wild California bay tree into commercial canola varieties results in a significant increase in the amount of the medium-chain fatty acids caprate (C10) and laurate (C12). Medium-chain fatty acids and medium chain triglycerides are used as nutritional supplements to treat dietary disorders and as a high-energy food source for postsurgical hospital patients. Increasing the amount of stearic acid present in canola would make the product suitable for margarine and confectionery products. Hydrogenation is frequently used to increase saturated fatty acids in margarine products, thus enhancing texture and consistency. However, hydrogenation also produces *trans* fatty acids that may raise concentrations of cholesterol in the blood (see Chapter 5). With genetic engineering, it is now possible to increase saturated fatty acids by six times without producing any *trans* fatty acids.

Research Opportunities

Develop basic tools for genetic manipulation of plants   Our basic understanding of the biochemistry and genetics of plant metabolism must be improved and important agronomic characteristics elucidated. Cloning systems applicable to monocots, including construction of appropriate vectors, more efficient gene transfer systems, and a better understanding of gene expression and regulation, must be developed. Tissue-specific promoters to control the timing and level of gene expression in organs and tissues need to be identified.

Custom design raw agricultural commodities   As we understand how more complex traits are regulated in plants, biotechnology could be used to modify structural, functional, and processing characteristics of interest to the food processor and the consumer. Improved nutritional quality (e.g., oil seeds with specific fatty acid profiles and vegetables with enhanced amounts of essential amino acids, vitamins, minerals, or other specific nutrients); naturally sweet or salty varieties; higher solids content; improved texture, color, flavor, or aroma; and extended shelf life are probably controlled by multiple genes and present a greater challenge to the plant biotechnologist. Antisense RNA technology will be used to inactivate enzymes involved in tissue softening (e.g., polyendogalacturonase in tomatoes), oxidative rancidity, natural toxicant production (e.g., alkyl isothiocyanate in garlic, capsaicin in chilies, d-limonene in oranges, psoralens in parsley, hydrazines in mushrooms, and solanine in potatoes), or other reactions that result in deterioration of quality.

Construct functional foods   The links between various dietary components and cancer continue to be elucidated. Over 600 plant-derived chemicals (phytochemicals) with chemopreventive properties have been identified. These include antioxidants such as beta-carotene and vitamins C and E; retinoids such as isotretinoin; flavonoids, mono- and triterpenoids, and isoflavones; hydrolyzable tannins such as ellagic acid; omega-3-fatty acids; sulfur-containing compounds from garlic and onion; and many others. Ultimately, genetic engineering will make it possible to modulate the content of these components in plants. Alternatively, it may be possible to use tissue cultures from plants to produce phytochemicals that can be added to foods as ingredients. The greatest challenge in engineering foods for dietary compliance will be to determine what compositional changes of crop plants are most desirable from a nutritional standpoint. In many cases, the basic information needed to make sound decisions on the role of diet in health and disease is lacking or changes when new studies are published.

Develop analytical methods of assessing the safety of engineered plants   Better analytical methods for comparing the composition of engineered and nonengineered plants and for assessing the impact of unanticipated multiple effects are needed. The fate and persistence of engineered proteins in plant parts throughout the life cycle of the plant (i.e., growth, fruit ripening, and senescence) and in processed foods must be investigated. *In vitro* and *in vivo* model systems for validating the safety of whole foods and food ingredients derived from genetically engineered plants must be developed. Genetic engineering will be used to introduce into plants proteins not previously part of the human diet. We need to develop testing methods to assess the potential allergenicity and toxicity of these proteins.

Plant Tissue Culture Technology

Plants are the source of many useful compounds and mixtures, including pharmaceuticals, flavors, fragrances, essential oils, enzymes, and pigments. Many of these compounds are considered secondary metabolites as they are generally not essential for cell growth. Production of secondary metabolites in plants is linked to cell differentiation (i.e., formation of roots, shoots, or fruit). Large markets exist for these secondary metabolites, which are commonly obtained commercially by extraction from intact plants. Many plant-derived ingredients used in foods are extracted from plants grown outside the United States; therefore, supplies are subject to political instability in the supplier countries, as well as natural catastrophes such as drought, floods, microbial and fungal diseases, and insect infestation.

Plant tissue culture (PTC) is a technique that allows plant cells to be grown in a solid (callus culture) or liquid (suspension culture) medium, in much the same manner as microorganisms. PTC may provide an alternative source of secondary metabolites. Because PTC involves growth of plant cells in contained and controlled fermentation vats, these systems require minimal land use, are independent of weather conditions, and do not require the use of agricultural chemicals. Examples of PTC-derived food ingredients include pigments (e.g., betalains, annatto, anthocyanins, betacyanin, betaxanthin, lycopene, and other carotenoids), flavor and aroma compounds (e.g., vanillin, ginger, and turmeric), essential oils (e.g., limonene, menthone, and methyl eugenol), enzymes, antioxidants, and sweeteners (e.g., stevioside and glycyrrhizin).

Research Opportunities

Identify triggers that uncouple cell differentiation from secondary metabolism   Creating growth conditions conducive to the production of secondary metabolites in PTC is frequently done empirically by manipulating growth media or environmental conditions; yet, metabolic pathways have not been elucidated for many of the secondary metabolites of commercial interest and optimum conditions vary for each. Identification of the metabolic trigger(s) that uncouples cell differentiation from secondary metabolism would make it possible for undifferentiated cell cultures to produce plant-derived compounds efficiently.

Elucidate important traits to target for genetic improvement, including the basic biochemistry and genetics involved in the metabolic pathways   Undifferentiated cultured plant cells can produce compounds that are never found in the differentiated field-grown plant. Over 80 new cell culture-associated, low-molecular-weight compounds have been compiled to date. It has been proposed that the process of dedifferentiation leads to the activation of dormant genes that yield new enzymes which divert the normal biosynthetic chain into new compounds not found in the differentiated plant. These new substances could have applications in the food and pharmaceutical industries. A basic understanding of the biochemistry of these metabolic systems provides a foundation for genetic manipulation of the pathways.

Develop methods for selecting stable, high-producing cell lines   Simple, rapid, and reliable methods for the selection and maintenance of high-producing cell lines need to be developed. There are no methods (e.g., freezing or freeze-drying) for long-term storage of PTC; therefore, cells must be subcultured on a regular basis to maintain viability. Unfortunately, continuous subculture leads to an unexplained loss of viability and productivity.

Develop improved bioreactors and downstream processing and purification systems for PTC-derived biological materials   Plant cells are fragile and require bioreactors that provide gentle agitation yet high oxygen-transfer rates. Significant improvements in plant cell bioreactors must be attained to make PTC an attractive economic alternative to extraction from intact plants. One approach for protecting cells is to immobilize or entrap cells within matrixes. It is critical to develop materials that protect plant cells yet allow rapid diffusion of nutrients and secondary metabolites in and out of cells. Processing and purification systems will need to be adapted to maintain the biological activity of PTC-derived materials.

Animal Biotechnology

Traditional breeding and selection techniques have been used to improve meat-producing animals (beef, swine, sheep, and poultry) and fish used as human and animal food sources. The basic principles of biotechnology can be used for genetic improvement of animals and fish. To date, biotechnology has been used to (1) produce growth promoters, vaccines, and other biologics by recombinant organisms, (2) produce transgenic animals with modified composition, and (3) construct transgenic animals to produce pharmaceuticals in their milk, blood, or urine.

Research Opportunities

Improve basic tools for the genetic manipulation of animals   Identification and understanding of the physiology of the major genes controlling growth and lactation, reproduction, and disease and stress resistance in animals are needed. The ability to produce transgenic livestock possessing traits of economic value is currently limited by our inability to maintain in culture pluripotent embryonic stem cells from any species except the mouse, by our lack of appropriate promoter-regulatory DNA to control expression of transgenes, and by the lack of knowledge about the physiological consequences of the expression of specific foreign genes. To advance the field, we also must develop a basic understanding of the biochemistry and genetics of traits controlled by multiple genes and develop cloning systems with acceptable, selectable markers. *In vitro* models of gene expression in animal systems and methods for assessing the overall impact of genetic modification on animal metabolism, including potential pleiotropic effects and nutritional implications, must be available.

Improve the productivity of meat-producing animals   The tools of biotechnology provide us with the opportunity to develop transgenic livestock that contain genes coding for improved growth characteristics, lactational performance, and resistance to disease and stress. Antimicrobial agents used as feed additives to alter intestinal microflora, improve absorption of nutrients, decrease protein requirements, and control subclinical diseases can be produced by genetically engineered organisms. In addition, other recombinantly derived drugs, monoclonal antibody vaccines, and immunomodulators derived from genetically engineered microorganisms could have an impact on animal health and meat quality. Safe, effective, reliable, and inexpensive diagnostics for disease detection, pregnancy tests, and detection of pathogenic organisms need to be developed.

Improve the nutritional quality of foods derived from animals   The cloning of genes coding for somatotropin or for enzymes that accelerate synthesis of beta-agonists into the germline of animals could accelerate growth and significantly improve the composition and nutritional quality of meat. Partitioning the fat and cholesterol in milk and meat and decreased fat content of these products would result in a healthier food supply more consistent with nutritional guidelines.

Fermentation

Bacteria, yeasts, and molds have been used for centuries as starter cultures for the production of fermented foods. Fermented foods provide a major contribution to human diets in all parts of the world because fermentation requires little energy and is relatively simple, natural, efficient, and inexpensive. Microbial metabolism is responsible for the production of the acids, carbon dioxide, and alcohol that function as preservative agents as well as enzymes that alter the flavor, texture, shelf life, safety, digestibility, and nutritional quality of fermented foods.

Microorganisms produce a variety of secondary metabolites which can be produced via fermentation and purified for use as food ingredients. Microorganisms are metabolically diverse, small, and easy to grow in large quantities on various substrates, making them ideal candidates for the production of secondary metabolites. The types of chemicals produced by microbial fermentation include acidulants, amino acids, vitamins, flavors, flavor enhancers, pigments, stabilizers, thickeners, surfactants, sweeteners, antioxidants, and preservatives.

Genetic engineering techniques offer more precise tools for improving food-grade microorganisms. Although significant research has been conducted on genetic engineering of food-grade microorganisms, no genetically engineered organisms have yet been approved by the FDA for use in foods. Several enzymes derived from genetically engineered organisms, including rennet (used in cheese making) and alpha-amylase (used for the production of high-fructose corn syrup), have been approved for use in the United States.

Research Opportunities

Develop basic tools for the genetic manipulation of microorganisms   The regulatory elements and signal sequences involved in control of gene expression in microbial systems need to be identified and isolated. This will make possible the construction of strains that excrete valuable secondary metabolites into the culture medium, from which they can be readily extracted and purified. Construction of multifunctional integrative cloning vectors will allow the transfer and stable integration into the chromosome of single genes as well as coding for entire metabolic pathways. Efficient and reliable gene transfer systems applicable to bacteria, yeast, and molds need to be developed.

Construct microorganisms with unique metabolic properties   Identification of microorganisms for metabolic screening will greatly expand the numbers and types of microorganisms that can be used in food fermentation and in the production of food ingredients. Genetic improvements will be targeted to a specific organism and fermentation system and may involve improved processing characteristics (e.g., more consistent and improved leavening of bread and accelerated ripening of cheese), decreased waste (e.g., bacteriophage-resistant organisms that eliminate economic losses caused by destruction of cultures by bacteriophage), enhanced food safety (e.g., microbial production of bacteriocin, which inhibits foodborne pathogens), improved nutritional quality (e.g., microbial production of amino acids or vitamins and engineered yeast for production of low-calorie beer), or enhanced bioavailability of nutrients (e.g., engineering of the meat factor influencing iron absorption into starter cultures and engineered starter cultures as delivery systems for digestive enzymes).

Understand the role of microorganisms as probiotics   Microorganisms have been reported to play key roles in maintaining the health of humans and animals by colonizing the gastrointestinal tract and controlling intestinal microorganisms capable of producing toxic effects in the host. Lactobacilli assist in the digestion of lactose, provide important digestive enzymes, inactivate toxins, bind cancer-causing chemicals, modulate the gut flora, deconjugate bile acids, and supply B vitamins. Further research is warranted, since the exact mechanisms for these effects are not well understood. Probiotic effects have been studied extensively in animals, and it is not uncommon to add certain organisms directly to animal feed to enhance digestibility of the feed and to protect the gastrointestinal tract from microbial invasion. The efficacy of this approach in human diets needs to be tested.

Enzymes and Protein Engineering

Enzymes are catalysts, generally proteins, that enhance the rate of the synthetic and degradative reactions of living organisms. The food-processing industry is the largest single user of enzymes, accounting for, on average, more than 50 percent of enzyme sales. Proteases, lipases, pectinases, cellulases, amylases, and isomerases are used extensively to control the texture, appearance, flavor, and nutritive value of processed foods. Although enzymes are produced by animals and plants as well as microorganisms, the enzymes from microbial sources are generally most suitable for commercial applications. Microbial products can be mass-produced without such limitations as season of the year or geographic location, which might be imposed by plant-derived enzymes. In addition, microorganisms grow quickly, and production costs are relatively low. In view of the metabolic diversity of microorganisms, nature has provided a vast reservoir of enzymes that act on all major biological molecules.

Unfortunately, enzymes frequently do not function optimally under the conditions of temperature and pH used in food processing. Chemical modification has been used successfully to improve enzymes; however, the general lack of specificity in the reagents and the requirement for difficult and tedious purification and characterization to insure homogeneity severely limits the power of the method for routine improvement of enzymes. Site-specific mutagenesis, a specialized form of genetic engineering, has been used to introduce in the structure of enzymes minor changes that have dramatic effects on substrate specificity, pH and thermal stability, and resistance of the enzyme to proteolytic degradation. For example, substitution of amino acids at specific key locations within the active site of the enzyme subtilisin demonstrated that properties of the enzyme could be altered dramatically, both positively and negatively, when compared to the native enzyme. Site-specific mutagenesis could improve the versatility of enzymes in food systems and decrease the cost of processing food. This technology could also be used to modify other proteins of interest to the food-processing industry, possibly altering functional properties or nutritive value.

Enzymes are frequently used in batch food-processing systems; however, they can be immobilized and used in continuous processing systems where applicable. For example, the enzymes used to convert starch in corn to high-fructose corn syrup and the enzyme rennet used in cheese manufacture have been immobilized and used continuously for weeks and sometimes months or years without substantial loss of activity. Cost savings in excess of 40 percent have been achieved by conversion from batch to immobilized enzyme systems.

Research Opportunities

Develop analytical tools to improve understanding of enzyme structure and function   Improved computer modeling systems are needed to predict the structural and functional impact of base pair or amino acid substitutions in DNA and protein, respectively. We need to develop models for evaluating the impact that structural changes in enzymes or proteins exert on their behavior in food systems (i.e., interactions with proteins, other macromolecules, and water) and chemical and physical tests for measuring properties directly associated with the desired changes in native plants and processed foods.

Design improved enzymes   Enzyme and protein engineering will make it possible to create tailor-made enzymes that function optimally under food-processing conditions. In addition to modifying reaction rate, pH and thermal stability, and resistance of the enzyme to proteolytic degradation, it may be desirable under certain circumstances to modify substrate specificity of enzymes. Theoretically, it will be possible to construct enzymes that modify fat, protein, or carbohydrates in ways not possible with enzymes that now exist in nature, creating the potential for new biological molecules in food systems. Enzymes could also be engineered to function in unusual environments, such as in organic solvents, or under extremes of pressure or temperature for unique food-processing applications. Protein engineering could be used to make noncatalytic proteins catalytic by attaching an active site to an existing protein. It may be possible to engineer antibodies that possess catalytic activity; their binding and recognition sites could be used to immobilize the enzyme for food-processing applications.

Improve enzymes in intact plants   Enzyme- and protein-engineering techniques, coupled with plant genetic engineering, could be used to modify enzymes and proteins in intact plants. For example, methods now exist to construct genes coding for synthetic proteins enriched in essential amino acids. Since cereal grains are deficient in one or more of the essential amino acids isoleucine, lysine, methionine, threonine, or tryptophan, transfer of these genes to plants deficient in these amino acids could improve their nutritive value. Many plant components used in food processing are chemically modified following extraction from the plant (e.g., hydrogenation of oils and cross-linking of starch). Engineering of plants with enzymes capable of chemically modifying starch or oils could eliminate the need for chemical modification after extraction.

MOLECULAR BASIS OF FOOD QUALITY

Clearly, these are exciting times for researchers involved in the study of the chemistry, physics, and biochemistry of foods. Quality and stability of food products are determined by the molecular properties of their constituents. However, the molecular properties often express themselves in unique, supramolecular structures that have an overriding influence.

Techniques for measuring chemical structure, reactivity, and physical properties have become available at an unprecedented rate, and there is every indication that developments will continue. Some, such as nuclear magnetic resonance (NMR) and electron paramagnetic resonance (EPR) imaging, are nondestructive, thus allowing for continuous monitoring of changes. Theoretical interpretation of data has been greatly improved by computer-assisted data processing. All of this promises to aid our understanding of the complex interactions of molecules that make up tissue or reformulated foods.

Improved understanding of the relationship between the molecular structure of food biopolymers and the functional properties of biopolymers in food products will be one important application of these new techniques. This will enable us to substitute more readily available, less expensive, or nutritionally or functionally superior ingredients in our food supply. A food biopolymer of particular interest is the class of cyclodextrins, which are six- to eight-membered donut-shaped rings of glucose molecules produced enzymatically from starch (Figure 4.3). They have the ability to bind noncovalently with many different types of molecules in their "core." In doing so, they alter the physical and chemical properties of the molecularly encapsulated "guest" molecules. Cyclodextrins have many potential applications in food products. For example, they can be used to carry flavors, enhance the solubility of otherwise water-insoluble compounds, and remove such undesirable compounds as cholesterol from food.

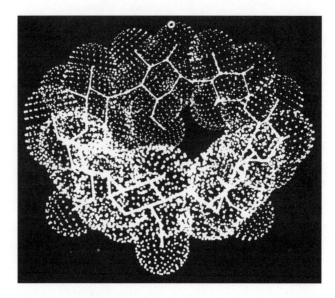

FIGURE 4.3 This molecular model illustrates the beta-cyclodextrin molecule and its ability to entrap materials in its hollow "core." Through available molecular modeling systems, it is possible to identify the uses of beta-cyclodextrins in specific applications.

Determination of the important properties of biopolymers such as proteins will make it possible to improve structure by biotechnological techniques, both genetic and enzymatic. For example, the use of magnetic resonance techniques in determining the types of interactions and molecular conformations of proteins in gels could allow for both higher quality and more economical production of these products.

Research Opportunities

Study the role of water in foods   One of the most important functional properties of food biopolymers is the ability to bind water. The amount, association with structural elements, distribution, and structure of water are without doubt critical to the quality of foods. It is perhaps not an exaggeration to suggest that in many ways water is the most important determinant of food quality. Water determines the structure of biopolymers and is both the medium of and a participant in most of the reactions that occur in foodstuffs. One of the difficulties in dealing with the problem of water structure in foods is that there is considerable uncertainty about the structure of water itself. Not only does water modify the structure of cellular components, the structure of water is in turn modified by the components of the cell.

The large surface area of cellular structures makes the effects at interfaces of particular importance. The more highly developed structure of water at these interfaces affects its function as a solvent and most likely reduces its ability to disassociate into hydrogen and hydroxyl ions. This latter is of critical importance in determining pH and chemical reactions. Methods for determining water structure are based primarily on relaxation techniques, measuring either the properties of water directly by proton magnetic resonance or the properties of molecules in water, such as the use of electron spin resonance (ESR) and NMR to study the translational or rotational movements of free radicals and other food constituents.

The rate of formation and growth of ice crystals is an important factor in the quality of frozen foods. Much attention has been paid recently to the extremely high viscosity of the glassy state of water in frozen foods. This phenomenon illustrates the importance of water in chemical reactions in foods and offers a potential for improved quality during frozen food storage. Techniques such as differential scanning calorimetry can distinguish between temperature-induced changes in the glassy state and phase changes brought on by melting of ice crystals.

In the 1980s, food scientists realized that they could better understand the relationships of food structure, food function, and water in food materials, products, and processes by applying polymer science, with its study of glassy states, glass transitions, and plasticization by water. Food polymer science, emphasizing the basic similarities between synthetic polymers and food molecules, provides a practical experimental framework to study real-world food systems that are not at equilibrium. It is being widely applied to explain and predict the functional properties of food materials during processing and storage of the final products.

Quantify the specific structural changes in the various levels of food macromolecular organization In spite of the potential promised by polymer science approaches to the study of water in foods, other lines of investigation should not be neglected. In particular, it should also be recognized that, in many cases, the relevant properties of food molecules result not from their generalized polymer behavior but rather from their specific molecular structure, as should be expected for biological macromolecules, with their well-known ability to assume diverse functions by varying their basic structure (in the case of polymers, their primary sequence). Such aspects are particularly important in foods containing components that retain significant aspects of biologically imposed structure: cells, membranes, fat globules, globular proteins, and so on. The specific details of the interaction of macromolecular functional groups with water are known to be crucial in biological self-organization and in maintaining viability, such as the role of hydrophobicity in protein conformation and membrane structure, the role of water structuring in ionic solvation, and specific hydration effects such as hydrogen bonding. Altering the hydration environment of food molecules, as in processing, often leads to irreversible and undesirable changes in food quality. In many cases, these changes cannot be understood in terms of general polymer theory but must be considered in terms of the specific structural details of the system under consideration. As a result, we need much more study of the molecular details of food polymer hydration—particularly under conditions of low water content or low temperatures.

Learn more about the behaviors of food components in solution   A related requirement is the need for greater basic work in simple model systems containing one or only a few components and variables. Until the behaviors of individual food components in solution are understood, and then the interactions of simple combinations of such polymers in solution, there is little hope of significant progress in understanding much more complicated systems. Much more needs to be learned about hydration forces, their role in colloidal stabilization, and whether these forces override more traditional models of colloidal interactions in food systems.

Explore mechanical-physical properties of foods related to bond energies   Often the properties of a food are more related to the unique supramolecular architecture of the major food polymers than to their specific molecular properties. Many food polymers like proteins and starches are extensive structures of interacting components joined by noncovalent bonds. Collagen and the contractile proteins of muscle are examples of this, as are the cellulose and hemicelluloses of plant cell walls. Many techniques, some rather elegant, have been developed to measure mechanical forces in processed foods. In addition, there has been good progress in understanding some of the chemical and physical changes occurring in individual molecules and supramolecular structures during processing.

What is lacking is a theory to relate the changes at the molecular or supramolecular level to the overall physical or mechanical properties of the food tissues. For example, how do the noncovalent bonds formed by protein denaturation and aggregation influence a physical measurement such as tensile strength? An understanding of these phenomena would make it possible to modify processing techniques and food formulations to produce foods with any desired physical attribute.

In a similar manner, it will be important to establish the contribution to these physical properties of covalent bonds in food biopolymers. Splitting of covalent bonds by hydrolysis of polymers is a technique that has been used for centuries to modify physical properties and produce products of desirable quality. Examples of this would be tenderization of meat by protein hydrolysis and increased yield and quality of fruit juices by hydrolysis of pectins. However, in most cases results have been achieved by trial and error, without a firm understanding of the number of bonds necessary to be broken to achieve optimal results.

Understand free-radical reactions in foods   Biopolymers play a critical role in determining the physical-mechanical properties of food tissues. Both covalent and noncovalent bonds between biopolymers govern these properties. An area of great importance in food processing is the effect that mechanical actions such as grinding and cutting have on these processes. It has been reported that this type of mechanical action can break covalent bonds and form free radicals, which have been associated with food deterioration. Little attention has been given to this phenomenon in food research, although the principle is well established with man-made polymers. Since many of our food products are subjected to these kinds of mechanical stresses, understanding the extent of the changes they cause is critical. Not only would the physical properties of various food polymers such as proteins be affected, but the formation of free radicals could set off chain reactions leading to degradation of lipids and other components in foods.

ESR spectroscopy is a powerful tool for measuring the production of radicals *in situ* and in real time. It measures free radicals directly, rather than just the decomposition products of the radicals. This type of kinetic information makes it possible to understand free-radical reactions occurring in food tissues without having to macerate and extract foods, processes that can themselves create free radicals. These *in situ* techniques should improve our understanding of other free-radical reactions as well. These other reactions would include those initiated by various forms of reactive oxygen species, thus allowing for improved strategies to counteract the effects of these free-radical oxidation processes.

Enhance understanding of biomembrane changes   Understanding of membrane structure and function has increased greatly in recent years, but much remains to be done. Good progress has been made in understanding the interactions of membrane proteins and lipids; however, interaction of membrane components with the proteins of the cell cytoskeleton is just beginning to be understood. These interactions will undoubtedly play a great role in the quality of foods.

To give some idea of the significance of membranes in food tissues, it can be calculated that 1 kilogram of lean beef has approximately 8,000 square meters of membrane surface. Thus, many of the reactions that go on in food result from the chemistry and enzymology of surfaces. Many of the functions of membranes in food tissues are an extension of their metabolic roles. These include energy production, the movements of ions and small and large organic molecules, receptor sites for hormones and therefore for cellular control responses, and involvement in the control of ionic composition and pH of cellular compartments. Membranes are responsible for postharvest vectorial metabolism and osmochemistry. In addition, the lipids of membranes are highly unsaturated and their extremely large surface area per unit of weight makes them particularly susceptible to oxidative reactions. These membrane processes are critical in the postharvest metabolism of fruits and vegetables and the postmortem control of calcium ion concentrations in the sarcoplasm of muscle tissue. Thus, quality control and maintenance are in large part a function of the membrane systems.

ENVIRONMENTAL ISSUES

Sustainability

Each step in the food system—production, transportation, processing, storage, and marketing—has some effect on the environment. Therefore, the concept of sustainability in the food system is critical to a finite world with an expanding population. An important challenge in this age of environmental and economic concerns is to identify, develop, and implement new systems for producing high-quality, economical, wholesome foods with reduced adverse effects on the environment and with better use of raw materials.

Sustainable agriculture attempts to minimize environmental degradation through a range of practices that includes integrated pest management; low-intensity animal production systems; crop rotations to reduce pest damage, improve crop health, decrease soil erosion, and (for legumes) fix nitrogen in the soil; and tillage and planting practices that reduce soil erosion and help control weeds. In the food-processing industry, processors are beginning to recycle more by-products that were formerly discarded. These by-products include the soluble materials in wastewater, such as sugar washed off peaches, tomato juice in flume water, starch removed from potatoes during washing and fluming operations, and solid materials such as corn husks and crab shells. If suitable uses can be found for these by-products, they can be converted to raw materials or ingredients in feed, food, or other products and removed from the waste stream.

An excellent example of sustainability exists in the fishing industry. In 1987, fish processors in Massachusetts designated fish waste disposal as one of their main future concerns. Regulations at that time prevented offshore disposal of the waste, and fees for landside disposal were steadily increasing, along with its potential for pollution. Scientists developed an economically viable liquid fertilizer from fish waste material for regional crops such as cranberries. Much of the fertilizer was liquefied using endogenous enzymes from the fish waste itself. They found that all plant material fertilized with the liquid fish fertilizer had equal or better growth than plants grown using commercial fertilizers. These and further studies have led to the addition of liquid fish fertilizer to the official list of approved cranberry fertilizers.

Research Opportunities

Develop alternative energy sources and agricultural chemicals U.S. agriculture depends heavily on fossil fuels to provide power for machinery, for the production and application of fertilizers and pest control chemicals, for crop drying, and for many other purposes. Improving our understanding of plant and pest interactions and the biology and genetics of insects and weeds will enable us to design integrated pest management strategies that reduce the need for pesticides. Advances in biotechnology should lead to the development of plants that are more resistant to pests and less dependent on the application of manufactured fertilizers. There is a need for new, effective pesticides that do not pose long-term health risks to consumers or to the environment. With additional research, we will learn how to collect and store solar, wind, and other sources of energy more reliably for applications on the farm, including the heating of livestock buildings and the drying of harvested crops.

Identify economically viable uses for by-products of the food industry and develop processes for separating them Information is needed on the identities, composition, and quantities of the solid and liquid by-products generated by the food industry. Research would help to identify the ways in which by-products can be incorporated into new foods, animal feed, or nonfood products. New technologies and devices such as membranes are needed to remove suspended and dissolved by-products from waste water and to separate by-products that become mixed together in a solid or liquid state.

Develop databases and water quality standards that will expand the use of water recycling and reuse technologies Food-processing operations are major users of water. Expanded use of water recycling and reuse technologies could reduce the quantity of water used and decrease the disposal of by-products of food-processing operations. Before these technologies can be widely expanded, however, the federal government must establish regulatory criteria governing their use. Before the government can do this, however, it must construct a database on the current use of these technologies. Minimum chemical and microbiological standards need to be established for water recycling and reuse. Also needed are residue and quality standards for finished products that come into contact with recycled and reused water.

CONCLUDING REMARKS

Food science and technology have made remarkable strides in providing people with high-quality, safe, and wholesome foods. Food chemists, food microbiologists, nutritionists, and food engineers have combined their skills and applied many of the basic science advances and new methods to produce today's food supply. It is hard to believe, walking the aisles of the average supermarket with more than 20,000 items, that the formalized field of food science is just over 50 years old. It evolved about the time that technologists were discovering how to fortify foods with iodine, vitamin D, iron, and B-complex vitamins.

Food science is a young, dynamic field facing many challenges. Consumers have always demanded an array of foods pleasing to the senses. They want food to be convenient and of a composition that enables them to more easily meet dietary guidelines. Many technologies are in place to respond quickly to consumer desires or public health needs. However, scientists must seize the newer techniques developed by molecular biologists to design functional foods for health needs. Food engineers and microbiologists must work together to optimize new processing techniques to ensure the safety of foods while reducing food and packaging waste. In addition, this field must apply its most creative minds to developing the equipment and technologies that will provide us with the value-added foods we need to compete successfully in world markets. Exciting advances certainly await us in the years ahead.

5

Understanding Diet, Health, and Disease Relationships

Classic nutrition, which focuses primarily on nutrient deficiencies, produced breakthroughs of great medical and public health significance, including the prevention and treatment of rickets, pellagra, beriberi, iron-deficiency anemia, and scurvy throughout most of the world. Advances in understanding the metabolic role of nutrients and the successful implementation of that knowledge by clinicians, public health practitioners, and food technologists led nutrition scientists to focus more attention on the role of diet in achieving and maintaining health by maximizing physiological functions and reducing the risk of chronic diseases (what some refer to as "optimal" health and development). Fortunately, clinical nutrition investigators are finding the tools, technologies, and opportunities to explore fundamental relationships between diet and long-term health to be increasingly accessible. We define clinical nutrition, the focus of this chapter, broadly to include concepts of health promotion as well as those pertaining to the dietary treatment of diseases and metabolic disorders—that is, disease prevention as well as therapeutics.

A person's age, sex, and stage of growth have a direct impact on his or her nutritional requirements; in turn, nutritional state may influence the rate of growth, development, and aging. However, until recently it was difficult to study the application of these concepts to well-being. Current research shows that undernutrition during the first three years of life is associated with a smaller body size and fat-free mass in later life, supporting the view that malnutrition during critical periods in early development has later consequences. These studies reaffirm the importance of good maternal nutrition during pregnancy and lactation and during childhood by identifying specific developmental outcomes that are affected by nutrient intakes during critical periods.

The aging process is also an exciting target of investigation. Animal studies show that aging is delayed by restricting food intake, though comparable studies in humans have not been done. Malnutrition may exacerbate or potentiate age-related chronic diseases that, in turn, accelerate aging. Malnutrition in later adult life also compromises function, with measurable consequences on morbidity, mortality, and quality of life.

Advances in the basic sciences challenge traditional paradigms of relationships between nutrients and their functions. In the case of vitamin D, for example, rickets and osteomalacia are the classic disease markers for insufficient intake. However, this nutrient appears to do more than simply facilitate calcium transport in the intestine. Several studies suggest that the active form of vitamin D has a direct effect on bone, helps regulate cell growth, and may affect immune function and cellular lipid metabolism. Vitamin D also affects vascular tissue; it enhances vasoconstriction, for example. These new findings call into question whether the amount of calcium in bone is the best indicator of vitamin D status for any individual.

Nutrients affect the central nervous system and immunological processes, but which nutrients are important and how they work requires further study. Individual nucleotides, amino acids, zinc, and several other nutrients seem to participate actively in immunological responses.

Food intakes can be related directly to neurotransmitter function in the brain. This arises from studies of the function of neuropeptides and amino acids as neurotransmitters and their role in neurodegenerative disease and from an increasing understanding of neurotransmitter receptors and the manner in which they are modulated by ions, free radicals, and the simultaneous action of other transmitters.

Information about how the body controls food intake is quite limited. We do not know all the signals that may arise in the intestine, whether and to what extent the liver and other organs are involved, whether and to what extent they may be under genetic control, or how various signals are integrated and processed in the brain and periphery. Furthermore, little is known about which potential regulatory molecules cross the blood-brain barrier, how they do so, where they exert their effects, or how they regulate function. Signals capable of affecting food intake also may arise from energy reserves in the form of glycogen or fat.

These and other comparable opportunities challenge us to examine broader relationships between nutrition and lifestyle. For example, nutrition scientists must ask how vitamin D adequacy can be defined in a context that includes an individual's dietary patterns, physical activity, and overall calcium status in order to promote optimal development and maintenance of the skeletal system, thereby preventing osteoporosis in late adult life. Other relationships between nutrients and serious clinical problems have been proposed, such as those between vitamin A and cancer, antioxidants and atherosclerosis and cataracts, and folic acid and neural tube defects. Sodium's role in hypertension may have been overestimated, while the role of other nutrients (e.g., calcium, magnesium, and potassium) may have been underestimated. Furthermore, these four nutrients are likely to interact. How this affects the risk of hypertension requires further study.

The complexity of relationships among food components and disease is demonstrated by the unfolding story of lipids and atherosclerotic heart disease. Early investigations discovered links between dietary cholesterol and saturated fats and atherosclerosis. Later, the role of polyunsaturates was explored. Those studies were followed by others exploring the role of monounsaturates, fish oils, and *trans* fatty acids. Most recently, levels of iron and ferritin in the body have been correlated with atherosclerotic heart disease. Clearly the picture is not complete, as there are conflicting data on the role of specific fats, other nutrients, food components, and dietary patterns and insufficient basic information on how atherosclerotic lesions evolve. Studies of relationships linking diet and heart disease show that sex, and perhaps racial and ethnic background, affect nutrient-outcome relationships and illustrate the need for more attention to these potentially important interactions. Personal behaviors also influence the risk of heart disease. For example, epidemiological studies demonstrate that even modest physical activity is protective. Much more investigation is needed before the relationship of diet and other variables to heart disease is fully explained.

The nutrition and food sciences have advanced to the point where we are able to investigate how dietary patterns—particularly the amounts and interactions of macro- and micronutrients consumed—can either promote health, increase the risk of disease, or increase disease severity. Understanding the mechanisms linking diet to disease and their dose-response relationships will lead to better dietary advice for individuals and populations. This chapter describes several opportunities for maximizing human function and reducing the risk of diet-related chronic diseases. Our examples were selected to represent major needs and promising opportunities and challenges for nutrition-related research. The past successes of the nutrition and food sciences have enabled us to eradicate or significantly reduce the incidence of straightforward nutrient deficiencies, uncover links between diet and chronic diseases, and begin to identify how dietary choices affect development throughout life. Today's science provides exciting challenges to the nutrition and food sciences for those committed to increasing healthy lifespans and who acquire the knowledge and tools to do so.

NEW OPPORTUNITIES: MAXIMIZING FUNCTION

Reproduction

Our understanding of nutrient function during various stages of the life cycle has advanced markedly during the past decade. It is now recognized that a woman's nutritional status at the time she conceives influences several aspects of her physiological response to pregnancy, relationships between her weight gain and the infant's birthweight, and the infant's anatomical development. Research now shows that, during lactation, mothers are generally able to produce milk of sufficient quantity and quality to support normal infant growth rates for at least the first three months of life, even when the mother's dietary supply of nutrients is limited, and for four to six months under the desirable conditions common in industrially developed countries. Breastfeeding confers several health benefits on the infant. It reduces the incidence and severity of certain infectious gastrointestinal and respiratory diseases and may lessen the infant's risk of immunologically related chronic diseases of later childhood and, in premature infants, may improve cognitive development.

Research Opportunities

Develop strategies that will enable women to gain appropriate amounts of weight during pregnancy   Weight gains during pregnancy may be either too small or too large. In the last few years, recommendations for weight gain during pregnancy have increased significantly, based on new research and a review of existing data. The recommended weight gain for women of normal pre-pregnancy weight is 25 to 35 pounds; for women of low pre-pregnancy weight, 28 to 40 pounds; for extremely obese women, at least 15 pounds; and for women carrying twins, 35 to 45 pounds. This weight should be gained gradually, through a nutritionally adequate diet. At a time when many women feel social pressure to be slender, more research is needed to develop strategies that succeed in encouraging women to try to achieve recommended weight gains during their pregnancy. It is also important to identify the number of women who gain excess weight during pregnancy and who do not lose it postpartum. Special treatments should be developed for these women. Physicians and nurses must be educated and trained to enhance their management skills related to gestational weight gain.

Research on weight gain during pregnancy must also address the question of the significance of the composition of this weight gain. Why do women in some industrially developed countries such as the United States and Sweden have higher fat gains than average? Is the gain in fat linked to food habits, the source of dietary energy, the amount of vitamins and minerals in the diet, or the result of weight fluctuations? What are the long-term consequences of high fat gains during pregnancy? Is there an optimal fat gain for pregnant women? These are all researchable questions.

Determine the effects of nutrition on embryogenesis   There may be important nutritional influences on embryogenesis, and disturbances of a nutritional-metabolic nature may lead to congenital malformations and limit behavioral development. For example, there is compelling evidence that giving vitamins, especially folate, to women around the time of conception decreases the risk of their babies developing neural tube defects. Others have related more subtle limits in cognitive performance to other micronutrient deficiencies and general undernutrition. Another example is the suggestive evidence that glucose concentrations in extracellular fluid are linked to the development of various fetal malformations. Several studies, though indirect or not optimally designed, imply that rigid glycemic control in diabetic women at the time of conception lowers the otherwise elevated incidence of fetal malformations. The changes in women's hormone production, and the resulting changes in metabolism, appetite, food tolerance, and dietary intake, need further study.

The primary research opportunity in this area is to define the molecular basis of these phenomena and how these mechanisms are influenced by overall dietary intake and food choices. This research bears directly on the issue of teratogenesis (the development of physical defects *in utero*), but it also will help in determining the benefits of dietary supplements during pregnancy.

Explore the relationship between calcium intake and risk of hypertensive disorders of pregnancy   There is an association between the status of calcium in the body and the development of acute hypertensive disorders of pregnancy, collectively known as preeclampsia. For example, epidemiological studies show an inverse relationship between calcium intake and the incidence of preeclampsia. Calcium supplements lower mean blood pressure in some people. In addition, preliminary clinical trials in which pregnant women were given calcium supplements suggest a lowered frequency of preeclampsia. If this relationship between calcium and preeclampsia exists, its mechanism is obscure. Identifying it would raise the hope of reducing the incidence of a disorder that accounts for a substantial proportion of morbidity and mortality among pregnant women and their fetuses.

Identify the relationship between lactation and calcium loss in the mother
Approximately 280 milligrams (mg) of calcium are secreted in breast milk
each day, resulting in significant stress on the mother's calcium stores. If
there is no adaptation to conserve calcium by the mother, then this loss
could lead to changes in calcium balance, resulting in bone demineraliza-
tion and increasing her future risk of osteoporosis. A primary physiological adaptation to lactation appears to be a decrease in calcium excretion
by the kidneys. Whether this decrease is a result of changes in calcitropic
hormones (such as parathyroid hormone) during lactation is not known. In
fact, an increase in bone mineral content after the baby is weaned has
been observed and appears to compensate, in part, for the loss that occurred during lactation. The extent to which the significant hormonal changes
that occur during lactation and weaning are involved in adapting to the
calcium loss imposed by lactation and the increase in bone mineral during
weaning needs to be clarified.

Once the mechanisms behind these alterations are known, it may be
possible to preserve, or even increase, bone mineral content during these
periods. Calcium kinetics can now be studied using stable isotopes, and
these should show how calcium compartments change during lactation
and weaning. More accurate methods of determining calcium status (including dietary intake) are being developed, and studies of the role of
calcitropic hormones, as well as estrogen and progesterone, in bone metabolism are proceeding. In addition, advances in technologies to measure
bone density are enabling investigators to study regional changes in both
trabecular and cortical bone. The radiation doses used in these technologies are now low enough to permit safe long-term studies of bone mineral
changes.

*Develop a better understanding of the role of nutrition in the etiology of
various other pregnancy-related outcomes and conditions*   Low-birthweight
infants, delayed onset of milk production, and maternal health problems
such as gestational diabetes are still prevalent in the United States. Furthermore, the etiologies of these problems are largely unexplained. What
maternal dietary and health behaviors are associated with these unfavor-
able outcomes? Does maternal dieting, both short- and long-term, influence the onset of these problems? What is the role of overall diet quality,
physical activity, occupation, stress, and quality of life? Are vitamin-min-
eral supplements beneficial during pregnancy and lactation and preferable to fostering improved nutrient intake through diet? If so, which ones
are beneficial and when? How much is needed? Are there any potential
health consequences from the long-term use of vitamin and mineral supplements, especially those containing iron? Are pregnant women more likely

VON GIERKE'S DISEASE:
A REVOLUTION IN TREATMENT

Nutritional therapy has had a very important impact on the lives of people with certain genetic diseases known as inborn errors of metabolism. One of the more common and most important of the inborn errors of metabolism affecting glycogen storage is glycogenosis type I. First described by Von Gierke in 1929, it is caused by a deficiency of glucose-6-phosphatase activity in the liver and kidneys. Affected children are unable to produce glucose from liver glycogen normally, and they consequently suffer from recurrent hypoglycemia. Their growth is stunted, and they have a host of secondary abnormalities, including serious clinical problems such as metabolic acidosis and recurrent nose bleeds. In the past, these children frequently died before puberty, and those who did survive almost invariably developed complications including multiple adenomas of the liver that could become malignant.

It has been well understood for some time that the continual provision of carbohydrate to children with this disorder by frequent feedings could ameliorate the biochemical abnormalities, such as lactic acidosis and high blood concentrations of uric acid and lipids. However, the introduction of nocturnal nasogastric feeding of a high-glucose formula in 1976 dramatically changed the outlook for children with Von Gierke's disease, so that most of them now live into adult life with markedly improved health and amelioration of all the consequences of sustained hypoglycemia. This form of treatment was largely superseded in 1984 when investigators reported that feeding affected individuals uncooked starch in a suspension of water maintained their blood glucose levels for up to six hours, because of the slow degradation of this form of starch by pancreatic amylase. Thus, the difficult nasogastric regimen that required intubation each night was replaced by a much simpler one that is virtually as effective.

Phenylketonuria was the first inborn error of metabolism treated successfully by nutritional means (by a diet low in phenylalanine). The dietary treatment of Von Gierke's disease is an equally impressive example of nutritional therapy based upon knowledge of metabolic pathways.

to adopt healthful behaviors? At what point after pregnancy and lactation is it best to initiate weight management?

Growth and Development

Growth and development are under genetic control, but they are modified by diet and the environment. Each developmental step is contingent upon the preceding one. This process probably accounts for the normal variation in maturation and likely influences the development of chronic diseases throughout life. Not well described are the mechanisms relating specific phenotypes to a person's genetic endowment (except in the case of certain inborn errors of metabolism), nutritional intake, and environment and the importance of specific dietary variables in determining individual risk of chronic disease.

Research Opportunities

Identify behavioral consequences of ingesting breast milk during infancy   Only now are the nonnutritive effects of milk ingestion and their underlying mechanisms being discovered. Milk, through its fat moiety, calms infants. Moreover, it reduces gross motor activity, reduces tachycardia, and doubles the pain threshold. These responses appear to be mediated by central opioid and cholecystokinin (CCK) receptors. One intriguing speculation is that these responses may influence long-term motivational systems.

One challenging opportunity is to identify the mechanism of how milk, within the context of its delivery by parent or caretaker, quiets the infant and thereby conserves energy while concomitantly providing energy. This may help us to treat low-birthweight infants with increased energy needs and provide an understanding of fundamental issues related to energy conservation and growth. Meeting this research challenge should reveal the earliest mechanisms that determine food intake and its affective consequences, including food selection, feeding disorders, and the development of obesity.

Develop a better understanding of the long-term consequences of nutritional insults on early development   The hypothesis that growth failure in early childhood predicts functional impairment at later ages has been substantiated recently in the follow-up to a supplementary feeding study conducted in Guatemala between 1969 and 1977. Length at age three was found to be independent of linear growth from age three to adulthood, indicating that individuals were unable to compensate for growth retardation incurred in early childhood. The degree of stunting at age three was related to measures of intellectual achievement such as literacy and highest grade completed. The relationships among early growth, diet, and later functional abilities remain to be elucidated. Especially important is the role of micronutrients in development; for example, recent investigations have related iron nutriture to cognitive development and subclinical vitamin A deficiency to mortality.

A number of questions illustrate the challenge presented by this opportunity. What are the vulnerable periods of development in humans? What type and degree of malnutrition affects development during specific periods of maturation? Is there a generational carryover in malnutrition? Does early malnutrition limit economic productivity in adults? What is the role of early overnutrition versus undernutrition on long-term function? Is exercise balanced with an increased energy intake essential to healthy development and normal function in children? What is the nature of parental influences on infants who fail to thrive?

Explore the relationship between early diets and metabolic "imprinting"   Changes in diet during the prenatal, sucking, and weaning periods may have a lasting impact on metabolic development. The activities of the rate-limiting enzymes of cholesterol and bile acid syntheses appear to be affected by diet during these periods of development. Similarly, studies of spontaneously hypertensive and salt-sensitive strains of rats also suggest that maternal diets during gestation and preweaning diets modulate blood pressure responses. Also, diets in early infancy can affect whether insulin-dependent diabetes develops in rat strains genetically predisposed to the abnormality.

Unfortunately, neither the mechanisms responsible for the apparent "imprinting" of metabolic responses by early diet nor the bases for the susceptibility to dietary influences during specific stages of development are known. Similarly, it is not clear whether we should extrapolate the results of animal studies of metabolic imprinting to humans. For example, while breastfeeding has been suggested to prevent or ameliorate atopic conditions, insulin-dependent diabetes, and some forms of childhood cancers, the evidence is not conclusive.

Identify the role of nutrition in prolonging the span of healthy lives   Overall health and function among the elderly are not linked to chronological age. Environmental and genetic factors also play an important role in the aging process. What factors contribute to variation in the aging process? How can we distinguish the pathologic from physiologic accompaniments of aging, such as changes in blood pressure and glucose tolerance? What long-term eating behaviors and lifestyles are associated with attaining a healthy old age? Undernutrition in animals slows the aging process. Will low intakes of specific nutrients also slow aging in humans? If so, at what cost to other functions? Does nutritional status influence the onset of menopause? If so, why? What is the role of antioxidants in aging? Do they exert an effect independent of their known physiological function and their role in the prevention of chronic disease? What effect does aging per se have on circulating concentrations of key metabolites used to assess health (e.g., cholesterol in the blood)? These and related questions illustrate important issues that will gain increasing attention as the population ages.

NUTRITION AND VISION-RELATED
DISORDERS OF AGING

The lens of the eye is designed to focus images on the retina. Aging compromises the function of both lens and retina. Age-related macular (i.e., retinal) degeneration (AMD) and age-related cataract are the major causes of blindness among the elderly. There are two forms of AMD. The more common is the "dry" form, characterized by a slow, insidious atrophy of the photoreceptors, retinal pigment epithelium (RPE), and choriocapillaries (the rich capillary bed that serves the photoreceptors, outer plexiform layer, and RPE). This atrophy severely compromises normal visual tasks such as reading, facial recognition, and depth perception. The atrophied area expands with time but rarely leads to total blindness. At present, there is no prevention or treatment for this condition. "Wet," or exudative, AMD is characterized by subretinal neovascularization, an aggressive growth of blood vessels from the choriocapillaris up through the retina that causes hemorrhage and scarring in the retina. Almost 90 percent of severe visual loss in AMD occurs in the 10 percent of cases with wet AMD. Dysfunction of the lens caused by partial or complete opacification is called cataract.

Research Opportunities

Explore the relationships between AMD and antioxidants AMD affects almost 30 percent of people in the United States over age 65, and the proportion of affected persons increases with age. AMD is also the primary cause of new blindness in persons over age 65. Clinicians estimate that by the year 2011, over 8 million Americans will experience some loss of vision due to AMD. Although careful monitoring and laser ablation slow the course of the exudative disease, this treatment may cause some immediate loss of vision, and it usually does not prevent the ultimate loss of central vision.

Although the pathogenesis of AMD has not been elucidated, it is believed widely that the primary lesion lies within the RPE cells and that excessive exposure to light and active forms of oxygen are involved. This is because the photoreceptors and RPE cells reside in a highly oxygenated environment subject to bright illumination.

As with cataract, oxidation appears to play a role in the etiology of AMD. Elevated concentrations of carotenoids, vitamin A, vitamin E, zinc, or all of these have been associated with diminished risk or progression of AMD in several preliminary reports. It is essential to examine the relationship between AMD and antioxidants for the prevention of AMD and to determine what concentrations of these antioxidants may be helpful.

Develop an improved understanding of the ability of antioxidants to prevent cataract formation Approximately 50 million persons in the world are blind from cataracts. More than 700,000 cataract extractions are performed annually in the United States. In fact, cataract extraction is the most frequently performed surgery among the elderly. In this country, the prevalence of senile cataract sufficiently severe to reduce vision is approximately 4.5 percent, 18 percent, and 45 percent among people age 52 to 64, 65 to 74, and 75 to 85, respectively. If cataracts could be delayed by only 10 years, the need for cataract extraction would be diminished by half. This would lead to considerable financial benefit, gains in productivity, and enhanced quality of life among the elderly. Although an awesome problem in the industrially developed nations, the situation is worse in the developing countries because (1) there is a dearth of ophthalmologists to perform the lens extractions and replacements, (2) cataracts are three to four times as common, and (3) cataracts develop earlier in life.

About 98 percent of the solid mass of the lens is protein. Lens proteins are extremely long-lived, therefore it is not surprising that in the aged lens the vast majority of protein matter may be damaged extensively. Much of the damage involves oxidation. The altered proteins accumulate, aggregate, and precipitate. Recent studies indicate that consumption of dietary antioxidants (vitamins C, E, and carotenoids) is associated with delay of cataract, but clinical trials must be completed.

Body Composition

Understanding the determinants of body composition is central to the nutritional sciences. In few other areas is the interplay between genetic endowment and the environment as evident as it is in the phenotypic expressions of diverse body compositions. Opportunities in the area of body composition assessment encompass a wide range of challenges in human physiology coupled with biophysics and bioengineering.

Research Opportunities

Explore relationships between lean body mass and selected functional indicators in late adult life Cross-sectional data show that loss of lean body mass (LBM) occurs with advancing age. The Baltimore Longitudinal Study on Aging showed an approximately 12 percent loss of LBM, determined anthropometrically, in men age 75 to 84 compared to men age 25 to 34. Using total body potassium as an indirect measure of LBM, one sees even more dramatic differences. Thus, it seems clear that erosion of LBM accompanies aging.

Decreased physical activity is a notable consequence of chronological aging and of most disease states. Decreased activity leads to loss of LBM, which makes exertion more difficult, leading to further atrophy. Sedentary people often ingest more calories than they use, leading to increased fat mass, with the risk of obesity and of associated disorders (e.g., diabetes, hyperlipidemia, and atherosclerosis).

Several observations support the contention that the amount of LBM has functional significance in aging. First, the amount of LBM—specifically, muscle mass—is the main determinant of physical strength. Second, interventions that increase muscle and lean mass improve strength and functional status in the aged. Third, reduced immune competence accompanies loss of LBM. LBM in the elderly can be increased by resistive exercise or administration of growth hormone, suggesting that loss of LBM is not an inevitable accompaniment of chronological aging. Much of the work done in this area is very recent, and the questions posed are central to the well-being of a growing number of the world's inhabitants.

Explore the relationship between lean body mass and the body's ability to respond to various physiological stresses   The functional significance of an adequate LBM is illustrated by data from starving and sick populations. The changes in LBM caused by starvation are similar to those seen in normal aging, but they can be reversed with food alone. Data from animal studies, autopsies of emaciated patients, and the records of Jewish physicians treating starving people in the Warsaw Ghetto between 1941 and 1943 show that a large amount of LBM is lost before death. Death occurred when losses of LBM reached approximately 40 percent. In aging, the situation is far more complex.

In intensive-care patients, erosion of LBM predicts mortality more accurately than any other independent variable. In cancer patients, any weight loss is associated with a 50 percent shorter median survival and worse functional status than patients with the same kind of tumor at the same stage but without weight loss. Similarly, loss of 40 percent of baseline LBM was found in patients dying of acquired immunodeficiency syndrome (AIDS). Depletion of LBM parallels reduction in immune competence and leads to complications, prolonged hospitalization, and death. The investigation of mechanisms responsible for these associations presents scientists with research questions relevant to clinical nutrition and patient management.

Explore relationships among body composition, cytokines, and immune responses   The immune system is a large component of the body's nonmuscle lean mass. Lymphocytes alone account for approximately 2 percent of total body weight and 8 percent of fat-free solids. The short half-life and active metabolism of many immune cells make the immune system very sensitive to variations in metabolism and nutrition. The status of the immune system is intimately related to body composition through the known effects of the cytokines IL-1-beta in muscle. This phenomenon is part of the acute-phase response triggered by exercise. In healthy people, exercise leads to more protein synthesis than degradation, with a subsequent increase in muscle mass. There is a two-way relationship between LBM and the immune system in that cytokines can alter body composition, and immune function can deteriorate when LBM is lost. These relationships are understood incompletely and present substantial challenges of importance to health promotion and improved patient care, particularly among the elderly.

Explore the relationship of the accumulation and distribution of body fat during childhood to long-term health   Adipose tissue is of interest because of well-established associations between the total amount and distribution of body fat (particularly deep visceral fat) and the risk of chronic diseases in adults, such as hypertension, diabetes mellitus, cardiovascular disease, and certain cancers. Body-fat distribution is measured effectively by imaging techniques and, clinically, by the waist-hip ratio and the abdominal sagittal diameter. However, the predictive value of such measures obtained in infancy through adolescence for long-term health is not known.

In addition to developmental changes in body fat, an individual's genotype and diet also influence fat accretion. Studies of twins raised separately or together suggest a very high heritability (60 to 70 percent) of body mass index. Adoption studies, however, yield a more probable heritability factor of about 40 percent. Genetic makeup also appears to determine distribution of body fat, thereby modulating the risk of various chronic diseases.

Understanding the interactions among diet, genes that regulate the accretion and distribution of adipose tissue, and lifestyle, and the relationship between fat distribution and chronic disease pose significant challenges to clinical and basic scientists.

Develop new methodologies for measuring and describing body composition and body fat distribution   Measurement of body composition has focused on ways to measure water, proteins, minerals, and fat. Methodologies include anthropometry, hydrodensitometry, dilution techniques, bioelectrical impedance, neutron activation, nuclear magnetic resonance, computerized tomography scanning, dual photon absorptiometry, and others. Two-compartment models (fat and nonfat) and more sophisticated multicompartment models, based on tissue, elemental, or chemical methods, have been developed.

Novel laboratory-based methods for assessing body constituents will provide opportunities to understand better the relationships among diet, targeted functions, the size and composition of functional and anatomical compartments of the lean and non-lean body mass, and the environment. There is also a great need for robust and reliable methods capable of measuring the principal components of body composition in nutrition surveillance and other types of survey and field studies.

Develop a better understanding of the dynamic composition of bone and the relationship between calcium status and long-term health   Osteoporotic fractures are a major cause of morbidity and mortality among the elderly. Since the population of the United States is aging rapidly (by the year 2050, almost one-quarter of the population is projected to be over age 65), the prevention of osteoporosis is a major public health goal. Although much is known about the biochemistry of bone mineralization and loss of bone mass, the actual causes of osteoporosis are not well understood. For example, there are racial and ethnic differences in the prevalence of osteoporosis that do not seem to be correlated with dietary calcium intake.

The problem of osteoporosis is generally more severe in women. Therefore, most of the research has been in women. Among the many risk factors identified are age, sex, race, genetics, reproductive factors, cigarette smoking, alcohol, physical activity, medical history (e.g., rheumatoid arthritis, insulin-dependent diabetes mellitus, or osteoarthritis), use of certain medications (e.g., steroids, estrogen, and thiazide diuretics), and immobility. Components of the diet that have been linked to the prevention or development of osteoporosis include calcium, fluoride, protein, phosphate, and vitamin D. However, there is not enough evidence to establish any component's role. While it is clear that the greater the peak bone mass achieved in early adult life the lower the risk of osteoporotic bone fractures later, it is not known how best to achieve peak bone mass. Supplemental estrogen in the postmenopausal years is the best known means of slowing the progressive loss of bone mass in elderly women. Much of the current research interest is in intervention, to test the effects of calcium (with or without vitamin D) and estrogen on bone loss.

Immune Function

The consistent impairment of a variety of immune responses in protein-energy malnutrition is established. Recent work has extended this observation to include the critical roles of individual nutrients in regulating immunity. Other factors that interact with nutrition and immunocompetence include age, physical activity, physical and emotional stress, drugs, infections, other systemic diseases, and trauma. Many of the commonly used immunological assays, such as lymphocyte response to mitogens, the production of antibodies, or the ability of phagocytes to kill ingested microorganisms, generally reflect the end point of a complex series of interactions between distinct cells and their products. Important areas posing interesting challenges and opportunities for future research are described below.

Research Opportunities

Explore the role of specific nutrients in maintaining mucosal barriers   Protein-energy malnutrition is associated with the incidence and increased severity of diarrheal and respiratory illnesses. The role of individual nutrients such as amino acids, carbohydrates, vitamins, and trace elements in mucosal infections is poorly understood. Areas that require further study are how various nutrients modulate the incidence and severity of virulence factors and how they influence the integrity of mucosal epithelial cells and the subsequent attachment of microorganisms to them. A greater understanding of these relationships should enhance strategies for the prevention of mucosal infections and improve clinical management when they occur.

Improve our understanding of the dependence on specific nutrients of unique immunorelated cellular and molecular events   It was suggested more than 30 years ago that there is an interaction among nutrition, immune responses, and infectious disease. Many nutrient deficiencies result in impaired defenses, and more than recommended levels of some nutrients appear to enhance the immune response beyond that observed with "adequate" levels of that nutrient. Conversely, both acute and chronic inflammatory conditions, as well as infectious and neoplastic diseases, result in several metabolic changes in the body that can adversely affect nutritional status. The roles of various nutrients in specific gene expression that regulate immunoactive cell functions, such as the production of cytokines and cell-cell interactions, are poorly understood. Recent advances in our understanding of the role of cytokines in mounting immune responses make the study of the nutritional modulation of these mediators essential (Figure 5.1). Focusing on cytokines whose roles in the modification of nutritional status have been either studied or implicated [interleukins (IL) 1, 2, and 6 and tumor necrosis factor (TNF)] is especially exciting.

Investigate the nutritional modulation of cytokines by dietary components   Production of IL-1 by monocytes in peripheral blood vessels is impaired by protein deficiency. This impairment appears specific to protein deficiency since IL-1 production by leukocytes from patients with

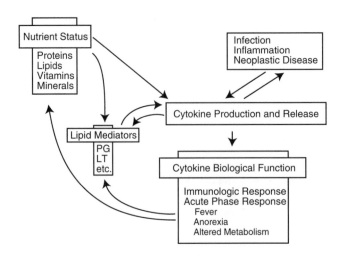

FIGURE 5.1 Interrelationships of nutrition with infectious and inflammatory diseases that are mediated by cytokines. PG = prostaglandin; LT = leukotriene. Source: Meydani, S.N. Nutr. Rev. 48(10):361-369, 1990. Reprinted with permission. Copyright International Life Sciences Institute, North America. All rights reserved.

marasmus is normal. Furthermore, the acute-phase response following injection of IL-1 is impaired in protein-deficient rabbits and guinea pigs.

Cytokines are also modulated by the consumption of selected fatty acids, fat, water-soluble vitamins, and trace elements. Eicosanoids are 20-carbon polyunsaturated fatty acids (PUFA) derived from essential fatty acids. Arachidonic acid is the main precursor of eicosanoid synthesis. This compound is metabolized enzymatically to prostanoids of the 2 series (e.g., prostaglandin E2 and thromboxane A2) and leukotrienes of the 4 series (e.g., leukotriene B4). These compounds are highly active substances with diverse biological actions. They are important in regulating immune and inflammatory responses and have been implicated in the pathogenesis of autoimmune, immunodeficiency, neoplastic, and inflammatory diseases (Figure 5.2). The limiting steps in eicosanoid production are precursor availability (determined by fatty acid composition of membrane phospholipids and activity of phospholipases), and activity of cyclooxygenases and various lipoxygenases. The long-chain fatty acids of the marine oils, namely eicosapentaenoic and docosahexaenoic acids, can replace arachidonic acid in membrane phospholipids, resulting in reduced production of prostaglandins of the 2 series and leukotrienes of the 4 series. Fatty acid replacement influences cytokine production and other aspects of immune and inflammatory responses. Furthermore, the activity of the synthesizing enzymes is influenced by lipid hydroperoxide levels and thus antioxidant status. Eicosanoid synthesis can therefore also be modified by dietary antioxidant nutrients such as vitamins C and E, selenium, and copper. Because lipoxygenase is a zinc-containing enzyme, its activity might be influenced by dietary zinc.

Micronutrients play other roles in cytokine modulation. The age-associated decline in T cell-mediated function has been attributed to defective IL-2 production and responsiveness. Vitamin E supplementation of the diets of aged mice doubled IL-2 production and increased ConA-stimulated lymphocyte proliferation and delayed-type hypersensitivity skin responses. Healthy elderly humans given vitamin E supplements [800 international units (IU) per day for 30 days] increased production of IL-2. This increase was accompanied by more active mitogenic responses to ConA and delayed-type hypersensitivity skin tests. Vitamin E supplementation did not affect IL-1 production. The effect of vitamin E on IL-2 production may be mediated by a decrease in prostaglandin E_2.

Reducing vitamin B_6 in the diets of healthy elderly subjects caused a significant drop in IL-2 production by mononuclear cells in peripheral blood vessels. Production returned to baseline after subjects were given

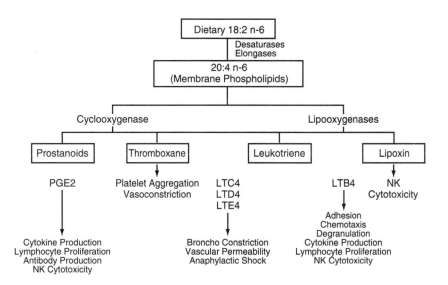

FIGURE 5.2 Role of eicosanoids in the regulation of immunological and inflammatory processes. PG = prostaglandin; LT = leukotriene; NK = natural killer cell. Source: Meydani, S.N. Nutr. Rev. 48(10):361-369, 1990. Reprinted with permission. Copyright International Life Sciences Institute, North America. All rights reserved.

vitamin B_6. A direct correlation was observed between concentrations of pyridoxal phosphate in plasma and IL-2 production.

Zinc deficiency in rats and humans was associated with a decrease in IL-2 production. Reduced IL-1 and IL-2 production contributes to impaired T cell-mediated function, and injection of human recombinant IL-1-alpha into pregnant rats increased zinc uptake by liver and bone marrow and increased expression of metallothionein 1 and 2 genes. Deficiencies of iron, copper, and magnesium also decrease IL-1 production.

The role of cytokines goes beyond functions associated with the usual immune responses. Two forms of tumor necrosis factor have been identified: TNF-alpha and TNF-beta. TNF-alpha, which may play a role in the development of adult-onset diabetes mellitus, appears to be overproduced by obese animals. This cytokine depresses the expression of a transport protein, glut4, that makes possible insulin-mediated glucose transport across cellular membranes. Researchers have found low concentrations of glut4 and high concentrations of TNF-alpha in obese animals with insulin-resistant diabetes.

Cognitive Function—Central Nervous System

No other organ system of the body depends more on nutrition than the central nervous system (CNS), nor does any system of the body have a greater effect upon nutrition. Interactions between the CNS and nutrition, therefore, offer a challenging array of opportunities for research.

Research Opportunities

Enhance our understanding of the role of nutrients and other food components in the development of the CNS and in treating developmental disorders of the CNS We understand the role of adequate maternal nutrition in preventing low-birthweight babies, but we are only beginning to elucidate the role of specific micronutrients in fetal development. An important example is the recent finding of the effectiveness of folic acid in preventing some neural tube defects. Similarly, we know that iodine deficiency impairs brain development. Iodine deficiency may well be the greatest cause of mental retardation in the world today. We do not have a precise understanding of the effects of iodine on the developing nervous system nor on its production of cognitive disabilities. Iron is another micronutrient essential to adequate cognitive development. The deleterious effects of iron deficiency in infancy are known. Five-year-old children whose iron deficiency anemia during infancy had been corrected were mentally disadvantaged compared to peers who had not suffered from anemia in their first year of life.

Establish requirements for the large number of nutrients whose effect on the development of the CNS is still uncertain   Docosahexaenoic acid is important to the development of photoreceptor cells during early development, but we do not yet know how to use this knowledge to develop dietary recommendations. Similar uncertainty surrounds the role of n-6 and other n-3 fatty acids in neural development. The list of nutrients affecting the development of the CNS is large and growing; further understanding of this area can pay large dividends in fostering improvements in growth and development.

A special case of nutritional requirements is presented by premature and low-birthweight babies who are maintained by nutritional support. Studies of the survival and cognitive development of these infants will increase the effectiveness of such support and provide insights into nutritional issues that are difficult to approach in normal children.

Explore potential links between nutritional status, aging, and brain function   Recent observations correlate a narrowing of the carotid arteries with elevated concentrations of homocysteine in the blood, concentrations that, in turn, are correlated with mild deficiencies of folate and vitamins B_6 and B_{12}. It is possible that nutrients influence the progression of cerebrovascular disease and thereby influence mental and cognitive functions. We need to conduct intervention trials to determine whether nutritional factors that decrease homocysteine levels—including betaine, folate, and vitamins B_6 and B_{12}—reduce the risk of cerebrovascular disease. Exciting opportunities exist to explore and define the relationship between methylation in the CNS and behavior and to understand the relationships among folate, B_{12}, methylation, and brain cell function.

Develop strategies to help individuals compensate for the diminished ability to smell and taste as they age   Aging is associated with decrements in taste and smell of at least 50 percent, decrements that may be increased considerably by the more frequent illness of the aged and by medications used to control these illnesses. This consequence of aging provides important opportunities for research. One example is to determine the extent to which diminution in olfaction and taste limits dietary intake. To what extent are modifications in taste a reflection of differences in nutritional status with respect to zinc, protein, and perhaps other nutrients? To what extent do these changes represent programmed loss of taste buds and other receptors? Similar questions can be posed with regard to olfaction. A decrement in olfaction is one of the earliest signs of Alzheimer's disease. Food scientists are manipulating food flavors and colors in an effort to improve the appeal of foods to people with diminished taste and smell acuity (see Chapter 4). The potential relationship between olfaction and nutrition should be explored to learn if olfactory changes contribute or follow nutritional depletion in patients with cognitive impairments.

Identify the key roles of the CNS in regulating food intake and body weight Whatever its metabolic determinants, food intake depends in the final analysis upon the CNS. It is clear that malfunctioning of the paraventricular nucleus or the ventral noradrenergic bundle results in over- or undereating. Recent research on the control of food intake goes far beyond earlier studies on the regulation of body weight to delineate neural networks that respond to specific nutrients and neurotransmitters that affect communications within the targeted network. For example, the neurotransmitter galanin is involved specifically in the ingestion of fats, whereas neuropeptide Y subserves carbohydrate intake. Early evidence that the opioid peptides increase food intake has been followed by indications that their effects are complex. They evidently are stimulated by the pleasurable qualities of food and increase ingestion of fatty and sweet foods, while having no effect on ingestion of low-fat or unsweetened foods. Many opportunities exist for further research in the area of neurotransmitter control of food intake.

Although it is clear that the energy output side of the energy balance equation is of critical importance, we know almost nothing about the effects of physical activity on the amount and choice of foods and nutrients. Since sustained physical activity is one of the very few predictors of maintenance of body weight following weight reduction by obese people, more information in this area would have immediate practical consequences as well as being of great theoretical value.

Major opportunities for the study of the role of specific nutrients and their metabolites in the modulation of specific CNS functions are provided by the rapidly developing field of neuroimaging. For example, neuroimaging has made it possible to move beyond animal studies of the neural circuitry mediating food intake and food choice to studies in humans. Recently, positron emission tomography scans have been used to show hypermetabolic activity in the temporal lobes of persons suffering from bulimia nervosa.

Food-Related Behaviors

The study of nutrition and behavior has dealt traditionally with the impact of certain foods or nutrients on brain function and their subsequent influences on behavior. Sugar and other carbohydrates, food colors, alcohol, and caffeine are among the food constituents evaluated for their potential influences on behavior. Much less attention has been paid to the ways in which behavior influences nutritional status. Research on food

preferences, food choices, and the selection of a habitual diet has sometimes been regarded as peripheral to the science of nutrition. Yet changing the food choices and dietary practices of individuals and populations is
a major factor in reducing the risk of obesity, coronary heart disease, and
cancer. For dietary interventions to be successful, we need a better understanding of the many factors that affect food preferences and diet
choice (see Chapter 6).

Research Opportunities

*Identify neurotransmitter functions that modulate food preference and
selection*   As noted above, a major area of current research is the identification of specific neurotransmitters subserving the ingestion of macronutrients (e.g., galanin for fats, neuropeptide Y for carbohydrates). There
have been reports that serotonin may give rise to an appetite for carbohy-
drate-rich foods. Animals injected with morphine selectively increase fat
intake, while the opioid antagonist naltrexone blocks overeating. Related
research indicates that endogenous opioid peptides may mediate overeating that is associated with exposure to sweet or high-fat foods. This new
area of study merits more detailed attention by nutrition scientists interested in neurophysiology.

*Improve our understanding of the links among the sense of taste, attitudi-
nal factors, and weight regulation*   Studies of taste responsiveness often
have been guided by the expectation that taste responsiveness is modulated by hormonal and metabolic factors. Recent studies have focused on
the roles of sugar and fat in determining sensory preferences and have
concluded that sensory preference for fat versus sugar depends to some
extent on body weight. While obese women preferred foods rich in fat,
anorectic women preferred sweet stimuli and showed an aversion to dietary fat. Other studies revealed that obese weight cyclers, or "yo-yo"
dieters, showed increased preferences for sweet, high-fat foods relative to
obese individuals of stable body weight. Sensory preferences appear to
differ among clinical populations of women at extremes of body weight
and may prove to be a valuable tool in distinguishing between potential
subtypes of human obesity.

Preferences for sugar-fat mixtures may be modulated by previous experience or may be contingent on attitudinal or social variables, including
attitudes toward body weight and dieting. For example, early (innate)
preference for fats is reinforced and maintained by the postingestional
consequences of fat intake. Fats absorb the smells and odors of foods and
are a salient target of food aversion in both pregnant women and cancer
patients undergoing chemotherapy. There are sex differences in food pref-

erences. Overweight men listed steaks and roasts, hamburgers, french fries, and pizza as preferred foods. In contrast, women listed bread, cake, cookies, ice cream, chocolate, pies, and other desserts.

Dietary restraint also influences food choices. In the extreme example of eating disorders, cognitive factors may override caloric depletion and physiological need; thus, anorexic women show a strong aversion to foods rich in fat and report liking only those foods that they view as nutritious and low in calories, for example, salads, vegetables, and fresh fruit.

Clinical opportunities are available to link physiological, psychological, and sociocultural variables. Capturing these opportunities will increase our understanding of how taste preferences link metabolic variables to food preferences and individual experiences in the regulation of eating behaviors.

NEW OPPORTUNITIES: UNDERSTANDING DIET AND DISEASE RELATIONSHIPS

Cancer

There is intense interest in the relationship of diet to cancer. Although much remains to be learned about the influence of specific dietary constituents and dietary patterns on cancer risk, diet may rank second only to cigarette smoking in its impact on cancer morbidity and mortality. Many food components of interest are not nutrients as classically defined, and the nature of their direct effects or interactions are little understood. In addition, we have only a rudimentary understanding of the psychological and sociocultural factors that should be considered in designing and implementing interventions to bring about dietary changes that can reduce cancer risk in the population.

Research Opportunities

Identify the role of fat in the etiology of cancer   Much effort in recent years has been devoted to studying the effect of dietary fat on cancer risk. While epidemiological data in humans and much animal laboratory research indicate that dietary fat contributes to cancer risk, findings are sometimes equivocal even for those sites that have been studied most (i.e., colon, breast, and prostate). There could be numerous reasons for such inconsistencies, including errors in measuring dietary intake, biased recollection of diet history, lack of specificity or inappropriate classification of fats (e.g., saturated vs. unsaturated, monounsaturated vs. polyunsaturated, omega-3 vs. omega-6, *cis*- vs. *trans*-fatty acids, etc.), inability to separate the effect of dietary fat from that of calories, poor measures of net energy balance in epidemiological studies, failure to deal adequately with the interactive effects of dietary and nondietary factors (including genetic polymorphisms affecting susceptibility), and others. Each of these possibilities provides key opportunities for research on the relationship between fat and cancer.

Identify the role of constituents of fruits and vegetables in determining cancer risk   Evidence that certain foods can protect against cancer is mounting rapidly. Indeed, one of the most consistent observations in epidemiological studies is the inverse relationship between consumption of fruits and vegetables and the occurrence of cancer. However, while many different constituents of these foods (such as beta-carotene, other carotenoids, indoles, flavones, and isoflavonoids and other phytoestrogens) have cancer-inhibitory properties, the specific agents responsible for these effects, the possible interactions among them, and their mechanisms of action have yet to be elucidated.

Develop useful biomarkers for the study of diet and cancer at specific sites   Biomarkers with potential use in population research on nutrition and cancer are now being identified. These markers include constituents of peripheral blood and tissues that reflect levels of exposure to various exogenous factors. Examples of markers include the CYP1A1 gene, a member of the cytochrome P450 family, whose inducibility may reflect exposure to polycyclic aromatic hydrocarbons, and the formation of DNA or hemoglobin adducts of aromatic amines to which individuals are exposed. Few biomarkers have been adequately characterized for use in population studies. Some of the issues that must be addressed before a marker can be applied to the study of nutrition and cancer relationships are intra- and interindividual variation in marker levels, range of responses detectable, specificity of the marker for a given exposure, reliability of laboratory assay methods, and feasibility for application to large population samples.

Apply advances in molecular biology to the study of gene-environment interactions in the etiology of cancer   Early population-based research on cancer (including descriptive studies of cancer patterns in migrants, temporal trends in incidence, and wide variations in incidence among geographically separated but ethnically similar groups) established the dominant role of environmental factors in the etiology of this disease. With recent advances in molecular biology, including the polymerase chain reaction (PCR), restriction fragment length polymorphism (RFLP) techniques, and the identification of specific genes and their alleles (variant forms), population research is able increasingly to focus on susceptible subgroups and determine actual concentrations of carcinogens in tissue.

The consequences of exposure to environmental chemicals (including food constituents) are determined by the biochemical pathways in which they are metabolized. Many of the genes controlling the enzymes that metabolically activate procarcinogens or detoxify carcinogens are polymorphic, and the variant forms of their enzyme products may have different catalytic properties. Furthermore, these enzymes may be inducible, and their level of activity may reflect exposure to the carcinogen of interest as well as to other substrates on which they act (e.g., drugs and alcohol). Conversely, several different isozymes (e.g., in the cytochrome P450 family) act on the same chemical substrate. Thus, determining the net effect of a particular exposure in an individual can be quite complex, since it involves genetic susceptibility, internal metabolic processes, and careful assessment of environmental exposure (e.g., by questionnaire or biomarker measurements). The need for research on these topics in the study of nutrition and cancer is paramount and offers many opportunities. Such research provides an interface among genetics, epidemiology, molecular biology, and nutritional science.

Diabetes

Type II (non-insulin-dependent) diabetes is among the most common metabolic diseases in the United States, affecting about 4 percent of the population and up to 11 percent of people age 70 and over. Some 70 percent of these diabetic persons are obese; about half would no longer be diabetic if they lost weight. Thus, nutrition poses a major challenge to our understanding of the pathogenesis of Type II diabetes and the development of new approaches to management.

Research Opportunities

Improve our understanding of the pathophysiology linking obesity and Type II diabetes   There is considerable epidemiological data on the primary genetic basis of obesity and of Type II diabetes. Dyslipidemia, hypertension, and hyperuricemia often afflict obese persons with Type II diabetes. These conditions are often familial and are associated with premature atherosclerosis, myocardial infarction, stroke, and peripheral vascular disease.

We need to clarify the molecular biology of the candidate genes and of population genetics to better understand the biological base for the associations between obesity, diabetes, and the other conditions mentioned above. The critical genetic mutations that result in the aggregation of these conditions and disorders are yet to be identified. Once they are, we should be able to design therapies for controlling the direct results of the primary defects and associated pathologies.

Explore molecular mechanisms related to insulin resistance   The role and importance of insulin resistance and hyperinsulinemia in the pathophysiology of the conditions discussed above need to be pursued. Recently accumulated evidence suggests that changes in insulin receptor expression, insulin receptor kinase activity, glucose transport regulation, and links in intracellular signaling are related to the insulin resistance of obesity and Type II diabetes. In addition, research has shown that there is a defect somewhere beyond the glucose transport step, reducing the ability to make glycogen. Similarly, scientists have begun to explore molecular mechanisms that link micronutrients, including trace minerals such as chromium and magnesium, to insulin action and secretion and carbohydrate tolerance. Delineation of these molecular mechanisms will improve our understanding of the pathogenesis and pathophysiology of Type II diabetes.

Improve dietary management of Type II diabetes   Restricted intake of energy-yielding nutrients and weight reduction will substantially improve insulin resistance and result in lower insulin concentrations. However, there is still debate regarding the relative amounts of dietary protein, carbohydrate, and fats that are optimum in the diet, as well as the ideal quantity and proportion of polyunsaturated versus saturated fatty acids. Recent recommendations limit protein intake to approximately 15 percent of total calories and fats to 30 percent. However, some scientists favor less carbohydrate and somewhat more fat. The role of omega-3 and omega-6 fatty acids also is debated. Contested issues center around the relative impacts of glycemic control, lipid concentrations in the blood, and cardiovascular disease.

We need to study the effects of diet on the development of several disabling complications of diabetes. For example, there is suggestive evidence that restriction of protein intake may be important in the prevention and treatment of kidney failure in diabetes. The recently reported Diabetes Control and Complications Trial showed clearly that glycemic control has a major influence on the development of kidney, eye, and nerve disease in insulin-dependent (Type I) diabetes. It is likely that improved glycemic control would have similarly favorable effects in Type II diabetes. More information is needed on the influence of glycemic control in the development of atherosclerotic disease.

Progress has been made in controlling body weight in Type II diabetes through behavioral approaches, which often leads to improved glycemic control. Further research into better methods for weight loss and maintenance will pay large dividends.

Hypertension

An estimated 25 million adults in the United States have definite hypertension, and an additional 17 million have borderline hypertension. The widespread adverse effects of hypertension involve multiple organ systems and increase the risk of stroke, coronary heart disease, congestive heart failure, peripheral vascular disease, and nephrosclerosis. Nutritional therapy holds great promise for the prevention and treatment of these common medical disorders. For example, a study of 300 obese hypertensives revealed that weight loss among those receiving medication radically reduced the need for medication and returned the blood pressure of almost all to normal levels. This suggests that one highly effective dietary treatment is already available to control hypertension. While studies are needed to clarify the roles of the various nutrients and their potential interactions, among the most pressing research needs is exploration of the molecular mechanisms by which nutrition can be used to control blood pressure and the mechanisms underlying the remarkable benefits of weight reduction in controlling this disorder.

Research Opportunities

Identify individuals with salt or sodium sensitivity   While salt is not the sole dietary factor in the development and treatment of hypertension, sensitivity to sodium chloride remains an important issue for large numbers of people with the disorder. There is little doubt that a subset of individuals is salt-sensitive and therefore at risk of hypertension because of excessive sodium intakes. A key challenge in this area is how to detect these individuals.

Explore the roles and interactions of electrolytes other than sodium in the development of hypertension   A new area of interest in nutrition and hypertension is the interactions of mineral electrolytes, principally potassium, calcium, and magnesium. In each case, numerous studies in recent years have identified the benefits of adequate intakes of these nutrients. Substantial work is required to identify the thresholds of these minerals in the human diet below which the risk of hypertension accelerates. A body of evidence has emerged in the last several years indicating that these nutrients do not act individually, but in a concerted, interactive fashion; thus, optimal blood pressure is dependent on adequate exposure to two or more of these electrolytes. For example, potassium's ability to cause vasorelaxation is dependent on calcium. From the clinical arena, reports recently have noted that salt sensitivity is only evident in populations on low-calcium and low-potassium diets.

Research is needed to identify the mechanisms whereby these electrolytes interact. Given the critical role that electrolytes play in signal transduction, enzyme activation, and control of gene expression, we need basic investigations to identify the mechanisms whereby specific concentrations of electrolytes reduce overall cardiovascular risk. For example, calcium intake in experimental models of hypertension can be manipulated to produce the optimal amount of calmodulin, a ubiquitous calcium-binding protein. Given the essential role of this protein in all cells, further exploration of the mechanisms whereby ingestion of dietary calcium results in increased cell production of calmodulin will enhance our understanding of how it and possibly other electrolytes influence regulation of blood pressure.

We need to find out whether sodium sensitivity could be eliminated completely if people simply maintain an adequate intake of these other electrolytes, and, perhaps most important, we must determine whether the protective action of calcium, magnesium, and potassium is somehow sodium-dependent. Studies of both humans and animals suggest that the ability of calcium and potassium, and possibly magnesium, to lower blood pressure may require an intake of 150 milliequivalents (mEq) of sodium per day. Studies to define this carefully may be of immediate value.

Identify the role of lipids and carbohydrates in the development of hypertension   Other dietary components also influence blood pressure. While there is little doubt that omega-3 fatty acids improve regulation of blood pressure, monounsaturated fatty acids, as well as saturated fatty acids, need to be investigated. The contribution of phenylated proteins, the metabolic offspring of the cholesterol pathway, also merits exploration. The influence of dietary fats on G proteins is postulated to be critical to the regulation of function of vascular smooth muscle.

The 80 percent concordance of essential hypertension and carbohydrate intolerance has been confirmed repeatedly. While much of the focus has been on insulin's potential for affecting regulation of blood pressure (primarily through sodium reabsorption in the kidneys), more recent investigations suggest that insulin may link abnormal carbohydrate metabolism and blood pressure directly. Careful examination of the impact of glucose itself and of general cellular metabolism is needed to delineate the role of carbohydrates in the control of blood pressure. In addition, the effects of various types of carbohydrates and their respective influences on tone of vascular smooth muscle and sympathetic muscle require further exploration.

Cardiovascular Disease and Arteriosclerosis

Strong correlations among the amounts and types of fat consumed by various populations and their rates of coronary heart disease (CHD) have directed attention to diet as a potentially important cause. Research has implicated numerous constituents of diet—such as saturated, monounsaturated, and polyunsaturated fatty acids; *trans*-unsaturated fatty acids; antioxidants; and various minerals and water-soluble vitamins. This research underscores the role of nutrition and the challenges to the field. Further, populations migrating from areas with a low incidence of CHD to high-incidence regions also experience substantial increases in CHD, emphasizing the importance of lifestyle over genetic factors in explaining many geographical differences.

Research Opportunities

Improve our understanding of the biological mechanisms linking CHD to the consumption of dietary fats   The intake of saturated fatty acids (saturated fat) has received the greatest attention as a potential cause of CHD because of its particularly strong geographical correlation with incidence rates. Although the ecological correlations are notably susceptible to confounding by other dietary and nondietary lifestyle factors, major support for the saturated-fat hypothesis derives from metabolic feeding studies indicating that saturated fats increase total and low-density lipoprotein (LDL) cholesterol, combined with firm epidemiological data relating these serum lipids to the risk of CHD. Nevertheless, the relation of saturated-fat intake to CHD risk appears more complex than previously thought. There are several reasons for this. For example, the chain lengths of saturated fatty acids influence their response to lipids in the blood. Some saturated fatty acids do not appear deleterious, indicating the need to reevaluate individual fatty acids in relation to specific lipid fractions. Since coronary thrombosis is a common precipitating event in the development of CHD, the adverse effect of any dietary factor on development of CHD need not be limited to its effect on serum cholesterol concentrations. Indeed, some investigators have suggested that saturated fats may promote coronary thrombosis. Unfortunately, remarkably few studies have evaluated this important question, and several of them have serious methodological limitations. Furthermore, randomized trials of dietary interventions for the prevention of CHD have often been complicated by simultaneous modification of multiple factors and have not provided any clear evidence of reducing saturated fat. Accumulated evidence of several types suggests that saturated fat intake plays a more complex role in the etiology of CHD than has often been assumed. Analogous issues relate to the study of the mechanisms linking CHD to the consumption of other fats, such as the n-3 fatty acids.

Define the role of linoleic acid in CHD prevention   A small quantity of linoleic acid (about 2 g per day) is required for human health. In one prospective study conducted in the 1950s to 1960s, when the average intake by the U.S. population was far lower than today, an inverse relation between linoleic acid intake and risk of CHD was observed. Similar results have been reported recently. When linoleic acid is substituted for saturated fatty acids in the diet, concentrations of cholesterol in the blood fall. The significance of its effect on specific lipid components is less clear. For example, linoleic acid can lower concentrations of high-density lipoproteins (HDL) as well as LDL. The previously stated goal of increasing polyunsaturated fat to 10 percent of total calories in the U.S. diet is being reconsidered, in part because of theoretical concerns regarding the long-term effects of such a diet on other health risks (e.g., possible increased risk for cancer and suppression of the immune system).

Explore the role of monounsaturated fatty acids in lipoprotein regulation   Monounsaturated fats have been considered neutral; they were thought neither to raise nor to lower serum cholesterol. In more recent studies, substituting monounsaturated for saturated fat decreased LDL cholesterol without decreasing HDL cholesterol, whereas substituting carbohydrates for saturated fats decreased both LDL and HDL. Furthermore, LDL particles rich in monounsaturated fatty acids appear to be more resistant to oxidation, which may make them less atherogenic, at least compared to LDL enriched in polyunsaturated fatty acids. These recent metabolic findings are consistent with the geographical association between high intakes of monounsaturated fat in the southern Mediterranean countries and low rates of CHD.

Assess the role of processed fats (e.g., trans-unsaturated fatty acids) in CHD   *Trans*-unsaturated fatty acids are formed by the partial hydrogenation of polyunsaturated liquid vegetable oils during the production of margarine and vegetable shortening. These products have the advantage of being devoid of dietary cholesterol and being generally low in cholesterol-raising saturated fatty acids. Although no consistent effect of *trans* isomers on total serum cholesterol was observed in several earlier studies, in more recent feeding studies, *trans* isomers of unsaturated fatty acids increased LDL and reduced HDL. These findings have caused concern about the ingestion of *trans* isomers, which today contribute about 3 percent of total calories to the U.S. diet.

Explore the role of micronutrients in CHD   In addition to the long-standing hypotheses relating type and amount of dietary fats to CHD, newer hypotheses have emerged in recent years. These do not necessarily conflict with, and may ultimately complement, relationships with dietary fats.

Several dietary antioxidants, particularly vitamins E, C, and beta-carotene, may reduce the oxidation of LDL particles and thereby interfere with the development of atherosclerosis. At present, epidemiological data are largely ecological in nature, but they support the hypothesis that high intakes of antioxidants may reduce the risk of CHD. This possibility represents one of the more exciting developments in nutritional research.

Rapidly accruing data also indicate that high concentrations of homocysteine in the blood are a risk factor for CHD (see box). An excess of this amino acid in plasma may directly damage the arterial wall which can promote atherogenesis. Supplementation with folic acid or vitamin B_6, or both, often reduces elevated homocysteine substantially. Whether such supplementation can reduce the risk of CHD remains unclear.

Understand the metabolic interrelationship between obesity and conditions related to increased CHD   The relationship between obesity and CHD is poorly understood. Obesity has several metabolic consequences that increase the risk of CHD, including dyslipidemia [higher very-low-density lipoproteins (VLDL), higher LDL, and lower HDL concentrations], hypertension, and insulin resistance. The more severe the obesity, the more severe the metabolic consequences. Whether obesity enhances the risk of CHD through other mechanisms (e.g., hyperinsulinemia or thrombogenesis) remains to be elucidated, but some authorities speculate that it does. Certainly, additional investigation of the impact of obesity on development of CHD is needed, together with research on the mechanisms of this relationship.

At least as important as the severity of obesity is the distribution of body fat. Even a modest increase in visceral fat increases all risk factors for CHD. In addition to the overall risk conferred by visceral fat in CHD, it has been implicated in several pathological conditions, such as familial combined hyperlipidemia. These abnormalities, and others related to obesity, seem to accelerate the development of atherosclerosis, dyslipidemia [characterized by small VLDL particles, increased intermediate-density lipoproteins (IDL), small-dense LDL, increased total apolipoprotein B, decreased HDL_2, and decreased apolipoprotein A-1], hypertension, and hyperuricemia. This aggregate of metabolic abnormalities appears with and without familial predispositions and is frequently associated with premature CHD, peripheral vascular disease, and stroke. Although visceral obesity alone appears to predispose people to these abnormalities, the particular pattern of abnormality that develops (e.g., dyslipidemia or hy-

HOMOCYSTEINE AND VASCULAR DISEASE

Abnormal homocysteine metabolism was first described in 1962 in two siblings with mental retardation who excreted large quantities of homocystine in their urine. Several years later, homocystinuria caused by an inherited defect in hepatic cystathionine beta-synthase was reported. Later, homocystinuria and vascular disease were also associated in patients with inherited defects in either hepatic cystathionine beta-synthase or methylenetetrahydrofolate reductase. When the pathology of these patients was reviewed, a causal association was proposed between arteriosclerosis and homocysteine elevation in blood. A possible relationship with nutritional cofactors folate, vitamin B_{12}, and vitamin B_6 was implicit in these original observations, and a number of early papers demonstrated some amelioration of activity of genetically defective pathways with large doses of these vitamins.

Recently, there has been increased interest in the relationship of moderate homocysteinemia to vitamin status and its association with cardiovascular disease. The serum protein-bound homocysteine concentration was related inversely to serum folate. This suggested that prolonged folate depletion, even at low normal levels, might lead to moderate or persistent homocysteinemia and hence to vascular disease. Homocysteinemia has been induced nutritionally in animals made deficient in either folate or vitamin B_6. High doses of folate or pyridoxine have been used in humans to lower concentrations of homocysteine in the blood. In addition, elevated homocysteine concentrations have been corrected with vitamin B_{12} therapy when those elevations were related to deficient or borderline concentrations of vitamin B_{12}. Thus, a clear theoretical basis for B_{12} regulation of homocysteine in the blood has emerged.

Plasma homocysteine concentrations were measured in surviving elderly members of the Framingham Study cohort, along with concentrations and dietary intakes of vitamins B_{12}, B_6, and folate. Homocysteine concentrations increased with age and lower B-vitamin status. The age association remained strong even after adjustment for B-vitamin concentrations. This increase in homocysteine with age, independent of B-vitamin status, may result from an age-related decline in cystathionine beta-synthase and possibly other enzymes involved in homocysteine metabolism.

We cannot yet conclude that lowering chronically elevated plasma homocysteine or increasing vitamin intake will cause regression of vascular disease. However, a strong case can be made for preventing the marginal or manifest vitamin deficiency states that may contribute substantially to this potentially important risk factor for cardiovascular disease, the largest cause of mortality among the elderly. Efforts to address the best means by which to prevent deficiencies of folate, vitamin B_{12}, and vitamin B_6 in the increasing number of our population over age 65 now have added impetus.

pertension) may be genetically determined. Modern molecular biological techniques may be especially useful for elucidating the genetic basis of these metabolic abnormalities.

Obesity

Obesity is one of the most important nutritional problems in this country, affecting over 25 percent of the population. In addition to being a direct risk to health, it increases the risk of chronic diseases such as coronary heart disease, Type II diabetes, hypertension, and several cancers. A major advance in our understanding of human obesity has been the recent demonstration of the importance of genetic factors in its etiology. Obesity is a disease whose origins lie in the interaction between genetic predisposition and environmental variables, chief among which are food intake and physical activity. It arises from periods of imbalance between energy intake and energy expenditure. However, we do not understand the causes of these imbalances or, indeed, how energy balance is regulated. Meeting challenges in each of these areas is crucial to unraveling the etiologies of this condition.

Research Opportunities

Enhance our understanding of the sociodemographic determinants of obesity   Obesity is increasingly prevalent in the United States and is more common here than in other industrially developed countries. It is particularly common in some subgroups, such as black women, in whom the prevalence (50 percent) is twice that in white women, and it is strongly inversely related to socioeconomic status in women of all races. What dietary behaviors predispose individuals to obesity? Does it reflect an increased reliance on fast foods or convenience foods, lack of opportunity or requirement for physical work, or all of these? How can obesity be prevented or treated? Obesity in children and teens can have a devastating effect on their self-esteem. What is the role of food behaviors (e.g., snacking) and limited physical activity in the etiology of obesity among children and teens? How can obesity be treated in this group without increasing the risk of eating disorders? These and related questions remain central to this area of investigation.

Improve our understanding of the control of food intake   Research is needed to clarify the controls on neurotransmitters and receptor systems in the central and peripheral nervous systems. Over the past two decades, considerable progress has been made in research on the roles of several peptides involved in the regulation of food intake—cholecystokinin and bombesin-like peptides, glucagon, neuropeptide Y, galanin, endorphins, calcitonin, and neurotensin. However, we have yet to establish the physiological relevance of these signals, their mechanisms of action, and their clinical utilities, especially the interactions, if any, among these systems and macronutrient intake to produce satiety. Much remains to be learned about their physiological interrelationships and how they can be affected pharmacologically. Further research in this area will be facilitated greatly by the genetic strains of animals predisposed to obesity now available and the development of others with anomalies in target receptor systems. Research is expected to yield pharmacological and dietary strategies for the prevention and treatment of obesity.

Develop a better understanding of metabolic strategies for short- and long-term control of food intake   It is likely that homeostatic controls on food intake can be disrupted when the caloric concentrations, sensory qualities, or both of the diet are enhanced. The result may be obesity among genetically vulnerable individuals. Determining the genetic and physiological basis of this vulnerability will improve our understanding of obesity and increase our understanding of the short- and long-term homeostatic controls of food intake.

Identify the metabolic role of energy reserves in the regulation of body composition and weight   A critical area for future research in obesity is regulation of body weight. Food intake in some individuals appears to vary widely over the short term, while body weight remains within narrow limits. What are the mechanisms that maintain body weight within relatively narrow limits despite seemingly wide fluctuations in food intake? In such cases, what signals occur and how are they processed? Whether energy reserves produce signals that might regulate intake is unknown. Also, there have been suggestions that circulating concentrations of carbohydrate, fat, and amino acids, as well as energy production, determine hunger and satiety. There is experimental evidence in favor of each of these possibilities, but we still do not understand fully why eating is initiated and terminated or how it is controlled over long periods of time.

Apply molecular genetics to decipher the roles of genetics and the environment in the development of human obesities   The tools of molecular genetics can greatly advance our understanding of obesity. Indeed, studies of obese animals provide the best evidence of interaction between genetic and dietary factors in the expression of obesity. Animal models of obesity show that the disorder can be caused by a single defective gene or by more than one defective gene. Twin and adoption studies show that genetic factors contribute significantly to the etiology of human obesity and suggest that a major gene may be responsible. The characterization of the human genome will help us identify genetic contributions to human obesity, particularly as phenotypic expressions of obesity are better understood.

The ob/ob mouse and the Zucker rat gain excess weight through overeating of any diet, whereas other animals' obesities are promoted by high-fat diets, sucrose solutions, or the so-called cafeteria diet. Diets containing high proportions of fat are more efficient in promoting obesity than are low-fat or fat-free regimens. While a portion of excess carbohydrate calories is lost as heat, fat calories tend to be deposited more efficiently as body fat. Elucidating the genetic endowments that predispose people to obesity and the metabolic mechanisms underlying the distinct characteristics of obesities of apparently diverse etiologies will represent a major advance in obesity research.

Explore the role of defects in energy expenditure in human obesities   Recent studies have suggested that decreased energy expenditure for a given lean body mass may contribute to the development of obesity in some individuals. Thus, pre-obese individuals may be metabolically more efficient. As a result, more energy is available for storage. These studies show, however, that the calories saved by the increased efficiency are inadequate to account for the weight gain and that increased energy intake probably plays the more important role. Thus, decreased energy expenditure may serve more as a marker of overeating than as the only cause of weight gain. This controversy provides significant challenges to understanding energy regulation.

Longitudinal studies of infants, children, and adults are needed to determine the relative contribution of different risk factors to the development of adiposity and obesity. Studies of persons at genetically determined high risk of obesity are particularly necessary; we need to learn the relative contribution of total energy expenditure, resting metabolic rate, and food intake on body composition during growth and development.

Learn more about the basic biology of adipose tissue   Regulation of lipolysis and lipogenesis is an important area of investigation. While a great deal is known about these processes, little information is available about interindividual differences and how they can affect the induction or maintenance of obesity. We need to know more about differences among obese and nonobese persons in lipoprotein lipase, hormone receptor number and regulation, glucose transporters, second messengers within the cell, and relevant enzymatic activation and inhibition, all of which may be important in the development of the condition. Our knowledge of differences in adipose cells (e.g., those associated with distinct anatomical locations such as visceral and subcutaneous abdominal sites) that may contribute to obesity is inadequate. The process by which a pre-adipocyte becomes an adipocyte and the stimulatory factors that promote this process at various sites in the body and at various ages needs to be explored in much more depth.

Develop improved treatments for obesity At the present time, over $30 billion is spent each year on programs and products designed to control body weight, and the market is growing. Yet the prevalence of overweight has increased over the past two decades. The treatment of obesity has improved during the past decade, and it is now possible to safely achieve weight losses of 20 kg (44 lbs) with some consistency. The major problem remaining in the treatment of obesity is maintenance of the weight loss. The major research priority in this area is the development of methods for long-term maintenance of weight control.

Diarrhea

While not a significant problem in the United States, diarrhea remains the most frequent cause of death of young children in the world. In addition to those who die, many more children suffer significantly impaired health, nutritional status, and development. The increased frequency of evacuation and the high fluid content of the feces that characterize diarrhea are usually caused by pathogens, including parasites, viruses, and bacteria, but they may also result from food intolerance or a variety of other functional, metabolic, or anatomical abnormalities.

Research Opportunities

Enhance our understanding of how specific nutrients modulate individual responses to diarrheas of specific etiology From a nutritional standpoint, the prevention and optimal management of diarrheal illness present important challenges. Information is needed regarding the mechanisms that determine nutrient absorption and utilization in diseases caused by specific pathogens. The precise role of micronutrients in immune function or epithelial cell replication is particularly important. Zinc, for example, appears to affect a number of immunological responses. Without adequate zinc, the ability of T cells to release autocrine-stimulating growth factors, such as IL-2, is impaired. Zinc deficiency may adversely affect the normal replacement of epithelial cells in the intestinal tract. Selenium affects the release of humoral immunoglobulins (particularly subclasses of IgG) and influences the production and release of IL-1, an important initial step in the immune response. The role of fat-soluble vitamins also merits increased scrutiny. Vitamins A and E appear to influence the release of interleukins from lymphocytes under mitogenic stimulation and to modulate the leukotriene prostaglandin system.

An example of more direct significance to industrially developed countries is the composition of infant formulas. Often, nucleotides are not provided to infants fed synthetic formulas, but recent information suggests that they may have important stimulatory effects on immune function, both systemic and gastrointestinal. Other nutrients known to be essential to epithelial function of the gastrointestinal tract, such as glutamine, also have a profound effect on the secretory IgA system.

Determine the mechanisms by which breastfeeding protects infants from diarrhea   At the interface of biological and behavioral research is the impact of breastfeeding on diarrheal disease. Breastfed infants are exposed to fewer foodborne pathogens. In addition, breastfeeding protects infants in other ways, although the mechanisms that underlie these modes of protection are not well understood. For example, the role of immunological agents in human milk has been the subject of numerous investigations, yet controversy remains as to which is more important: the passive transmission of protection to the infant gut's lumen or the transmission of factors that may induce the infant's own immune system to respond more effectively to infectious challenges. Similarly, there is little consensus regarding the role of growth factors in milk in promoting the maturation of the infant's gastrointestinal epithelium (thereby augmenting mucosal barriers against the penetration of the gastrointestinal tract by antigens) versus promoting the renewal of injured intestinal mucosa.

Develop new strategies for preventing and managing diarrhea that incorporate key behavioral variables   The association between nutritional status and diarrhea is strongly influenced by cultural, social, and economic factors that affect feeding practices. The following algorithm illustrates the kinds of behavioral issues that require attention.

- Are foods that are appropriate for the young child available in the community?
- Are they available in the household?
- Are foods stored and prepared in ways that maximize nutritive content?
- Does the child receive the appropriate foods?
- Does the child eat the foods if they are offered?

To develop interventions that will reduce the sickness and death caused by diarrhea and other infectious diseases, we must understand the factors involved in the five questions above. For example, anorexia often accompanies diarrheal illness, but because the basis for it is poorly understood, the role of caregiver behavior in managing the problem cannot yet be specified. Similarly, interventions to improve the energy and nutrient density of foods given to young children may require reallocation of household resources and maternal time and changes in beliefs about what constitutes appropriate foods and feeding practices for children. Furthermore, to deal effectively with these problems, it also is necessary to develop food-processing technologies appropriate to specific settings and to provide foods with acceptable storage stability, adequate energy and nutrient density, and appropriate preparation time and fuel-use requirements for cooking and hygiene purposes.

CONCLUDING REMARKS

In this chapter, our examples of opportunities and challenges have focused on the nutritional well-being of individuals. We chose examples in two categories: research targeting ways to maximize functions important to well-being and optimal development (in the areas of reproduction, growth and development, body composition, immune function, central nervous system function, and food-related behavior) and research that focuses on disorders and diseases influenced by diet (cancer, diabetes, hypertension, cardiovascular disease and arteriosclerosis, vision-related disorders of aging, obesity, and diarrhea in infancy and early childhood). These examples suggest important strategies for improving our understanding of food behavior, diet, health, and disease relationships. The challenges and opportunities demonstrate the value of multidisciplinary research for the future application of new knowledge in the basic sciences. They stress the knowledge base and skills needed to assess the relevance of new information to the individual and to make use of it efficaciously. In addition, the challenges and opportunities illustrate the seamless continuity of the importance of diet to health promotion and disease prevention throughout the life cycle. This characteristic is of special relevance because of the marked changes in the age structure of populations throughout the world. While we know how to avoid frank nutrient deficiencies, we cannot achieve maximal function or avoid diet-related diseases effectively without a closer and more sophisticated attention to diet.

6

Improving the Diet and Health of Individuals and Populations

Until quite recently, eliminating nutritional deficiencies was the major focus of community or population nutrition programs. From a public health perspective, dealing with these conditions was relatively straightforward, through governmental requirements for food fortification and the use of vitamin and mineral supplements in high-risk persons.

Over the past several decades, a new era of nutritional science has unfolded. Researchers have begun to detect important relationships between diet and the development of major chronic diseases, such as coronary heart disease, diabetes, hypertension, and cancer. In many instances, the diet-disease relationships reflect nutrient excesses rather than deficiencies. However, dealing with these diet-disease relationships from a public health perspective is not straightforward. Manipulating the food supply and using supplements alone cannot ensure adequate or "optimal" nutriture to prevent these diseases, which constitute the major causes of mortality in the United States. Individual responsibility for appropriate food selection must be an essential aspect of nutrition intervention programs. Yet food choices depend on many factors, including nutrition knowledge, motivation, economics, food availability, and others. Furthermore, as outlined in earlier chapters, our increased scientific sophistication is making it possible to stratify the population based on genetically determined susceptibility factors, so interventions may not have to be applied equally to everyone. Exciting opportunities for research in public health nutrition related to diet and disease interactions are numerous and hold vast potential for improving the health of the nation.

While a portion of the U.S. population suffers from diseases often related to excess consumption of certain food components, others go hungry. The extent of hunger and food insecurity in this country is unknown, but awareness of the problem is growing as it receives more public and scientific attention. Understanding the causes and consequences of food insecurity and hunger and developing effective interventions are major challenges facing public health nutritionists. Since an uneven distribution of the food supply is thought to be the underlying cause of this problem, federal food assistance programs have been implemented over the past 20 years to improve access to food for the most vulnerable groups, such as infants, pregnant and lactating women, the poor, and the aged. While effective, a contemporary evaluation is needed of the impact of these programs in the context of today's social and economic problems.

Better measuring tools are required to monitor the impact of intervention programs, whether they provide food and services or promote behavior change through education, price incentives, convenience, or modification of the food supply. Ideally, nutrition assessment tools and methods should be simple, accurate, inexpensive, specific, and sensitive to small changes. Our knowledge of food composition needs to be enhanced, and databases must include nonnutritive components of food that influence health (e.g., fiber). New biological markers of nutrient intakes will be especially useful to validate dietary assessment methods.

Evaluating programs includes studying their operations, logistics, organizational behavior, and personnel motivation. Evaluating participation in intervention programs and their systems of food delivery requires studying the various determinants of household and individual behavior. Evaluating strategies for promoting behavior change requires an assessment of the determinants of, and constraints on, the behaviors of interest. Investigators need a wide range of skills and knowledge to perform these assessments, yet all fall outside the traditional field of nutritional science. What is required is a new kind of nutrition professional who combines these areas of training. Current attempts by nutritional professionals to increase the prevalence of breastfeeding in the United States have been relatively unsuccessful in the past decade. This may be due in part to the fact that the need or desire for women to work outside the home has not been considered and incorporated into breastfeeding promotion efforts. Nutrition professionals must be able to integrate nutrition science with the beliefs and values of society in order to motivate behavior change.

Chapter 2 highlights some of recent accomplishments in the nutrition and food sciences and identifies research needed to implement effectively new laboratory findings in these disciplines. Iron nutriture is a particularly challenging issue discussed in that chapter. Iron deficiency is of special concern because it may affect the physical and mental development of infants and young children. However, as many as 10 percent of the U.S. population is at risk for hemochromatosis and iron overload. Intervention approaches need to be developed and tested that ensure that iron-fortified foods reach the population at risk of iron deficiency without putting those with hemochromatosis, or those prone to the disorder, at risk.

Recently, epidemiological studies have shown that some neural tube defects (NTDs) can be prevented by folic acid when taken prior to and during the first trimester of pregnancy (see Chapter 2). Fortification of foods with folic acid is a potential intervention, therefore, to reduce the risk of NTDs. However, this kind of intervention presents difficult public policy issues because it would lead to most people consuming more folic acid than they do now. This could pose risks to some, especially those with underlying vitamin B_{12} deficiency. Alternatively, all fertile women may be advised to take a folic supplement or to increase their intake of folate-rich foods. The choice is one of altering the food supply or altering the nutrition messages for women of childbearing age and motivating them to change their food habits. The costs and benefits of each approach needs to be investigated, not only for this particular issue, but for many other public policy issues in nutrition as well.

Information provided in Chapter 4 shows that food science and technology has made enormous strides in providing high-quality, safe, and wholesome food that has been modified to help consumers more easily meet dietary recommendations. For example, the number of low-fat food items available in supermarkets and restaurants has increased substantially in recent years. However, only a minority of individuals in this country meet dietary recommendations. This is because modification of the food supply is only part of the process. In addition, consumers need the knowledge to make healthy food choices in supermarkets and restaurants, the motivation to make changes in food selection practices, and the availability of health-promoting foods to maintain the changes over the long term. Actions based on a comprehensive understanding of the interaction between economic and health policies, societal values, and individual and household behaviors and food attitudes must be combined with efforts of the food industry to alter the food supply. Research bridging the gap between the biological science of nutrition and the behavioral and social sciences is required to accomplish the complicated task of influencing long-term choices in food habits.

The special concerns of the most vulnerable groups in the population (infants, pregnant and lactating women, the poor, and the aged) are outlined in Chapter 5. Nutritionists charged with the responsibility for improving the dietary and health of groups in the future need to do more than simply provide information. Instead, the information needs to be presented in a manner that makes it relevant to the recipient, which includes integrating the messages into the cultural and social values of the group. In other words, the messages need to be tailored to the values of specific communities and population groups. For example, the increasing prevalence of obesity among the poor reflects, at least in part, the absence of effective communication between nutrition professionals and the disadvantaged. The development of models or approaches for modifying nutrition messages that better fit a community or specific minority group is an important research challenge for the future.

A new kind of nutrition investigator is needed who researches issues at the interface between the nutrition and populations and the behavioral and social sciences. This chapter identifies selected research opportunities for this new breed of nutrition scientist in three general areas—reducing the risk of diet-related disease, reducing the risk of food insecurity and hunger, and improving the methods and tools for nutritional assessment, monitoring, and evaluation. Several interesting and exciting needs and opportunities for research are identified for each area. Our examples are meant to be illustrative, not comprehensive.

REDUCING THE RISK OF DIET-RELATED DISEASE

Research during the past several decades has identified several important relationships between diet and chronic disease, such as coronary heart disease, diabetes, hypertension, and cancer. Few of these relationships have been established with absolute certainty, and they are constantly being refined. Nevertheless, a large literature on diet and chronic disease now exists and provides a basis for interim dietary recommendations to the public. Three influential reports have helped establish a consensus on dietary patterns to promote health and reduce the risk of chronic disease—the 1988 *Surgeon General's Report on Nutrition and Health*, the 1989 National Research Council report *Diet and Health: Implications for Reducing Chronic Disease Risk*, and the 1990 *Dietary Guidelines for Americans* by the U.S. Departments of Agriculture (USDA) and Health and Human Services. Their recommendations include maintaining appropriate weight, reducing consumption of fats and cholesterol, and eating a variety of foods, notably more grain products, fruits, and vegetables. While there is broad agreement as to what constitutes a healthful diet, motivating people to adopt healthful lifestyles remains a formidable challenge for nutrition professionals.

Three strategies to meet this challenge were proposed by the Food and Nutrition Board in its 1991 report *Improving America's Diet and*

Health: From Recommendations to Action. This report identifies the government, the food industry, health-care professionals, and educators as key groups to implement dietary recommendations. It calls for (1) government and health-care professionals to become more active as policymakers, role models, and agenda setters, (2) improving the public's knowledge of nutrition and increasing their opportunities to practice good nutrition, and (3) increasing the availability of health-promoting foods.

We discuss below the research opportunities for motivating individuals to meet dietary recommendations. We consider two general factors that influence food habits—sociocultural and behavioral.

Sociocultural Factors in Diet Selection

While genetic and physiological determinants shape individual food preferences and aversions, the translation of these into behavior—diet selection—is mediated by sociocultural factors. Research on diet selection has traditionally focused on identifying factors that result in similarities in food consumption patterns among people in groups. More recent work has (1) broadened the array of variables used to differentiate people into food-consuming groups, (2) begun to focus on sources of variation in behavior within groups, and (3) sought to identify factors in the larger society that regulate continuity and change in food behavior, both in the lifetimes of individuals and through time in groups.

Research Opportunities

Define intergroup variables that determine variation in food consumption Foodways have long been recognized as powerful metaphors of group identity. Consumption of, and preference for, a particular cuisine have been used to attribute group membership to individuals. In the United States, it has been assumed consistently that ethnic groups, regional populations, and rural or urban distinctions were the primary lines along which eating could be differentiated. Anthropological work during World War II reinforced this assumption by using such groups as units of analysis. Classic studies in this country documented the conservative nature of foodways even as groups migrated.

The assumption that ethnic and regional foodways are strictly conservative is now being challenged. Recent research shows that food consumption patterns are dynamic, responsive, and continually shaped and reinforced by social interaction. The extent to which foodways remain unchanged is determined by the pattern of activities of group members. Outmigration, intermarriage, and occupational and educational mobility are all factors that change social interaction and thus tend to be followed by change in foodways. Investigations are needed to establish the circumstances under which foodways are likely to be most dynamic and how the direction of change can be predicted and modified.

The variables now seen as critical in differentiating Americans into food-consuming groups are more structural than cultural. For example, gender-based differences in control of household resources and control of decisions about food consumption have been implicated in the food habits and nutritional status of women and children. At the same time, research shows that there are gender-specific ideologies for classifying foods. Such ideologies form part of the cognitive framework within which food consumption choices are made.

Age is another factor instrumental in determining food consumption patterns. Certain foods are consumed more frequently by older people than the rest of the population, and the patterns of consumption (e.g., meals vs. snacks and timing of eating) vary with age. Research is needed to disentangle biological effects of aging (such as sensory and digestive changes) from social effects (such as changes in household composition) and from cohort, or age-group, effects. The latter are particularly important in understanding food behavior because the food experiences of cohorts differ dramatically and shape current preferences. Other significant cohort similarities, such as the availability of particular foods or food technology, may affect food habits.

Research on nutrition that takes social class differences in the United States as its point of departure finds that certain food habits may be better explained by a combination of class attributes such as income, education, and occupation than by the more traditional ethnic distinctions. For example, trends in breastfeeding incidence and duration during the last several decades follow income and education lines, with better-educated women and those with higher incomes leading the trend toward bottle-feeding in the 1950s and 1960s, then back to breastfeeding in the 1970s and 1980s. In all areas of public health nutrition, research is needed to determine when social class influences food consumption through attitudes toward and beliefs about food and when it acts as a constraint through low income and education on the ability to obtain adequate food and nutrients.

Determine factors that modify intragroup or individual variation in food consumption   A recent refocusing of attention in the social sciences toward small-group and individual analyses promises to be especially important for understanding food consumption and developing interventions to modify food habits. Through both qualitative and quantitative studies, researchers have established ways of detecting sources of intraindividual as well as intracultural variation. This change in focus is reflected in the movement from seeking meaning and explanation of food consumption and nutrition at group levels to an emphasis on the household as the arena in which food consumption takes place. Similar households develop distinctive strategies of acquiring and distributing food to household members. These patterns may reflect preferences by age or gender of household members, stages of the family developmental cycle, or more subtle and idiosyncratic behavioral patterns. The impact of intrahousehold differences in food consumption should be a focus for both domestic and international research on child health and survival.

Research on cyclic patterns of food consumption reflects attempts to understand sources of intragroup variation. Particularly for agricultural populations, seasonal cycles of labor and food availability are critical determinants of food consumption. Even within industrialized populations, cycles of food consumption have been found, reflecting patterns of work, leisure, ritual, and life-cycle events.

There is clear evidence that food consumption by individuals or groups cannot be viewed in isolation. Sociocultural factors such as age, gender, and income play a part in determining food choice. But food consumption must also be viewed as part of a larger system within which individuals make choices. This system sets several parameters for food choice: economic (e.g., how much income is available for food purchases?), environmental (e.g., what foods are readily available?), and ideological (e.g., what foods are considered appropriate and good to eat?). Research is needed that considers all of these parameters as viable explanations for food consumption patterns. A better understanding of the sources of intragroup variation in food consumption could be obtained through multiple-method research designs that integrate qualitative and quantitative techniques.

Behavioral Strategies for Lifestyle Change

While improving the public's diet and health is the major goal of public health nutrition, motivating and assisting people to translate dietary guidelines into permanent dietary change remains a formidable challenge to health professionals. Recent dietary recommendations emphasize the need for individuals to reduce fat consumption to 30 percent or less of total daily calories. Attempts to achieve this goal have been only partly successful. The observed decline in consumption of some overt sources of fat (e.g., red meat and whole milk), especially among women, has been offset by increased intake of fats and oils, other dairy products, and frozen desserts. Total fat consumption has not declined substantially, and experts fear that consumers have simply learned to replace one fat source with another (which may or may not be advantageous to health).

Implementing dietary recommendations on a population-wide basis provides exciting new areas for collaboration between nutrition specialists and behavioral scientists. Diet, of course, is only one factor influencing health and well-being. Other personal health behaviors (e.g., not smoking and getting exercise) and the appropriate use of health-care services are also linked to disease risks and should not be overlooked in health promotion efforts.

Research Opportunities

Identify the barriers to changing food habits Implementing dietary guidelines across the United States requires that many sectors of the population modify their eating habits toward a more healthy diet. However, most people find that reducing the consumption of foods rich in total fat and saturated fat and increasing consumption of vegetables, fruits, grains, and legumes is no easy task. There are many barriers to healthy behavior change that range from lack of motivation and not perceiving immediate improvements in health to long-standing food preferences and socially influenced dietary patterns. The traditional strategy for dietary change has been nutrition education. However, improving knowledge is not sufficient. Consumer attitudes, beliefs, and motivations must be changed as well.

Strategies for health behavior change have been based on a variety of theoretical constructs and models. These include the health belief model, which explains health-related behavior largely in terms of individual attitudes and beliefs. The theory of reasoned action addresses the attitudes to a given behavior and evaluations of probable behavior outcome. The intention to act is determined by a respondent's attitudes toward the action and their perception of likely outcome relative to some subjective norm. The social learning theory predicts consumer behavior by employing such key constructs as incentives, outcome expectations, and self efficacy. A more recent cognitive-behavioral model of relapse prevention addresses such concepts as self esteem and loss of control. Additional theoretical frameworks include the stages of change model, the diffusion theory, and the social support model, to name a few.

For the most part, these models and strategies address behavioral change at the behavioral level. The health belief model was initially applied to compliance with prescribed medical regimens and the use of medical care and other health services. The stages of change model was developed originally to study behaviors associated with smoking cessation by individuals. Other models have been variously applied to smoking cessation, addictive behaviors, seat-belt use, adherence to exercise programs, and weight loss.

There have been many fewer studies on the applications of the existing strategies for behavioral change to dietary interventions, either in individuals or in communities. Several studies have applied the theory of reasoned action to predict the consumption of high-fat foods. They reported individual beliefs and outcome evaluations linked to the consumption of milk, cheese, ice cream, and other high-fat foods. Other studies have attempted to use attitudes to dietary fats as a potential predictor of fat consumption.

Very few studies have addressed the application of the strategies for behavioral change to the dietary behavior of populations. One critical question is whether the stages of change model can be generalized to dietary behavior change in communities. Given the complexity of food habits, it is unclear how the progress from one stage to the next is to be defined, monitored, and evaluated. Another critical question concerns motivation and the recruitment of populations at risk from the precontemplation stage to contemplation and to action.

Food habits at the community level are influenced by social nutrition. Studies on dietary change need to examine those cultural and environmental factors that promote or prevent the initial dietary change and its maintenance. Some interventions have been based on societal or system changes, addressing the role of grocery stores, restaurants, schools, daycare programs, and senior-citizen centers in improving the diet of individuals and groups. In some studies, dietary interventions have been targeted to point-of-purchase selections in supermarkets. Dietary-change studies have also involved the workplace, community organizations, and social groups. Among the topics for research are the acculturation of newly arrived immigrants and ethnic minorities and its impact on nutrition and the role of community organization and community structures in promoting better nutrition.

Initiate and evaluate population-based dietary intervention programs   Most past intervention programs have focused on reducing or eliminating alcohol and drug use, smoking cessation, and weight loss. Applying behavioral change strategies to specific dietary interventions in communities is relatively new. While eating and smoking behaviors are fundamentally distinct, it may be that some of the basic tenets of population-based approaches to smoking cessation may be adapted to dietary change. Among potential options are the workplace approach, community organization approach, and use of the mass media, all of which have been used in smoking-cessation studies.

Behavioral scientists view the workplace as being midway between the individual process of behavior change and the more complex community or social setting. Past workplace interventions have addressed smoking cessation, high blood pressure control, increasing physical activity, and weight loss. Community organization has been one strength of the Minnesota Heart Healthy Program, which was designed to lower the risks of coronary heart disease through intervention at the community level. The Stanford Five-City Multifactor Risk Reduction Project was a 14-year program of community organization and education, largely through the mass media, that successfully lowered risk factors such as smoking, blood pressure, and blood cholesterol concentrations.

While applications of the existing models and approaches to dietary behavior change open new opportunities for nutrition research, it is important to note that eating behaviors are in many ways unique and present specific challenges. First, food habits and body weight are likely to be influenced by genetic, physiological, and other biological factors that dietary interventions must take into account. Second, barriers to dietary change may be psychological, cultural, social, economic in nature, or some combination of these. Efforts to change dietary behavior must be sensitive to issues of age, gender, income, ethnic background, and religion. Third, while the goal of drug abuse or smoking programs is the elimination of the behavior, that is not the case for eating behaviors; the goal is not cessation but modification toward some agreed-upon optimum. Since there is little agreement regarding desirable body weights or amount of fat in the diet, for example, dietary goals often appear ill-defined. Fourth, the link between diet, nutritional status, and chronic disease varies among individuals. Some are resistant to dietary interventions and show no improvement in cardiovascular-disease risks even after adhering to dietary guidelines. The individual variability of response is very likely to affect participant compliance with a dietary intervention. Consequently, an integral component of population-based dietary interventions is an evaluation of the efficacy of the proposed dietary change and its impact on community health.

REDUCING THE RISK OF FOOD INSECURITY AND HUNGER

It is ironic that in a country where there is a surplus of food, some people go hungry. A markedly uneven accessibility characterizes the food supply in the United States. This problem has been recognized over the past several decades but is now coming into sharper perspective with renewed public and scientific attention. It will continue to pose challenges for both research and practice in public health nutrition into the next century.

Research Opportunities

Document the extent of food insecurity and hunger in the United States
The first step in addressing issues related to food distribution is to clarify

the definitions used. Nationwide surveys searching for malnutrition as measured by anthropometric techniques and clinical tests typically find it to be a rare condition. As measurable malnutrition may be the end of a continuum of food availability, it has been argued that "hunger" may be a more appropriate term and that it should include an inability to obtain adequate food even if the shortage is not prolonged enough to cause health problems. Further refinement of the definition has resulted in a conceptual framework identifying four components of hunger at both individual and household levels: (1) quantity of food (Is the household supply depleted? Is individual intake sufficient?), (2) quality of food (Is household food suitable? Are individual diets adequate?), (3) psychological (Is there general anxiety about food? Do individuals feel deprived and lacking in choice?), and (4) social (Must unacceptable means be used to acquire food? Are eating patterns disrupted?). Together, these components make up what has come to be termed "food security" or "food insecurity." Nutritionist Cathy Campbell states that:

> Food security is access by all people at all times to enough food for an active, healthy life, and at a minimum includes the following: 1) the ready availability of nutritionally adequate and safe foods and 2) the assured ability to acquire personally acceptable foods in a socially acceptable way. Food insecurity exists whenever the availability of nutritionally adequate, safe foods or the ability to acquire personally acceptable foods in socially acceptable ways is limited or uncertain.

Hunger as a physical sensation caused by lack of food need not be present for persons or households to lack food security. Further, aspects of personal and social values and preferences are integral to the definition of food security. This means that measures of food security specific to different population segments need to be developed. Some research has been conducted to develop measures for women and children and rural populations, but more are needed for the elderly, ethnic minorities, the homeless, and other hard-to-reach groups.

Once appropriate measures of food security have been developed, they must be integrated into existing nutrition monitoring and surveillance programs. Some measures were introduced and pilot-tested in the Third National Health and Nutrition Examination Survey (NHANES III), but they need to be developed and refined further.

Investigate the causes and consequences of food insecurity and hunger
These will be major tasks for future public health nutritionists, requiring a modification of the research designs typically used by investigators in the field. Survey methods as traditionally used in national or state probability samples are frequently not adequate to document many groups at risk of

food insecurity. For example, Native Americans living on reservations and Native Hawaiians are usually excluded from sampling frames. Sampling frames for migrant populations and for the homeless do not exist or would be difficult to develop because these groups lack a usual residence from which they can be selected. Many other groups at risk are covered proportionately by probability samples, but the resulting sample sizes of those who lack food security are too small to permit meaningful analysis. These groups include infants, pregnant and lactating women, the chronically poor, and the mentally and physically impaired. Sample sizes for groups such as undocumented aliens and substance abusers are often inadequate, because of inadequate identification or cooperation. As a result, there is still no clear understanding of how individuals come to be food insecure, nor what this status means for their physical, social, and psychological well-being.

Efforts to modify research methodology in the area of food security have focused on three alternatives to the standard probability survey. The actual choice depends on the type of difficulty in sampling the population of interest. First, one can supplement an existing survey by adding special questions or oversampling a specific population segment. This can be accomplished only if the group of interest, albeit rare, is included in the sampling frame. If not, it is sometimes possible to add a more suitable sampling frame. However, it is often not possible to carry out exactly the same procedures as will be used in the larger survey, and the integrity of the entire survey may be threatened.

A second approach is to conduct special-purpose surveys in which it is possible to develop a sampling frame. It might be necessary, for example, to screen a large number of households to identify high- or low-density clusters of the group of interest within the larger population. Multiphase sampling of these two kinds of clusters may then be done. Such a technique might be useful in studying food security of minority mothers of small children, where young families and minorities are clustered within specific neighborhoods. Sometimes social networks can be used to identify members of rare groups, and sampling can be done from the networks.

A third approach is the use of nonprobability methods. Such methods become necessary when the cost of probability methods based on the previously mentioned strategies becomes too high. The use of nonprobability measures requires a researcher who is quite familiar with the population of interest. Expert judgment is needed to minimize investigator bias in the choice of respondents. It is sometimes possible to introduce randomization, even in a nonprobability sample. For example, if a survey of food insecurity among the homeless were conducted, it might be advisable to interview random respondents in places such as community shelters where large numbers of potential respondents are found.

In addition to these survey methods, qualitative or ethnographic techniques may help to understand the causes and consequences of food insecurity. Such methods are important for identifying causal factors unique to particular population segments. Ethnographic methods are frequently used in conjunction with surveys, both to inform the design of the survey and to help interpret its results.

In sum, the research skills necessary to confront the problems of hunger and food security in the United States go beyond those traditionally found among public health nutritionists. It will be necessary for them to enlist the help of, or master some of the skills of, statisticians, anthropologists, and sociologists.

Develop effective food programs and policies to prevent hunger   Research on food security must involve an investigation of various programs and policies to determine which approaches are the most effective for preventing hunger among specific U.S. populations. Public health nutritionists along with other social scientists should be involved in the development, implementation, and evaluation of this research.

The two major influences on nutrition in the United States are agricultural and health policy. Insofar as economic, social, and political factors affect agricultural and health policies, they also affect nutrition policies. Components of a comprehensive nutrition policy include: (1) availability of food to everyone, (2) assurance of the quality, safety, and wholesomeness of the food supply, (3) consumer education about appropriate food choices to promote health and prevent disease, (4) improved means by which individuals can put their increased awareness and dietary knowledge into practice, (5) access to nutrition services in preventive health care and the medical care system, and (6) effective food assistance programs for those in need. Federal food assistance programs are an important means of ensuring that access to an adequate, safe, nutritious, and reliable food supply is available to all at reasonable cost.

The four major federal food assistance programs [school feeding programs, the Food Stamp Program, the Special Supplemental Food Program for Women, Infants, and Children (WIC), and the Congregate and Home-Delivered Meals Programs] have a variety of goals, services, delivery models, and eligibility criteria. Most are intended to improve the nutrition and health status of recipients by improving their access to food, thus improving food security. With the exception of the Congregate and Home-Delivered Meals Programs for the elderly, federal food assistance programs are administered by USDA and have a second explicit aim of supporting agriculture. In the United States, one in six persons receives government-sponsored food assistance at some point during the year.

The Food Stamp Program and WIC increase the food-buying power of recipients.° In contrast, school meals programs, nutrition programs for the elderly, and emergency food programs provide food directly. Together, these programs play an important role in many U.S. households in reducing hunger and worry about obtaining food.

Little is known about the impact of food assistance programs on reducing the risks of food insecurity. An understanding of these components is crucial to structuring or restructuring these programs so they can effectively meet nutritional and other goals and be acceptable to users. Using a broader definition of food security to include the psychological and social components of hunger may be useful in fully evaluating and tailoring these programs to their participants' needs.

Cost-benefit and cost-effectiveness analyses can be used to quantify the value of federal food assistance programs for recipients, government, and taxpayers. Cost-effectiveness or economic analyses consider the outcomes of alternative actions or programs on consumers and society and the inputs required to deliver and manage the programs over time. Cost-benefit research must first assess the direct effects of a food assistance program and other intended and unintended consequences. Then these effects must be related to costs for each program alternative.

With such data in hand, it is possible to evaluate the effectiveness of a program. When applied to food insecurity, a program is considered to be effective when the marginal (i.e., additional) benefits of lessening food insecurity are equal to or greater than the marginal cost of the program to bring about the change and when the program stays within budgetary constraints and achieves benefits in a reasonable amount of time. Since there are many causes of, and risks from, food insecurity in households, different modes of intervention may be necessary.

Unfortunately, many cost-benefit analyses focus on the short term. While some food assistance programs have shown very favorable short-term payoffs (e.g., WIC), the intermediate and long-term indirect and overall costs and benefits should be observed and documented. Studies

---

°The Food Stamp Program issues monthly allotments of coupons that participants can redeem at retail food stores. Eligibility is determined by income. WIC is designed to improve the health of pregnant, lactating, and postpartum women and of infants and children up to five years of age by providing supplemental foods, nutrition education, and access to health services. Eligibility is determined by income and evidence of nutritional risk. Participants receive vouchers redeemable at retail food stores for specified foods that provide nutrients in which their diets are likely to be low.

should consider the outcomes experienced by program participants and their families. For example, is there evidence that the food habits of the next generation in the household are modified? Is there a long-term impact on the socioeconomic status of the household? Long-term benefits to food program providers and other human services providers, groups throughout the food system, the education sector, employers, and taxpayers also need to be considered. For example, is the educational performance of the recipients altered? Is there a shift in the unemployment index? Is there evidence that the program increases or decreases the tax burden of the U.S. population? Addressing these research questions and many others would provide data to assess the cost-benefit and cost-effectiveness of the federal food assistance programs.

Knowledge about the food-related behaviors of low-income and disadvantaged people is limited. Efforts to promote dietary guidance have been directed toward middle- and upper-income groups and the cultural majority. Interdisciplinary training programs may be necessary to acquaint nutritionists with economic models and broader social models for conceptualizing and studying the full impact of nutrition interventions and food assistance programs.

Evaluate existing food assistance programs   The National School Lunch Program (NSLP), the most wide-ranging effort to support the nutrition of children, is available to 90 percent of all schoolchildren (approximately 24 million). It has been modified in recent years to adjust to changing food preferences and practices in an effort to control food waste and allow participants more choice. The regulations changed from the requirement that all five components of the meal be served (meat or meat alternate, bread or bread alternate, milk, and two fruits and vegetables) to offering all components and serving at least three to each child. In addition, a la carte lines, salad bars, and "hamburger basket" (hamburger and french fries) options are used to appeal to the preferences of high school students. We need to evaluate the impact of the shift from "serve" to "offer" and of other innovative changes. It is not known how these changes in regulations have altered the nutrient intakes of school children who consume these midday meals. The emerging scientific findings linking saturated fat and other dietary components to the development of chronic diseases bring new meaning to the NSLP's goal of "safeguarding the health of the nation's children through the provision of nutritious foods."

Because school nutrition programs reach a great proportion of the nation's children, the lunchroom provides an ideal laboratory in which to replace foods high in animal and hydrogenated fats and low in nutrients with more healthful alternatives and test innovative strategies for influencing the food preferences and food choices of children. Research in the

1970s showed how much more effective nutrition education was in the classroom when coupled with more nutritious food choices in the lunchroom. Continuing research is needed on the impact of nutrition education on the choices children and teachers make in the school meals programs, especially when school cafeterias provide the more healthful alternatives. Frequently, food service operators hesitate to offer more healthful options for fear they will not sell.

Research indicates that the Food Stamp Program benefits families because it increases their spending on nutrient-dense food. It also benefits the agricultural sector through increased demand for agricultural products. The most positive outcomes were documented early in the history of this program, when nutrition education was an integral component. We need to know why only one-half of eligible people participate in this entitlement program. Reports that are primarily anecdotal in nature suggest that poor outreach, administrative hassles, and the social stigma of using stamps are barriers to participation.

Participants in the Food Stamp Program are free to choose the foods they want. However, they must be provided with information and guidance to increase their consumption of fruits, vegetables, and other foods that help them to meet dietary guidelines. If a stigma associated with using stamps is a barrier to participation, then electronic "credit cards" and other innovations should be evaluated. The administrative hassles associated with the use of food stamps stem from the lack of administrative accountability. The possibility of balancing the need for administrative accountability with a simplified application and eligibility verification procedure should be investigated. There has been discussion about "cashing out" the food stamp program—that is, eliminating the program and increasing the cash grant to dependent families for an amount equal to their food needs. Early studies found food stamps to be twice as effective as cash in increasing food expenditures, but the effect of "cashing out" coupled with broad-based nutrition education needs further evaluation. The components of comprehensive programs that provide electronic credit cards, nutrition education, and vouchers or food packages should be tested individually to sort out the distinct effects of each intervention. The potential of using the Food Stamp Program to provide dietary guidance to low-income families needs to be evaluated. The impact of various strategies on food choices, nutrients consumed per dollar spent, and other desired outcomes should be studied.

WIC is the most thoroughly evaluated of all federal food assistance programs. However, although the program is targeted for pregnant and lactating women, infants, and children, evaluations have focused on pregnant women and the outcome of pregnancy. The evaluation of WIC participation on children was cancelled by Congress in 1992 on the grounds that there was no need to prove the obvious (that WIC is good for children). In addition to supplemental food, the program provides nutrition education and facilitates contact with the health-care system. WIC is widely regarded as an important and effective program. About three dollars are saved in morbidity, mortality, and hospitalization costs for every dollar spent on WIC benefits. WIC staff have been given additional responsibilities, such as immunization outreach, drug and alcohol screening, cholesterol screening, and determining the eligibility of participants for food stamps and Medicaid. These requests and mandates come in response to the recent emphasis on one-stop services and the opportunity to reach young families for other health promotion purposes. We need to study the impact of these additional activities on the efficiency and effectiveness of WIC. Although WIC programs have been the target of three large evaluations, none of them has studied the long-term effects of WIC participation on growth, social and cognitive development, nutrition knowledge, food selection and preparation practices, nutrient consumption, health status, educational attainment, and employment. The current WIC food package, established in 1972, needs to be evaluated in light of current knowledge about nutrients in short supply in the U.S. diet and the links between diet and chronic disease.

Title III of the Older Americans Act is designed to provide meeting places where older adults can receive a nutritious meal and nutrition education and an opportunity for socializing and recreation. Congregate dining and home-delivered meals programs provide some food security and bring elderly persons into regular contact with others. Through social contact, other needs can be identified and solutions sought. The meals programs also provide an opportunity for healthy elderly people to do productive work as volunteers. We need to assess the effects of congregate dining on quality of life, both physiologically and psychologically, and on longevity. Does the program prevent or delay entry into nursing homes for the frail elderly? Also, studies are needed to determine whether congregate dining and home-delivered meals programs are accessible to, and used by, the neediest elderly in the community. If not, barriers to access need to be determined and reduced. The impact of nutrition education provided with congregate dining and home-delivered meals has not been assessed. We need to know if this education affects food consumption outside of the program and contributes to the dietary, health, and social aims of the program.

The Child and Adult Care Food Program is designed to ensure nutritious meals for children to age 12, the elderly, and certain handicapped individuals who participate in a nonprofit, licensed, or approved day-care program. This program serves 1.5 million participants daily, only 1 percent of whom are elderly. Research needs to be done to determine why participation by the elderly is so low and, if they have a need for this program, how to improve participation. Data on the quality of nutrition education provided in the program and its benefit to the well-being of recipients are limited. For example, studies need to be conducted of the program's impact on growth and development of the children and the overall well-being of the elderly and handicapped individuals.

Assess government policies related to food assistance The two aims of food assistance programs—enhancing the nutritional quality of the diet and supporting agricultural prices—are often in conflict. This conflict is illustrated by the commodity donation program and WIC, which have been criticized for providing and encouraging consumption of high-fat, protein-rich foods such as cheese and whole milk. Critics claim that U.S. agricultural policy is geared more toward the needs of food producers than consumers. Nevertheless, the majority of USDA's food assistance programs are directed toward consumers rather than food producers. Studies need to be undertaken to determine what incentives can be provided to farmers to produce more of the foods that form the basis of healthful diets.

Another important issue in agricultural policy is the extent to which food assistance programs increase the amount of food consumed (supplementation) or alter dietary patterns (substitution). To support agriculture, increased demand (i.e., supplementation) is desired. From a nutritional standpoint, supplementation covers shortfalls in energy and nutrient intake, but substitution is desired when caloric needs are met or exceeded. The availability of surplus agricultural and price-supported commodities does not always improve the dietary patterns of recipients. We need to find ways to integrate nutritional goals with the aims of agricultural price supports in federal food assistance programs.

Surveys show that food insecurity is becoming more prevalent in the United States. At the same time, the national debt is increasing and federal support for assistance programs is becoming more limited. To increase the availability of, and access to, food for those in need, we need to determine what combination of social and economic indicators best predicts the need for assistance. Many of the current food assistance programs were designed in the 1970s, and it is uncertain whether they meet the needs of the disadvantaged today. For example, do the programs consider adequately the fact that most married women who have children under six years of age also work outside the home, that one in four children is born to an unwed mother, and that one child in nine lives in a household headed by only one adult?

Most federal food programs require that recipients have an address, which eliminates the homeless, one of the neediest groups in the United

States. In sum, we need to evaluate the design and effectiveness of federal food assistance programs in the context of today's social and economic problems.

IMPROVING METHODS AND TOOLS FOR NUTRITIONAL ASSESSMENT, MONITORING, AND EVALUATION

Nutritional assessment is typically defined as the interpretation of information obtained from dietary, biochemical, anthropometric, and clinical assays of nutritional status. This information is used to assess the health status of individuals or populations as influenced by their intake and utilization of nutrients. Nutrient deficiencies in the United States are most often associated with poverty. Pregnant women, infants, young children, the elderly, alcohol and drug abusers, and persons suffering from prolonged injury or illness are at greatest risk of malnutrition caused by dietary deficiencies. Nutritional assessment of individuals is an essential component of health care and forms the basis for nutritional intervention in clinical or home-care settings.

The components of nutritional assessment are sensitive to different stages of nutritional deficiency. Generally, clinical symptoms or classic anatomical signs that are apparent during a medical examination (e.g., xerophthalmia) reflect prolonged and severe nutritional deficiencies. Earlier stages of nutritional deficiencies are detected through biochemical or laboratory assessment methods. Advances in assessing the unique biochemistry of individuals should enable nutrition experts in the future to provide dietary recommendations tailored to a particular person.

Research Opportunities

Develop biochemical markers of nutritional status   Some period of depletion of body nutrient stores precedes the signs and symptoms of nutritional deficiencies. Laboratory tests of nutritional status are typically based on (1) nutrient concentrations in body fluids or tissues, (2) urinary excretion of nutrients or their metabolites, (3) nutrient-dependent enzyme activities, (4) metabolic responses to a nutrient load, and (5) nutrient-dependent physiological functions such as immune function and taste acuity. Static biochemical tests include assays of albumin or iron concentrations in serum, vitamin A concentrations in plasma, zinc in hair, and concentrations of creatinine in urine. Functional tests focus on nutrient-dependent physiological functions in tissues or the entire body. For example, one method of diagnosing vitamin A deficiency is to measure the time to see a dim light after bleaching totally the rhodopsin in the eye. This functional test is called the dark adaptation response. The ability to detect or to discriminate tastes has been used to evaluate zinc status.

Biochemical tests of nutritional status are often influenced by physiological factors other than the depletion of nutrient stores. These may include diurnal variation, physical exercise, hydration status, drug use, disease state, or even the habitual diet. For example, urinary creatinine or the creatinine-height index can help to estimate the muscle mass of individuals who consume little or no animal protein. However, this test is not appropriate for those consuming creatinine-containing animal products. Other factors influencing the usefulness of biochemical tests are the precision, specificity, and sensitivity of the analytical method.

Many research opportunities exist to design and develop laboratory assays of nutritional status. Ideally, such tests should be simple, accurate, and reproducible methods of detecting initial stages of nutrient depletion. Assays for use in large population-based studies should also be inexpensive, rapid, minimally invasive, and preferably automated.

Research in this area has focused on developing novel biomarkers of nutritional status. For example, concentrations of metallothionein, a zinc-binding protein, depend on dietary zinc status. Metallothionein assays in erythrocytes may prove to be a much needed biomarker of zinc nutriture in humans. Similarly, understanding the role of vitamin E in lipid peroxidation has led to the development of the breath pentane test and the release *in vitro* of malondialaldehyde from erythrocytes. Another new technology for assessing nutritional status involves the use of stable isotopes. For example, the use of deuterium-labeled vitamin A provides an accurate, reproducible method of measuring total body vitamin A stores *in vivo*.

Medical technology has translated successfully some biochemical assays of nutritional status into automated assays suitable for field use. For example, plasma glucose and cholesterol concentrations can be measured rapidly using minimal amounts of blood. New applications of medical technology will permit rapid screening of large population samples in epidemiological studies and lead to better identification of subgroups at risk.

Develop simple, specific anthropometric measures of nutritional status
Anthropometric measures are widely used to assess body composition and growth. Nutritional anthropology is defined as the measurement of the physical dimensions and the composition of the human body at different ages and degrees of nutrition.

Anthropometric measures typically used in clinical assessments include weight and stature, skinfold thickness at multiple sites, and mid-arm circumference. They may be used, respectively, to calculate body mass index (BMI = weight/height^2, a measure of overweight), and to estimate total body fat, and to gauge muscle mass. Measures for use with children include weight for age, height for age, and head circumference for age, the latter used as an index of protein status during the first two years of life.

Generally, anthropometric data are interpreted using reference standards that are most often cross-sectional data from national or international surveys. NHANES data are a common reference source for heights and weights of children, while Metropolitan Life Insurance tables (the 1959 or 1983 versions) remain useful guidelines for adults.

Clinical assessments of body composition use numerous labor-intensive and invasive procedures, ranging from underwater weighing to total body potassium measures, total body water, total body electrical conductivity, computerized tomography, and ultrasound. Such methods are often based on specific assumptions, each with limitations. Methods of assessing body composition are often developed and validated using healthy young men as subjects. Their applicability to the body composition of pregnant women, infants, children, and older individuals is sometimes unclear. Biological methods for measuring body composition, with rare exceptions (such as the bioelectric impedance measure, which is, however, sensitive to hydration status), are unsuitable for use outside the laboratory. Field researchers still rely on anthropometric measures of height and weight, skinfold thickness, and waist and hip circumferences to assess nutritional status.

Anthropometric measures typically use cutoff points to classify individuals by nutritional status. Those points are somewhat arbitrary and are often established by reviewing anthropometric characteristics of individuals with clinically significant malnutrition. Few stepped cutoff points are suitable for use over the entire range of nutritional status, from adequate to malnourished to severely deprived. Another research challenge is posed by the need to develop reference standards for anthropometric measures that are age- gender-, and race-specific. The development of minimally invasive body-composition assays for use with large populations would also help epidemiological studies.

Improve the sensitivity and specificity of dietary intake assessment methods   The first stage of a nutritional deficiency is identified by dietary assessment methods. In clinical settings, this assessment is usually performed in a face-to-face interview between patient and a trained dietitian. The standard dietary history method estimates typical patterns of food consumption over a two-week period, and it is generally used in conjunction with a computerized analysis of nutrient intake. The dietitian uses the results of this assessment to provide the patient with specific dietary advice.

An alternative procedure using multiple-day food records or food diaries places a greater burden on the subject. Following appropriate instructions, the subject maintains a record of his or her food consumption over a period of days (generally four or seven), making entries at the time food is consumed. This is the preferred procedure in many clinical settings. Food records are also the chief means of data collection in some epidemiological studies of food consumption, such as USDA's Nationwide Food Consumption Survey. Major limitations of this technique include the need for high motivation and literacy by participants and substantial costs in collecting and processing the diet records.

As might be expected, the larger the population sample, the shorter the time interval required to assess accurately population (not individual) food intakes. Large-scale epidemiological studies such as NHANES II, with upward of 20,000 respondents, have tended to rely on interviews using a single 24-hour recall. In this procedure, respondents are asked to recall all foods and beverages consumed within the previous 24 hours.

Self-administered food frequency questionnaires (FFQs) have become a popular method of assessing habitual food intakes over time, usually a period of one year. FFQs typically consist of a list of food names, a semiquantitative estimate of portion size, and a set of response options. They force subjects to give precoded responses but have the advantage of being readable through optical scanners and processible by computers. Studies of FFQs indicate that carefully designed forms provide adequate information at very low cost, making large studies possible. Such questionnaires provide data on the consumption of specific food groups and nutrients, which can be useful in studies of disease causation. However, because FFQs may be insensitive to unusual foods, portions, or methods of preparation, they may not be suitable for comparisons among various ethnic and cultural groups.

One problem with the classic techniques of dietary intake assessment is their reliance on the respondents' memory, which can be remarkably selective. Subjects overreport the consumption of health-promoting foods, while downplaying or omitting altogether the consumption of foods high in calories, fat, sugar, and salt.

Among the research challenges are development of rapid and accurate measures of dietary intake. One recent development is the use of repeated telephone-administered 24-hour food recalls, increasingly used instead of food records. Since keeping food records may alter dietary patterns, some investigators believe that unscheduled telephone interviews provide a more reliable assessment of food intake. Some FFQs have been shortened and redeveloped for administration over the phone. Validating dietary assessment tools is always difficult. New biomarkers of nutrient intakes are needed to validate new methods for assessing intakes.

Another research opportunity is the study of people's attitudes toward nutrition and diet. Cognitive bias may result in under- or overreporting of food intake. The frequency estimates of food consumption using an FFQ are especially susceptible to reporting errors, and different types of bias may operate for men and women. Studies on this topic would combine both psychology and nutrition and offer an ideal opportunity for collaboration across disciplines.

A third research opportunity is provided by the study of nutrient interactions. Generally, FFQs and other techniques for assessing dietary intake are used to correlate nutrient intake with nutritional status and the risk of chronic disease. However, foods or nutrients should not be viewed in isolation, since absorption of nutrients from one food may be influenced by other foods in the diet. A classic example is that essential amino acids must be present in order for the body to make optimum use of protein. A recent paper on the absorption of beta-carotene makes a similar point: absorption of beta-carotene was minimal when this antioxidant was taken during fasting, but it increased sharply when accompanied by a meal containing 200 g of fat from ice cream. Nutrient status may depend on the consumption of foods that, while not sources of that nutrient, influence its absorption.

Dietary intake assessments usually depend on two steps: determining food intake using one of the techniques described above and calculating nutrient intake based on the nutrient composition of the foods consumed. At present, information on nutrients in foods is provided through updates of USDA Handbook No. 8. Recent updates include data on the fatty acid and fiber contents of selected foods. However, information for some nutrients is very incomplete. For example, the USDA database does not distinguish between complex and simple carbohydrates. It often cannot supply information on the amount of the antioxidant nutrients in foods that are the subject of much research (see Chapters 2, 3, and 5). Little information is available on the composition of ethnic foods. Major research opportunities in this area include determining the nutrient composition of foods consumed almost exclusively by minorities and new immigrants to this country.

Develop standards for assessing dietary intakes of individuals   The interpretation of information from dietary surveys must sometimes be compared to one or more recognized standards of adequate nutrient intake. Nutrient intakes in the United States are usually compared to the recommended dietary allowances (RDAs). But since RDAs are typically set at levels that exceed the estimated average need of the nutrient, intakes below the RDAs do not necessarily indicate nutrient deficiency.

Research opportunities in this area include development of standards for nutrient intake that quantitate the probable risk of nutrient deficiencies. Furthermore, with the current emphasis on disease prevention, consideration should be given to developing recommended intakes for food components that are not essential nutrients (e.g., carotenoids and dietary fiber) but whose consumption may influence nutritional status and health. Standards defining excessive intake of nutrients are also needed.

Develop new tools for nutrition monitoring Nutrition monitoring is defined as the ongoing description of nutrition conditions in the population for the purpose of planning interventions, analyzing the effects of policies and programs, and predicting future trends. Assessing the diet of population subgroups defined in socioeconomic terms helps to determine the nutritional needs of groups at risk because of policy or economic reasons and to design and evaluate intervention programs.

Nutrition monitoring typically encompasses five types of measurements: health and nutritional status, food consumption, dietary knowledge and attitudes, food composition, and food supply measurements. Some of these measurements were reviewed earlier in this chapter. Measurements are made at different points along a "nutrition continuum" that ranges from food production to consumption and eventually to the health status of individuals and groups.

Information derived from nutrition monitoring forms the basis for policy decisions such as those on food fortification, food safety, food labeling, nutrition education, public health interventions, and food assistance. Therefore, all surveys and surveillance systems must be firmly grounded in research. Methods of assessing dietary intakes and nutritional status, food composition databases, and reference standards are all products of basic and applied research. These products must rest on a firm foundation of fundamental research that ranges from basic biochemistry to epidemiology, encompassing food composition, nutrient bioavailability, nutrient requirements, and the role of nutrition and diet in the etiology of chronic disease.

The current research challenges for nutrition monitoring arise from the changing food supply and rapidly changing demographic profile of the U.S. population. The introduction of new products into the food supply, such as reduced-calorie foods, biotechnology-derived foods, and foods produced using new processing techniques, makes it difficult to keep food composition databases up-to-date and for people to describe accurately what they have eaten. The increasing ethnic diversity of our society and the increasing consumption of meals away from home seem to require the development of novel methods of data collection and analysis that are sensitive to the issues of ethnicity, gender, education, and socioeconomic status.

Research opportunities in this area include gathering more comprehensive data on populations that are at highest nutritional risk. Such populations include infants, adolescent girls, pregnant and lactating women, and the elderly, as well as groups not adequately covered in current nutritional surveys, including Native Americans and other ethnic minorities, newly immigrated ethnic groups, and the homeless. New sampling techniques need to be developed to reach these populations, and questions of adequate sample size need to be studied in greater detail. For example, how precisely do we need to estimate intake for each demographic group? How finely do these groups need to be characterized by such variables as race, age, gender, income, education, or religion? To what degree can statistical modeling be used to identify subgroups at risk? How useful is the currently used telephone screening method for identifying subgroups at risk and targeting them for more detailed study and potential nutritional intervention?

Novel methods of data collection are needed to characterize issues of literacy and cultural differences in food preparation. Innovative ways of collecting food intake data from the very young and the very old need to be developed. The validity of proxy reports by parents regarding the dietary intakes of young children has been called into question, especially if the children are away from their parents in day care or at school. Efforts should be made to test the validity of proxy reports or to find alternative ways of obtaining dietary information. Identifying effective ways of collecting food intake data from elderly persons who require long-term care is another priority area for further research.

Develop new strategies for evaluating nutrition interventions   The goal of many nutritional interventions is to improve health behaviors. While the basis for nutrition interventions may be clinical, laboratory, and epidemiological studies, successful implementation often falls within the purview of the social and behavioral sciences.

The nutrition community has been criticized for its failure to evaluate the effectiveness of its intervention programs. One important reason for this failure may be that nutrition professionals often lack training in the social and behavioral sciences. The successful implementation of nutrition programs depends on many factors, which may include an accurate assessment of staff requirements in relation to staff availability; costs in relation to cost constraints; availability of other resources, including equipment, supplies, and infrastructure; and political pressures and constraints. In addition, the needs, practices, and constraints on the target population need to be considered. Examples of these include the direct and indirect cash costs of participation, time costs of participation, level of knowledge and information about the intervention, conformity with the habits and preferences of the population, cultural expectations, and issues of social acceptability.

Many programs have failed because of one or more of these factors. Participation in the Food Stamp Program has been limited by the inconvenience and length of time it takes for certification as well as by lack of knowledge about the program, particularly by non-English-speaking immigrants new to this country. The essentially obsolete Commodity Food Distribution Program had limited effect because of the inconvenience to participants of receiving a month's worth of food at once and because some participants were unfamiliar with the foods and did not know how to prepare them. Efforts to promote breastfeeding have often been unsuccessful because the educational messages did not help the target groups overcome important cultural and social constraints.

Many nutrition interventions require the target population to change its behavior in some way, usually by altering food consumption patterns. For example, the nationwide Five-a-Day for Better Health program aims to increase the consumption of fruits and vegetables to five or more servings per day. However, this goal is well above the current estimates of fruit and vegetable consumption in the U.S. population. The USDA's own data have shown that the consumption of fruits and vegetables among women actually declined between 1977 and 1985, with the greatest drop (approximately 20 percent) among low-income respondents.

Attempts to change dietary behaviors cannot succeed without an understanding of the network of causal factors that determine food choice and the contexts in which the dietary behaviors take place. Studies of taste and the development of food preferences (see Chapter 5) fall outside the traditional field of nutrition science. The fields of program operations and logistics, personnel motivation, and organizational behavior have also been outside the purview of nutrition science, even though they are an integral component of nutrition practice. Future nutrition professionals should combine these areas of training at the graduate level.

Develop methods for assessing creative new interventions using computer-assisted decision-making models Health and nutrition interventions are of three general types. There are those that deliver services and provide food, such as WIC, or provide food only, such as the various school-based and other child-feeding programs and the Food Stamp Program. There are also those that promote behavior change through education in schools and by the media, by providing information through nutrition labels and advertising, or by incentives that may include lower prices or added convenience. Finally, there are interventions that attempt to change dietary patterns without requiring much conscious behavior change, such as nutrient fortification or altering the composition of foods.

The design and evaluation of successful health and nutrition interventions requires an expanded understanding of national agricultural and economic policies, individual and household behavior, and their determinants. The complex interaction between national food policies, household and individual behavior, and the health and nutritional status of the individual are depicted in Figure 6.1. Evaluation of this entire spectrum is, of course, beyond the means of a single investigator. However, mathematical modeling techniques, driven by advances in computer technology, allow information from large-scale surveys to be integrated with household or indi-

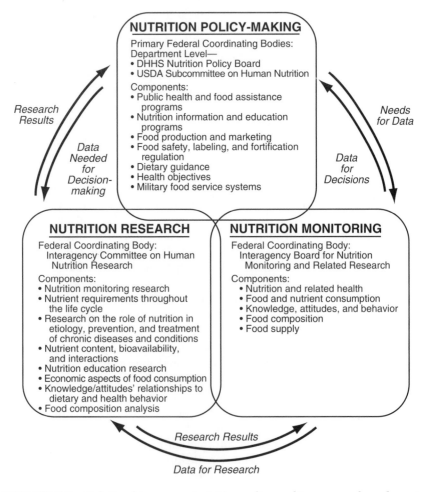

FIGURE 6.1   Relationships among nutrition policy-making, research, and monitoring. From Fed. Reg. 56(209):55716-55767.

vidual data. For example, a model of the socioeconomic, nutritional, and health status of a specific population group can be formulated using survey data from several sources. This model can then be used to test several potential nutritional intervention programs with the help of computer-assisted decision-making modeling techniques. Based on the outcome of this initial testing, one or more programs may be selected for field testing. The results of those field tests could be incorporated into the computer model to refine and target the intervention further before it is widely implemented.

Using this technology requires skills not ordinarily learned in nutrition science programs—survey techniques in contrast to laboratory research techniques, economic and other social science approaches to understanding behavior in contrast to laboratory and clinical measurements, and familiarity with mathematics and computer science technology in contrast to biological procedures. The developers of successful intervention strategies in the future are likely to be those who have learned these skills and have specialized knowledge of nutrition, food consumption, and health status.

CONCLUDING REMARKS

Developing successful and comprehensive programs to improve the diet and health of populations involves four distinct steps: (1) identification of the problem, (2) development and implementation of an intervention, (3) evaluation of the response, and (4) modification of the intervention, based on the response. Specific and sensitive tools to monitor and assess the physiological response of individuals and populations are required for this process. Central to the long-term success of any public health program is incorporation of successful aspects of the program into food and nutrition policies of governmental agencies and food industries.

Challenges in public health nutrition for the future include developing successful interventions and policies to reduce the risk of diet-related diseases and the incidence of hunger and food insecurity and monitoring the impact of those policies. New computer technologies are enabling scientists to estimate food and nutrient intakes of large groups, to store and interpret a vast array of survey data, and to build decision-making model systems for testing potential interventions. Complex and multidisciplinary interventions in the future may be evaluated in the laboratory using computer-assisted models before expensive field trials are undertaken.

Previous nutritional interventions, which used either food fortification or vitamin and mineral supplementation approaches, were relatively easy to carry out and their results were easily observed. The nutritional challenges of today are much more complex, spanning dietary excesses and disease to inadequate food distribution and hunger. The targets of potential interventions range from the macro level of national agricultural and health policies to the micro level of household and individual food behaviors. Future interventions to deal with these complex problems will need to integrate findings from the basic behavioral sciences with agriculture, economics, political science, and the other social sciences. This process will provide many new, exciting research opportunities for nutrition and food scientists.

7

Education and Training in the Nutrition and Food Sciences

To meet the research opportunities and challenges identified in the previous four chapters, it is vital to the future of the nutrition and food sciences to attract motivated, achievement-oriented students into these disciplines and provide them with high-quality education and training. In colleges and universities across the United States, there are approximately 92 programs in or departments of nutrition, 29 in food science, and 27 joint departments or programs. The American Institute of Nutrition (AIN) estimated in 1989 that there were almost 2,000 students in master's degree programs in nutrition and about 600 in doctoral programs. The National Center for Education Statistics reports that in the 1990-1991 academic year, 305 students received master's degrees in food science and 124 received doctorates.

Many professionals have been trained at both the undergraduate and graduate levels in nutrition or food science. However, a substantial number of prominent nutrition and food scientists have developed their professional identification later in their careers, frequently at the postbaccalaureate level and not uncommonly at the postdoctoral level. This reflects the fact that nutrition and food science are multidisciplinary areas of research and learning and that these disciplines can attract scientists at a variety of stages of career and intellectual development. For this reason, academic programs in the nutrition and food sciences must always remain open and adaptable to talented and qualified individuals. Nutrition and food scientists can be trained in a variety of ways, but for these disciplines to maintain their identity and become most effective in generating new knowledge, a substantial number of individuals should be trained as nutrition and food scientists.

Undergraduate and graduate programs in the nutrition and food sciences exist in research-oriented colleges and universities, professional schools, and liberal arts institutions. Almost all land-grant universities and colleges in each of the 50 states offer training in the nutrition sciences, food sciences, or both. Within an institution, these programs may be found in colleges of human ecology, home economics, agriculture, or health sciences or in schools of medicine, public health, or nutrition. Thus, the composition and location of educational and training programs in the nutrition and food sciences vary among institutions. Some of the strengths and weaknesses of the various structures are discussed later, in the section on graduate education.

Current institutional infrastructures need to be examined as the nutrition and food sciences advance to meet the research challenges identified in this report—in the basic biological sciences of nutrition, food science and engineering, the clinical nutrition sciences, and the behavioral and social sciences of nutrition. The expertise required to meet these challenges goes beyond the traditional qualifications of faculty in nutrition, food science, medical school, or public health programs. Expertise from scientists in related fields is necessary. In other words, nutritionists and food scientists must engage in interdisciplinary efforts with each other and with basic biological and social scientists. For example, research in the biological sciences shows that some nutrients play key roles in regulating metabolism. Future efforts to identify nutrient-gene interactions will require the attention of nutritionists well trained in molecular, cellular, and integrative biology. Although the work of food scientists has expanded and improved our food supply, many new challenges remain. Collaboration among engineers, microbiologists, molecular biologists, food scientists, and nutritionists is needed to create new foods that are nutritious, palatable, and safe. Clinical nutritionists have demonstrated the role of diet in maintaining physiological function and preventing chronic disease, but future advances in understanding these relationships require joint efforts with physicians and biologists. Designing successful public health and community intervention programs requires an understanding of human behavior, economics, epidemiology, anthropology, and political science. Interdisciplinary efforts among nutritionists and behavioral and social scientists are needed to meet this challenge. It is essential, therefore, that students in the nutrition and food sciences develop an understanding of the basic science of a related discipline such as molecular biology, microbiology, biochemistry, chemistry, engineering, medical science, sociology, or political science.

One way to extend the boundaries of a nutrition or food science department to include related fields is to develop graduate programs that are offered by groups of faculty with a common interest in nutrition or food science rather than by a specific department or division. Such group programs have been used successfully for the basic biological sciences of nutrition and the food sciences, clinical nutrition, and social sciences of nutrition. In these programs, graduate study is organized in "fields" that cut across departmental boundaries. Thus, it is as easy to combine nutrition with biochemistry and physiology as it is to combine nutrition with anthropology and economics, or any other possibilities of interest to the student. These interdisciplinary groups can expand the opportunities within an institution as well.

Another approach for extending the boundaries of nutrition or food science departments into related disciplines is to hire faculty from those disciplines into the department. This is a good method to ensure integration of related disciplines into the curriculum when the department is large enough to accommodate this diversity. However, this approach is limited by the few available positions for new faculty in any one department and the fact that faculty may wish to associate with others from their discipline rather than individuals in a related science. When departmental size is a factor, it may be more practical to have students learn the theory of related disciplines from faculty in these related departments. It then becomes the responsibility of the nutrition or food science faculty to link and integrate that knowledge into food and nutrition theory.

UNDERGRADUATE EDUCATION

Many students who enter programs in the nutrition and food sciences as undergraduates do not plan to pursue graduate studies and hope to become employed in a related activity after graduation. Departments of nutrition usually provide two undergraduate tracks: one focused on nutrition science and the other on the practice of nutrition (i.e., dietetics); students in the latter category are less likely to go to graduate school. Students in nutrition science use the degree as preprofessional training for graduate school in biomedical science or to enter the job market or business administration. According to a recent survey by the American Dietetic Association (ADA), the highest degree received by almost half the country's registered dietitians (R.D.) is the baccalaureate. Undergraduate nutrition programs are frequently oriented toward these students, training them for employment as practitioners and administrators in, for example, hospitals, industry, and government food programs. As a result, dietetics programs are not designed to meet the needs of students who plan to go on to graduate and other professional programs. Furthermore, the perception of many undergraduates and their faculty advisors is that nutrition and food science are not as challenging as are traditional sciences such as biology or chemistry. This incorrect perception discourages many students from choosing to major in these disciplines.

The best undergraduate programs in the nutrition and food sciences draw upon the biological, chemical, physical, and behavioral sciences to help students understand the interrelationships of nutrition, food, and health and to develop critical-thinking and problem-solving skills. We believe that faculty should identify nutrition and food science undergraduates who intend to go to graduate school and ensure that their coursework follows this model, encourage them to specialize, and offer all students opportunities to conduct independent research under the guidance of a professor. We recommend a core curriculum for these students with the following courses: general chemistry, organic chemistry, and biochemistry; biology and integrative biology (e.g., physiology); nutrition science; microbiology; food chemistry; mathematics through elementary calculus; physics; statistics; and behavioral sciences. Students interested in food science need the same basic science training in biology, chemistry, and physics, plus food engineering, food processing, and coursework in regulatory policy. Where possible, freshmen should take an introductory course in the nutrition and food sciences to provide an early grounding in their chosen discipline and to learn the relevance and importance of the basic sciences.

Since nutrition and food science majors are required to complete prerequisite work in the basic sciences during the first two or three years of their undergraduate education, there is a tendency for some of them to lose interest and change their major. To prevent this from happening, general courses or seminars focusing on popular issues in nutrition or food science could be offered for students each semester or quarter. At least one institution offers an introductory course to freshmen geared to the nutritional issues of interest to an educated layperson. In the second year, after the students have had a year of biology and a course in the behavioral sciences as freshmen, they take a course on the influence of the social sciences on the foodways and nutritional health of populations. These courses give a broad perspective on the diet-related interests of concern to individuals and populations before they enroll in nutritional biochemistry and metabolism. Another institution offers one- or two-unit seminars open to all students on campus on popular topics in foods and nutrition, such as nutrition and physical fitness, nutrition and heart disease (or cancer or obesity), food safety, maternal and infant nutrition, nutrition and aging, and social influences on eating habits and access to food.

Many fine research universities and colleges do not have specialized undergraduate programs in nutrition or food science. A major challenge is to identify students in these settings who may have interests in the critical problems of food and nutrition, excite their curiosity, and identify opportunities for them to begin to study these issues within their institutions. Students need a foundation in nutritional biochemistry and metabolism, molecular biology, and the integrative biological sciences. In addition, they should have experience in conducting research, including experimental design, data analysis, and development of inferences. These students may need to take advantage of opportunities outside their institution to receive specialized training in the nutrition and food sciences.

Summer Training Programs

Summer courses in the nutrition and food sciences could provide great opportunities to acquaint undergraduates—both nutrition and food science majors as well as interested students at institutions with or without programs in these disciplines—with a range of research problems in the nutrition and food sciences and with the approaches and technology being used to solve these problems. We believe that these summer training programs exist in two different forms. The first form is represented by the highly successful summer courses such as those offered at the Marine Biological Laboratory (Woods Hole, Massachusetts) and Cold Spring Harbor Laboratory (Cold Spring Harbor, New York), that cover areas of biology from parasitology to computational neuroscience to the genetics of yeast or mice and are intense versions of graduate-level laboratory courses. It is generally not possible to organize such high-powered courses with the fiscal and personnel resources available at most undergraduate institutions. For the best of these courses, highly qualified researchers and teachers are recruited from around the country to organize and conduct these summer courses. The formal lectures and laboratory sessions last from six to eight weeks. In the laboratory, students work in groups on a series of projects spanning current research in an area. Such a training program could give students hands-on experiences in structured laboratory of field-based settings and acquaint them with a range of research problems and tools used by investigators in the nutrition and food sciences. Formal examinations should provide a measure of the student's achievement and should become a permanent part of the student's academic record.

An alternative program would be modeled after summer undergraduate research experiences that are organized and offered by many university science departments in the United States. These programs differ considerably from the type discussed above because they emphasize research experience for individual students in individual research laboratories. Rather than having a set of organized laboratory experiences, students work on specific, specialized research problems for an entire summer (10 to 12 weeks). As a general rule, these programs also have didactic components in which faculty give lectures about their own research or some related specialized area of research. Usually these lectures involve only one or two hours per week, with the balance of time spent in a specific research laboratory. Although less broad than the more structured courses described above, the advantage of these programs is their emphasis on ongoing research in a realistic laboratory setting. For some undergraduates, a better balance could be achieved in these programs by including an intensive lecture course (four to six hours per week) that covers a specialized area of interest to the faculty. Unlike the structured program, formal examinations are not appropriate to measure the accomplishments of the student. At the end of a summer research program that emphasizes experience in a research laboratory, each student should give an oral presentation on his/her research results to the faculty, staff, and other trainees of the program. The program faculty and the faculty mentor should provide a formal evaluation of the student's accomplishments based on the oral presentation and their knowledge of the student's laboratory accomplishments.

The two models described above are suitable for undergraduate students (and occasionally beginning graduate students) of different types. Thus, students, majoring in nutrition or food science may already have taken courses that would be covered in a program of formal lectures and structured laboratory exercises. These students would likely be better served by an intensive exposure to a research laboratory and to seminars on current research of the faculty. On the other hand, science students who do not major in the nutrition or food sciences or who are educated at institutions that do not have nutrition or food science departments may gain more from the structured laboratory experience, where breadth is emphasized.

Summer training programs conforming to both of these models should be organized and offered by nutrition science and food science departments. We recommend that these programs be offered by the U.S. Department of Agriculture (USDA) as well. Competitively awarded fellowships would allow selected undergraduates to gain experience at nutrition departments and food science departments or at the five Human Nutrition Research Centers (HNRCs) and five Regional Research Centers (RRCs) located throughout the United States (see Chapter 8). Professional societies in the nutrition and food sciences, industry, USDA, and the National Institutes of Health (NIH) should provide support for establishing these programs, especially for the more structured courses where the organization and execution will be more expensive. For both types of programs, these same groups should provide competitively awarded travel grants and fellowships to enable talented undergraduates with demonstrated interest in these disciplines to participate.

Accreditation

A significant source of tension may exist between institutions that offer baccalaureate degrees in the nutrition and food sciences and the ADA and Institute of Food Technologists (IFT), which accredit or approve many of the programs. Both disciplines benefit from this credentialing or approval process, but meeting the requirements outlined by these professional associations makes demands on departmental curricular resources and may limit student development.

ADA has an extensive set of highly structured curricular requirements and faculty-supervised criteria that leads to the credentialing of students as R.D.s. Credentialing requirements may serve the practical needs of students and employers, but they do not ensure that the academic accomplishments of undergraduates are comparable to those of students in the basic sciences. Credentialing requirements also may have the effect of encouraging undergraduates who desire an R.D. to focus on vocational needs rather than fully explore the basic sciences and more specialized aspects of human nutrition. Furthermore, paths taken by various institutions to meet credentialing requirements increase the difficulty of completing an undergraduate degree in four years. An additional consequence of ADA requirements is that they diffuse resources away from departmental or institutional efforts to begin training students to critically evaluate research in the nutrition and food sciences and to become competent investigators.

Programs that lead to a bachelor's degree and an R.D. tend to be more popular than nutrition science programs because the former are more directly linked with immediate career opportunities, and are therefore important to nutrition departments that offer undergraduate degrees. However, when financial resources are reduced or limited, nutrition departments walk a tightrope between the potential loss of "practitioner" faculty and the need to maintain a rigorous, science-oriented major.

IFT requirements for programs in food science are more general, compared to ADA certification requirements, but they too reduce the flexibility of undergraduate programs and may diminish the enthusiasm or ability of faculty in the vanguard of their field to develop and introduce demanding academic courses at the early stages of a student's career. Thus, the brightest undergraduates in food science may not be sufficiently stimulated and may have more limited intellectual horizons than some of their peers in other areas of science.

We recommend that departments of nutrition and food science with high-quality research programs take the initiative and develop, in cooperation with the appropriate professional societies (e.g., ADA, IFT, and AIN), a credentialing and approval process that is fully congruent with future opportunities in the nutrition and food sciences, clearly allied to the rapid advancements in knowledge and technology, and increasingly competitive in attracting bright undergraduates who wish to pursue advanced degrees. This could be accomplished by ADA and IFT task forces, each composed of representatives of the association and faculty chairs whose departments are affected significantly by association requirements. Each task force could examine how issues of certification and accreditation are handled in other professions. Given ADA's and IFT's stated commitment to enhance the research base of dietetics and food science and technology, we urge ADA and IFT to permit greater flexibility in the undergraduate curriculum. Increased flexibility would permit a greater emphasis on basic science preparation and improve the research base for the practice of dietetics and food science. In addition, it would ensure that nutrition and food science majors trained in the best research-oriented departments would enjoy the benefits of an exciting and rigorous undergraduate major and still have a reasonable chance of passing the R.D. qualifying examination. Any concerns that some majors would escape a particular kind of practical experience could be met by specialty exams given by employers or a professional society.

GRADUATE EDUCATION

Graduate education and training in the nutrition and food sciences are configured, in part, around a student's undergraduate background and career goals. Without question, opportunities abound in these disciplines. In fact, few disciplines that offer a graduate degree provide recipients with such a wide spectrum of career opportunities. These careers include academic and industrial research in various fields of basic biological and biomedical science, administration and nutrition research in business, public health nutrition specialists in the United States and abroad, specialists in nutrition and international development, product development in industrial research, food policy analysis, and investigation into the basic aspects of cultural nutritional practices.

Because applicants to graduate programs in nutrition or food science come from a variety of backgrounds, admission requirements tend to be flexible. Most programs require a basic understanding of biology, chemistry, and mathematics. Students frequently have undergraduate coursework similar to that recommended for premedical students. The didactic phases of graduate education in the nutrition or food sciences usually have three components: (1) field-related core graduate courses, (2) basic graduate level courses, usually in basic science, and (3) courses related to career goals such as molecular biology or epidemiology. Examples of generic doctoral programs for nutrition science, food science, and public health nutrition are shown in Tables 7.1, 7.2, and 7.3, respectively. Each program is filled out with the area of specialization to conform to a student's career goals.

Required courses in nutrition often include graduate-level basic cellular and molecular biology, biochemistry, physiology, perhaps genetics and epidemiology, and one or more courses in the social sciences. In food science, core courses include graduate-level food chemistry, food microbiology, food engineering, and basic science or engineering. After prerequisites have been satisfied, students select courses that fit their career objectives. An important aspect of graduate training, particularly at the doctoral level, is the development of an in-depth knowledge base necessary for independent research. Doctoral students in nutrition science or food science may have research dissertation topics as diverse as the interaction between a nutrient and a nuclear receptor leading to gene transcription to the influence of food selection practices on the nutritional status of migrant farm workers.

TABLE 7.1 Example of a Doctoral Program for Nutrition Science

---

Prerequisites
Bachelor's degree with a strong background in the biological and physical sciences

Recommended Courses
Advanced Metabolism and Biochemistry
Carbohydrate and Lipid Nutrition
Mammalian Physiology
Mineral Nutrition
Nutritional Sciences Seminar
Proteins and Amino Acid Nutrition
Research Planning and Ethics
Statistical Methods
Vitamin Nutrition

Areas of Specialization
Nutritional Biochemistry
    This specialization may require additional courses in biochemistry, molecular and cell biology, immunology, genetics, and endocrinology.
Clinical and Human Nutrition
    This specialization may require additional courses in clinical nutrition, food chemistry, microbiology, epidemiology, endocrinology, genetics, and social sciences.

TABLE 7.2 Example of a Doctoral Program for Food Science

Prerequisites
Bachelor's degree with a strong background in the biological and physical sciences

Recommended Courses
Advanced Food Chemistry
Advanced Food Processing
Carbohydrates in Food Systems
Food Lipids and Flavor Chemistry
Food Science Seminar
Food Toxicology
Principles of Food Microbiology
Proteins and Enzymes in Food Systems
Psychophysical Aspects of Foods
Research Planning and Ethics
Statistics

Areas of Specialization
Food Chemistry/Biochemistry
    This specialization may require additional courses in chemistry, biochemistry and
    molecular biology, microbiology, nutrition science, fisheries and aquatic sciences, and
    computer science.
Food Processing/Engineering
    This specialization may require additional courses in chemistry, computer science,
    agricultural or other engineering departments, horticulture, and animal science.
Food Safety
    This specialization may require additional courses in chemistry, biochemistry and
    molecular biology, physiology, toxicology, microbiology, and environmental engineering
    sciences.

Graduate education programs in nutrition and food science departments (separate or combined) usually draw strength from graduate-level courses in the basic sciences such as biochemistry and molecular biology. They tend to have strong programs of didactic instruction and provide rich research experiences with faculty committed solely to these disciplines. When these programs are at institutions with medical programs, students can also elect to take courses that emphasize disease and its treatment as part of their didactic program. Students in all of these programs are encouraged to become fluent in the language of related disciplines (e.g., biochemistry, molecular biology, immunology, and epidemiology) through seminar programs and other contacts with scientists in these cognate areas to augment their training and career opportunities.

Students considering graduate programs should assess the extramural funding base of these programs. Extramural research grants can be used to support doctoral and postdoctoral trainees, and this would extend and

TABLE 7.3   Example of a Doctoral Program for Public Health
Nutrition

Prerequisites
Strong background in the biological and social sciences. Undergraduate study of nutrition
is preferred.

Recommended Courses
Assessment of Nutritional Status
Behavioral Science
Biostatistics (basic and multivariate)
Epidemiologic Methods and Analysis
Health Education (theory and methods)
Health Policy and Administration
Human Nutrition and Metabolism
Intervention Programs (design and evaluation)
Nutrition Seminar
Research Methods and Ethics

Areas of Specialization
Nutritional Epidemiology
    This specialization may require additional courses in biostatistics, epidemiology, human
    genetics, environmental health, disease surveillance, international health, computer
    science, and the basic biological sciences.
Nutrition Policy
    This specialization may require additional courses in public policy, economics,
    communication, health education, community organization, organizational behavior,
    computer science, mathematical modeling, and other behavioral and social sciences.
Behavioral Science and Nutrition
    This specialization may require additional courses in anthropology, psychology,
    education, communication, organizational behavior, computer science, mathematical
    modeling, and other behavioral and social sciences.

strengthen training opportunities in modern research techniques. Interaction with postdoctoral trainees will supplement the graduate student's formal and informal training provided by the research faculty. It is useful for potential students to determine the diversity of options and philosophies of the research faculty for their graduate work.

Academic Structures for Education in the
Nutrition and Food Sciences

Many different academic structures have been used to provide education and training in the nutrition and food sciences. Each has its strengths and weaknesses. The structures are based on institutional considerations that are usually both historical and fiscal. Institution involvement ranges from small centers or programs with no formal commitment of funds or faculty to those where multiple specialties exist within one administrative unit and with a substantial concomitant budget and faculty size. The extent of education and training opportunities also varies widely, ranging from a few undergraduate or graduate students to large programs with undergraduate course enrollments of 1,000 or more and 50 or more graduate students. The following description of four types of academic structures for the nutrition and food sciences provides an overview.

Departments of Nutrition

Undergraduate and graduate programs in nutrition science are offered by departments of nutrition or nutritional sciences. Administratively, they are usually in colleges of agriculture, home economics, or public health, but occasionally in colleges of medicine. Each program will reflect the research interests and expertise of its faculty. Ideally, it should support at least 15 faculty members with diverse interests in order to provide the breadth and depth of training required of students. Departments of nutrition tend to provide undergraduate-level courses in basic human nutrition that frequently serve as science electives. The courses increase the student contact hours for each department and contribute to the undergraduate experience. Student-to-faculty ratios should be about 10-to-1 overall in these departments.

Because department-based nutrition graduate programs depend on the availability of related courses elsewhere on campus, they also reflect the general nature of the institution in which they reside. It is extremely helpful if the institution with a graduate program in nutrition also has a school of medicine, veterinary medicine, public health, or department of animal science, or all of these. Faculty in those schools or departments can be given joint appointments in the nutrition department, and vice versa.

Departments of Food Science

A viable department of food science requires faculty with specialized training in chemistry, microbiology, engineering, and biotechnology. Expertise in nutrition is necessary if there is no program or department on campus. Faculty frequently hold joint appointments in other science or engineering departments related to food science. A desirable student-to-faculty ratio is 10-to-1 (including undergraduate and graduate students), primarily because of the large number of laboratory courses and hands-on laboratory training that students need.

Frequently, food science departments do not offer large survey courses unless they are linked to nutrition science. As with nutrition departments, food science departments are aided, particularly at the graduate level, by on-campus schools of medicine and engineering and by departments with applied orientations, such as animal science. Strengths of these arrangements include the applicability of research to the marketplace and the excellent potential of industrial support. Weaknesses include a limited basic focus so that financial support from NIH and the National Science Foundation (NSF) is difficult to obtain. These departments need to be of sufficient size so that the spectrum of the food sciences (in, for example, the areas of chemistry, processing, and safety) is represented to spur student interest and teach the discipline effectively.

Combined Departments of Nutrition and Food Sciences

Combined departments of nutrition and food science evolve from mergers of a variety of academic units, frequently joining faculty with similar interests from home economics or foods, biochemistry, and commodity-based departments emphasizing food processing (e.g., horticulture, poultry science, and dairy chemistry). Faculty in a combined department usually number 20 or more and have diverse research interests. This diversity increases the likelihood that a student's interests will be represented in the department, but it tends to polarize faculty as well. Faculty from combined departments often have joint appointments in other departments or schools within the institution, such as biochemistry, medicine, or toxicology. Occasionally, a few faculty members have interests at the interface between nutrition and food science. The heterogeneous nature of these combined departments can be minimized if the nutrition and food science components are represented equally. Combined departments can be located within one college or budgetary unit (e.g., college of agriculture) or within two or more colleges (e.g., college of agriculture and college of human ecology). However, it may be difficult administratively to provide unity within the department if the chair must report to deans of two colleges.

Combined departments usually have undergraduate and graduate programs. Even in combined departments, each discipline has its own unique set of course and laboratory requirements to provide in-depth training. The ability of these departments to attract research funds from extramural sources (e.g., NIH and USDA) is based upon individual faculty orientation.

Medical School and Medical Center Nutrition Programs

Several medical schools have graduate programs in nutrition. However, very few of them maintain a separate academic department of nutrition. There is much structural variety in graduate nutrition programs in medical schools, reflecting both the lack of nutrition departments and a school-by-school approach to developing the medical nutrition curriculum. Thus, the affiliation of one or more key faculty members may strongly influence its shape and location within the medical school. Some of these departments have other college affiliations and provide applied undergraduate training (e.g., dietetics). Graduate nutrition programs may be linked to another basic science discipline such as biochemistry or they may exist in liaison with a clinical program such as gastroenterology or pediatrics, with administrative oversight through an interdisciplinary graduate group in the graduate school. Most such administrative units have no graduate nutrition program. Some institutions have established an institute, center, or program of human nutrition with responsibility for graduate and clinical education in nutrition. Although there is an obvious lack of uniformity among nutrition programs in medical schools, their diversity offers prospective graduate students a variety of programs from which to choose, ranging from those that emphasize biochemical nutrition and human clinical studies to nutritional epidemiology and public health.

Graduate training leading to the Ph.D. in nutrition science often draws strength from the course offerings that already exist for medical students, including courses in biochemistry, physiology, cell biology, microscopic anatomy, histology, microbiology, and immunology. Whereas the nutrition curricula of medical schools are typically less rich in didactic instruction for graduate students than the curricula of nutrition departments in nonmedical settings, the opportunities for research in biomedical nutrition are often very strong. Medical schools tend to emphasize an understanding of disease processes. As a result, they provide students with opportunities to work closely with other health professionals on research relevant to human health and disease. The ability to attract extramural funding is usually very good for faculty in these programs. Program weaknesses center on the secondary nature of the nutrition mission within the school or center. In addition, faculty lines, which are usually based on support provided by research or training grants, are inherently unstable. Medical school- or medical center-based nutrition programs usually have good student-to-faculty ratios.

Schools of Public Health

Several graduate nutrition departments are located within schools of public health. These schools address community health needs and train practitioners who can identify the needs of diverse populations and plan, implement, and evaluate programs to address those needs. Because of their small size, most public health nutrition programs have opted to specialize in such areas as nutritional epidemiology, international nutrition, clinical nutrition, nutrition education, or community nutrition. Given the importance of nutrition to health, it is difficult to imagine a school of public health without a strong human nutrition component. Yet nutrition is not one of the five basic public health disciplines (biostatistics, epidemiology, environmental health sciences, health services administration, and the social and behavioral sciences) required for accreditation as a school of public health. We recommend that schools of public health incorporate nutrition as a sixth basic public health discipline.

TRENDS IN DOCTORATES EARNED IN THE NUTRITION AND FOOD SCIENCES AND RELATED FIELDS

The National Research Council conducts an annual survey of the number and types of doctoral degrees awarded at U.S. universities. Doctoral degrees covered in this survey include the Ph.D., Sc.D., D.Sc., and Ed.D.; professional degrees such as the M.D. and D.D.S. are excluded.

Figure 7.1 presents the number of doctorates awarded in the nutritional sciences and food sciences between 1970 and 1991. The number has increased in both disciplines over time.

Doctorates awarded between 1970 and 1992 in the allied fields of biochemistry, cellular biology, molecular biology, public health and epidemiology, and home economics are shown in Figure 7.2. The number of doctorates awarded in biochemistry exceeds by far the number awarded in these other fields and increased substantially between 1987 and 1991. Doctorates awarded in molecular biology have steadily increased between 1979 and 1992. The number of doctorates awarded in cell biology

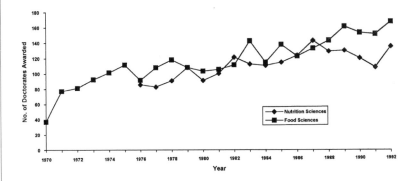

FIGURE 7.1 Number of doctorates awarded in the United States in the nutrition and food sciences, 1970-1972. National Research Council, Survey of Earned Doctorates 1970-1972. Data on doctorates awarded in the category of nutrition sciences became available in 1976.

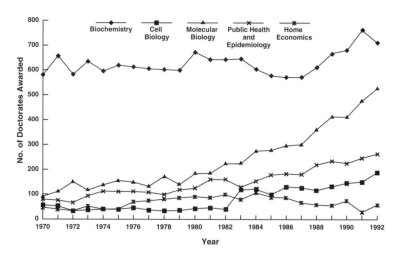

FIGURE 7.2 Number of doctorates awarded in the United States in biochemistry, cell biology, molecular biology, public health and epidemiology, and home economics, 1970-1972. National Research Council, Suvey of Earned Doctorates, 1971-972.

and public health and epidemiology has increased over the past 22 years; in contrast, doctorates awarded in home economics have not increased.

Table 7.4 presents doctorates awarded by sex in the seven fields described above for selected years. Since 1976, the nutrition sciences have shifted from awarding approximately equal numbers of doctorates to men and women to more than twice as many doctorates to women as men. More men than women receive doctorates in the food sciences, biochemistry, cell biology, and molecular biology, but the proportion of women in these fields between 1970 and 1992 has generally increased. In contrast, this 22-year period has seen the field of public health and epidemiology change substantially, from one awarding doctorates to more than three times as many men as women to one awarding 50 percent more to women than men.

The committee encourages efforts to recruit more women into the nutrition and food sciences (broadly defined), particularly as investigators, in order to achieve roughly equal numbers of men and women in these disciplines. The nutrition and food sciences are probably ahead of many other areas of science and engineering in regard to recruiting women.

Table 7.5 presents doctorates awarded in the seven fields described above by race and ethnic background for selected years. In general, relatively few Asians, blacks, and Hispanics have received doctorates in the nutrition and food sciences over the past 23 years. Of particular note, however, is the sixfold increase (from 6 to 37) in the number of Asians receiving doctorates in molecular biology between 1976 and 1992.

TABLE 7.4 Sex of Doctorate Recipients in Selected Fields for Selected Years, 1970-1992

Field	1970	1976	1980	1985	1990	1991	1992
Nutrition Sciences							
Men	—	41	28	41	30	35	37
Women	—	44	62	72	88	71	96
Food Sciences							
Men	33	70	78	103	95	101	103
Women	4	21	24	33	56	48	62
Biochemistry							
Men	486	476	485	397	441	477	432
Women	97	141	188	184	237	285	282
Cell Biology							
Men	39	32	31	61	76	87	108
Women	17	14	13	39	69	63	80
Molecular Biology							
Men	70	105	123	182	261	299	332
Women	25	43	60	95	152	182	194
Public Health and Epidemiology							
Men	63	72	70	74	89	108	106
Women	18	44	58	105	136	140	159
Home Economics							
Men	4	8	13	13	12	2	9
Women	46	60	77	77	62	28	49

SOURCE: National Research Council, Survey of Earned Doctorates, 1970-1992. Data on doctorates in the category of nutrition sciences became available in 1976.

The committee believes strongly that recruiting more racial and ethnic minorities into the nutrition and food sciences is necessary for this country to improve the diet and health of its citizens. Many nutrition problems, such as undernutrition, malnutrition, obesity, and diet-related diseases, fall disproportionately on racial and ethnic minorities, particularly those of low socioeconomic status. With more minority practitioners and researchers in the nutrition and food sciences, we would be able to develop more effective and sensitive interventions and policies.

Table 7.6 presents doctorates awarded in the seven fields described above by citizenship for selected years. Doctorates have been awarded to an increasing number of temporary residents in this country over the past several decades in most of these seven fields. This trend is particularly pronounced in the food sciences, where the number of doctorates awarded to temporary residents exceeds those awarded to U.S. citizens by more than 50 percent.

TABLE 7.5 Race and Ethnic Background of Doctorate Recipients in Selected Fields for Selected Years, 1970-1992

Field	1976	1980	1985	1990	1991	1992
Nutrition Sciences						
Asian	9	6	5	8	7	7
Black	2	3	4	I	2	3
Hispanic	I	I	2	3	5	3
Native American	0	I	0	0	I	0
White	54	66	72	73	60	82
Unknown	2	2	5	2	0	3
Food Sciences						
Asian	8	10	9	10	9	14
Black	I	0	4	4	I	2
Hispanic	I	I	I	7	3	2
Native American	0	I	I	I	I	0
White	54	49	64	47	49	50
Unknown	2	3	0	0	2	2
Biochemistry						
Asian	44	35	34	33	58	39
Black	4	7	6	12	7	11
Hispanic	6	5	8	5	12	14
Native American	0	I	2	0	I	I
White	462	517	441	459	473	446
Unknown	19	43	9	10	7	7
Cell Biology						
Asian	I	4	4	7	7	11
Black	2	0	I	2	I	0
Hispanic	0	I	2	4	4	4
Native American	0	0	I	I	0	0
White	35	33	81	104	103	130
Unknown	19	43	9	10	7	5
Molecular Biology						
Asian	6	8	15	15	37	37
Black	4	5	I	I	5	8
Hispanic	0	2	3	7	5	11
Native American	0	0	3	0	3	2
White	124	138	218	300	309	315
Unknown	4	12	4	4	7	6
Public Health and Epidemiology						
Asian	5	5	4	10	15	11
Black	7	4	9	9	15	14
Hispanic	0	2	4	5	5	5
Native American	0	0	I	0	2	0
White	83	102	126	159	153	169
Unknown	2	6	0	0	7	6
Home Economics						
Asian	0	0	3	2	0	3
Black	3	3	3	4	2	2
Hispanic	0	0	4	0	0	I
Native American	I	0	0	2	0	0
White	62	80	72	56	22	40
Unknown	0	4	0	I	0	0

SOURCE: National Research Council, Survey of Earned Doctorates, 1970-1992. Data on race and ethnic background were not available for 1970. Data for race and ethnic background are for U.S. citizens and permanent residents only.

TABLE 7.6 Citizenship of Doctorate Recipients in Selected Fields for Selected Years, 1970-1992

Field	1970	1976	1980	1985	1990	1991	1992
Nutrition Sciences							
U.S. citizens	—	58	75	86	79	65	85
Permanent residents	—	10	4	2	8	10	13
Temporary residents	—	16	9	24	26	29	46
Unknown	—	1	2	1	5	2	3
Food Sciences							
U.S. citizens	24	53	52	66	51	52	54
Permanent residents	7	13	12	13	18	13	16
Temporary residents	6	25	38	53	77	80	93
Unknown	0	0	0	4	5	4	2
Biochemistry							
U.S. citizens	470	493	589	472	487	520	482
Permanent residents	39	42	19	28	32	38	36
Temporary residents	69	57	53	69	149	198	183
Unknown	5	17	12	12	10	9	13
Cell Biology							
U.S. citizens	49	40	38	87	114	109	144
Permanent residents	3	3	4	4	5	7	6
Temporary residents	4	0	2	7	19	32	38
Unknown	0	3	0	2	7	1	0
Molecular Biology							
U.S. citizens	81	130	158	240	314	337	354
Permanent residents	7	8	7	4	13	29	25
Temporary residents	7	9	18	30	86	114	146
Unknown	0	1	0	3	0	1	1
Public Health and Epidemiology							
U.S. citizens	62	92	114	137	172	172	192
Permanent residents	3	5	5	7	11	25	13
Temporary residents	15	12	8	23	38	48	56
Unknown	1	7	1	12	4	2	4
Home Economics							
U.S. citizens	40	66	87	79	65	24	45
Permanent residents	2	0	0	3	0	0	1
Temporary residents	8	2	2	6	9	5	11
Unknown	0	0	1	2	0	0	1

SOURCE: National Research Council, Survey of Earned Doctorates, 1970-1992. Data on doctorates in the category of nutrition sciences became available in 1976.

TRAINING OF SPECIFIC TYPES OF INVESTIGATORS

Graduate education and training in the nutrition and food sciences varies depending on the focus and specialty of the student. This section addresses some of the expectations of students who wish to obtain graduate training in clinical investigation, public health nutrition, or food science.

Clinical Nutrition Investigators

Clinical nutrition has been traditionally concerned with basic knowledge relating to the diagnosis and treatment of diseases that are affected by the intake, absorption, and metabolism of food constituents. These concerns have been expanded to include health promotion and disease prevention, thus underpinning the emphasis on prevention that characterizes current discussions of health-care reform. The clinical nutrition researcher is usually an M.D. with primary training in internal medicine, pediatrics, or surgery who then undergoes further training in nutrition. Alternatively, he or she may be a Ph.D. who focuses in an area of nutrition and becomes knowledgeable about clinical aspects; such a person is likely to have received graduate training in nutrition, although some may have been trained in biochemistry, dietetics, epidemiology, molecular biology, or pharmacology. While clinical nutrition is not a recognized board under the American Board of Medical Subspecialties, the American Board of Nutrition over the past 40 years has influenced standards and guidelines for training clinical-nutrition specialists.

Generally, support for health professionals in most clinical research is fragmented, undervalued, and underfunded, particularly support for research on patients. No organized body focuses attention on and provides support to clinical investigators to ensure their survival and growth in numbers at a time of unprecedented explosions of knowledge in molecular biology, genetics, medicine, and medical information systems.

Students may come to this specialty training from a wide range of disciplines. Therefore, each student requires a specialized curriculum to be certain that he or she is trained adequately, possesses the tools to work at the frontiers of research, and has the knowledge to ask important questions. Training is required in four areas:

•   Basic biomedical science: This area includes study of biochemistry, physiology, cellular and molecular biology, and genetics.
•   Basic nutrition science: This area includes study of the biochemistry and physiology of nutrient absorption and metabolism, principles of nutritional assessment, the nutritional consequences of critical illness, and nutrition throughout the life cycle.

• Clinical knowledge: This is obtained by exposure to health promotion programs and to patients with medical, pediatric, and surgical illnesses in which nutrition plays a role. Students should also learn about the connection between eating habits in the United States and health and have a familiarity with national nutrition policies as well as food science and the food supply.

• Basic and clinical research: This training should take place under the supervision of a senior faculty investigator and include experience in basic laboratory techniques, experimental design, statistics, interpretation of data, making oral and written presentations, research ethics, and preparing grant applications.

Clinical Nutrition Research Units (CNRUs) and Obesity Nutrition Research Centers (ONRCs) can provide ideal settings for the training of clinical nutrition investigators because they support interdisciplinary research, bringing together a variety of basic scientists and clinical investigators (see Chapter 8). The training functions of CNRUs and ONRCs should be expanded and strengthened. Involvement in both formal didactic and laboratory-based training would enhance the trainees' expertise in nutrition. It would also increase the possibility that when trainees join medical and other professional and academic faculty, they will be active in the nutrition education of physicians and other health professionals.

Nutritionists in the Behavioral and Social Sciences

Nutritionists with expertise in the behavioral and social sciences are frequently trained in schools of public health that are affiliated with medical schools not directly associated with comprehensive universities. Thus, these students may have strong backgrounds in the biological sciences and basic human nutrition but lack opportunities to develop expertise in a field of social science, such as social and cultural anthropology, psychology, behavioral science, political science, health policy, communication science, or health education. In the future, schools of public health should consider offering two emphases within their graduate nutrition programs. Those affiliated with medical schools may want to develop an emphasis in the biological aspects of nutrition of populations. Students in these programs would be trained to investigate the links between public health problems and medical practice and, as professionals, would be expected to conduct research in clinical nutrition focused on individuals or populations. Schools of public health at institutions with social science departments may wish to develop an emphasis in the social and psychological influences on the nutrition of populations. Students in these programs would study the links between public health nutrition and economic and social policies. A few schools of public health may be located at institutions that would allow them to offer both the biological and social science emphases. Students in both emphases will need to develop a thorough understanding of epidemiology and biostatistics to conduct nutrition research in the biological and social sciences. In all cases, graduate students in public health nutrition should have access to a department with ongoing research in basic human nutrition.

Food Scientists and Technologists

At the graduate level in food science, research is typically conducted in specific scientific areas such as engineering, chemistry, microbiology, biotechnology, or food safety. The best departments recruit graduate students from the basic biological and physical science and engineering undergraduate programs, as well as food science and nutrition science undergraduates who have excellent backgrounds in basic science. These students are well prepared to apply their knowledge to the many research challenges in graduate programs in food science and technology. To prosper, food science departments must increase their efforts to recruit the best students. This may be accomplished, in part, through summer programs of the kind discussed earlier in this chapter and by providing increased numbers of graduate fellowships.

Food science and technology is inherently interdisciplinary. In fact, many faculty received their degrees in programs such as engineering or microbiology. The challenge is to provide training programs that include both the interdisciplinary subjects that make up the disciplines (i.e., food chemistry, food microbiology, food engineering, and nutrition) as well as advanced courses in the specialty area of study (e.g., engineering). Students will also need to acquire skills in statistics, critical thinking, technical speaking and writing, and computer technology.

Food science departments should promote interactions between their students and faculty in the traditional agriculture departments (e.g., animal science, horticulture, and agronomy) and the basic science departments (e.g., chemistry, biochemistry, and engineering). Students must be able to communicate with, associate with, and learn from students and faculty in those departments. For example, a student carrying out a biotechnological research project to increase the production of ethanol from corn should be consulting with microbiologists, biochemists, chemical engineers, and agronomists.

Efforts are under way in many departments to focus part of the training on group problem solving or group projects. This can be accomplished through a seminar course or a product development competition at the university, regional, or national level. For example, IFT sponsors a product development competition each year and encourages groups of undergraduate and graduate students at a university to join forces to create a product from concept to final package. Issues addressed by the team include engineering and processing, raw materials, cost accounting, packaging, safety, advertising, product stability, and environmental impact.

Because the food and drug industries support some of the research in food science departments and hire many of their graduates, students should take opportunities to communicate with industry personnel. Many departments bring in a variety of industrial speakers on formal and informal bases to speak with students. Summer internships with industry provide a valuable training experience for both undergraduate and graduate students in food science.

SUPPORT OF GRADUATE EDUCATION IN THE NUTRITION AND FOOD SCIENCES

The future vitality of the nutrition and food sciences will be shaped by today's students, because they become tomorrow's investigators. To encourage more students to begin careers as investigators in the nutrition and food sciences, it is imperative that funds be available to support at least partially the costs of their graduate education and training. Government funds for this purpose come almost entirely from the NIH and USDA. A brief description of their various award programs is provided in the box. Further details about the level of support are found in Chapter 8.

In FY 1991, NIH support for students and trainees at all levels in the nutrition and food sciences totaled $4.1 million. Comparable figures for USDA support in FY 1992 were $2.3 million. These sums are grossly inadequate to attract a new generation of outstanding investigators to the nutrition and food sciences—investigators who, for example, can take advantage of the biological revolution that is opening up new opportunities to study fundamental life processes at the genetic and molecular levels or who can integrate this knowledge with applications in clinical nutrition and public health. Furthermore, in many cases support of training is insubstantial and separate from the exciting advances being made in biology and technology. We believe that a program with new mechanisms would augment the current programs and provide much better linkage between the biological revolution and resulting technologies and the nutrition and food sciences.

A National Combined Pre- and Postdoctoral Program

A common theme in the comments we received from biologists around the country was that we should recommend the creation of new graduate programs for research in the nutrition and food sciences. Molecular and

NIH AND USDA SUPPORT OF
GRADUATE AND POSTGRADUATE EDUCATION

National Institutes of Health

The training of scientists for careers in the behavioral and biomedical sciences is supported primarily through National Research Service Awards (NRSAs). Training grants are awarded to institutions, and fellowships are awarded to individuals. NRSAs have two major objectives: to (1) increase the number of individuals trained for research and teaching in specifically designated biomedical areas, and (2) improve the environment in which the biomedical training is conducted. Several of the most common types of NRSA awards are described, as well as the Clinical Investigator Award.

Postdoctoral Individual (F32) NRSAs

Commonly known as fellowships, these awards provide postdoctoral research training for qualified individuals who have received a Ph.D., M.D., D.D.S., or equivalent degree. Recipients are biomedical scientists, clinicians, and others who carry out supervised research to broaden their scientific backgrounds and expand their potential for research in health-related areas. Each applicant must arrange to work with a sponsor who is affiliated with an institution that has the staff and facilities needed for the proposed training. There is national competition for these awards.

Institutional (T32) NRSAs

Commonly known as training grants, these are awarded to nonprofit, private, and nonfederal public institutions to support a training program in biomedical research at the predoctoral and postdoctoral levels. The applicant institution must have or be able to develop the staff and facilities required for the proposed program and is responsible for the selection and appointment of trainees. Institutional grants may be made for periods of up to five years and may be renewed. However, an individual may not receive more than eight years of support in the aggregate from an NRSA (five years predoctoral support and three years postdoctoral support) unless a waiver is granted.

Senior Fellowships

Senior fellowships are designed to provide opportunities for experienced scientists to make major changes in the direction of their research careers, to acquire new research capabilities, to broaden their scientific background, to enlarge their command of an allied research field, or to take time from regular professional responsibilities to increase their capabilities for engaging in health-related research.

Clinical Investigator (K08) Award

This award is designed to provide an opportunity for promising clinically-trained individuals to develop into independent biomedical investigators. It enables candidates to investigate a well-defined problem under a competent sponsor. The award is intended to facilitate the transition from postdoctoral training to a career as an independent investigator. Applicants for the award should have completed their clinical training and have had some postdoctoral research experience.

U.S. Department of Agriculture

Training of scientists for careers in human nutrition and food science is supported primarily through the National Needs Graduate Fellowships Program and the Agricultural Research Enhancement Awards.

National Needs Graduate Fellowships Program

This program, begun in 1984, awards grants to colleges and universities to encourage outstanding students to pursue and complete graduate degrees in an area of agricultural science for which development of scientific expertise has been designated by USDA as a national need. Human nutrition and food science is one of six such areas.

Agricultural Research Enhancement Awards

USDA's National Research Initiative Competitive Grants Program (NRICGP) supports training through Agricultural Research Enhancement Awards (AREA), which were first awarded in fiscal year (FY) 1991. These awards are designed to help institutions develop competitive research programs and attract scientists to careers in the agricultural sciences. AREA provides support for postdoctoral fellows and new faculty. It also includes Strengthening Awards to enhance the research capabilities of individuals at smaller institutions and those in states that have had limited success in obtaining NRICGP grants. By federal law, at least 10 percent of NRICGP funds go to AREA.

cellular biology, biochemistry, systems physiology, chemistry, toxicology, biotechnology, microbiology, and engineering were elements described as central to a graduate program in the nutrition and food sciences. In this section we describe a structured monetary incentive that, in the short term, should increase the number of scientists with expertise in nutrition or food science, or both, and in complementary disciplines such as molecular genetics, biochemistry, chemical engineering, physical anthropology, selected behavioral sciences, epidemiology, and selected areas of economics.

In the long term, it should ensure the growth of nutrition and food science departments and interdepartmental programs with state-of-the-art graduate curricula. Such support for graduate training, in turn, should ensure a continuous supply of well-trained scientists poised to apply the latest technologies to research problems in the nutrition and food sciences.

Either of the two commonly used types of administrative structures for nutrition and food science programs was considered appropriate to achieve the goals outlined above. The first would involve existing departments of nutrition and food science that had redefined or more gradually evolved scientific areas of interest to include molecular biology or the behavioral and social sciences. In the immediate future, such departments will need to strengthen faculty representation with expertise in the relevant biological, engineering, behavioral, and social sciences with research commitment to questions of significance to the nutrition or food sciences. These needs appear to be especially critical in disciplines related to molecular biology. While the overall graduate curriculum in a nutrition or food science department is expected to have a strong bias toward cellular and molecular biology, biochemistry, and systems physiology (or toward the physical sciences for food engineers), the behavioral sciences also serve as key disciplines.

The second organization would be appropriate for institutions without formal nutrition or food science departments. In such cases, establishing interdepartmental programs should be considered. A truly interdisciplinary curriculum would ensure an appropriate balance of basic biology, molecular biology, biochemistry, physiology, the behavioral and social sciences, and, particularly for food science, the physical sciences and engineering-related disciplines. In both organizational schemes, the best and most economical solution would be to tap into existing interdisciplinary curricula or to encourage the institution to develop new ones. Several existing departments and programs would be able to take advantage of such interdepartmental curricula. This approach integrates nutrition and food science graduate students with students in the basic biological sciences or other fields of study. Some existing examples of these types of organizations are described in this chapter.

Description of Program

The key feature of this program would be guaranteed stipends for the last three years of graduate work and the first three years of postdoctoral work. To create and maintain a viable program, at least 10 awards should be provided per year. We envisage the program being funded by NIH and USDA, perhaps with the help of NSF and private foundations. Fellowships should be awarded on a national basis to ensure that only students of the highest caliber participate. The competition would be much the same as that for individual NRSAs. Application to such a program would be restricted to graduate students in their second or third years of study, when most students are able to choose a future course for their training. In addition, the students' coursework and initial research activities should be well under way, making it possible to select students on a more informed basis than just grade-point average or Graduate Record Examination scores. Under most circumstances, a student's existing graduate program would sponsor the application and would be where the ensuing work took place.

The postdoctoral laboratory and institution would not be selected until about one year before completion of the Ph.D. and would preferably be different from the student's graduate institution. This arrangement is generally better for development of a student's research career because it permits experiences in a variety of different scientific environments. Choice of the postdoctoral laboratory would be made by the student, with advice from faculty in his or her predoctoral program. The head of the laboratory chosen for the postdoctoral training and a national monitoring committee of the granting agency would have to concur in the proposed training program. The role of this monitoring committee would be primarily to ensure adherence to the philosophy of the combined pre- and postdoctoral program. The national monitoring committee should be composed of extramural scientists who are expert in the nutrition and food sciences, since agency and foundation administrators might not be sufficiently knowledgeable to prevent abuses. Failure to work in a laboratory approved by the national monitoring committee would trigger payback, as would failure to continue in research.

The national program would work in two ways. First, a student would obtain a Ph.D. degree in nutrition or food science. Then he or she would enter a postdoctoral laboratory in a complementary discipline that is not located in a nutrition or food science department. The research program of the laboratory chosen as the site for postdoctoral training and the fellow's research topic should have a clear relation to the nutrition or food sciences. (Benefits of the student's training in nutrition or food science to the postdoctoral training should be identifiable.) In this scenario, the student gets training in nutrition or food science during the Ph.D. program and advanced training in a complementary discipline during the postdoctoral program. Formal instruction during the postdoctoral period would be as required to support the approved research project.

In the second scheme, a student would obtain sound academic and research training in a supporting discipline (e.g., molecular biology, physical anthropology, or engineering). The student would then select a postdoctoral laboratory within a department or program in nutrition or food science. As expected from the first scheme, anticipated benefits of the student's doctoral training should be evident from the application. In this second scheme, formal instruction in nutrition or food science would be required. In nutrition, such courses should emphasize experimental nutrition and systems physiology; in food science, they should emphasize food engineering and food chemistry.

If the national program proved successful, it might be possible to establish training programs on an institutional level. These would involve formal agreements between institutions to provide pre- or postdoctoral training, or both, on a reciprocal basis or interinstitutional training programs. Such local programs could take advantage of special training environments or research emphases to recruit students with specific interests.

CONCLUDING REMARKS

In this chapter, we have made recommendations to attract motivated and achievement-oriented students to the nutrition and food sciences and improve their education and training at the undergraduate and graduate levels. Implementing them should increase the pool of competent, successful investigators whose research advances these disciplines. The future vitality of the nutrition and food sciences also depends on sufficient financial resources from government, industry, and private nonprofit organizations to support research, education, and training of students and the institutions where these activities take place. We turn to these topics in Chapter 8.

8

Support of the Nutrition and Food Sciences

Since World War II, the United States has produced the world's pre-eminent health research enterprise, funded almost entirely by three autonomous sources: government, industry, and private nonprofit organizations. These sources fund and conduct research in the nutrition and food sciences; however, precise data on funding are not available for all of them.

RESEARCH AND FUNDING OF RESEARCH BY GOVERNMENT

The federal government estimates its annual expenditures on research and research training in the nutrition and food sciences to be more than one-third of a billion dollars each year. Because the National Institutes of Health (NIH) and U.S. Department of Agriculture (USDA) provide approximately 90 percent of these funds, we focus on these two agencies in this chapter. Tables 8.1 and 8.2 summarize federal expenditures, in actual and constant dollars, respectively, on nutrition research and training. In fiscal year (FY) 1991 (the most recently available data), these expenditures totaled $421 million, an increase of 20 percent in constant dollars from FY 1983, when these expenditures were first reported. Federal expenditures in constant dollars reached a peak in FY 1988, declined for two years, then increased somewhat in FY 1991, indicating overall that

TABLE 8.1 Actual Federal Expenditures (in millions of dollars) to Support Human Nutrition and Nutrition Research Training

	FY 1983	FY 1984	FY 1985	FY 1986	FY 1987	FY 1988	FY 1989	FY 1990	FY 1991 (estimated)
NIH	$ 164	$ 193	$ 207	$ 213	$ 261	$ 276	$ 287	$ 292	$ 311
USDA	49	53	60	61	68	70	65	62	64
Other DHHS agencies	8	10	14	18	20	24	26	25	37
Other non-DHHS agencies	9	12	10	12	8	14	11	8	9
TOTAL	$ 231	$ 268	$ 292	$ 304	$ 357	$ 384	$ 389	$ 387	$ 421

NOTE: NIH: National Institutes of Health. USDA: U.S. Department of Agriculture. Other DHHS agencies: National Center for Health Statistics; Food and Drug Administration; Health Resources Services Administration; Centers for Disease Control; and Alcohol, Drug Abuse, and Mental Health Administration. Other non-DHHS agencies: includes U.S. Departments of Commerce, Defense, and Veterans Affairs; U.S. Agency for International Development; National Aeronautics and Space Administration; and National Science Foundation.

SOURCE: Annual reports of NIH Nutrition Coordinating Committee, *National Institutes of Health Program in Biomedical and Behavioral Nutrition Research and Training.*

TABLE 8.2 Federal Expenditures (in millions of constant dollars) to Support Human Nutrition and Nutrition Research Training

	FY 1983	FY 1984	FY 1985	FY 1986	FY 1987	FY 1988	FY 1989	FY 1990	FY 1991 (estimated)
NIH	$164	$182	$186	$184	$214	$215	$213	$205	$206
USDA	49	50	54	53	56	55	48	43	42
Other DHHS agencies	8	9	13	16	16	19	19	18	24
Other non-DHHS agencies	9	11	9	10	7	11	8	6	6
TOTAL	$231	$253	$263	$263	$292	$300	$288	$271	$278

NOTE: Calculations are based on NIH Biomedical Research and Development Price Index. FY 1983 = 100%. NIH: National Institutes of Health. USDA: U.S. Department of Agriculture. Other DHHS agencies: National Center for Health Statistics; Food and Drug Administration; Health Resources Services Administration; Centers for Disease Control; and Alcohol, Drug Abuse, and Mental Health Administration. Other non-DHHS agencies: includes U.S. Departments of Commerce, Defense, and Veterans Affairs; U.S. Agency for International Development; National Aeronautics and Space Administration; and National Science Foundation.

SOURCE: Annual reports of NIH Nutrition Coordinating Committee, *National Institutes of Health Program in Biomedical and Behavioral Nutrition Research and Training.*

investments in nutrition and food science research are not keeping pace with inflation.

Several government reports of the late 1970s concluded that human nutrition research activities by the federal government were fragmented, uncoordinated, and generally unresponsive to the changing health problems of Americans. In partial response to this criticism, the Interagency Committee on Human Nutrition Research (ICHNR) was established, along with the computerized database known as the Human Nutrition Research Information Management System (HNRIMS).

The ICHNR exists to improve the coordination and increase the effectiveness and productivity of federal agencies engaged in nutrition research. It also coordinates the collection, compilation, and dissemination of information on nutrition research. The committee is co-chaired by the Assistant Secretary for Health of the Department of Health and Human Services (DHHS) and the Assistant Secretary for Science and Education of USDA. Members include representatives of DHHS (NIH and the Food and Drug Administration), USDA (Agricultural Research Service and the Human Nutrition Information Service), National Science Foundation, Department of Defense, Agency for International Development, Department of Veterans Affairs, National Aeronautics and Space Administration, Office of Science and Technology Policy, and Department of Commerce. The HNRIMS computer database provides an accounting of the government's human nutrition research activities. It is maintained and updated by NIH's Division of Nutrition Research Coordination (DNRC) under the auspices of the ICHNR. Descriptions of each research project are available through the publicly available online retrieval system of DIALOG Information Services, Inc.

The National Institutes of Health (NIH)

NIH, the principal biomedical research arm of DHHS, contributed three-quarters of total federal expenditures in support of nutrition research and training in FY 1991. Tables 8.3 and 8.4 summarize (in actual and constant dollars, respectively) NIH expenditures by institute, center, and division in support of nutrition research and training. NIH nutrition research and training dollars have increased steadily from $144.3 million in FY 1982 to $343.8 million in FY 1992. In constant dollars, this represents an increase in funding of 43 percent over 10 years. NIH reports that expenditures for nutrition research and training have consistently represented approximately 4 percent of total NIH obligations during that time. It coordinates its nutrition research, training, and educational activities through its DNRC.

NIH has made major contributions in developing the scientific base for modern nutrition science and in translating these findings to the public. Most NIH institutes have made significant contributions. For example, NIDDK is a leader in supporting many fundamental areas of nutrition research, and most recently research on obesity. NHLBI and NCI are central players in efforts to alter dietary practices in this country to prevent and treat cardiovascular disease and cancer, the two major causes of death. NICHD has been active in developing our understanding of the role of diet in early life. NIA supports and conducts research to determine the ways that nutrition influences the onset and progression of aging.

NIH defines nutrition research as that "designed to assess the consequences of food or nutrient intake and utilization in the intact organism, including humans, and the metabolic and behavioral mechanisms involved. These studies encompass investigation of nutrient variables at the cellular or subcellular level." This definition also includes:

• Research designed to elucidate the metabolic role or function of nutrients in both animal models and humans.

• All studies concerned with genetic-nutrient-environmental interactions where a nutrient is a variable.

• Dietary studies expected to produce significant changes in health status, including the maintenance of health and the treatment of disease in humans. Such studies might include clinical trials, epidemiological studies, metabolic studies, surveillance, and nutritional status monitoring studies.

• Research on factors related to the causes, prevention, and treatment of obesity.

Table 8.5 provides figures for the number of NIH grants and contracts in the classification categories used by HNRIMS. In the 41 research categories, six areas received more than 300 grants or contracts in FY 1992: cardiovascular disease; cancer; other diseases; other conditions; lipids; and disease prevention. Fewer than 10 awards were made in effects of technology on foods and diets; other research in food science; other research in nutrition education; and effects of government policy and socioeconomic factors.

NIH supports both extramural and intramural research. Of the $343.8 million spent by NIH on nutrition research and training in FY 1992, approximately 95 percent went to extramural projects. It supports extramural nutrition research through research project grants, program project grants, center grants, contracts, cooperative agreements, training grants, fellowships, and other awards. Awards for extramural research are based on peer-review assessments of scientific merit and relevance to NIH programs. Table 8.6 provides the most recent figures available for NIH ex-

TABLE 8.3 Actual NIH Expenditures (in millions of dollars) to Support Human Nutrition and Nutrition Research Training

	FY 1982	FY 1983	FY 1984	FY 1985	FY 1986
NCI	$ 30.6	$ 37.3	$ 50.1	$ 45.2	$ 46.2
NHLBI	35.4	38.4	44.6	45.7	49.3
NIDR	1.5	2.1	1.4	1.8	1.2
NIADDK	27.0	33.3	36.0	46.0	—
NIDDK	—	—	—	—	44.7
NINCDS	2.8	2.5	2.7	2.9	2.2
NINDS	—	—	—	—	—
NIAID	1.9	1.6	1.6	1.7	1.8
NIGMS	1.8	2.1	2.3	2.3	2.3
NICHD	18.4	20.2	24.1	26.8	27.7
NEI	5.3	5.6	4.6	5.5	5.2
NIEHS	1.6	1.4	1.8	5.4	4.5
NIA	3.3	4.4	4.8	4.6	5.3
NIAMS	—	—	—	—	2.8
NIDCD	—	—	—	—	—
DRR	14.8	15.4	18.9	19.4	19.5
NCRR	—	—	—	—	—
FIC	—	0	0.1	0	0.1
NCNR	—	—	—	—	0.3
TOTAL	$ 144.3	$ 164.3	$ 192.9	$ 207.3	$ 213.0

NOTE: NCI: National Cancer Institute; NHLBI: National Heart, Lung, and Blood Institute; NIDR: National Institute of Dental Research; NIADDK: National Institute of Arthritis, Diabetes, and Digestive and Kidney Diseases; NIDDK: National Institute of Diabetes and Digestive and Kidney Diseases; NINCDS: National Institute of Neurological and Communicative Disorders and Stroke; NINDS: National Institute of Neurological Disorders and Stroke; NIAID: National Institute of Allergy and Infectious Diseases; NIGMS: National Institute of General Medical Sciences; NICHD: National Institute of Child Health and Human Devel-

penditures by category of support. While the number of projects increased slightly, their dollar value increased substantially.

In 1979, as a means of initiating or supporting multidisciplinary research in clinical nutrition at biomedical research institutions, NIH established Clinical Nutrition Research Units (CNRUs), followed more recently by Obesity Nutrition Research Centers (ONRCs). Related functions of these nutrition/obesity research centers are to enhance patient care and promote good health while improving the education of medical students, house staff, practicing physicians, and allied health personnel in clinical nutrition. CNRUs and ONRCs bring together basic scientists and clinical investigators within a university medical center to conduct collaborative

FY 1987	FY 1988	FY 1989	FY 1990	FY 1991	FY 1992 (estimated)
$ 52.7	$ 59.6	$ 64.5	$ 67.0	$ 74.8	$ 83.7
57.3	60.3	64.3	61.8	58.0	65.1
1.8	1.5	1.6	1.8	2.4	3.4
—	—	—	—	—	—
54.7	60.2	64.0	67.5	70.2	74.8
3.4	3.2	—	—	—	—
—	—	1.1	1.1	1.9	1.9
2.7	3.5	3.8	4.1	4.4	5.2
2.7	2.5	2.0	2.3	2.5	2.8
32.9	34.4	31.2	28.9	31.7	32.9
6.5	6.9	6.1	9.0	11.7	15.0
12.9	9.9	10.3	8.6	4.1	4.0
6.9	7.6	8.5	10.1	15.7	19.2
3.4	4.1	4.1	4.4	4.8	5.2
—	—	1.2	2.0	2.1	2.4
22.1	22.1	23.8	—	—	—
—	—	—	23.1	25.3	25.0
0.1	0	0.1	0.1	0.1	0.1
0.5	0.4	0.5	0.7	1.1	3.4
$ 260.6	$ 276.2	$ 287.0	$ 292.4	$ 310.8	$ 343.8

opment; NEI: National Eye Institute; NIEHS: National Institute of Environmental Health Sciences; NIA: National Institute on Aging; NIAMS: National Institute of Arthritis and Musculoskeletal Diseases; NIDCD: National Institute on Deafness and Other Communication Disorders; DRR: Division of Research Resources; NCRR: National Center for Research Resources; FIC: Fogarty International Center; NCNR: National Center for Nursing Research.

research in clinical nutrition, thereby increasing the potential for accomplishments greater than those possible through individually conducted projects. Today, there are eight CNRUs and four ONRCs. NIDDK established five of the eight CNRUS and the four ONRCs; these latter centers focus on obesity and related eating disorders. The remaining three CNRUs, established by NCI, focus on cancer. CNRUs and ONRCs have increased the scope and intensity of education in nutrition for health professionals and have pioneered new research areas by providing seed funds for pilot studies that form the basis for more thorough investigations over time. Special core facilities are available at each of the CNRUs and ONRCs as a shared resource for researchers and clinicians to apply state-of-the-art techniques.

TABLE 8.4 NIH Expenditures (in millions of constant dollars) to Support Human Nutrition and Nutrition Research Training

	FY 1982	FY 1983	FY 1984	FY 1985	FY 1986
NCI	$ 30.6	$ 35.2	$ 44.7	$ 38.4	$ 37.7
NHLBI	35.4	36.2	39.8	38.8	40.2
NIDR	1.5	2.0	1.2	1.5	1.0
NIADDK	27.0	31.4	32.1	39.0	—
NIDDK	—	—	—	—	36.4
NINCDS	2.8	2.4	2.4	2.5	1.8
NINDS	—	—	—	—	—
NIAID	1.9	1.5	1.4	1.4	1.5
NIGMS	1.8	2.0	2.1	2.0	1.9
NICHD	18.4	19.1	21.5	22.8	22.6
NEI	5.3	5.3	4.1	4.7	4.2
NIEHS	1.6	1.3	1.6	4.6	3.7
NIA	3.3	4.2	4.3	3.9	4.3
NIAMS	—	—	—	—	2.3
NIDCD	—	—	—	—	—
DRR	14.8	14.5	16.9	16.5	15.9
NCRR	—	—	—	—	—
FIC	—	0	0.1	0	0.1
NCNR	—	—	—	—	0.2
TOTAL	$ 144.3	$ 155.0	$ 172.1	$ 176.0	$ 173.6

NOTE: Calculations are based on NIH Biomedical Research and Development Price Index. FY 1982 = 100%.

A major function of the nutrition/obesity research centers is the education of health professionals as well as the public in improved nutritional practices.

In April 1993, NIH announced the formation of a Bionutrition Initiative to expand the science base of human nutrition; increase our knowledge of nutritional interventions to prevent, cure, or treat nutrition-related afflictions; and use this knowledge to improve and refine dietary guidance for the public. The term "bionutrition" was coined to designate the special opportunities that molecular and genetic techniques offer for enriching the nutrition sciences. A Bionutrition Advisory Council composed of academic scientists is being established to help design and implement the Initiative. NIH plans to establish an identifiable intramural presence to support bionutrition research, stressing collaborative research opportunities within NIH and with other relevant federal agencies.

FY 1987	FY 1988	FY 1989	FY 1990	FY 1991	FY 1992 (estimated)
$ 40.7	$ 43.9	$ 45.1	$ 44.3	$ 47.2	$ 50.4
44.3	44.4	45.0	40.9	36.6	39.2
1.4	1.1	1.1	1.2	1.5	2.0
—	—	—	—	—	—
42.3	44.3	44.8	44.6	44.3	45.0
2.6	2.4	—	—	—	—
—	—	0.8	0.7	1.2	1.1
2.1	2.6	2.7	2.7	2.8	3.1
2.1	1.8	1.4	1.5	1.6	1.7
25.4	25.3	21.8	19.1	20.0	19.8
5.0	5.1	4.3	6.0	7.4	9.0
10.0	7.3	7.2	5.7	2.6	2.4
5.3	5.6	5.9	6.7	9.9	11.6
2.6	3.0	2.9	2.9	3.0	3.1
—	—	0.8	1.3	1.3	1.4
17.1	16.3	16.7	—	—	—
—	—	—	15.3	16.0	15.0
0.1	0	0.1	0.1	0.1	0.1
0.4	0.3	0.3	0.5	0.7	2.0
$ 201.5	$ 203.3	$ 200.8	$ 193.4	$ 196.3	$ 206.9

Committee Recommendations to NIH

Increase the level of support of nutrition research and training through the Bionutrition Initiative We recognize the long-term commitment to nutrition research and training by NIH and commend the promise of an even greater intellectual and financial commitment through the Bionutrition Initiative. Five of the 10 leading causes of death in the United States are diet-related, and a large portion of the nation's health-care bill results from diseases that can be prevented or ameliorated in part through diet. Thus, the nutrition sciences really do need increased research emphasis.

Approximately four cents of every $100 spent on health care in this country is directed to nutrition research. This level of funding is in stark contrast to the much greater amount spent by the public on dietary nostrums and products of questionable value. It is important that NIH generously support a balanced portfolio of research in key nutrition areas through

TABLE 8.5 Number of NIH Grants and Contracts in FY 1983 and FY 1992 to Support Human Nutrition and Nutrition Research Training, by HNRIMS Classification Category

HNRIMS Classification Category	FY 1983 Grants and Contracts	FY 1992 Grants and Contracts (estimated)
Maternal nutrition	98	126
Infant and child nutrition	325	219
Adolescent nutrition	33	62
Adult nutrition	28	92
Nutrition of the elderly	109	153
Cardiovascular disease and nutrition	293	467
Cancer and nutrition	694	501
Other diseases and nutrition	245	490
Trauma (burns) and nutrition	33	34
Infection, immunology, and nutrition	148	115
Obesity, anorexia, and appetite control	235	233
Genetics and nutrition	256	139
Nutrition and function	311	159
Nutrient-nutrient/drug/toxicant interactions	315	237
Other conditions and nutrition	41	362
Research on nutritional status	302	129
Carbohydrates	100	165
Lipids (fats and oils)	331	363
Alcohols	32	13
Proteins and amino acids	232	230
Vitamins	417	281
Minerals and trace elements	213	259
Water and electrolytes	96	86
Fiber	25	10
Other nutrients in food	17	16
Food composition	34	14
Bioavailability	48	25
Effects of technology on foods/diets	13	3
Other research in food science	10	7
Food consumption surveys, research, and development	23	10
Research on dietary practices, food consumption, etc.	57	100
Methods for educating and informing the public	77	32
Other research in nutrition education	9	6
Effects of government policy and socioeconomic factors	2	3
Parenteral, enteral, and elemental nutrition	75	48
Prevention of disease	1,161	402
International research	37	27
Epidemiological research	176	99
Education for professionals	68	39
Education for the public	16	36
Clinical trials	—	94

SOURCE: Annual reports of the Division of Nutrition Research Coordination, *National Institutes of Health Program in Biomedical and Behavioral Nutrition Research and Training.*

TABLE 8.6 Actual NIH Obligations (in millions of dollars) in FY 1983 and FY 1992 to Support Human Nutrition Research and Training, by Number of Grants and Contracts and Category of Support

Category of Support	FY 1983	FY 1992	FY 1983 Expenditures	FY 1992 Expenditures (estimated)
Extramural				
Research grants	1,355	1,691	$ 87.4	$ 204.6
Program projects	83	87	19.2	38.9
Contracts	108	149	13.0	31.9
Centers	66	56	12.5	15.4
Research resources support	274	133	15.6	24.7
Reimbursement agreements	15	27	1.0	5.5
Career development awards	57	77	1.2	3.0
New investigator research awards	76	—	2.3	—
Facilities renovation/repair	—	—	—	—
Training (training grants and fellowships)	100	84	3.4	3.9
Intramural				
Projects	91	112	$ 8.1	$ 15.9
Training	10	3	0.7	Not available
TOTAL			$ 164.3	$ 343.8

SOURCES: Annual reports of the Division of Nutrition Research Coordination, *National Institutes of Health Program in Biomedical and Behavioral Nutrition Research and Training* and personal communication with Dr. Susan M. Pilch, Deputy Coordinator of the DNRC, March 1993.

the mechanisms of individual research (R01) grants, center grants, program project grants, and clinical trials. In addition, NIH support for nutrition training programs should be enhanced. This support is required to train new investigators in nutrition at the cutting edge of science (e.g., in areas such as molecular biology, molecular genetics, and biophysics) so that they can compete with other applicants for NIH research funds.

Ensure that nutrition scientists are adequately represented in NIH study sections that evaluate proposals for nutrition research All research proposals submitted to NIH for grant or contract funding are peer reviewed. The first, most important level of review is performed by scientific review committees, composed primarily of nonfederal scientists with expertise in the areas for which the group has review responsibilities. The 17-member Nutrition Study Section seems appropriately composed. However, many of the other 83 study sections that evaluate proposals with significant nutrition components—including those on behavioral medicine, biopsychology, epidemiology and disease control, general medicine, metabolic pathology, and metabolism—may not have sufficient representation. We recommend that a panel of extramural scientists containing a majority of nutrition experts review the actual composition of each study section and advise NIH as to the appropriate numbers of reviewers with nutrition expertise for each.

Ensure that the nutrition sciences have strong representation in NIH   The nutrition sciences must be represented more strongly within NIH through means that go beyond the DNRC. One way to do this is to establish an advisory group on nutrition, similar to the National Diabetes Advisory Board within NIDDK, which advises and makes recommendations to the NIH director, NIDDK director, and the heads of other appropriate federal agencies. Another option is to establish a Division of Nutrition within an institute, probably NIDDK, since it contributes more of its funds (11.3 percent) to nutrition research than any other NIH institute. Its research programs would gain in coherence and in the competition for support if a Division of Nutrition were formed and directed by a strong leader. This division could initiate calls for specific research, oversee program and center grants, nurture training programs and act as an advocate for young investigator awards, and possibly develop clinical trial initiatives. A Division of Nutrition within NIDDK could be a great stimulus for support of nutrition research.

We encourage the other institutes of NIH—including NHLBI, NCI, NICHD, NIGMS, and NIA—to develop organized programs in nutrition. The disciplines with which the above-named institutes are concerned relate to nutrition in important ways yet do not have the coherent programs or divisional status that would ensure the development and maintenance of adequate nutrition programs. Ideally, these programs would include program project grants, centers, and R01 awards.

Initiate a process to evaluate the efficacy of increasing support to current CNRUs and ONRCs and determine the appropriate number of nutrition/ obesity research centers   The eight CNRUs and four ONRCs in operation have succeeded in gathering together critical masses of scientists in their institutions to develop centers of excellence for research and training in nutrition. This kind of success is all too rare in medical schools around the country. CNRUs and ONRCs are effective mechanisms for expanding nutritional science and for putting the results into medical practice, but they may require strengthening of personnel and support for fundamental work to make up for funding cuts of previous years. At present, the average annual grant to the CNRUs and ONRCs is approximately

$500,000 per year, with a maximum of $700,000. It is likely that CNRUs and ONRCs should receive more funding and that the desirable number is substantially more than the 12 that exist today. We recommend that NIH initiate a process (perhaps through the American Society for Clinical Nutrition) to evaluate the efficacy of increasing support to CNRUs and ONRCs and determine the number needed to enhance research and training in clinical nutrition by making a real impact in the training of new researchers, in the initiation of new research, and in the development of new treatment modalities.

Establish new Specialized Centers of Research (SCORS) in nutrition through requests for applications (RFAs) and peer review SCORS, funded by various NIH institutes, have generally been a great success in providing opportunities for collaborative basic and clinical research on particular problems. SCORS encourage outstanding research and provide a venue for outstanding training of investigators. Much of the research within SCORS is at a more fundamental level than that conducted in the CNRUs and ONRCs. In some medical schools they may be based in a basic science rather than a clinical department. We also recommend that NIH initiate a process, similar to the one recommended above for CNRUs and ONRCs, to determine the number of SCORS needed to enhance training in fundamental biomedical and clinical nutrition.

Ensure that the NIH Women's Health Agenda and Minority Health Initiative have strong nutrition components NIH has established the Women's Health Agenda (WHA) and Minority Health Initiative (MHI) to support research that facilitates prevention strategies and clinical therapies to eradicate disease and improve the quality of life for women and minorities. Another important purpose of these programs is to recruit more women and minorities to careers in the biomedical sciences. Given that the nutrition and food sciences play such a critical role in preventing disease and disability in these populations, the WHA and MHI should support extensive research in these disciplines and create incentives to attract more women and minorities to them for careers as investigators.

U.S. Department of Agriculture

For more than a century, USDA has supported research in the nutrition and food sciences, primarily through its state agricultural experiment stations. Wilbur O. Atwater, the first director of USDA's Office of Experiment Stations, studied energy metabolism and the composition of foods. In 1884, at the urging of Atwater and his supporters, Congress for the first time provided USDA with funds earmarked for nutrition and food science research, specifically on the nutritive value of foods and on developing economical ways of building nutritious diets. Then, in the first half of this century, USDA and its experiment stations supported what turned out to be a very exciting period of discovery of essential nutrients, elucidating their metabolic roles and quantitating their presence in foods. In 1977, Congress designated USDA as the lead federal agency for nutrition research.

Today, however, USDA contributes only about 16 percent of total federal expenditures for human nutrition research. Tables 8.7 and 8.8 summarize USDA expenditures, in actual and constant dollars, respectively, for nutrition. While the dollar amount has grown from $43.5 million in FY 1982 to $72.2 million in FY 1991, that represents less than a 5 percent increase in funding in constant dollars over a 10-year period. In contrast to research, its expenditures for human nutrition education and information totaled $178.2 million in FY 1991.

A USDA scientist recently prepared a 10-year summary of funding and scientist-years committed to food, nutrition, and other agricultural research in the United States (Table 8.9). This analysis is particularly valuable because, in addition to accounting for USDA intramural and extramural funds, it accounted as best it could for state appropriations and miscellaneous funds to universities that complemented the USDA extramural funds. Between 1981 and 1991, total agricultural research system expenditures increased from $1,551.7 billion to $2,833.0 billion, while the total system commitment in scientist-years remained relatively constant (11,716 to 11,212). During this same period, the percentage of funds spent by USDA on intramural agricultural research declined from 36.7 percent to 29.9 percent. The summary report concludes that food science and technology research (which includes food safety, food processing, and food quality maintenance) declined from approximately 5.2 percent of total agricultural system research expenditures in 1981 to 4.7 percent in 1991. The number of scientist-years committed to this research decreased from 677 to 550. Similarly, research in human nutrition (which includes human nutrition and food choices) declined from approximately 3.6 percent of total agricultural system research expenditures in 1981 to 3.3 percent in 1991. The number of scientist-years committed to this research decreased from 341 to 268.

This trend of decreased federal funding (when adjusted for inflation) and effort is disturbing because of the exciting challenges and opportunities in the nutrition and food sciences that we face today and that lie ahead. Returns on investment of research in both of these areas should be excellent in terms of improving the health of Americans and expanding production and export of value-added food products.

USDA human nutrition research and education activities focus on the

TABLE 8.7 Actual USDA Expenditures (in millions of dollars) to Support Human Nutrition Research

	FY 1982	FY 1983	FY 1984	FY 1985	FY 1986	FY 1987	FY 1988	FY 1989	FY 1990	FY 1991
ARS	$ 25.5	$ 31.7	$ 34.3	$ 36.9	$ 37.8	$ 40.6	$ 44.3	$ 45.7	$ 47.9	$ 49.6
CSRS	8.7	7.8	7.7	7.7	7.5	7.5	7.7	6.9	8.1	10.7
HNIS	8.0	6.7	5.3	6.0	12.8	6.1	7.1	7.7	7.9	8.5
ERS	1.4	0.9	0.7	0.7	1.1	1.2	0.8	0.9	0.9	1.1
FNS	0	0.7	5.4	1.4	1.5	0.5	0.5	0.6	2.8	2.3
TOTAL	$ 43.5	$ 47.8	$ 53.4	$ 52.7	$ 60.7	$ 55.9	$ 60.4	$ 61.8	$ 67.6	$ 72.2

NOTE: Figures include both intramural and extramural research. ARS: Agricultural Research Service; CSRS: Cooperative State Research Service; HNIS: Human Nutrition Information Service; ERS: Economic Research Service; FNS: Food and Nutrition Service.

SOURCE: Annual reports of USDA to Congress, *Report on USDA Human Nutrition Research and Education Activities*.

TABLE 8.8 USDA Expenditures (in millions of constant dollars) to Support Human Nutrition Research

	FY 1982	FY 1983	FY 1984	FY 1985	FY 1986	FY 1987	FY 1988	FY 1989	FY 1990	FY 1991
ARS	$ 25.5	$ 29.9	$ 30.6	$ 31.3	$ 30.8	$ 31.4	$ 32.6	$ 32.0	$ 31.7	$ 31.3
CSRS	8.7	7.4	6.9	6.5	6.1	5.8	5.7	4.8	5.4	6.8
HNIS	8.0	6.3	4.7	5.1	10.4	4.7	5.2	5.4	5.2	5.4
ERS	1.4	0.8	0.6	0.6	0.9	0.9	0.6	0.6	0.6	0.7
FNS	0	0.7	4.8	1.2	1.2	0.4	0.4	0.4	1.9	1.5
TOTAL	$ 43.5	$ 45.1	$ 47.6	$ 44.7	$ 49.6	$ 43.2	$ 44.5	$ 43.2	$ 44.8	$ 45.6

NOTE: Calculations are based on NIH Biomedical Research and Development Price Index. FY 1982 = 100%.

TABLE 8.9　USDA and University-Supported Research (in millions of dollars) in the Nutrition and Food Sciences

Research Expenditure	1981	1983	1985	1987	1989	1991
Total agricultural	$1,551.7	$1,739.7	$1,957.3	$2,143.2	$2,447.7	$2,833.0
Total food science and technology	80.5	84.8	90.7	95.6	108.0	133.4
Food safety	33.9	36.3	37.7	37.8	43.0	57.4
Food processing	42.9	45.4	50.1	54.1	60.7	69.6
Food quality maintenance	3.7	3.1	2.9	3.7	4.3	6.4
Total human nutrition	55.9	60.0	74.6	82.1	85.4	94.0
Human nutrition	47.1	54.7	63.3	70.4	77.0	84.5
Food choices	8.8	5.3	11.3	11.7	8.4	9.5

SOURCE: Current Research Information System (CRIS). Research in food science and technology includes the categories of food safety, food processing, and food quality maintenance. Research in human nutrition includes the categories of human nutrition and food choices; research in this latter category includes identifying the determinants of dietary patterns and developing methods to overcome obstacles to adopting healthful food habits.

nutritive value of foods, human nutritional needs, the kinds and amounts of foods that Americans consume relative to their needs, and strategies for improving diets and the food supply. The purpose of its nutrition research activities is to understand the relationship of food and its nutrients to health promotion in individuals at all stages of life. USDA categorizes its human nutrition research support into five categories: Nutrient requirements and health maintenance, nutritional status and food intake, use of food and food choices, nutrient composition and bioavailability, and nutritional impacts of programs.

Approximately two-thirds of USDA funds for human nutrition research supports intramural research; the remainder supports extramural research. The Agricultural Research Service (ARS) is the principal intramural nutrition research agency within USDA; its work is largely conducted at five Human Nutrition Research Centers (HNRCs): the Beltsville (Maryland) HNRC, Grand Forks (North Dakota) HNRC, Western (San Francisco) HNRC, the HNRC on Aging (at Tufts University, Boston), and the Children's Nutrition Research Center (affiliated with the Baylor College of Medicine, Houston). ARS conducts agricultural and food-related research at five Regional Research Centers (RRC): Eastern (Philadelphia) RRC, Southern (New Orleans) RRC, Western (Albany, California) RRC, National Center for Agricultural Utilization Research (Peoria, Illinois), and the Richard B. Russell Center (Athens, Georgia). The Cooperative State Research Service (CSRS) administers and coordinates funds appropriated by Congress through the 1862 Hatch Act to state agricultural experiment stations in land-grant institutions, 1890 schools through the Evans-Allen Act, and Tuskegee University for research on food, agriculture, and human nutrition.

Competitive Research Grants in Human Nutrition

After passage of the 1977 Farm Bill, CSRS established the Competitive Research Grants Office (CRGO) in 1978 with a competitively awarded research grants program for agriculture, food, and the environment. Of the $15 million congressional appropriation to this office, $5 million was designated for human nutrition research, a level of funding that over the years dwindled to a low of $1 million in FY 1989.

In 1989, the National Academy of Sciences' (NAS) Board on Agriculture criticized USDA's competitive grants research program for its limited resources and the short duration of its awarded grants. The program awarded far fewer grants than the number of meritorious proposals submitted, few significant experimental results were obtained during the period of the grant, and few talented postdoctoral fellows were attracted to the program. The Board on Agriculture recommended that USDA support for research be increased to $500 million annually and focused in several areas, including nutrition, food quality, and health, and in engineering, products, and processes. The Board also recommended that the size and duration of the average USDA competitive grant award be increased substantially.

USDA endorsed the Board on Agriculture's recommendations. The National Research Initiative Competitive Grants Program (NRICGP) was established, replacing the CRGO program, to support primarily basic research in the six areas described by the Board. In the 1990 Farm Bill, Congress authorized a $500 million annual budget for this program but appropriated only $73 million in FY 1991. In FY 1992 and 1993, Congress set the spending level for the NRICGP at $97.5 million, with at least 20 percent of these funds to support multidisciplinary team research.

The NRICGP Division of Nutrition, Food Safety, and Health supports research in two program areas, Improving Human Nutrition for Optimal Health (IHNOH) and Ensuring Food Safety (EFS). While funding for this division in FY 1992 and FY 1993, at $6.5 million, was the highest it has ever been and represented 6.7 percent of total NRICGP funding, the total is minuscule in relation to national needs.

Improving Human Nutrition for Optimal Health   The current research emphasis of IHNOH, as described in its title, is to improve our understanding of the relationship between optimal nutrition and optimal health.

Among the research areas it supports are nutrient bioavailability and interrelationships, nutrient requirements of healthy people, mechanisms underlying the relation between diet and health (such as the effects of nutrients on the immune system), and the cellular and molecular mechanisms underlying nutrient requirements (including the modulation of gene expression by nutrients). In FY 1993, it began to support research in an area it calls "food consumer behavior," which includes identifying and developing ways to overcome obstacles to adopting healthful food habits, to convey knowledge to target audiences, and to ascertain what factors affect food choices. In FY 1992, IHNOH awarded $3.7 million in grant support for 29 projects, with an average annual award of $60,166 for 2.1 years.

Ensuring Food Safety   This program area was established in FY 1991 to increase understanding of the disease-causing microorganisms that contaminate food and to thereby decrease foodborne illnesses. Among the research areas it supports are the identification of mechanisms of pathogenesis, prevention, and control of microorganisms; development or improvement of rapid, reliable methods to detect and quantify pathogenic organisms in food; and the effects of genetic and biotechnological modifications on the safety of food products. In FY 1992, EFS awarded $2.2 million in grant support for 16 projects, with an average annual award of $130,360 for 2.4 years.

Processing for Adding Value or Developing New Products   This program area, while not part of the NRICGP Division of Nutrition, Food Safety, and Health, is pertinent to our discussion. Its stated purpose is to improve the competitiveness of U.S. agricultural products in global markets. Examples of research in this area include the use of magnetic resonance imaging to study moisture and temperature gradients in food, which should lead to the design of more efficient processes and processing equipment, and to examine the effectiveness of alternative modes of selling processed foods in overseas markets. In FY 1992, the first year of this program area, it awarded $3.6 million in grant support for 26 projects, covering both food and non-food products, with an average annual award of $134,575 for 2.5 years.

Committee Recommendations Pertaining to USDA

Carry out strategic planning to identify more clearly priorities for research in the nutrition and food sciences   With the enormous advances being made in bio- and food technology and human nutrition and the loss of dominance of U.S. agriculture in the world economy, it is urgent for

USDA to develop a strategic plan that will place research in the nutrition and food sciences more in the center of its agricultural research initiatives. Several reports by the congressional General Accounting Office have pointed to the need for USDA to revitalize itself for the twenty-first century, from its organizational structure and management systems to research priorities. Funding of human nutrition research within USDA has remained constant for the past decade, and research in human nutrition, food science, and food technology has decreased both in dollars and scientist-years as a percentage of total agricultural system research expenditures. Furthermore, most of USDA's nutrition and food science research is conducted internally rather than externally through competitively awarded grants to outstanding scientists for cutting-edge research. The NRICGP does provide USDA with important opportunities (see recommendation below). Just as NIH recently began to develop a strategic plan to guide its activities in bionutrition into the next century, so a similar effort should prove valuable to USDA, particularly if it is conducted internally with opportunities for extensive outside input. Any USDA strategic plan to identify research priorities in the nutrition and food sciences should be coordinated with the NIH Bionutrition Initiative.

Congress should provide full funding to the NRICGP, and USDA should direct a substantial amount of these funds to its programs in human nutrition and processing for adding value or developing new products We recognize the long-term commitment of USDA to research in the nutrition and food sciences and note that the NRICGP represents an important opportunity to raise the priority of nutrition and food science research within USDA. Of the $500 million per year authorized to the NRICGP, Congress has allocated only $97.5 million per year to date. The human nutrition and food safety program areas, however, receive only $6.5 million (6.7 percent) of this total, while the processing for adding value or developing new products program receives only $4 million (4.1 percent). USDA has projected that the proportional funding of its NRICGP Division of Nutrition, Food Safety, and Health will double to 13 percent (to $65 million) and its processing for adding value or developing new products division will almost triple to 11 percent (to $55 million) when the NRICGP is funded in full. We urge Congress to provide full funding to the NRICGP and USDA to allocate at a minimum the sums it has projected for its two programs. This funding increase should be in addition to the approximately $31 million for USDA's intramural research program in human nutrition.

Increase substantially the size and duration of the average USDA competitive grant award In FY 1992, the average award in the IHNOH program area was $60,166 per year for 2.1 years. Within the EFS program area, the respective figures were $130,360 for 2.4 years. The NAS Board on Agriculture recommended in 1989 that each grant award be at least $100,000 per year per principal investigator and be given for at least three years. We agree with the Board and believe that implementing its recommendation will help to attract more nutrition and food scientists and doctoral and postdoctoral students to these disciplines.

Consider increasing the amount of Hatch Act support from CSRS to the nutrition and food sciences Each state receives Hatch Act funds on a formula basis and distributes them, along with additional funds from the state, to its various agricultural experiment stations at land-grant universities. In the past several years, only 2 to 4 percent of Hatch funds has supported nutrition and food science research. We recommend that USDA consider increasing this small level of support in one or both of the following ways. The level of support could be doubled to approximately 10 percent of Hatch funds. Alternatively, more Hatch funds could be allocated to research on crops and animals used as human food, particularly in biotechnology, to improve the nutritional quality and yield of these products.

Improve the relationships between the Human Nutrition Research Centers (HNRCs) and the Regional Research Centers (RRCs) and their universities The HNRCs and RRCs and the universities with which most are affiliated are staffed with highly educated, well-trained, and world-renowned biomedical nutrition investigators. The RRCs, which focus a portion of their research activities on food science, nutrition, and food safety issues, have less formal relationships with universities. The quality of the research activities within the HNRC and RRC will be enhanced if investigators have frequent opportunities for contact and networking with their academic colleagues. At the same time, universities must be sensitive to the needs of HNRCs to meet national research needs, respond to USDA priorities, and serve as a visible and independent example of this country's commitment to a strong research program in human nutrition. The summer training programs described in Chapter 7 would provide excellent opportunities for interaction and networking to take place.

Expand the National Needs Graduate Fellowship Program This program awards grants to colleges and universities for outstanding graduate students in the food and agricultural sciences, including human nutrition. To date, this program has funded 150 fellows in human nutrition and food science. Currently, the awards support up to four doctoral-level fellows, providing $17,000 per year to each fellow for three years, plus a $1,000 cost-of-education allowance each year to the fellow's institution. When the program began in 1984, $1.1 million was spent to support 71 fellows (20 at the master's level and 51 at the doctoral level). Budget constraints led to eliminating support for master's students in 1988. By 1990, a strategy had been developed to rotate the funding for each area of national need in alternate years; thus, no human nutrition and food science fellowships were awarded in 1991 or 1993. In 1992, the program supported 10 doctoral fellows in food science and 11 fellows in human nutrition at a total of $1.1 million. The national need areas of human nutrition and food science will be supported again in FY 1994. We recommend that the budget for this program be at least doubled and that once again awards be made annually.

Increase publicity for the Agricultural Research Enhancement Awards (AREAs) We commend Congress and USDA for establishing AREAs in 1991 to strengthen the research capacity of individuals and institutions (see Chapter 7). By federal law, at least 10 percent of NRICGP funds are targeted to AREAs. In FY 1992, AREAs supported 186 individuals with a total of $16.1 million (including 15 postdoctoral fellows at $1.2 million, 45 new investigators at $5.6 million, and 126 faculty members at smaller institutions and those in states with limited success in obtaining NRICGP grants at $9.1 million). USDA should publicize this new awards program better, in order to attract more high-quality candidates, particularly in food science and food engineering. Publicity will become increasingly important as the program expands with more financial support from Congress to the NRICGP.

Increase support for cost-effective research on value-added foods and supporting technologies In the 1980s, the United States lost its preeminent position in world agricultural trade, as many nations that had been our best agricultural customers became competitors. Many of these competitors have focused on exporting value-added foods that meet consumer demands. As noted in Chapter 4, adding value to raw agricultural commodities through processing not only provides employment opportunities (especially for well-trained food scientists and food engineers), but also improves a country's economic health and balance of payments. In FY 1992, however, USDA spent only $3.6 million in its program area on processing for adding value or developing new food and non-food products. A high-priority area of USDA research in food science should be to develop and apply new and emerging food and engineering technologies to develop value-added products.

Widen the scope of research and evaluation of food assistance programs by involving more outside investigators in identifying the questions and conducting the studies   In FY 1993, USDA spent approximately $20 million on research, demonstration projects, and evaluations of its food assistance programs, including the Special Supplemental Food Program for Women, Infants, and Children (WIC), the Food Stamp Program, and the School Lunch Program. While the regulations for some of these programs specify that monies be spent in these areas, funding is determined by Congress each year. These congressionally appropriated funds are not reported as part of USDA's expenditures in human nutrition research. Currently, USDA identifies the research and evaluation needs of its food assistance programs. Many of them pertain to assessing program participation and operations. USDA performs some of this research and evaluation; most of the remainder is done by contractors through open-bid awards. Very little money is made available for these purposes in grants to academically based researchers. USDA argues that its research needs are very specific and are covered best with contracts to firms that specialize in providing the data it needs.

Many opportunities exist to study food assistance programs in terms of their nutritional and health impact on participants and how this impact could be improved. For example, we know little about the extent to which these programs affect participants' nutritional and health status and their food selection skills and dietary patterns, or the effects on these outcomes of variations in program characteristics or service delivery. We urge USDA to allocate a substantial amount, perhaps 25 percent of its food assistance assessment funds, to grants for investigators interested in improving the nutritional outcomes of these programs. USDA should document funds for these grants as part of its expenditures for human nutrition research.

National Science Foundation (NSF)

NSF supports both basic research and science education across broad categories of science and engineering, primarily by funding the research of university-based investigators. It does not have a research program devoted to human nutrition or food science research, and therefore its direct support of research in these areas is small—less than $1 million per year. For example, in FY 1991, NSF funded seven projects with nutrition as a component at a total of $356,033; all were in the social science areas of cultural or physical anthropology and economics. In the food safety area, NSF provides approximately $100,000 per year to support the Center for Aseptic Processing and Packaging Studies at North Carolina State University. In the food engineering area, NSF is providing $97,852 per year between 1993 and 1995 to an investigator at the University of Missouri studying adaptive control development of food manufacturing. It appears that NSF provides approximately $500,000 in direct grants to investigators in the nutrition and food sciences.

In fact, most of NSF's support to the nutrition and food sciences is indirect. It provides, for example, training grants to minorities as well as graduate student support and dissertation support grants. In addition, NSF provides equipment grants to institutions to enable them to upgrade their research facilities. Some of the research it funds in biotechnology, environmental biology, risk assessment, and several other areas are of tangential relevance to the nutrition and food sciences.

Committee Recommendations Pertaining to NSF

Develop a new initiative to support food science and food engineering Approximately 40 universities in the United States have recognized food science and food engineering as distinct, multidisciplinary fields. Food engineering in particular deals with manufacturing operations involving biological materials and thus requires solutions to problems that are substantially different from those in conventional engineering. Pre- and postdoctoral programs in food science and food engineering are poorly supported. NSF support could therefore markedly increase the availability of personnel in these fields, as was shown with NSF support of material science and engineering. NSF should recognize food science and engineering as part of the nation's science, mathematics, engineering, and technology priorities and provide support to students in these fields through its Graduate Research Traineeship Program. In addition, NSF should establish at least one Center of Excellence in Food Engineering, similar to the centers it supports in other engineering fields.

Ensure that nutrition and food scientists are adequately represented on NSF advisory panels that evaluate proposals in these areas Because NSF has no research program in the nutrition and food sciences, it is important that recognized members of these disciplines be members of NSF advisory panels that review proposals submitted for funding. The presence of such individuals on these panels should help to increase NSF's support for basic food science and food engineering research and basic behavioral research related to food intake patterns and other sociocultural determinants of food behavior.

Enhancing the Nutrition and Food Sciences within the Federal Government

The federal government clearly is, and will continue to be, the major funder of research and training in the nutrition and food sciences. Imple-

RESEARCH IN THE NUTRITION AND FOOD SCIENCES BY GOVERNMENT AGENCIES (EXCLUDING NIH, USDA, AND NSF)

In FY 1991, as noted in Figure 8.1, DHHS agencies other than NIH spent $37 million to support human nutrition and nutrition research training; non-DHHS agencies other than USDA spent $9 million. Here we provide examples of some of the research activities of these agencies in the nutrition and food sciences.

DHHS Agencies

Alcohol, Drug Abuse, and Mental Health Administration (ADAMHA)

ADAMHA is comprised of the National Institute of Mental Health, the National Institute on Drug Abuse, and the National Institute on Alcohol Abuse and Alcoholism. Their nutrition research programs tend to focus on the biological, behavioral, and psychological factors involved in food and nutrition-related behaviors. ADAMHA's interests include alcohol use and nutritional deficits and the relationships between eating disorders and mental disorders. In October 1992, ADAMHA was reorganized into the Substance Abuse and Mental Health Services Administration (SAMHSA). As part of the reorganization, the three research institutes are transferred to NIH.

Centers for Disease Control and Prevention (CDC)

CDC conducts applied nutrition research related to its responsibilities to monitor, at the national and state levels, the health and nutritional status of vulnerable groups (e.g., dieters and mothers and their children) and to assess the health-related behaviors and practices of consumers. Its surveillance studies help to identify and refine the relationships of various risk factors to disease outcomes. In addition, it conducts validation studies of surveillance tools to assess and improve their reliability. CDC conducts most of its research intramurally and through cooperative agreements with schools of public health across the country.

Food and Drug Administration (FDA)

Among FDA's primary missions in the nutrition and food areas are to safeguard the nutritional quality of the nation's food supply, protect the public from fraudulent or harmful food products, and improve the public's understanding of the importance of diet to health. FDA supports research activities relating to the development of policy in the areas of food fortification, food safety, food quality, food labeling, and foods used for the dietary management of patients with serious diseases and injuries.

Health Resources Services Administration (HRSA)

HRSA's research activities in the nutrition and food sciences are focused primarily within the Indian Health Service. It supports surveys to assess the health of American Indians and research to improve their health status and reduce their risks of developing diet-related diseases.

National Center for Health Statistics (NCHS)

NCHS is the agency most responsible for assessing the nutritional status of the U.S. population. It performs this function primarily through the National Health and Nutrition Examination Surveys (NHANES). NCHS also conducts national surveys to identify health-related behaviors of the public, including their dietary practices.

Non-DHHS Agencies

Agency for International Development (AID)

The nutrition research effort of AID is focused on providing more effective programs to combat malnutrition in developing countries by improving the knowledge base needed to analyze and understand the causes of malnutrition. It supports: (1) research in the biomedical, behavioral, and food sciences, (2) nutrition monitoring and surveillance, (3) nutrition education, and (4) the effect of government policies on food consumption and nutrition. AID supports linkage grants between U.S. universities and developing countries as well as some graduate student training in this country and in developing countries. It plans to launch a $58 million grant program to investigate micronutrient problems in developing countries over the next five years, of which $8 million is planned for research.

Department of Commerce (DOC)

Within DOC, the National Marine Fisheries Service (NMFS) has responsibility for ensuring the safety of seafood. NMFS conducts periodic national surveys of seafood consumption and has a strong interest in the development of research information on the role of fish oils in the prevention and treatment of cardiovascular disease and related conditions.

Department of Defense (DOD)

Military nutrition and food science research within the DOD began in 1917 and is now headquartered at the U.S. Army Natick Research, Development and Engineering Center in Natick, Massachusetts. While the majority of this research is conducted intramurally, DOD has numerous cooperative and collaborative agreements with academic institutions as

continued

well as research contracts with industry and academia. Its nutrition research is directed to develop nutritional strategies to optimize the mental
and physical performance of soldiers by (1) defining nutritional standards
for their food rations, (2) evaluating ration and feeding systems for their
effects on nutritional status, health, and performance, and (3) developing
nutritional strategies to sustain and enhance military performance in extreme environments (e.g., desert or Arctic regions). DOD also conducts
research in food engineering as it relates to the development, processing,
preservation, and packaging of foods required to meet the unique military
feeding requirements.

Department of Veterans Affairs (DVA)

The DVA cares for veterans of the armed services. The medical
arm of the DVA consists of medical centers and satellite or independent
outpatient clinics. The majority of the centers and some clinics have
medical research programs, some of which focus on nutrition or have
nutritional components. Research projects in this area tend to focus on
total parenteral and enteral nutrition, nutrition in the alcoholic, micronutrients, and nutrition in disease. The diseases of interest are those most
likely to be encountered by older people, such as heart disease, cancer,
and diseases of the gastrointestinal tract.

National Aeronautics and Space Administration (NASA)

NASA research activities in the nutrition and food sciences relate
primarily to the development of food products for manned space missions. These products must fulfill a crew's nutritional needs; be able to be
stored for months with negligible risk of spoilage; have minimum weight,
volume, and packaging; be of sufficient quality, variety, and presentation
to contribute positively to crew morale; have minimal preparation and
cleanup requirements; and leave little waste after being consumed.

menting the following three recommendations will enable the government
to strengthen its efforts in these areas.

Committee Recommendations Pertaining to the Federal Government

*Award extramural grants for research through open, competitive means
and peer review* The best way to ensure high-quality research in the
nutrition and food sciences (and all sciences) is to have funding by all
agencies awarded competitively through peer-review processes. Over the
past decade, congressional earmarking of funds to universities for specific
projects, centers, and studies—often referred to as pork barreling—has
become commonplace. Because earmarking bypasses all scientific merit

and technical review criteria, it ultimately benefits only a few institutions and not necessarily those with the most worthy or innovative projects. Earmarking of funds should be very limited and well defined, leaving funding to be competitively awarded on the basis of peer review.

Improve the documentation of government support of the nutrition and food sciences   Precise data on funding for research in the nutrition and food sciences are not available. The difficulty of obtaining this information is partly inherent; given that the nutrition and food sciences represent a wide collection of interests centering around food and its relationship to health and well-being, it is often difficult to characterize research in these areas. Furthermore, data are not available from all funders and may not be directly comparable because of differences in calculating expenditures. Over the past decade, the federal government has clearly improved the coordination of its nutrition and food-related research activities. Unfortunately, it is still not possible to estimate accurately the total resources applied to this research, in part because HNRIMS does not include state and private sector investments in research and does not impose uniform requirements on agencies reporting data. Documenting the government's research effort would be substantially improved if federal agencies were to use the same definitions of nutrition- and food-related research, become consistent in the inclusion or exclusion of overhead costs in their estimates of research costs, and use the same system throughout government to account for their contributions. Ideally, such a system could be used by the private sector and nonprofit institutions as well.

Invigorate the Interagency Committee for Human Nutrition Research   As described earlier, the ICHNR works to improve the coordination and increase the productivity of nutrition research within the federal government, in part by identifying research needs and eliminating unnecessary duplication of work. The effectiveness of ICHNR and its success as an advocate for more research in the nutrition and food sciences are determined largely by the Assistant Secretaries of DHHS and USDA; they co-chair the ICHNR, direct its activities and the pace at which they are carried out, and, most importantly yet indirectly, determine the vigor with which the committee develops and implements initiatives. The ICHNR performs best when the Assistant Secretaries have a special interest in advancing the nutrition and food sciences and move the committee accordingly. We recommend that Congress request that ICHNR evaluate NIH's and USDA's research initiatives in the nutrition and food sciences and prepare a report. ICHNR should be asked to assess the magnitude and focus of each agency's efforts in relation to public health needs and recommend improvements.

RESEARCH AND FUNDING OF RESEARCH BY THE FOOD INDUSTRY

The food industry's total expenditure on research and development is not known with certainty, but it probably ranges from $560 million to almost $2 billion. (It is worth noting that even the low end of this range is substantially more money than that spent by the entire U.S. government for the support of human nutrition and nutrition research training.) What is clear and disturbing, however, is that industrial funding of research has been declining in the 1990s, after growing and then leveling off in the 1980s. The situation is even worse for the food industry; its investment in food-processing research as a percentage of sales lags behind the industrial sector as a whole (0.6 percent vs. 4.8 percent) and grew from 0.4 percent to only 0.6 percent between 1963 and 1988. Reacting to corporate restructuring and the recession of the past few years, the funding priorities of companies have shifted even further away from basic research and development to support current business, respond to government regulations, and focus on core technologies. Most of this investment is used internally on applied and developmental research.

Committee Recommendations Pertaining to the Food Industry

Establish Better Links with Academic Departments of Food Science and Nutrition

As the explosion of biomedical discoveries fuels the need for even more research dollars, it is advantageous to both the private sector (the food industry as well as food-related industries with higher profit margins, such as pharmaceuticals and biotechnology companies) and universities to establish better relationships. These alliances offer great promise to universities as sources of new funds in the face of stable or decreasing federal support, as a way to keep their best and brightest faculty, and as a way to speed the transfer of research results from their laboratories to the marketplace. Industry, in turn, has a larger pool of qualified food and nutrition scientists from which to select. The private sector can provide support to academia through competitive grants programs, core support for departments, joint training of graduate students, and other means. For example, the idea should be explored of having at least some food science students advised by both a faculty member and a food industry representative (i.e., the representative would be a co-advisor). This initiative, which might be very attractive to industry, could provide students with a wide variety of views on course selection, options for student placements, and career opportunities.

Fortunately, there is a growing trend among university-based food-science departments to develop interdisciplinary centers for specific purposes that in turn help to attract industry funding. These centers include the Center for Value Added Research at Michigan State University, the Center for Nutritional Science at the University of Florida, the Food Research Institute at the University of Wisconsin, the Center for Aseptic Processing and Packaging Studies at North Carolina State University, the Center for Food Safety and Quality Enhancement at the University of Georgia, and six National Dairy Research Centers. We encourage the development and expansion of these centers and of other initiatives that promote academic-industry associations. We encourage Congress to explore the possibility of providing tax incentives to industry to encourage it to (1) develop these associations, (2) conduct more basic research in the nutrition and food sciences in its laboratories, and (3) increase its financial support to professional societies (such as the American Institute of Nutrition and the Institute of Food Technologists) that have mechanisms to use these funds to help outstanding students and academic investigators with promising proposals.

Increase Spending on Research Related to Value-Added Processing to Increase This Country's International Competitiveness and Trade Balance

As described in Chapter 4, this country is fast becoming primarily a supplier of basic, relatively inexpensive unprocessed agricultural commodities to the world and an importer of relatively expensive value-added products made from these commodities. Unfortunately, our food industry is increasingly looking outside the United States for cutting-edge technologies for food manufacturing and processing (e.g., removing caffeine using carbon dioxide rather than solvents). One indication of this is the patents awarded in food technology; the number awarded to U.S. firms is decreasing in relation to the number awarded to foreign-owned firms. U.S. firms are increasingly likely to turn to foreign countries for advanced technologies rather than invest to develop or improve them here. It may be necessary for the government to provide tax incentives to industry and encourage greater government-industry cooperation to meet this recommendation. The governments of many countries around the world encourage government-industry cooperation and provide incentives for industry to participate.

Commodity Checkoff Programs

Several commodity boards (for beef, eggs, pork, dairy products, potatoes, watermelons, soybeans, pecans, and mushrooms) have formed to support product promotion, the provision of consumer and industry information, research, and foreign marketing. Each board is financed by assessments (checkoffs) on the price of the commodity sold by producers; these checkoff programs are administered by USDA. Each commodity board determines the amount and kind of research it will fund, while USDA ensures that the research is permitted by the specific regulations of each checkoff program. A board typically supports research in two ways: (1) through targeted research, where it develops specific proposals to which interested investigators respond, and (2) through open solicitations, in which investigators are invited to submit research projects that will help support or promote the commodity. Most of the available monies appear to be competitively awarded.

Several of the commodity checkoff programs fund considerable research and are therefore an important component of the infrastructure of nutrition and food science research. The Beef Promotion and Research Board, for example, consists of 111 members representing all segments of the beef industry and oversees the national, one-dollar-per-head beef checkoff program. For fiscal year 1993, it approved $3.5 million for research projects, including $1.42 million for market research to define the forces affecting the beef market, market distribution, and consumer behavior, $1.17 million for product technology research, and $901,000 for nutrition research. The National Dairy Promotion and Research Board in FY 1993 approved $10.2 million for dairy foods research (to encourage development of new dairy products, processes, and packaging technologies) and nutrition research (to identify and clarify the nutritional attributes of new dairy foods that offer opportunities for promotion and positioning). All research proposals are reviewed for scientific merit by panels of scientists and industry representatives. Approximately $2.8 million per year is used to fund six centers of dairy product research and development located at 12 universities throughout the United States. These centers are funded with equal contributions from the board, the universities, and the local dairy industry.

We commend the various commodity groups that fund peer-reviewed research and hope that funding will increase each year. Those boards that do not support research at the present time—such as those for potatoes, watermelons, and mushrooms—should consider doing so in the future. We recommend that more commodity groups establish USDA-administered checkoff programs to promote their products, in part by funding research on their properties, composition, and applications. USDA should work together with the various commodity boards to identify important research needs and to promote a balance in the use of funds (among research, marketing, and product promotion) that is favorable to research.

RESEARCH AND FUNDING OF RESEARCH BY NONPROFIT ORGANIZATIONS

Foundations (both community and corporate-sponsored), voluntary health agencies (sometimes called operating foundations), and other nonprofit organizations (such as medical research organizations) play an important role in sponsoring health-related research and development, particularly in filling gaps in the nation's research agenda and in sponsoring new initiatives. Foundations often support individual research project grants, predoctoral and postdoctoral fellowships, equipment grants, publication expenses, special library collections grants, and conferences or workshops. Foundation support often helps to give nutrition and food science a visible presence on campus; this seed money often leads to the receiving institution's providing even more funds for research in these areas. Voluntary health agencies are active in promoting public awareness and education, providing continuing education for health professionals, making patient referrals, providing research and training grants, and lobbying to increase federal funding for disease-specific research.

Many foundations (such as the Pew Charitable Trusts, Rockefeller, Kellogg, and Heinz) and other nonprofit organizations (such as the American Heart Association, the Howard Hughes Medical Institute, and the American Cancer Society) have long been important supporters of research and training in the nutrition and food sciences. For example, American Heart Association expenditures on research in 1991-1992 were $101.3 million, a significant though unquantifiable portion of that research in the nutrition and food sciences.

In 1986, the Pew Charitable Trusts began what turned out to be a very successful National Nutrition Program to help several institutions develop and give direction to their nutrition and food science programs. Over 70 institutions applied to receive a grant of up to $1 million; a scientific advisory committee to the foundation selected five institutions to receive the funds. These five institutions received awards ranging from $600,000 to $1 million to be used over five years. Pew also provided fellowships to 25 individuals in the early stages of their careers. The total costs of the Pew initiative were about $5 million.

The committee recommends that new initiatives along the lines of the Pew program be developed and supported by other foundations. We also encourage foundations to provide matching funds and to continue and expand equipment grants that are vital to academic institutions in strengthening their technology base.

CONCLUDING REMARKS

This chapter has given an overview of the activities of, and support provided by, the federal government, food industry, and private nonprofit organizations to conduct research in the nutrition and food sciences and to educate and train students in these disciplines. Our recommendations to these funders, if enacted, will increase support and help them use their limited financial resources effectively to advance the nutrition and food sciences and lead to further improvements in public health.

Sources and Suggested Reading

SUMMARY AND CONCLUSIONS

FCCSET (Federal Coordinating Council for Science, Engineering, and Technology). 1993. An Overview of Federal Food Safety Research, Including Research Needs for the Future. A report by the Committee on Food, Agricultural, and Forestry Research, FCCSET. Office of Science and Technology Policy, Washington, D.C.

Vonnegut, K. 1985. Galápagos. Dell Publishing Co., Inc., New York.

CHAPTER 1: INTRODUCTION

Harper, A.E. 1969. Nutrition: where are we? Where are we going? Am. J. Clin. Nutr. 22:87-98.

IOM (Institute of Medicine). 1991. Improving America's Diet and Health: From Recommendations to Action. Report of the Committee on Dietary Guidelines Implementation, Food and Nutrition Board. National Academy Press, Washington, D.C.

Kretchmer, N. 1993. Forty years of *The American Journal of Clinical Nutrition*. Am. J. Clin. Nutr. 57:2.

CHAPTER 2: ACCOMPLISHMENTS IN THE NUTRITION AND FOOD SCIENCES

Folate and Neural Tube Defects

IOM (Institute of Medicine). 1990. Nutrition During Pregnancy: Weight Gain and Nutrient Supplements. Report of the Subcommittee on Nutritional Status and Weight Gain During Pregnancy and the Subcommittee on Dietary Intake and Nutrient Supplements

269

During Pregnancy, Committee on Nutritional Status During Pregnancy and Lactation, Food and Nutrition Board. National Academy Press, Washington, D.C.

IOM (Institute of Medicine). 1992. Nutrition During Pregnancy and Lactation: An Implementation Guide. Report of the Subcommittee for a Clinical Applications Guide, Committee on Nutritional Status During Pregnancy and Lactation, Food and Nutrition Board. National Academy Press, Washington, D.C.

Oxidative Damage to DNA, Proteins, and Fats

Ames, B.N., M.K. Shinega, and T.M. Hagen. 1993. Oxidants, antioxidants, and the degenerative diseases of aging. Proc. Natl. Acad. Sci. USA 90:7915-7922.

Orr, W.C., and R.S. Sohal. 1993. Effects of Cu-Zn superoxidase dismutase overexpression on life span and resistance to oxidative stress in transgenic Drosophila melanogaster. Arch. Biochem. Biophys. 301:34-40.

Witztum, J.L. 1993. Role of oxidized low density lipoprotein in atherogenesis. Br. Heart J. 69(1 Suppl.):S12-S18.

Sensory Biology and the Development of New Foods

DHHS (U.S. Department of Health and Human Services). 1988. The Surgeon General's Report on Nutrition and Health. DHHS (PHS) Publication No. 88-50210. U.S. Government Printing Office, Washington, D.C.

Drewnowski, A. 1987. Fats and food texture: Sensory and hedonic evaluations. Pp. 217-250 in H.R. Moskowitz, ed. Food Texture. Marcel Dekker, New York.

NRC (National Research Council). 1989. Diet and Health: Implications for Reducing Chronic Disease Risk. Report of the Committee on Diet and Health, Food and Nutrition Board. National Academy Press, Washington, D.C.

Biotechnology

Bills, D.D., and S.-D. Kung, eds. 1992. Biotechnology and Nutrition: Proceedings of the Third International Symposium. Butterworth-Heinemann, Stoneham, MA.

Harlander, S.K. 1989. Food biotechnology: yesterday, today, and tomorrow. Food Technol. 43:196-202,206.

Harlander, S.K. 1991. Biotechnology—means for improving our food supply. Food Technol. 45:84, 86, 91-92,95.

Oral Rehydration Therapy

Farthing, M.J.G., ed. 1990. Oral rehydration therapy: past, present, and future. Clin. Ther. 12:1-142 (Supplement A).

Vitamin A

Sommer A. 1982. Nutritional Blindness: Xerophthalmia and Keratomalacia. Oxford University Press, New York.

Sommer A., and S.L. Zeger. 1991. On estimating efficacy in clinical trials. Stat. Med. 10:45-52.

West, K.P., G.R. Howard, and A. Sommer. 1989. Vitamin A and Infection: Public health implications. Annu. Rev. Nutr. 9:63-86.

New Concepts of Nutrient Requirements

King, J.C. 1990. Assessment of zinc status. J. Nutr. 120:1474-1479.

CHAPTER 3: UNDERSTANDING GENETIC, MOLECULAR, CELLULAR, AND PHYSIOLOGIC PROCESSES

Brown and Goldstein and Lipid Metabolism

Brown, M.S., and Goldstein, J.L. 1986. A receptor-mediated pathway for cholesterol homeostasis. Science 232:34-47.
Hobbs, H.H., D.W. Russell, M.S. Brown, and J.L. Goldstein. 1990. The LDL receptor locus in familial hypercholesterolemia: mutational analysis of a membrane protein. Annu. Rev. Genet. 24:133-170.

Retinoic Acid

Eichele, G. 1989. Retinoids and vertebrate limb pattern formation. Trends Genet. 5:246-251.
Giguère, V., E.S. Ong, P. Segui, and R.M. Evans. 1987. Identification of a receptor for the morphogen retinoic acid. Nature 330:624-629.
Lehmann, J.M., M.I. Dawson, P.D. Hobbs, M. Husmann, and M. Pfahl. 1991. Identification of retinoids with nuclear receptor subtype-selective activities. Cancer Res. 51:4804-4809.
Petkovich, M., N.J. Brand, A. Krust, and P. Chambon. 1987. A human retinoic acid receptor which belongs to the family of nuclear receptors. Nature 330:444-450.
Summerbell, D., and M. Maden. 1990. Retinoic acid, a developmental signalling molecule. Trends Neurosci. 13:142-147.

Cloning the First Nuclear Retinoic Acid Receptor (RAR)

Giguère, V., E.S. Ong, P. Segui, and R.M. Evans. 1987. Identification of a receptor for the morphogen retinoic acid. Nature 330:624-629.
Petkovich, M., N.J. Brand, A. Krust, and P. Chambon. 1987. A human retinoic acid receptor which belongs to the family of nuclear receptors. Nature 330:444-450.

Vitamin D—Receptors and Metabolism

DeLuca, H.F. 1988. The vitamin D story: a collaborative effort of basic science and clinical medicine. FASEB J. 2:224-236.
Dintzis, F.R., and J.A. Laszlo, eds. 1989. Mineral Absorption in the Monogastric GI Tract: Chemical, Nutritional, and Physiological Aspects. Plenum, New York.
Kumar, R. 1991. Vitamin D and calcium transport. Kidney Int. 40:1177-1189.
Wasserman, R.H., C.A. Smith, M.E. Brindak, N. de Talamoni, C.S. Fullmer, J.T. Penniston, and R. Kumar. 1992. Vitamin D and mineral deficiencies increase the plasma membrane calcium pump of chicken intestine. Gastroenterology 102:886-894.

Neurotransmitters—Regulation and Action

Beal, M.F. 1992. Mechanism of excitotoxicity in neurologic disease. FASEB J. 6:3338-3344.
Hoebel, B.G., L. Hernandez, G.P. Mark, et. al. 1990. Brain microdialysis as a molecular approach to obesity: serotonin, dopamine, cyclic-AMP. Pp. 45-61 in Bray, G., D. Ricquier, and B. Spiegleman, eds. Obesity: Toward a Molecular Approach. UCLA Symposia New Series, Volume 132. Wiley Liss Inc., New York.
Olney, J.W. 1990. Excitotoxic amino acids and neuropsychiatric disorders. Annu. Rev. Pharmacol. Toxicol. 30:47-71.

Iron Metabolism and Regulation

Klausner, R.D., T.A. Rouault, and J.B. Harford. 1993. Regulating the fate of mRNA: the control of cellular iron metabolism. Cell 72:19-28.
Munro, H.N. 1990. Iron regulation of ferritin gene expression. J. Cell. Biochem. 44:107-115.
Ponka, P., H.M. Schulman, and R. C. Woodworth. 1990. Iron Transport and Storage. CRC Press, Boca Raton, FL.
Worwood, M. 1989. An overview of iron metabolism at a molecular level. J. Intern. Med. 226:381-391.

Genetics

McKusick, V.A. 1992. Mendelian Inheritance in Man: Catalogs of Autosomal Dominant, Autosomal Recessive, & X-Linked Phenotypes, 2 vols., 10th edition. Johns Hopkins University Press, Baltimore, MD.
Risch, N. 1990. Linkage strategies for genetically complex traits. II. The power of affected relative pairs. Am. J. Hum. Genet. 46:229-241.
Todd, J.A. 1992. Diabetes mellitus. Curr. Opin. Genet. Dev. 2:474-478.

Identification, Isolation, and Tracking of Specific Cell Types

Brundage, R.A., K.E. Fogarty, R.A. Tuft, and F.S. Fay. 1991. Calcium gradients underlying polarization and chemotaxis of eosinophils. Science 254:703.
Connor, J.A., W.J. Wadman, P.E. Hockberger, and R.K.S. Wong. 1988. Sustained dendritic gradients of Ca^{++} induced by excitatory amino acids in CA1 hippocampal neurons. Science 24:649-653.
Cornell-Bell, A.H., S. Finkbeiner, M.S. Cooperr, and S.J. Smith. 1990. Glutamate induces Ca^{++} waves in cultured astrocytes: long-range glial signalling. Science 247:470-473.
Inoue, S. 1986. Video Microscopy. Plenum Press, New York.
White, J.G., W.B. Amos, and M. Fordham. 1987. An evaluation of confocal versus conventional imaging of biological structures by fluorescence light microscopy. J. Cell Biol. 105:41-48.

Animal Models

Brown, M.S., and J.L. Goldstein. 1992. Koch's postulates for cholesterol. Cell. 71:187-188.
Darling, S.M., and C.M. Abbott. 1992. Mouse models of human single gene disorders. I: Nontransgenic mice. BioEssays. 14:359-366.

Johnson, P.R., M.R. Greenwood, B.A. Horwitz, and J.S. Stern. 1991. Animal models of obesity: genetic aspects. Annu. Rev. Nutr. 11:325-353.
Smithies, O. 1993. Animal models of human genetic disease. Trends in Genetics 9:112-116.

Imaging Technologies for Metabolic Studies

Gardner, S.F., J.A. Green, E.M. Bednarczyk, L. Farnett, and F. Miraldi. 1992. Principles and clinical applications of positron emission tomography. Am. J. Hosp. Pharm. 49:1499-1506.
Shulman, R.G., A.M. Blamire, D.L. Rothman, and G. McCarthy. 1993. Nuclear magnetic resonance imaging and spectroscopy of human brain function. Proc. Natl. Acad. Sci. USA 90:3127-3133.

Gene Therapy

Anderson, W.F. 1992. Human gene therapy. Science 256:808-813.
Valle, D. 1991. Treatment of genetic disease: Current status and prospects for the future. Semin. Perinatol. 15(Suppl. 1):52-56.

The Human Genome Project and Nutrition

Gilbert, W. 1991. DNA sequencing, today and tomorrow. Hospital Practice 26:165-169, 172, 174.
Oliver, S.G., Q.J. van der Aart, M.L. Agostoni-Carbone, M. Aigle, L. Alberghina, D. Alexandraki, G. Antoine, R. Anwar, J.P. Ballesta, P. Benit, et al. 1992. The complete DNA sequence of yeast chromosome III. Nature 357:38-46.

Gene Expression and Gene Manipulations

Goodridge, A.G. 1990. The new metabolism: molecular genetics in the analysis of metabolic regulation. FASEB J. 4:3099-3110.
Smithies, O. 1993. Animal models of human genetic disease. Trends in Genetics 9:112-116.

Structural Biology

Matthews, C.K., and van Holde, K.T. 1990. Biochemistry. 1129 pp. Benjamin/Cummings, Redwood City, CA.

Stem Cell Biology

Baum, C.M., I.L. Weissman, A.S. Tsukamoto, A.M. Buckle, and B. Peault. 1992. Proc. Natl. Acad. Sci. USA 89:2804-2808.
Kirschner, M. 1992. The cell cycle then and now. Trends Biochem. Sci. 17:281-285.
Potten, C.S., and M. Loeffler. 1990. Stem cells: attributes, cycles, spirals, pitfalls and uncertainties. Lessons for and from the crypt. Development 110:1001-1020.
Huang, S., and L.W. Terstappen. 1992. Formation of haematopoietic microenvironment and haemateopoietic stem cells from single human bone marrow stem cells. Nature 360:745-749.

Nutrient Transport Systems of the Blood-Brain Barrier

Neuwelt, E.A., ed. 1991. Implications of the Blood-Brain Barrier and Its Manipulation, Vol. 1: Basic Science Aspects. Plenum Medical Book Co., New York.

Segal, M.B., ed. 1992. Barriers and Fluids of the Eye and Brain. CRC Press, Boca Raton, FL.

Prevention and Repair of Oxidative Damage

Byers, T., and G. Perry. 1992. Dietary carotenes, vitamin C, and vitamin E as protective antioxidants in human cancers. Ann. Rev. Nutr. 12:139-159.

Chisolm, G.M., K.C. Irwin, and M.S. Penn. 1992. Lipoprotein oxidation and lipoprotein-induced cell injury in diabetes. Diabetes 41(Suppl. 2):61-66.

Dorgan, J.F., and A. Schatzkin. 1991. Antioxidant micronutrients in cancer prevention. Hematol. Oncol. Clin. North Am. 5:43-68.

Retinoic Acid-Regulated Nuclear Receptors

Lehmann, J.M., B. Hoffmann, and M. Pfahl. 1991. Genomic organization of the retinoic acid receptor gamma gene. Nucleic Acids Res. 19:573-578.

Ross, A.C. 1993. Cellular metabolism and activation of retinoids. Roles of the cellular retinoid-binding proteins. FASEB J. 7:317-327.

Sucov, H.M., K.K. Murakami, and R.M. Evans. 1990. Characterization of an autoregulated response element in the mouse retinoic acid receptor type beta gene. Proc. Natl. Acad. Sci. USA 87:5392-5396.

Haq, R., M. Pfahl, and F. Chytil. 1991. Retinoic acid affects the expression of nuclear retinoic acid receptors in tissue or retinol-deficient rats. Proc. Natl. Acad. Sci. USA 88:8272-8276.

Warrell, Jr., R.P., H. de Thé, Z-Y. Wang, and L. Degos. 1993. Acute promyelocytic leukemia. N. Engl. J. Med. 329:177-189.

CHAPTER 4: ENHANCING THE FOOD SUPPLY

The Food-Processing Industry

Conner, J.M. 1988. Food Processing: An Industrial Power House in Transition. Lexington Books, Lexington, MA.

Elitzak, H. 1991. Food costs beyond the farm gate. FoodReview, July-September:34-37.

Gallo, A.E. 1991. The food marketing system. FoodReview, July-September:38-41.

Fortification and Enrichment

Bauernfeind, J.C., and P.A. Lachance, eds. 1991. Nutrient Additions to Food: Nutritional, Technological, and Regulatory Aspects. Food and Nutrition Press, Trumbull, CT.

Bodwell, C.E. and J.W. Erdman, eds. 1988. Nutrient Interactions. Marcel Dekker, New York.

Smith, K.T. 1988. Trace Minerals in Foods: Their Relationship to Health and Nutrition. Marcel Dekker, New York.

Low-Fat and Low-Calorie Foods

Friedman, M. 1991. Healthy foods find cross-category niches. Prepared Foods 160(10):61.
Institute of Food Technologists. 1989. Low-Calorie Foods. Food Technol. 43(4):113-125.

Sensory Needs of the Elderly

Clydesdale, F.M. 1991. Meeting the needs of the elderly with the foods of today and tomorrow. Nutr. Today 26(5):13-20.
Clydesdale, F.M., ed. 1993. Sensory Perception in Aging: Special Issue. Crit. Rev. Food Sci. Nutr. 33(1).
Murphy, C., W.S. Cain, and D.M. Hegsted, eds. 1989. Nutrition and the Chemical Senses in Aging: Recent Advances and Current Research Needs. Ann. NY Acad. Sci., Vol. 561.

Functional Foods for Health

Caragay, A.B. 1992. Cancer-preventive foods and ingredients. Food Technol. 46(4):65-68.
Schmidl, M.K., and T.P. Labuza. 1992. Medical foods. Food Technol. 46(4):87-96.
NRC (National Research Council). 1989. Recommended Dietary Allowances, 10th ed. Report of the Subcommittee on the Tenth Edition of the RDAs, Food and Nutrition Board, Commission on Life Sciences. National Academy Press, Washington, D.C.

Microbiological Food Hazards

Cliver, D.O., ed. 1990. Foodborne Diseases. Academic Press, San Diego.
Doyle, M.P., ed. 1989. Foodborne Bacterial Pathogens. Marcel Dekker, New York.
Jay, J.M. 1992. Microbiological Food Microbiology, 4th ed. Van Nostrand Reinhold, New York.

Methods of Preservation

Fellow, P. 1988. Food Processing Technology: Principles & Practice. VCH Pubs., New York.

Physical and Engineering Properties

Jowitt, R., ed. 1987. Physical Properties of Food 2. Elsevier, New York.
Rao, M.A., and S.S.H. Rizvi, eds. 1986. Engineering Properties of Foods. Marcel-Dekker, New York.

Separation

King, C.J. 1991. Separation Processes, 2nd ed. McGraw-Hill, New York.

Biosensors and Process Control

Seborg, D.E., T.F. Edgar, and D.A. Mellichamp. 1989. Process Dynamics and Control. John Wiley and Sons, New York.

Luyben, W.L. 1990. Process Modeling, Simulation, and Control for Chemical Engineers, 2nd ed. McGraw Hill, New York.

Rheology

Moskowitz, H. 1987. Food Texture: Instrumental and Sensory Measurement. Marcel Dekker, New York.

Peleg, M., and E.B. Bagley. 1983. Physical Properties of Food. AVI, Westport, CT.

Schwartzberg, H.G., and R.W. Hartel. 1992. Physical Chemistry of Foods. Marcel Dekker, New York.

Packaging

Downes, T.W. 1989. Food packaging in the IFT era: Five decades of unprecedented growth and change. Food Technol. 43(9):228-240.

OTA (Office of Technology Assessment). 1992. Green Products by Design: Choices for a Cleaner Environment. Report No. OTA-E-541. U.S. Government Printing Office, Washington, D.C.

Biotechnology

Bills, D.D., and H.-D. Kung, eds. 1992. Biotechnology and Nutrition: Proceedings of the Third International Symposium. Butterworth-Heinemann, Stoneham, MA.

OTA (Office of Technology Assessment). 1992. A New Technological Era for American Agriculture. Report No. OTA-F-474. U.S. Government Printing Office, Washington, D.C.

Goldberg, I., and R. Williams, eds. 1991. Biotechnology and Food Ingredients. Van Nostrand Reinhold, New York.

Marx, J.L., ed. 1989. A Revolution in Biotechnology. Cambridge University Press, New York.

Molecular Basis of Food Quality

Levine H., and L. Slade, eds. 1991. Water Relationships in Foods: Advances in the 1980s & Trends for the 1990s. Plenum Press, New York.

Schwartzberg, H.G., and R.W. Hartel, eds. 1992. Physical Chemistry of Foods. Marcel Dekker, New York.

Slade L., and H. Levine. 1988. Non-equilibrium behavior of small carbohydrate-water systems. Pure Appl. Chem. 60:1841-1864.

Symons, M.C.R. 1988. Formation of radicals by mechanical processes. Free Radic. Res. Commun. 5:131-139.

Environmental Issues

NRC (National Research Council). 1989. Alternative Agriculture. Report of the Committee on the Role of Alternative Farming Methods in Modern Production Agriculture, Board on Agriculture. National Academy Press, Washington, D.C.

CHAPTER 5: UNDERSTANDING DIET, HEALTH, AND DISEASE RELATIONSHIPS

Reproduction

IOM (Institute of Medicine). 1990. Nutrition During Pregnancy: Weight Gain and Nutrient Supplements. Report of the Subcommittee on Nutritional Status and Weight Gain During Pregnancy and the Subcommittee on Dietary Intake and Nutrient Supplements During Pregnancy, Committee on Nutritional Status During Pregnancy and Lactation, Food and Nutrition Board. National Academy Press, Washington, D.C.

IOM (Institute of Medicine). 1991. Nutrition During Lactation. Report of the Subcommittee on Nutrition During Lactation, Committee on Nutritional Status During Pregnancy and Lactation, Food and Nutrition Board. National Academy Press, Washington, D.C.

Growth and Development

Ciba Foundation Symposium. 1991. The Childhood Environment and Adult Disease: Symposium 156. John Wiley and Sons, New York.

Pollitt, E., K.S. Gorman, P. Engle, R. Martorell, and J. Rivera. Early Supplementary Feeding and Cognition: Effects Over Two Decades. Monographs of the Society for Research in Child Development, in press.

Box: Nutrition and Vision

Sauberlich, H.E., and L.J. Machlin, eds. 1992. Beyond Deficiency: New Views on the Function and Health Effects of Vitamins. New York Academy of Sciences, New York.

Taylor, A., P.F. Jacques, and C.K. Dorey. 1993. Oxidation and aging: impact on vision. Toxicol. Ind. Health 9:349-371.

Body Composition

Shephard, R.J. 1987. Physical Activity and Aging, 2nd edition. Aspen Publishers, Rockville, MD.

Immune System

Chandra, S., and R.K. Chandra. 1986. Nutrition, immune response and outcome. Prog. Food Nutr. Sci. 10(1/2):1-65.

Meydani, S.N. 1990. Dietary modulation of cytokine production and biologic functions. Nutr. Rev. 48(10):361-369.

Roitt, I.M., J. Brostoff, and D. Male. 1989. Immunology, 2nd edition. Gower Medical Publishing, New York.

Cognitive Function—Central Nervous System

Krieg, J.C. 1991. Eating disorders assessed by cranial computerized tomography (CCT, dSPECT, PET). Adv. Exp. Med. Biol. 291:223-229.

Cancer

Amos, D.I., N.E. Caporaso, and A. Weston. 1992. Host factors in lung cancer risk: a review of interdisciplinary studies. Cancer Epidemiology, Biomarkers & Prevention 1:505-513.

Idle, J.R., M. Armstrong, A.V. Boddy, C. Boustead, S. Cholerton, J. Cooper, A.K. Daly, J. Ellis, W. Gregory, H. Hadidi, C. Hofer, J. Holt, J. Leathart, N. McCracken, S.C. Monkman, J.E. Painter, H. Taber, D. Walker, and M. Yule. 1992. The pharmacogenetics of chemical carcinogenesis. Pharmacogenetics 2:246-258.

NRC (National Research Council). 1982. Diet, Nutrition and Cancer. Report of the Committee on Diet, Nutrition and Cancer, Food and Nutrition Board. National Academy Press, Washington, D.C.

NRC (National Research Council). 1989. Diet and Health: Implications for Reducing Chronic Disease Risk. Report of the Committee on Diet and Health, Food and Nutrition Board. National Academy Press, Washington, D.C.

Hypertension

Criqui, M.H., R.D. Langer, and D.M. Reed. 1989. Dietary alcohol, calcium, and potassium: independent and combined effects on blood pressure. Circulation 80:609-614.

Karppanen, H. 1991. Minerals and blood pressure. Ann. Med. 23:299-305.

Luft, F.C., and D.A. McCarron. 1991. Heterogeneity of hypertension: the diverse role of electrolyte intake. Annu. Rev. Med. 42:347-355.

NRC (National Research Council). 1989. Diet and Health: Implications for Reducing Chronic Disease Risk. Report of the Committee on Diet and Health, Food and Nutrition Board. National Academy Press, Washington, D.C.

Cardiovascular Disease and Arteriosclerosis

NRC (National Research Council). 1989. Diet and Health: Implications for Reducing Chronic Disease Risk. Report of the Committee on Diet and Health, Food and Nutrition Board. National Academy Press, Washington, D.C.

The Trials of Hypertension Prevention Collaborative Research Group. 1992. The effects of nonpharmacologic interventions on blood pressure of persons with high normal levels. J. Am. Med. Assoc. 267:1213-1220.

Willett, W.C. 1989. Nutritional Epidemiology (Monographs in Epidemiology and Biostatistics: No. 15). Oxford University Press, New York.

Box: Homocysteine and Vascular Disease

Lindenbaum, J., D.G. Savage, S.P. Stabler, and R.H. Allen. 1990. Diagnosis of cobalamin deficiency: II. Relative sensitivities of serum cobalamin, methylmalonic acid, and total homocysteine concentrations. Am. J. Hematol. 34:99-107.

McCully, K.S. and R.B. Wilson. 1975. Homocysteine theory of arteriosclerosis. Atheriosclerosis 22:215-227.

Obesity

Bjorntorp, P., and B.N. Brodoff, eds. 1992. Obesity. Lippincott, Philadelphia, PA.

Bouchard, D., ed. 1993, in press. Genetics of Obesity. CRC Press, Boca Raton, FL.

Stunkard, A.J. and T.A. Wadden. 1993. Obesity: Theory and Therapy. Raven Press, New York.

Diarrhea

IOM (Institute of Medicine). 1992. Nutrition Issues in Developing Countries. Report of the Subcommittee on Nutrition and Diarrheal Diseases Control and the Subcommittee on Diet, Physical Activity, and Pregnancy Outcome, Committee on International Nutrition Programs, Food and Nutrition Board. National Academy Press, Washington, D.C.

Walker, W.A., P.R. Harmatz, and B.K. Wershil, eds. 1993. Immunophysiology of the Gut. Bristol-Myers Squibb/Mead Johnson Nutrition Symposia, Vol. II. Academic Press, New York.

CHAPTER 6: IMPROVING THE DIET AND HEALTH OF INDIVIDUALS AND POPULATIONS

Reducing the Risk of Diet-Related Disease

DHHS (U.S. Department of Health and Human Services). 1988. The Surgeon General's Report on Nutrition and Health. DHHS (PHS) publ. 88-50210. U.S. Government Printing Office, Washington, D.C.

NRC (National Research Council). 1989. Diet and Health: Implications for Reducing Chronic Disease Risk. Report of the Committee on Diet and Health, Food and Nutrition Board, Commission on Life Sciences. National Academy Press, Washington, D.C.

Institute of Medicine (IOM). 1991. Improving America's Diet and Health: From Recommendations to Action. Report of the Committee on Dietary Guidelines Implementation. National Academy Press, Washington, D.C.

Sociocultural Factors in Diet Selection

Brown, L.K., and K. Mussell. 1985. Ethnic and Regional Foodways in the United States: The Performance of Group Identity. University of Tennessee Press, Knoxville.

Quandt, S.A., and C. Ritenbaugh, eds. 1986. Training Manual in Nutritional Anthropology. American Anthropological Association, Washington, D.C.

Sharman, A., J. Theophano, K. Curtis, and E. Messer, eds. 1991. Diet and Domestic Life in Society. Temple University Press, Philadelphia, PA.

Behavioral Strategies for Life-Style Change

Marlett, G.A., and J.R. Gordon, eds. 1988. Relapse Prevention: Maintenance Strategies in the Treatment of Addictive Behaviors. Guilford Press, New York.

Prochaska J.O., W.F. Velicer, C.C. DiClemente, and J. Fava. 1988. Measuring processes of change: applications to the cessation of smoking. J. Consult. Clin. Psychol. 56:520-528.

Rogers, E.M. 1983. Diffusion of Innovations, 3rd ed. Free Press, New York.

Steckler, A.B., I. Dawson, B.A. Israel, and E. Eng. 1993. Community health development: an overview of the works of Guy W. Steuart. Health Education Quarterly (Suppl. 1):S1-S150.

Reducing the Risk of Food Insecurity and Hunger

Anderson, S.A. 1990. Core indicators of nutritional state for difficult-to-sample populations. J. Nutr. 120:1559-1600.

Campbell, C.C. 1991. Food insecurity: a nutritional outcome or a predictor variable? J. Nutr. 121:408-415.

Dietz, W.H., ed. 1991. Symposium: Nutritional Assessment and Intervention: Interface of Science and Policy. J. Nutr. 131:401-429.

Society for Nutrition Education. 1992. Hunger in the '80s and '90s. J. Nutr. Educ. 24(1).

Improving Methods and Tools

American Dietetic Association. 1993. The Research Agenda for Dietetics: Conference Proceedings. The American Dietetic Association, Chicago.

Gibson, R.S. 1990. Principles of Nutritional Assessment. Oxford University Press, New York.

Mason, J.B., J.P. Habicht, H. Tabatabai, and V. Valverde. 1984. Nutritional Surveillance. World Health Organization, Geneva.

Olson, J.A. 1982. New approaches to methods for the assessment of nutritional status of the individual. Am. J. Clin. Nutr. 35:1166-1168.

CHAPTER 7: EDUCATION AND TRAINING IN THE NUTRITION AND FOOD SCIENCES

NRC/SED (National Research Council Survey of Earned Doctorates). 1970-1992. Survey of Earned Doctorates, sponsored by five Federal Agencies (National Science Foundation, National Institutes of Health, U.S. Department of Education, National Endowment for the Humanities, and the U.S. Department of Agriculture), and conducted by the National Research Council. National Academy Press, Washington, D.C.

CHAPTER 8: SUPPORT OF THE NUTRITION AND FOOD SCIENCES

IOM (Institute of Medicine); Bloom, F.E., and M.A. Randolph, eds. 1990. Funding Health Sciences Research: A Strategy to Restore Balance. Report of the Committee on Policies for Allocating Health Sciences Research Funds, Division of Health Sciences Policy. National Academy Press, Washington, D.C.

NIH (National Institutes of Health). 1992. National Institutes of Health Program in Biomedical and Behavioral Nutrition Research and Training, Fiscal Year 1991. Report of the NIH Nutrition Coordinating Committee, Division of Nutrition Research Coordination. NIH Publication No. 92-2092. National Institutes of Health, Bethesda, MD. (Publication is revised annually.)

NRC (National Research Council). 1989. Investing in Research: A Proposal to Strengthen the Agricultural, Food, and Environmental System. A report of the Board on Agriculture. National Academy Press, Washington, D.C.

USDA (U.S. Department of Agriculture). 1992. 1991 Report on USDA Human Nutrition Research and Education Activities: A Report to Congress. U.S. Government Printing Office, Washington, D.C. (Publication is revised annually.)

Acronyms

ACN	American College of Nutrition
ACS	American Cancer Society
ADA	American Dietetic Association
ADA	Adenosine deaminase
AHA	American Heart Association
AIDS	Acquired immunodeficiency syndrome
AIN	American Institute of Nutrition
AJCN	American Journal of Clinical Nutrition
ALS	Amylotrophic lateral sclerosis
AMD	Age-related macular degeneration
AMP	Adenosine monophosphate
AMPA/KA	Alpha-amino-3-hydroxy-5-methyl-4-isoxazole propionic acid/kanic acid
APL	Acute promyelocytic leukemia
AREA	Agricultural Research Enhancement Awards, USDA
ARS	Agricultural Research Service, USDA
ASCN	American Society for Clinical Nutrition
BA	Board on Agriculture, NRC
BBB	Blood-brain barrier
BHA	Butylated hydroxyanisole
BHT	Butylated hydroxytoluene
BMI	Body mass index

BST   Bovine somatotropin

C   Carbon
Ca   Calcium
CAT   Chloramphenicol acetyltransferase
CCK   Cholecystokinin
CDC   Centers for Disease Control and Prevention, DHHS
cDNA   Complementary DNA
CHD   Coronary Heart Disease
CNRU   Clinical Nutrition Research Unit, NIH
CNS   Central nervous system
CRGO   Comptetitive Research Grants Office, USDA
CRIS   Current Research Information System, USDA
CSF   Cerebrospinal fluid
CSRS   Cooperative State Research Service, USDA
Cu   Copper

DHHS   U.S. Department of Health and Human Services
DNA   Deoxyribonucleic acid
DNRC   Division of Nutrition Research Coordination, NIH

EFS   Ensuring Food Safety, USDA
ELISA   Enzyme-linked immunosorbent assay
ES   Embryo-derived stem cells
EPR   Electron paramagnetic resonance
ESR   Electron spin resonance

FACS   Fluorescence-activated cell sorting
FASEB   Federation of American Societies for Experimental Biol-
                       ogy
FCCST   Federal Coordinating Council for Science, Engineering,
                       and Technology
FDA   Food and Drug Administration, DHHS
FD&C   Food, Drug & Cosmetic (for coloring agents)
FFQ   Food frequency questionnaire
FH   Familial hypercholesterolemia
FIC   Fogarty International Center, NIH
FNB   Food and Nutrition Board, IOM, NAS
FNS   Food and Nutrition Service, USDA
FSIS   Food Safety and Inspection Service, USDA
FY   Fiscal year

g   Gram

| GABA | Gamma amino butyric acid |
| GNP | Gross National Product |

H	Hydrogen
HACCP	Hazard Analysis and Critical Control Points
HDL	High-density lipoprotein
HNRC	Human Nutrition Research Center, USDA
HNRIMS	Human Nutrition Research Information Management System, NIH
HMG-CoA	3-hydroxy-3-methylglutaryl coenzyme A
H_2O_2	Hydrogen peroxide

ICNHR	Interagency Committee on Human Nutrition Research
IDL	Intermediate-density lipoprotein
IFT	Institute for Food Technologists
IgA	Immunoglobulin A
IgE	Immunoglobulin E
IgG	Immunoglobulin G
IHNOH	Improving Human Nutrition for Optimal Health, USDA
IL	Interleukin
IOM	Institute of Medicine
IRE	Iron-responsive elements
IRE-BP	Iron-responsive-element-binding protein
IU	International Units

| kcal | Kilocalorie |
| kg | Kilogram |

LBM	Lean body mass
Lbs	Pounds
LDL	Low-density lipoprotein

M.D.	Medical doctor
mEq	Milliequivalents
mg	Milligram
MHI	Minority Health Initiative, NIH
mRNA	Messenger RNA

N	Nitrogen
NaCl	Sodium chloride
NAS	National Academy of Sciences
NCEP	National Cholesterol Education Program, NIH
NCI	National Cancer Institute, NIH

NCNR	National Center for Nursing Research, NIH
NCRR	National Center for Research Resources, NIH
NE	Norepinephrine
NEI	National Eye Institute, NIH
NHANES	National Health and Nutrition Examination Survey, DHHS
NHLBI	National Heart, Lung, and Blood Institute, NIH
NIA	National Institute on Aging, NIH
NIADDK	National Institute of Arthritis, Diabetes, and Digestive and Kidney Diseases
NIAID	National Institute of Allergy and Infectious Diseases, NIH
NIAMS	National Institute of Arthritis and Musculoskeletal Diseases, NIH
NIDCD	National Institute on Deafness and Other Communication Disorders
NICHD	National Institute for Child Health and Development, NIH
NIDDK	National Institute of Diabetes and Digestive and Kidney Diseases, NIH
NIDDM	Non-insulin dependent diabetes mellitus
NIDR	National Institute of Dental Research, NIH
NIEHS	National Institute of Environmental Health Sciences, NIH
NIGMS	National Institute of General Medical Sciences, NIH
NIH	National Institutes of Health, DHHS
NINCDS	National Institute of Neurological and Communicative Disorders and Stroke, NIH
NINDS	National Institute of Neurological Disorders and Stroke, NIH
NMDA	N-methyl-D-aspartic acid
NMR	Nuclear magnetic resonance
NRC	National Research Council, NAS
NRICGP	National Research Initiative Competitive Grants Program, USDA
NRSA	National Research Service Awards, NIH
NSF	National Science Foundation
NSLP	National School Lunch Program
NTD	Neural tube defect
O	Oxygen
ONFS	Opportunities in the Nutrition and Food Sciences
ONRC	Office of Nutrition Research Coordination, NIH
ORT	Oral rehydration therapy
OSEP	Office of Science and Engineering Personnel, NRC
OSTP	Office of Science and Technology Policy, Executive Office of the President

P	Phosphorus
PCR	Polymerase chain reaction
PET	Positron emission tomography
pH	Hydrogen ion concentration
PHS	Public Health Service, DHHS
PKU	Phenylketonuria
PST	Porcine somatotropin
PTC	Plant tissue culture
PTH	Parathyroid hormone
PUFA	Polyunsaturated fatty acid(s)
RAR	Retinoic acid receptor
R.D.	Registered Dietitian
RDA	Recommended Dietary Allowance
RFA	Requests for applications
RFLP	Restriction fragment length polymorphism
RNA	Ribonucleic acid
RPE	Retinal pigment epithelium
RRC	Regional Research Center, USDA
RRC	Report Review Committee, NRC, NAS
SCORS	Specialized Centers of Research
TNF	Tumor necrosis factor
UNICEF	United Nations International Children's Emergency Fund
U.S.	United States
USDA	U.S. Department of Agriculture
USRDA	U.S. Recommended Daily Allowance
VLDL	Very-low-density lipoprotein
WIC	Special Supplemental Food Program for Women, Infants, and Children, USDA
WHA	Women's Health Agenda, NIH
WHO	World Health Organization
5HT	5-hydroxy-tryptophan (serotonin)

APPENDIX

B

Contributors to the Report

During the course of this study, many nutrition professionals and bio-medical scientists contributed their views and ideas about the content of this report. Some provided material or advice at our invitation, others responded to our widely publicized questions, and some reviewed parts of this report or the entire report. We carefully considered all comments, but did not adopt all the advice and suggestions provided. We apologize for the likelihood that we have overlooked some individuals from our listing.

The following individuals gave invited presentations to the committee or its working groups:

David H. Alpers, Washington University, St. Louis
Jacqueline Dupont, U.S. Department of Agriculture
Richard W. Hanson, Case Western Reserve University
Van S. Hubbard, National Institutes of Health
Samuel G. Kahn, U.S. Agency for International Development
Lynn A. Larsen, U.S. Food and Drug Administration
Melvin M. Mathias, U.S. Department of Agriculture
Michael K. May, National Institutes of Health
Donald B. McCormick, Emory University
Susan M. Pilch, National Institutes of Health
Robert L. Riemer, National Academy of Sciences

David D. Schnakenberg, U.S. Army Medical Research and Development Command
John W. Suttie, University of Wisconsin, Madison
James E. Tavares, National Academy of Sciences

The following people provided the committee with information or other forms of help upon request:

Barbara Abrams, University of California, Berkeley
Sharon Akabas, Teachers College, Columbia University
Olav Alvarez, University of Texas-Houston
Richard Atkinson, Eastern Virginia Medical School, Hampton
Janet K. Baltzell, U.S. Department of Agriculture
Oded Bar-Or, McMaster University
Arthur L. Beaudet, Baylor College of Medicine
Robert E. Black, Johns Hopkins University
Steven Blair, Institute for Aerobics Research, Dallas
Elliott Blass, Cornell University
Gladys Block, University of California, Berkeley
John W. Brady, Cornell University
Judith Brown, University of Minnesota, Minneapolis
Kenneth H. Brown, University of California, Davis
John Brunzell, University of Washington, Seattle
Carol Bryant, University of South Florida
Doris H. Calloway, University of California, Berkeley
Mary Carey, Massachusetts General Hospital
Kenneth K. Carroll, University of Western Ontario, Canada
Richard Cash, Harvard University
Ranjit K. Chandra, Janeway Child Health Center, St. John's, Newfoundland
Ronald Chez, University of South Florida, Tampa
Barton Childs, Johns Hopkins University
Dennis W. Choi, Washington University
Frank Chytil, Vanderbilt University
Julie E. Clarke, National Academy of Sciences
John Connor, Purdue University
Isobel Contento, Teachers College, Columbia University
Catherine Cowell, Columbia University
Audrey T. Cross, Columbia University
Richard J. Deckelbaum, Columbia University
Hector F. DeLuca, University of Wisconsin, Madison
Dominick DePaola, Baylor College of Dentistry
Kathleen M. DeWalt, University of Pittsburgh

Salvatore Dimauro, Columbia University
Charles A. Dinarello, Tufts University
Doris D. Disbrow, University of California, Berkeley
Michael P. Doyle, University of Georgia, Griffin
Gregor Eichele, Baylor College of Medicine
Cyril Enwonwu, Meharry Medical College
William Evans, USDA Human Nutrition Research Center on Aging, Boston
Mark L. Failla, University of North Carolina, Greensboro
Philip M. Farrell, University of Wisconsin, Madison
John D. Fernstrom, University of Pittsburgh
L. Frank Flora, U.S. Department of Agriculture
James Gibbs, Cornell Medical Center
Sandy Gillespie, Atlanta Diabetes Association
Jonathan D. Gitlin, Washington University
Walter H. Glinsmann, U.S. Department of Health and Human Services
Jeffrey I. Gordon, Washington University
Richard J. Grand, New England Medical Center Hospitals, Boston
Danielle Greenberg, Cornell Medical Center
Janet Grommet, Teachers College, Columbia University
Scott M. Grundy, University of Texas, Dallas
Joan D. Gussow, Teachers College, Columbia University
Jere D. Haas, Cornell University
Peter Hahn, University of British Columbia, Vancouver
K. Michael Hambidge, University of Colorado, Denver
Colleen E. Hayes, University of Wisconsin, Madison
Robert P. Heaney, Creighton University
H.O. Hultin, University of Massachusetts, Amherst
Robert L. Isaacson, State University of New York at Binghamton
Khursheed N. Jeejeebhoy, University of Toronto
Karl F. Jensen, U.S. Environmental Protection Agency
Norge Jerome, Kansas State University
C. Ronald Kahn, Joslin Diabetes Center, Boston
John T. Kalberer, Jr., National Institutes of Health
James Kendig, University of Rochester
Mohammed Khaled, University of Alabama, Birmingham
Janice Kiecot-Glaser, Ohio State University
Michael S. Kilberg, University of Florida, Gainesville
John E. Kinsella, University of California, Davis
Harry R. Kissileff, Columbia University, New York
Penny Kris-Etherton, Pennsylvania State University
Sally A. Lederman, Columbia University
Fred D. Ledley, Baylor College of Medicine

Sheryl Lee, Arizona Department of Health Services, Tempe
Sarah F. Leibowitz, Rockefeller University
R.E. Levin, University of Massachusetts, Amherst
David A. Levitsky, Cornell University
Jerry B. Lingrel, University of Cincinnati
Irwin Mandel, Columbia University Dental School
Reynaldo Martorell, Cornell University
Joel B. Mason, New England Medical Center Hospitals, Boston
Catherine McCarroll, Georgia State Office of Nutrition
David A. McCarron, Oregon Health Sciences University
J. Denis McGarry, University of Texas, Dallas
Paul McHugh, Johns Hopkins University
Alfred H. Merrill, Jr., Emory University
Timothy H. Moran, Johns Hopkins University
Arno G. Motulsky, University of Washington, Seattle
Rebecca Mullis, Centers for Disease Control and Prevention, Atlanta
Hamish N. Munro, USDA Human Nutrition Research Center on Aging,
    Boston
Juan Navia, University of Alabama, Birmingham
Marion Nestle, New York University
Abraham M.Y. Nomura, Kuakini Medical Center, Honolulu, Hawaii
Robert E. Olson, State University of New York at Stony Brook
David E. Ong, Vanderbilt University
Grace L. Ostenso, U.S. House of Representatives
Daniel M. Pasquini, National Academy of Sciences
Mulchand S. Patel, Case Western Reserve University
Evan Pattishall, National Institutes of Health
Micha Peleg, University of Massachusetts, Amherst
Roy Pitkin, University of California, Los Angeles
Henry C. Pitot, University of Wisconsin, Madison
Kathleen M. Rasmussen, Cornell University
Sue Ann Ritchko, U.S. Department of Agriculture
Cheryl Ritenbaugh, University of Arizona
Beatrice L. Rogers, Tufts University, Boston
Jeffrey Rosen, Baylor College of Medicine, Houston
Steven M. Rothman, Washington University
Robert B. Rucker, University of California, Davis
Robert Russell, USDA Human Nutrition Research Center on Aging,
    Boston
Zack I. Sabry, University of California, Berkeley
Susan Schiffman, Duke University
Robert T. Schimke, Stanford University
Ruth Schwartz, Cornell University

Nevin S. Scrimshaw, Massachusetts Institute of Technology
Charles R. Scriver, McGill University
Barry Shane, University of California, Berkeley
Richard Shekelle, University of Texas, Houston
Laura S. Sims, University of Maryland, College Park
Harold Slavkin, University of Southern California, Los Angeles
Bonny L. Specker, University of Cincinnati
Arthur A. Spector, University of Iowa, Iowa City
Patricia L. Splett, University of Minnesota, Minneapolis
Steve L. Taylor, University of Nebraska, Lincoln
Delores H. Thurgood, National Academy of Sciences
Nylda Tirado, Cornell Cooperative Extension, New York
Kay Umeakunne, Emory University
Dennis E. Vance, University of Alberta
W. Alan Walker, Massachusetts General Hospital, Boston
Huber R. Warner, National Institutes of Health
Robert H. Wasserman, Cornell University
Savio L.C. Woo, Baylor College of Medicine, Houston
Richard J. Wood, USDA Human Nutrition Research Center on Aging,
    Boston
Bonnie Worthington-Roberts, University of Washington, Seattle
Elizabeth A. Yetley, U.S. Food and Drug Administration
Lillian Yung, Teachers College, Columbia University

The following people responded to generic requests for information
made at professional meetings and in various professional journals and
newsletters:

Steve Austin, Western States Chiropractic College
June A. Beckford, Brooklyn, New York
Gerald S. Berenson, Tulane University
Jane Bowers, Kansas State University
Alfred A. Bushway, University of Maine, Orono
Francis F. Busta, University of Minnesota, St. Paul
Dorice Czajka-Narins, Texas Woman's University
Peter D'Adamo, *Journal of Naturopathic Medicine*
Suzanne Hendrich, Iowa State University, Ames
Charlotte Hennessy, Grants Pass, Oregon
Mary K. Hunt, Dana-Farber Cancer Institute, Boston
Joseph J. Jen, University of Georgia, Athens
Susan G. Kordish, Clearfield County Area Agency on Aging, Inc.,
    Pennsylvania
Theodore P. Labuza, University of Minnesota, St. Paul

Paul A. Lachance, Rutgers University
Chong M. Lee, University of Rhode Island, West Kingston
Anthony L. Pometto III, Iowa State University, Ames
Barry M. Popkin, University of North Carolina, Chapel Hill
Lowell D. Satterlee, North Dakota State University, Fargo
Karen M. Schaich, Rutgers University
Barbara O. Schneeman, University of California, Davis
LuAnn Soliah, Baylor University, Waco, Texas
Linda Van Horn, Northwestern University
Mary Wagner, General Mills, Minneapolis, Minnesota
Robert G. Zimbelman, American Society of Animal Science, Bethesda,
    Maryland

Many scientific and professional societies provided information and help to the committee. We particularly appreciate the help of Richard G. Allison of the American Institute of Nutrition and S. Stephen Schiaffino of the American Society for Clinical Nutrition. We also wish to thank the American Dietetic Association, American Society for Parenteral and Enteral Nutrition, Institute of Food Technologists, and the Society for Nutrition Education for their help and support of this study.

C
Biographies of Committee
Members and Staff

FERGUS M. CLYDESDALE is Professor and Head, Department of Food Science and Nutrition at the University of Massachusetts, Amherst. His research interests involve the basic chemical changes in processed foods and their effect on quality, nutrition, and acceptability, with particular emphasis on the maximization of technology to improve nutrition and quality. Dr. Clydesdale has received the Nicholas Appert Award and the Babcock-Hart Award from the Institute of Food Technologists. He is the editor of *Critical Reviews in Food Science and Nutrition* and the CRC Book Series in Food Science and Nutrition. He holds a B.A. and M.A. in Food Chemistry from the University of Toronto, Canada, and a Ph.D. in Food Science and Technology from the University of Massachusetts, Amherst.

ROBERT J. COUSINS is Boston Family Professor of Nutrition and Director of the Center for Nutritional Sciences, University of Florida, Gainesville. His area of expertise is nutritional biochemistry, particularly the metabolism and molecular biology of trace elements. He is especially interested in the regulatory and mechanistic aspects of absorption, metabolism, and function of dietary zinc. Dr. Cousins is the recipient of both the Mead Johnson Award and the Osborne and Mendel Award from the American Institute of Nutrition. He is a past-president of the Federation of American Societies for Experimental Biology. Dr. Cousins is an Associate Editor of *The Journal of Nutrition* and serves on the editorial boards of many journals, including the *Annual Review of Nutrition*. He holds a B.A. in

Zoology and Chemistry from the University of Vermont, Burlington, and M.S. and Ph.D. degrees in Nutritional Biochemistry from the University of Connecticut, Storrs. He received postdoctoral training in biochemistry at the University of Wisconsin, supported by an NIH Postdoctoral Fellowship.

ADAM DREWNOWSKI is Professor of Community Health Programs and Director, Human Nutrition Program, School of Public Health, University of Michigan, Ann Arbor. He is also Associate Professor in the Department of Psychiatry, University of Michigan Medical School. His areas of research expertise include taste and food preferences in obesity and eating disorders, dietary intake assessments, and the effects of dieting on alcohol and drug use in young women. He holds B.A. and M.A. degrees in Biochemistry from Balliol College, Oxford University, England; and a Ph.D. in Psychology from Rockefeller University, New York.

ROBERT EARL (*FNB Staff, Staff Officer*) is Project Director of the FNB's Food Forum and was staff officer for the studies by the Committee on the Nutrition Components of Food Labeling and the Committee on State Food Labeling. Prior to joining the Institute of Medicine, Mr. Earl was Administrator of Government Affairs for the American Dietetic Association in Washington, D.C. Previously, he was statewide nutrition consultant for adult health, chronic disease, and health promotion programs with the Texas Department of Health, Austin. Mr. Earl is currently President of the District of Columbia Metropolitan Area Dietetic Association and is a member of Delta Omega National Public Health Honorary Society. Mr. Earl holds a B.S. in Human Nutrition from the University of Michigan, Ann Arbor; an M.P.H. in Public Health Nutrition from the University of North Carolina at Chapel Hill; and is working on a doctorate at the Institute for Public Policy at George Mason University, Fairfax, Virginia.

JOHN W. ERDMAN, Jr. (*Committee Vice Chair*) is Professor of Nutrition in Internal Medicine and Professor of Food Science at the University of Illinois at Urbana, where he has been on the faculty since 1975 and is now Director of the Division of Nutritional Sciences. Dr. Erdman has served on the editorial boards of a number of food science and nutrition journals, including the *Journal of Nutrition*. He has received numerous awards and honors and was recently made a Fellow in the Institute of Food Technologists. Dr. Erdman's research interests are the effects of food processing upon nutrient retention, the metabolic roles of vitamin A and beta-carotene, and the bioavailability of minerals from foods. He currently serves on the Institute of Medicine's Food and Nutrition Board and was a member of the FNB's Committee on the Nutrition Components of Food Labeling and Committee on State Food Labeling. He also has been a member of the Subcommittee on Bioavailability of Nutrients of the Committee on Animal Nutrition of the National Research Council's Board on Agriculture. Dr. Erdman holds B.S., M.S., M.Phil., and Ph.D. degrees in Food Science from Rutgers University.

CUTBERTO GARZA (*Committee Vice Chair*) is Professor of Nutrition and Director of the Division of Nutritional Sciences, Cornell University. Prior to coming to Cornell, he served as Associate Director of the U.S. Department of Agriculture Children's Nutrition Research Center, Houston, Texas, and as Director of the Nutrition and Gastroenterology Laboratory at Baylor College of Medicine, Houston, Texas. Dr. Garza's research areas are in pediatrics, lactation, infant nutrition, composition of human milk, breastfeeding, energy intake of infants and young people, and metabolism. He serves on the editorial board of the *American Journal of Clinical Nutrition*, and is a recipient of many honors and awards, including the M.I.T. Health Science Foundation Award, and the Distinguished Achievement Award from Baylor University. Dr. Garza holds a B.S. degree from Baylor University, an M.D. from the Baylor College of Medicine, and a Ph.D. in Nutritional Biochemistry from the Massachusetts Institute of Technology.

ALAN G. GOODRIDGE (*Committee Vice Chair*) is Professor and Head of the Department of Biochemistry at the University of Iowa, Iowa City. His areas of expertise are metabolism, molecular biology, and endocrinology. His research interests are in the nutritional and hormonal regulation of gene expression. Dr. Goodridge is an Associate Editor of *The Journal of Biological Chemistry*, serves on the editorial board of the *Annual Review of Nutrition*, and is President-elect of the Association of Graduate and Medical Departments of Biochemistry. Dr. Goodridge was a Josiah Macy Jr. Faculty Scholar at the Institute of Molecular Biology in Paris in 1975-1976. He holds a B.S. in Biology from Tufts University and M.S. and Ph.D. degrees in Zoology from the University of Michigan, Ann Arbor.

M.R.C. GREENWOOD (**FNB Liaison to Committee**) is Dean of Graduate Studies and Professor of Nutrition and Internal Medicine at the University of California at Davis. Dr. Greenwood is currently Chair of the Food and Nutrition Board and is a member of the Institute of Medicine. Previously she was Professor of Biology at Vassar College. Her research interests are in physiology and nutrition and behavior. Her research has been conducted in obesity; food-motivated behavior; genetic-hypothalamic obesity; lipid metabolism; and childhood obesity. She is a recipient of the American Institute of Nutrition's Award in Experimental Nutrition and was a Mellon Scholar-in-Residence at St. Olaf College, Northfield, Minnesota. Dr. Greenwood has served on the editorial board of the *Proceedings of the Society for Experimental Biology and Medicine, Nutrition and Behavior,* and on the Advisory Board of the *International Journal of Obesity.* Dr. Greenwood holds an A.B. in Biology from Vassar College and a Ph.D. in Physiology, Nutrition and Behavior from Rockefeller University.

SUSAN K. HARLANDER is Director of Dairy Foods Research and Development, Land 'O Lakes, Inc., Minneapolis, Minnesota. She was previously an associate professor in the Department of Food Science and Nutrition, University of Minnesota, Minneapolis. Her research interests are genetic engineering, food biotechnology, and the interface of biotechnology and food science. Dr. Harlander has received the Distinguished Teacher Award from the University of Minnesota. She serves on the editorial boards of *Critical Reviews in Food Science and Nutrition, Advances in Food and Nutrition Research,* and *Dairy Field Today.* She holds a B.S. in Biology from the University of Wisconsin, Eau Claire, and an M.S. in Microbiology and Biochemistry and a Ph.D. in Food Science from the University of Minnesota.

RICHARD J. HAVEL (*Committee Chairman*) is a Professor of Medicine at the University of California at San Francisco. Until recently he was also Director of UCSF's Cardiovascular Research Institute, where he heads a Specialized Center of Research in Arteriosclerosis. Dr. Havel, a member of the National Academy of Sciences and Institute of Medicine, is a former chairman of the Food and Nutrition Board. His research interests are intermediary and lipoprotein metabolism, with emphasis on the metabolism of triglyceride-rich lipoproteins and the role of the liver in lipoprotein catabolism. He has chaired the Advisory Board of the *Journal of Lipid Research* and recently served on the Adult Treatment Panel of the National Cholesterol Education Program. Currently, he also directs a program of the Agency for International Development to reduce cardiovascular and cerebrovascular disease in the Czech Republic. Dr. Havel is a past recipient of the Bristol Meyer Squibb Award for Distinguished Research in Nutrition, the National Cholesterol Award for Scientific Achievement of the National Conference on Cholesterol and High Blood Pressure Control, and the McCollum Award of the American Society for Clinical Nutrition.

JANET C. KING, (*Committee Vice Chair*) is Professor and Chair, Department of Nutritional Sciences, University of California at Berkeley.

Her research interests are the nutritional requirements for protein, energy, and trace elements in nonpregnant, pregnant, and lactating women, and zinc utilization in healthy adults. Dr. King has been honored as the Frances Fisher Memorial Lecturer, sponsored by the American Dietetic Association Foundation, and has received the Lederle Laboratories Award in Human Nutrition, presented by the American Institute of Nutrition. She is an Assistant Editor of the *American Journal of Clinical Nutrition.* Dr. King holds a B.S. in Dietetics from Iowa State University, Ames, and a Ph.D. in Nutrition from the University of California at Berkeley.

LAURENCE N. KOLONEL is Professor of Public Health and Director, Epidemiology Program, Cancer Research Center of Hawaii, University of Hawaii, Honolulu. His research interests are the dietary etiology of cancer, ethnic variations in cancer risk, and the effects of migration on cancer incidence. Dr. Kolonel is an Associate Editor of *Cancer Research* and serves on the editorial boards of the *American Journal of Epidemiology, Cancer Epidemiology Biomarkers and Prevention, Cancer Causes and Control,* and *Nutrition and Cancer.* He currently serves on the IOM's Food and Nutrition Board and was a member of the FNB's Committees on Diet, Nutrition and Cancer and on Diet and Health. Dr. Kolonel holds a B.A. in Chemistry from Williams College, Williamstown, Massachusetts, an M.D. from Harvard Medical School, and M.P.H. and Ph.D. degrees from the School of Public Health, University of California at Berkeley.

GILBERT A. LEVEILLE is Vice President for Research and Technical Services, Nabisco Foods Group, RJR-Nabisco, Inc., East Hanover, New Jersey. He previously served as Director, Nutrition and Health Science of General Foods Corporation, and was Professor and Chair, Department of Food Science and Human Nutrition at Michigan State University, East Lansing. His research interests are lipid, protein, and amino acid nutrition and metabolism, atherosclerosis, and obesity. Dr. Leveille is a member of Sigma XI Honor Society and has received the Poultry Science Research Award, the Mead-Johnson Award from the American Institute of Nutrition, and the Carl R. Fellers Award from the Institute of Food Technologists. He has served on the editorial board of *Drug-Nutrient Interactions,* the *Journal of Environmental Pathology and Toxicology,* the *Journal of Nutrition,* and *Nutrition Reviews.* He is currently an Associate Editor of *Nutrition and Cancer.* Dr. Leveille holds a B.V.A. (Bachelor of Vocational Agriculture) from the University of Massachusetts, Amherst, and M.S. and Ph.D. degrees in Nutrition and Biochemistry from Rutgers University.

F. XAVIER PI-SUNYER is Director of the Obesity Research Center and Chief of Endocrinology, Diabetes and Nutrition at St. Luke's-Roosevelt

Hospital Center, and Professor of Medicine at the College of Physicians and Surgeons, Columbia University, New York. His research interests are the hormonal control of carbohydrate metabolism, diabetes mellitus, obesity, and food intake regulation. Dr. Pi-Sunyer is a past president of the American Society for Clinical Nutrition, has been honored as a Fellow of the Fogarty International Center of the National Institutes of Health, and serves on the Board of Directors of the American Diabetes Association, of which he was president in 1992-93. He is Associate Editor of *Obesity Research* and is presently Vice-President of the North American Association for the Study of Obesity. He holds a B.A. in Chemistry from Oberlin College, an M.D. from Columbia University, and an M.P.H. from Harvard University.

MARTHA CONSTANTINE-PATON is a Professor in the Department of Biology at Yale University. Her research is in the cellular interactions involved in patterned synaptogenesis and the regulation of glutamate receptor function during the early development of the vertebrate nervous system. Dr. Paton is a recipient of a Solowey Award in Neuroscience, the Young Investigator Award of the Society for Neuroscience, the Young Investigator NIH Postdoctoral Award Society for Neuroscience, a John Simon Guggenheim Fellowship, and a National Merit Award from the National Eye Institute. She has served as a member of the Society for Neuroscience Council, as a Director of a course on neural systems and behavior at the Marine Biology Laboratory at Woods Hole, and as a Director of the Interdepartmental Neuroscience Program at Yale University. She holds a B.S. in Biology from Jackson College of Tufts University and a Ph.D. in Neurobiology and Behavior from Cornell University.

SARA A. QUANDT is Associate Professor, Department of Anthropology, and a member of the Graduate Faculty in Nutritional Sciences at the University of Kentucky, Lexington. Her research interests are the sociocultural dimensions of nutrition, infant feeding practices, nutrition and aging, and methodologies of dietary and nutrition assessment. Dr. Quandt is currently President of the Council on Nutritional Anthropology. She serves on the editorial boards of *Medical Anthropology Quarterly* and *Practicing Anthropology*. Dr. Quandt holds a B.A. in Anthropology from Lawrence University, Appleton, Wisconsin; and M.A. and Ph.D. degrees in Anthropology (with a minor in Human Nutrition) from Michigan State University.

SYED S.H. RIZVI is Professor of Food Engineering, Department of Food Science at Cornell University, Ithaca, New York. His research interests are engineering properties of biomaterials, bioseparation processes, process control, and packaging. Dr. Rizvi is a recipient of the Excellence in Teaching Award from the Institute of Food Science, and is a Merit Professor with the College of Agriculture and Life Sciences at Cornell University. He has served on the editorial boards of the *Journal of Food Process Engineering*, the *Journal of Plastic and Film Sheeting*, and the *International Journal of Food Sciences and Nutrition*. Dr. Rizvi holds B.S. and M.S. degrees in Technology from Punjab University, India; a M.Eng. from the University of Toronto, Canada; and a Ph.D. in Food Engineering from The Ohio State University.

IRWIN H. ROSENBERG is Director, U.S. Department of Agriculture Human Nutrition Research Center on Aging and is Professor of Nutrition at the Tufts University School of Nutrition, Boston, Massachusetts. His research interests are gastroenterology, the study of intestinal absorption and malabsorption, and human nutrition, with emphasis on metabolic and nutritional aspects of gastrointestinal disease. He is a recipient of the NIH Career Development Award, Josiah Macy Faculty Scholar Award, the Grace Goldsmith Award of the American College of Nutrition, and the Robert H. Herman Memorial Award of the American Society for Clinical Nutrition. Dr. Rosenberg, a past chairman of the Food and Nutrition Board, serves on several U.S. government advisory panels and committees. He is Editor-in-Chief of *Nutrition Reviews*, and has served on editorial boards of the *Journal of Nutrition*, the *American Journal of Clinical Nutrition*, the *Journal Laboratory of Clinical Medicine*, and the *ISI Atlas of Science and Medicine*. Dr. Rosenberg holds a B.S. in Biology and History from the University of Wisconsin, Madison, and an M.D. from Harvard University Medical School.

A. CATHARINE ROSS is Professor of Biochemistry and Director of the Division of Nutrition, Department of Physiology and Biochemistry, and is Professor of Nutrition, Department of Pediatrics, at the Medical College of Pennsylvania, Philadelphia. Her research interests are molecular and cell biology, intracellular binding for retinol and retinoic acid, retinol deficiency, and vitamin A and immunity. Dr. Ross is a recipient of the NIH Research Career Development Award and the Mead-Johnson Award of the American Institute of Nutrition. She has served on the editorial board of the *Journal of Lipid Research*, and *Nutrition Reviews*. Dr. Ross holds a B.S. in Zoology from the University of California at Davis; an M.N.S. from the Cornell University Graduate School of Nutrition; and a Ph.D. in Molecular and Cell Biology from Cornell University.

SACHIKO TOKUNAGA DE ST. JEOR is Professor of Clinical Medicine and Director of the Nutrition Education and Research Program in the School of Medicine and Professor of Nutrition in the College of Human and Community Sciences at the University of Nevada. Her research interests are weight management, obesity, nutrition assessment, cancer prevention, and nutrition education in medical schools. Dr. St. Jeor has been honored as an outstanding alumnus from both the College of Health and Human Development at Pennsylvania State University and the College of Health at the University of Utah. She also received the Award for Excellence in the Practice of Dietetic Research and chaired the Council of Research, American Dietetic Association and is a founding member of the Council on Renal Nutrition of the National Kidney Foundation. She is a Visiting Professor of Nutrition with the National Dairy Council and has served on the Behavioral Medicine Study Section and Clinical Applications and Prevention Advisory Committee for the National Heart, Lung, and Blood Institute, National Institutes of Health. She has served on the editorial boards of *Behavioral Medicine Abstracts*, *Clinics in Applied Nutrition*, the *Weight Control Digest*, and the *Journal of the American Dietetic Association*. Dr. St. Jeor holds a B.A. in Nutrition from the University of Utah, Salt Lake City; an M.S. in Nutrition from the University of Iowa, Iowa City; and a Ph.D. in Nutrition from Pennsylvania State University, University Park.

ALBERT J. STUNKARD is Professor of Psychiatry and former Chairman of the department at the University of Pennsylvania. His research has investigated sociological, psychological, metabolic, and genetic determinants of human obesity and treatment of the disorder by behavioral, dietary, pharmacological, and surgical measures. He has twice been awarded the Annual Prize for Research of the American Psychiatric Association and received the Joseph Goldberger Award in Clinical Nutrition of the American Medical Association. He serves on several editorial boards and is Executive Editor of *Appetite*. He is a member of the Institute of Medicine and is Past President of the American Psychosomatic Society, the Society of Behavioral Medicine, and the Association for Research in Nervous and Mental Disease. He holds a B.S. from Yale University and an M.D. from Columbia College of Physicians and Surgeons.

PAUL R. THOMAS (*FNB Staff, Project Director*) is Project Director of the FNB's Committee to Develop Criteria for Evaluating the Outcomes of Approaches to Prevent and Treat Obesity. He was previously Project Director for the Committee on Dietary Guidelines Implementation and served as editor of their report, *Improving America's Diet and Health: From Recommendations to Action*, and assisted the FNB subcommittee that produced the *10th Edition of the Recommended Dietary Allowances*. Prior to coming to the FNB, he established and directed the

Division of Nutrition Services at the Monongalia County Health Department in Morgantown, West Virginia. Dr. Thomas is co-editor of the FNB publication *Eat For Life, the Food and Nutrition Board's Guide to Reducing Your Risk of Chronic Disease.* He is also co-author of *The Nutrition Debate: Sorting Out Some Answers,* with Joan Dye Gussow, Ed.D. Dr. Thomas holds a B.A. degree in Biology from the State University of New York at Buffalo; an M.S. degree in Public Health Nutrition from Case Western Reserve University, Cleveland; and an Ed.D. degree in Nutrition Education from Teachers College, Columbia University, New York.

DAVID VALLE is Professor of Pediatrics, Molecular Biology and Genetics and a Howard Hughes Medical Institute Investigator at the Johns Hopkins University School of Medicine, Baltimore, Maryland. Dr. Valle's research interests are pediatric research, genetic diseases (particularly inborn errors of metabolism), cloning and analysis of genes, mutation detection, and inherited retinal degeneration. He holds a B.S. in Zoology from Duke University and an M.D. from the Duke University Medical School.

WALTER C. WILLETT is Frederick Stare Professor of Nutrition and Epidemiology at the Harvard School of Public Health and Professor of Medicine at Harvard Medical School. His research interests are the development of methodologies to measure dietary factors in epidemiologic studies, and etiologies of coronary heart disease and cancer, with particular emphasis on dietary causes. Dr. Willett studied food science as an undergraduate at Michigan State University, East Lansing, and holds an M.D. from the University of Michigan, Ann Arbor; and M.P.H. and Dr.P.H. degrees from the Harvard School of Public Health.

CATHERINE E. WOTEKI (*FNB Director*), prior to joining the IOM, was Deputy Director of the Division of Health Examination Statistics, National Center for Health Statistics, U.S. Department of Health and Human Services. She has served in important health posts at the Office of Technology Assessment of the U.S. Congress and at the U.S. Department of Agriculture's Human Nutrition Information Service. Dr. Woteki is co-editor of the FNB publication *Eat For Life: The Food and Nutrition Board's Guide to Reducing Your Risk of Chronic Disease.* She was a recipient of an IOM Distinguished Staff Award in 1991 and holds various honors from the Public Health Service, U.S. Department of Health and Human Services. Dr. Woteki currently serves as a member of the Council on Research of the American Dietetic Association and on the editorial advisory board of the American Institute of Nutrition. Dr. Woteki holds a B.S. in Biology and Chemistry from Mary Washington College, Fredricksburg, Virginia; and M.S. and Ph.D. degrees in Human Nutrition from Virginia Polytechnic and State University, Blacksburg, Virginia.

Index

Five-a-Day for Better Health, 205
Flavor and flavorings, 41, 102-103, 107-108
Fluorescence-activated cell sorting (FACS), 71
Folate and folic acid, 35-36, 101, 103, 161, 173
 and neural tube defects, 35, 101, 145, 160, 182
Food and Drug Administration (FDA), 101, 109, 260
Food assistance programs, 3, 6, 21, 28, 181, 192-198
 evaluation of, 193-197, 204-205, 257-258
Foodborne disease, *see* Microbiological food hazards
Food consumption, 5, 20, 144, 162
 assessment and measurement, 5, 200-204
 neurological regulation, 5, 162
 and oxygen intake, 27
 preferences, 5, 6, 20, 38-39, 163-164
Food frequency questionnaires (FFQs), 201-202
Food industry, 6-7, 21, 100-101
 research support, 1-2, 12, 21, 264-267
 summer training support, 8, 214, 231
 see also Processed foods and processing
Food safety, 3, 7, 21, 110-116
 and biotechnology, 41, 109-110, 128, 132
 microbiological hazards, 110-112, 116-117, 124
 NSF support, 258
 USDA support, 11, 254
Food sciences, 1*n*, 142
 graduate education, 8-9, 218, 220-221
 undergraduate education, 7-8, 211-216
Food stamp program, 192, 193, 195, 205, 258
Food supply, 2, 5, 6-7, 13, 20-21
 USDA research, 11
Fortified foods, 6, 28, 33, 35-36, 43, 101-103
Foundations, 1-2, 9, 12, 267-268
Free-radical reactions, 7, 58, 139
Fried foods, 106
Frozen foods, 28, 104, 117, 137
Fruits, 21, 40, 93-94, 102, 165, 205
Functional foods, 6, 25, 108-110, 128
Funding of research, 1-3, 9-10, 12-13, 28-29
 academic, 12, 218-219

 federal, 1-2, 9, 10-11, 28, 237-264
 by food industry, 1-2, 12, 21, 264-267
 by foundations, 1-2, 9, 12, 267-268
Fuzzy logic, 121-122

G

Gamma amino butyric acid (GABA), 57
Gender, *see* Sex-related differences
Gene expression regulation, 4, 29, 40, 47-48, 61-66, 84-86
 and vitamin A, 43, 51
 and vitamin D, 23, 53-56
Gene knockout, 63, 66, 73, 80
Gene mapping, 67, 83-84
Gene therapy, 5, 75, 81-83
 for cancer, 63, 83
Genetic engineering, 21, 39, 108, 114, 115-116
 animals, 40-41, 130-131
 microorganisms, 39, 41, 131-133
 plants, 39-40, 113, 126-130, 134-135
Genetics, 4, 8, 15, 18, 29, 47, 217
 and atherosclerosis risk, 24
 basic research, 61-68, 78-88
 and chronic disease, 4-5, 15-16, 19-20, 29, 32-37
 and diabetes, 33-34
 and food preferences, 5, 20
 and hemochromatosis, 32, 33
 multifactorial disorders, 67-68, 75
 neural tube defects, 35
 and obesity, 20, 67, 68, 87, 175-176
Gene transfer, 25, 39, 61-65
Germline gene therapy, 81-82
Glutamate, 45-46, 57, 93
Graduate education, 7, 8-9, 209, 210, 211, 216-227, 229, 230
 see also Fellowships and grants
Grants, *see* Fellowships and grants; Funding of research
Growth, *see* Development and growth

H

Handicapped persons, 196-197
Hatch Act, 253, 256
Hazard analysis and critical control points (HACCP) procedures, 112, 117
Health Resources Services Administration, 261

Tissues, 4, 80-81, 94
culture of, 71-73, 129
Toxicology, 29, 114, 233
Toxins, naturally occurring, 7, 58, 112-114
Training of scientists, 1, 2, 7, 209-211
behavioral and social science, 229-230
clinical nutrition, 228-229
federal support, 221, 239
food science, 230-231
see also Academic research programs;
Fellowships and grants; Graduate
education; Undergraduate
education
Transferrin, 32, 59-61
Transgenic animals and organisms, 40-41,
63-65, 79, 81-82, 130-131
Tryptophan, 126

U

Undergraduate education, 7-8, 209, 210,
211-213
accreditation, 8, 215-216
summer training, 8, 213-215, 230
U.S. Department of Agriculture (USDA),
192-193
fellowships and grants, 231, 233, 234-
236, 256-257
Human Nutrition Research Centers, 8,
214, 252-253, 256
Regional Research Centers, 8, 214,
252, 256
research support, 11, 237, 238, 239,
249-258
summer training support, 8, 214
U.S. Government, *see* Federal government

V

Value-added foods, 6, 116-124
industry research support, 12, 265
USDA research support, 11, 254, 257
Vegetables, 21, 93-94, 102, 205
and biotechnology, 6, 40
Viral vectors, 62-63
Vitamin A, 4, 6, 18, 37, 50-51, 96, 178
deficiency, 42-44, 50, 198-199
Vitamin B complex, 36, 58, 101, 103, 159-
160, 173

Vitamin C, 103
antioxidant properties, 4, 19, 24, 37,
40, 46, 93, 128, 159
Vitamin D, 22-23, 48, 51, 53-56, 101, 144-
145
Vitamin deficiency, 27, 28, 45-46, 160, 198-
199, 200-203
A, 42-44, 50, 198-199
B complex, 36, 58, 173
iron, 29, 32, 33, 58, 102, 160, 181-182
and parenteral and enteral feeding,
45-46
Vitamin E, 159, 178
antioxidant properties, 4, 19, 24, 37,
40, 46, 93, 94, 128
Voluntary health agencies, 12, 267-268
Von Gierke's disease, 149

W

Waste, 7, 41, 120, 123, 141
from farm animals, 41, 140-141
Water in food, 7, 118, 136-137
Water pollution, 41, 141-142
Wernicke-Korsakoff syndrome, 58
White House Conference on Food,
Nutrition, and Health, 3
WIC, 192, 193, 195-196, 197, 258
Women
and folic acid, 35-36
iron deficiency, 29, 32, 102
nutrition careers, 224, 225, 249
see also Osteoporosis; Pregnancy
Women's Health Agenda, 249
Workplace interventions, 188-189
World Health Organization (WHO), 42, 43

X

Xerophthalmia, 42
X-ray diffraction, 76-77

Z

Zinc, 4, 6, 36, 44-46, 102, 103, 159, 160,
177, 199